ALL THE KINGS' HORSES

Also by Amanda Murray

Race to the Finish

ALL THE KINGS' HORSES

Amanda Murray

A Celebration of Royal Horses from 1066 to the Present Day

Preface by Sir Michael Oswald KCVO,
former Stud Manager to Her Majesty the Queen

ROBSON

First published in the United Kingdom in 2006 by
Robson Books
151 Freston Road
London
W10 6TH

An imprint of Anova Books Company Ltd

ISBN 1 86105 930 2

A CIP catalogue record for this book is available from the British Library.

10 9 8 7 6 5 4 3 2 1

All images © CORBIS

Typeset by SX Composing DTP, Rayleigh, Essex
Printed and bound by MPG Books Ltd, Bodmin, Cornwall

This book can be ordered direct from the publisher.
Contact the marketing department, but try your bookshop first.

www.anovabooks.com

Contents

Acknowledgements

I have a great many to thank for their help with this book. I have drawn from literature both past and present, from Sir John Evelyn's diaries of the seventeenth and eighteenth centuries to Ian Balding's reminiscences of the twenty-first century, and from newspapers, historical documents and Internet websites containing snippets of local history that have proved invaluable.

My thanks also go to Sir Michael Oswald, the former stud manager to Her Majesty the Queen, who provided the Preface to this book and who has been kind enough to share his knowledge with me. My thanks go to Timothy Cox, who owns one of the largest private libraries on horse-racing and the history of the horse in this country; and by the same token, Jeanette Laird, who also made her private collection of books available to me. In addition are the staff of the following museums, societies and record offices, for whose time, assistance and patience I am grateful: the Humanities and Reference Section of Liverpool Central Library, the Natural History Museum, the National Horseracing Museum, the Society of Authors, the Public Record Office, the House of Lords Record Office, Lancashire Record Office, East Sussex Record Office, Cheshire and Chester Archives and Local Studies Service, West Sussex Record Office, Warwickshire County Record Office, Staffordshire Record Office, the Jockey Club and Pamela Clark of the Royal Archives, Windsor Castle.

I wish to thank my publisher, Jeremy Robson, and Melanie Letts, Jennifer Lansbury, Alan Heal and Barbara Phelan at Robson Books. Finally, I want to thank my family – both at home and in Israel – for their support; all my friends in the file-management and summons teams at Tithebarn House for their support, their interest in my work and especially their friendship; and in particular, computer experts Tom Oglesby and Keith Ellis for fixing my computer.

Preface

This book records the great alliance between horses and royalty. The two have been close companions for centuries – in battle, in sport and in ceremonial situations – and this alliance is as strong today as it ever has been.

The Queen has ridden all her life, and few people have a greater under-standing of the handling and welfare of the horse, while the Duke of Edinburgh is a successful competitive carriage driver of international calibre and, at the age of 84, is still one of the sport's leading lights. In eventing, the Princess Royal has represented Great Britain in the Olympics, while her daughter Zara Phillips will be a strong contender for the British team in the next Games. Polo has seen the Duke of Edinburgh and Prince Charles as leading players and is now the favourite sport of his sons, Prince William and Prince Harry.

If polo is the sport of princes, then horse-racing is the sport of kings. For over 400 years it has been the recreation that the British royal family has enjoyed and patronised above all others. Henry VIII and Elizabeth I bred racehorses at Hampton Court and imported stallions and mares from North Africa and the Middle East in order to improve the breed and performance of the native English horse. James I and Charles I continued this practice, and it was under their patronage that this importation of Barbary and Arab blood was expanded. Since those early times, the history of the Royal Stud has been closely interwoven with the evolution of the racehorse, and no other breeding establishment has played such an important role in its development.

Charles II, although not involved with the breeding of horses, established Newmarket as the headquarters of racing, and under the reign of William III and Queen Anne the mothballed Royal Stud at Hampton Court resumed operations. Later, George II's second son, William, Duke of Cumberland, bred the great stallions Eclipse and King Herod at his stud in Windsor Great Park, two stallions from which descend 98 per cent of all thoroughbreds in the world today.

Queen Victoria is the only person to have bred winners of both the Derby and the Oaks in the same year and also bred La Flèche, the greatest racing filly of the nineteenth century. Indeed, more champion racehorses all over the world have descended from mares at Hampton Court than from any other stud, while the most important sire of the twentieth century, Phalaris, owed 63 per cent of his pedigree to the stud there.

PREFACE

The studs at Sandringham and Wolferton in Norfolk were started by King Edward VII, who also bred the Derby winners Persimmon and Diamond Jubilee and who also owned Minoru – another Derby winner – and the Grand National winner Ambush II. His successor, King George V, bred and owned the Classic-winning filly Scuttle and bought the great foundation mare Feola, whose daughter Hypericum was a Classic winner for King George VI and became the grandmother of Aureole and the great American racehorse and sire Round Table. Hypericum was also the great-grandmother of the Queen's outstanding filly Highclere.

The Queen also inherited a fine stud of broodmares and twice became the leading owner in the 1950s. At the same time, Queen Elizabeth, the Queen Mother, became the most loved patron of racing over jumps, winning over 460 steeplechases and hurdle races. The last thirty years, however, have seen sweeping changes to the whole pattern of racing and breeding with the proliferation of air travel and the arrival of Arab owner/breeders with international operations on a scale ten times larger than had ever been seen before.

Against this background, the royal studs have continued to operate on much the same scale as they have in the past. The emphasis on quality remains unabated, however, and the Queen has bred and raced the dual Classic winners Highclere and Dunfermline, while the former's daughter Height of Fashion became one of the world's greatest broodmares. With the highly successful Sandringham stallions Bustino and Shirley Heights being succeeded by 2005's Derby winner, Motivator, the worldwide influence of the royal studs looks set to continue.

What is certain is that, whether in the field of racing, polo, three-day eventing or just riding for pleasure, royalty and horses will remain in a happy partnership, continuing the story that this book tells so well.

Sir Michael Oswald KCVO

Introduction

Since 1066 there have been 42 monarchs in Britain – each different from the last, with their own ideals and priorities. Some have not even been born in this country and have hailed from France, Germany and Holland. Each monarch has been an individual whose likes and dislikes have dominated their courts down the centuries, yet the one thing that has always linked them has been a major fascination for horses – from their use in war and pageantry to sport and leisure – and they have contributed to the development of the thoroughbred industry.

I have not sought to improve on the wealth of outstanding literature that already exists on the history of horses and horse-racing, but have sought instead to look at how the British royal family's interest in horses has fitted in with their everyday lives and their royal duties over the centuries, and how the royal household has developed to accommodate their activity. My book looks at the horsemanship of each monarch, from King William I to Queen Elizabeth II, and how their skills helped to raise the profile of the monarchy in the social context, while certain individuals within the royal households (such as William Cavendish, 1st Duke of Newcastle, Robert Dudley, Earl of Leicester, Gervaise Markham and Richard Marsh) helped to shape thinking on horsemanship. With horsemanship came horse breeding and management, which from the earliest days the monarchy was very much involved in, either directly or by encouraging the work of others – from Prospero D'Osma to George Villiers, 1st Duke of Buckingham, and from James D'Arcy to William Augustus, 1st Duke of Cumberland, to name but a few.

Throughout history there are breathtaking stories concerning individual monarchs, for instance: how a tournament was used to lure a royal favourite to his death; how a member of the St Leger family rebelled against King Richard III; how a Master of the Horse (a senior role, overseeing the care and management of the royal horses) sought the downfall of a king and was beheaded; how a royal duke came to breed one of the greatest racehorses that ever lived; how a king, interested in hunting, discovered a corner of England that has since become synonymous with horse-racing; and how a princess sought to become an Olympian. Then there are the simpler tales, of how a prince was a proficient blacksmith, how a farmhouse came to accommodate some of the grandest stables in the country, how the side-saddle was introduced, how a visit to the races caused a person to be exiled, how a Russian

Grand Duke became associated with the British Jockey Club, and how horsemanship has always had close links with architecture.

Of course, the British monarchy has always been associated with horse-racing and has been highly successful in this regard, although there have been ups and downs. I have sought to examine the Chifney affair of 1791 by looking at Samuel Chifney's autobiography, *Genius Genuine*, as well as the newspaper accounts of the day. I have also looked at how some monarchs sought to distance themselves from the seedier side of horse-racing – in particular, how Prince Albert, the Prince Consort, tried to raise the monarchy above the sport in an effort to reform the royals' image during the 'Filthy Forties', while his son, King Edward VII, sought to raise the profile of both the monarchy and the sport, so that they complemented each other, thus setting the seal once and for all on the Royal Family's involvement in horseracing and its responsibility towards it – especially during the First and Second World Wars. It is a responsibility that has extended to the present day and not just towards horse-racing, but towards all equine sports, horses and those who take care of them. The Royal Family is the most enduring institution that we have in this country and I include here a brief history of the monarchy since 1066.

The Romans left Britain before AD 600 and in their wake left a land divided. For the next 400 to 500 years the many peoples of England, Ireland, Scotland and Wales fought the Vikings, the French and each other, and England was split with separate rulers. The independent kingdoms of Essex, Sussex and Wessex were brought together through conflict, but there was no true stability. In the 1060s the crown of England was promised by Edward the Confessor to the Duke of Normandy, called William. But when Edward died, the throne was usurped by Harold Godwinson – Harold II – so it was up to William of Normandy to take his inheritance back, which he did by invading the British Isles in 1066 and confronting Harold at the Battle of Hastings on 14 October, resulting in Harold's death that same day.

Thus known as the Conqueror, King William I's rule of England was akin to of an absentee landlord. He did, however, establish some kind of order as his followers arrived and settled, and in 1086 he commissioned the *Domesday Book*, which was completed within six months and detailed the wealth of the country. When William died in 1087 he was not mourned. His successor, his son William – known as Rufus because of his red hair – reigned until 1100 when he was killed in a hunting accident. With unseemly haste his brother declared himself King – Henry I – and he reigned for many years. His son died, so he declared that his daughter Matilda, Empress of Germany, should become Queen in her own right, but on Henry's death, his nephew Stephen was

INTRODUCTION

declared King instead. There then followed a power struggle between Stephen and Matilda, which resulted in Stephen making Matilda's son, Henry, his royal heir.

On Stephen's death, Matilda's son Henry Plantagenet became King Henry II, the head of a dynasty that would rule England until 1485. Henry and his wife, Eleanor (in her own right Duchess of Aquitaine in France), had eight children. The two eldest sons, Henry and Geoffrey, died in their father's lifetime, so it was his third son, Richard, who succeeded as Richard I. He drained the country's economy through his obsession with Christian crusades in the east and he seldom visited England, eventually dying in France in 1199. His brother John succeeded him and is remembered for the Magna Carta. In 1216 John died and was succeeded by his young son Henry – Henry III – who as a child was subject to a regency until he came of age. He ruled for many decades and was succeeded by Edward I, who was followed by Edward II, who was deposed by his wife, Isabella, and her lover, and later murdered. Isabella acted as regent over her son, Edward III, who later became the father of the Black Prince. As the Black Prince died in his father's lifetime, it was *his* son, a child of about eight, who succeeded Edward III and later became King Richard II. However, he was later usurped by his distant cousin, Henry Bolingbroke, who declared himself King Henry IV and established the House of Lancaster, splitting the Plantagenet line. Henry IV was the father of Henry V, a born warrior whose main ambition in life was to realise his belief that the kings of England were also the true kings of France. He died soon after achieving success at the Battle of Agincourt, leaving an infant son to succeed him – Henry VI – who was dominated first by his mother, Katherine de Valois, and later his wife, Margaret Beaufort. Henry VI's reign was not a secure one in that the other side of the Plantagenet line, the House of York, led by Edward, Duke of York, was determined to oust Henry and so began a war which would last for some thirty years and would become known as the Wars of the Roses (1455–85). Henry was executed and the son of the Duke of York, also called Edward, became King Edward IV, but he did not live long to enjoy his reign, dying in April 1483. His twelve-year-old son became Edward V, whose regency was a source of contention between his mother's family, the Woodvilles, and his father's brother, Richard of Gloucester, who had the young king and his brother, Richard, Duke of York, taken to the Tower of London and kept there. Within weeks Richard of Gloucester had declared himself king – Richard III – and the two boys, the Princes in the Tower, had disappeared. Since it was believed that the boys had been murdered, a rebellion, led by the Duke of Buckingham, took place in November 1483, but its failure resulted in the execution of him and other rebels. Even so, within two years the Yorkist Richard III himself was dead after facing the Lancastrian Henry Tudor at the Battle of Bosworth, thus bringing an end to the Plantagenet line.

The Tudors reigned from 1485 to 1603. Henry VII was a shrewd administrator whose main objective was to restore the wealth of the country after so many years at war. His son Henry VIII, as a new Renaissance prince, spent all the new-found wealth and, in order to acquire a divorce from his first wife, broke from the Church of Rome and took the wealth of the monasteries in England. He married six times but had only three legitimate children to succeed him: Edward VI, who died at the age of fifteen; Mary I, who became known as 'Bloody Mary'; and Elizabeth I, who reigned from 1558 to 1603. Elizabeth died without issue and the throne of England passed to her distant cousin, King James VI of Scotland, who was the son of Mary, Queen of Scots (Mary Stuart), the great-granddaughter of Henry VII.

James became King James I of England. An attempt to blow up him and his parliament failed in 1605 and he continued his reign until his death in 1625. He was succeeded by his second son, who became Charles I. His reign was dominated by the English Civil War (1642–9), and his execution in January 1649 paved the way for eleven years of Parliamentary rule under Oliver Cromwell as Lord Protector. Cromwell died in 1658 and the monarchy was restored in 1660 under Charles I's son, Charles II, who acted as the eleventh-hour hero during the Great Fire of London in 1666. After his death in 1685 he was succeeded by his brother James – James II – who, because of his Catholic faith, was deposed in 1688 and succeeded by his daughter Mary and her husband, William of Orange – Mary II and William III. They died without issue and in 1702 Mary's sister, Anne, became Queen, but her reign was short lived and, after eighteen pregnancies, many of which resulted in miscarriage, she died in 1714 also without issue.

The throne of England therefore passed to the great-grandson of James I through his daughter Elizabeth: George Louis of Hanover in Germany. Aged in his mid-fifties, he became King George I and was at the head of a family that would rule England, as well as Hanover, from 1714 to 1901, ending with the death of George's great-great-great-granddaughter Queen Victoria. The reign of the Hanoverians was not easy and was noted for its profligate living, scandal, debts – and madness. So, after George II, George III, George IV and William IV, Victoria's accession at the age of eighteen was seen as a sign of new hope. It also ushered in the longest reign in British history and saw Britain become an empire.

Victoria died in January 1901 and was succeeded by her eldest son, Albert

INTRODUCTION

Edward, who became King Edward VII and the head of the Saxe-Coburg-Gotha family – since his mother, although a Hanoverian, had married Prince Albert, a prince of the German duchy of Saxe-Coburg and Gotha. King Edward would reign for only nine years, but his was the Gilded Age of society and wealth. He was also known as the 'Peacemaker' for his efforts to maintain peace in Europe through diplomatic means, but he was only holding off what had become inevitable. In 1910 Edward died and was succeeded by his son, who became King George V, but within four years England, France and Russia were at war with Germany and Austria, and by 1917 the whole world was at war and it did not end until 1918. The House of Saxe-Coburg-Gotha in England changed its name to Windsor in 1917, and the family name has remained so ever since.

George V reigned for almost 26 years, dying in January 1936, and by December of that year his eldest son, King Edward VIII, had abdicated in order to marry American divorcée Wallis Simpson. Edward was succeeded by his brother, who became King George VI and helped to maintain morale during the darkest days of the Second World War. His work, however, took its toll. Never a strong man but a heavy smoker, George died in February 1952, to be succeeded by the UK's present queen, Elizabeth II, who has reigned for over fifty years and celebrates her eightieth birthday in 2006. To this day, the Queen has maintained and enhanced the royal family's deep interest in and responsibility towards horses and horsemanship.

1
The Normans

Horses were instrumental in securing victory for William, Duke of Normandy, in his resolve to conquer England. A soldier first and foremost, he understood their importance in the face of war, and this was to provide him with an advantage over King Harold II when the time came to invade England. Coming from a warrior-like people, William was ambitious and uncompromising, and the success of his invasion of England lay in his preparation against a country that did not have the resources to defend itself. Good warhorses were essential.

It is believed that Duke William brought with him, on 700 small sailing ships, some 3,000 horses, of which some 2,000 were full stallions, fully prepared to be used as cavalry in battle, not as transport horses. This meant that the Normans did not need to depend on using local English horses after their arrival in England. The Bayeux Tapestry, the Norman version of events, on which 190 horses appear, is testament to their own horses' important role in the overall conquest of England.

The Tapestry provides an interesting insight into the type of equipment supplied for the horses. The horses had saddles, bridles and stirrups that appear to have been lightweight and flexible – not so much for speed as to allow both the horse and rider freedom of movement.[1] The Norman saddles had been adapted for warfare, with pommels to allow the armed soldier to stand up in the stirrups while maintaining balance and leaning forward comfortably.[2] Their triangular or pyramid style of stirrups, with long leathers,[3] reflects that the Normans valued practicality and flexibility in battle.[4] In contrast, the Englishmen's stirrups, looking more like modern stirrups, were descended from those used by the Vikings, with side bars hanging below the tread, and they were decorated, revealing a pride in horsemanship and status. The Tapestry shows that the Normans' weaponry, in particular the shield, depicted heraldry and colours that would be recognised on sight.[5] The Normans' horses also look much larger than their opponents', and altogether would certainly have provided an impressive sight, but how did the Normans develop such large horses when much of the north of Europe possessed horses no bigger than Shetland ponies?[6]

Some years before the invasion of England, the Normans had taken part in the re-conquest of Spain and had come across horses that had been brought there, originally, by the Arabs, who had initially merged the horses into their armies and then brought them along the African coast and into Spain. The peoples of the Middle and Near East[7] had discovered the horses in West Central Asia, so the horses had come a great distance and had been developed along the way.[8] The Normans wished to develop them further and found that the countryside in France was favourable for horse breeding, so throughout the eleventh century the horse continued to be developed and was bred to a bigger size.[9] The Normans were admired for their new war machine and many foreigners wanted to join their armies. Since horses had to be effective in battle, breeding the right type of horse was essential. They were bred to be strong and powerful, but at this stage there was no emphasis on speed. From the eleventh century the emphasis was on the size of the horse: the bigger the horse, the more damage it could inflict. It seems that by 1066 they were managing to breed horses that were significantly larger than the Englishmen's horses as depicted in the Bayeux Tapestry – although this could be more to do with perception than reality as the horses were not as important as the soldiers riding them.

Duke William and his armies had a clear advantage over Harold in the final confrontation when, on 14 October 1066, the Battle of Hastings resulted in Harold's death. William, Duke of Normandy, became King William I of England, and today is more popularly known as William the Conqueror. But William did not have any particular interest in the place he had just conquered. A warrior by nature (his royal seal showed an image of him riding to war), the trappings of kingship held few charms for him and especially in a country that was totally foreign to him and not even considered as important as his duchy in France.

The French had a sophistication about them that contrasted with what England seemed to offer. Its horse population was quite small (as were the horses themselves) and there may have been more horses in some parts of the country than others. They certainly existed in the east and south-east of England as the lords and peasants there were able to use horses to farm the land and grew oats to feed them. The horse would later become popular in the East Midlands,[10] but in the scheme of things they rated lower than other domestic animals, probably because they were so expensive to keep. In England at this time and for a long time afterwards, sheep were the most valuable commodity, followed by goats and cattle. Even oxen were considered cheaper to keep and just as good at pulling ploughs, so it seems that the importance of the horse depended upon where the farmer lived and worked. Elsewhere, horses were wild and seemed particularly prevalent in Wales. Given what the French had achieved thus far with the horses they had originally acquired in Spain, England presented a blank canvas upon which to create and develop a new kind of horse.

Once William had command of the kingdom, the whole of its land was seized by him and his followers. He himself had royal estates in 29 counties and was addicted to hunting,[11] since it was seen as the ideal training for war. His hunting reserves included Hatfield Forest in Hertfordshire (which had also been the property of King Harold), Neroche Forest in Somerset and Feckenham in Worcestershire. These and the other forests in William's possession had harsh laws, known as the Forest Laws, to keep the local peasantry out. Incidentally, the Normans brought with them a phrase used to warn huntsmen that a deer had been sighted: 'Ty a Hillaut' was later anglicised to the more recognisable 'Tally Ho'.[12]

The Hastings campaign in 1066 and the subsequent Northern Battles of 1069 meant that the English countryside was devastated, and despite the constant need for warhorses there was no constructive system for breeding them, so English horses continued to run wild in the forests or were captured by sheriffs and landowners. In fact, the horse population in the Norfolk Broads would drop from 359 to 139 between 1066 and 1086 – thanks to one sheriff, Roger Bigod,[13] a shrewd character who had been a poor nonentity but who grew in wealth and prestige after 1066, not because of military success, but through acquiring land. His estate comprised small landholdings that were scattered about the country and were worth a lot. He became powerful, but he abused his power and status by taking whatever land he liked and charging high rents elsewhere. The *Domesday Book* records that he had six lordships in Essex, 117 in Suffolk and 187 in Norfolk. He was sheriff of the last two, so if the numbers of horses fell he was probably selling them off rather than becoming involved in any breeding programme. However, the King's comrade Roger de Boulogne – now Earl of Shrewsbury – introduced Spanish horses to his new estates,[14] so the Conquest did succeed in bringing in fresh strains of blood.

Twenty-one years after successfully invading England, William directed that a statement of lands and resources be drawn up and a record kept of the land's wealth. This became known as the *Domesday Book* and would be completed in the relatively short space of two years.[15] It was designed primarily to see how much tax William was actually receiving; he was under threat from all sides – particularly from King Cnut of Denmark and King Olaf of Norway – so part of England's taxes went towards staving off marauding armies.

From the *Domesday Book* we can learn a little about how some of our present-day racecourse locations were back then. Lewes, Cheltenham, Chepstow, Doncaster, Epsom, Maghull (just ten minutes from Aintree and the original home of the Liverpool Steeplechase), Kempton, Leicester, Lincoln, Thirsk, Uttoxeter, Plumpton, Warwick and York were all agricultural lands held by noblemen either for themselves or 'in demesne' for the monarch (Lambourn was one such place). Gloucester had been quite wealthy in Edward's day, dealing in iron for the King's ships and in honey, while Tewkesbury was known for its slaves – the Book recorded fifty of them. The Church also held a great deal of land, including Epsom, which was in the control of the local abbey. William I himself held Sandown – which had previously been held by Edward the Confessor through a nobleman called Walnoth – and Windsor, although that was held for him in demesne. The Saxon kings who had hunted there had built a house by the Thames at a village called Windsor, after which the forest was named. When Edward the Confessor had died the property came under the authority of Westminster Abbey, but William bought it back. He considered the whole area fit for hunting and decided to build a castle there – a wooden castle, which would eventually be reconstructed in stone and is the present day Windsor Castle.[16]

King William did not live to see the completion of the *Domesday Book*. In 1087, while riding through the streets of Mantes in France, his horse stumbled among the burning ashes of the city he had just helped to destroy and he was thrown against the pommel of his saddle.[17] He died several days later on 9 September 1087[18] and was not particularly mourned. In fact, as a final insult, his body was robbed of its clothing and left naked for some time before eventually being interred.

Before his death William had decided that his eldest son, Robert, would inherit the Duchy of Normandy and not the throne of England. Normandy, after all, was still considered the more important of the two, so the kingdom of England went to the Conqueror's second son, also called William.

William II, also known as William Rufus because of his red hair, was the youngest king since the sons of Cnut.[19] He was in his late twenties when he became King, although his exact age at the time is unknown as the exact date of his birth is not known – somewhere between 1056 and 1060. He was a warrior prince like his father and possessed all of his dubious virtues: tyranny, cruelty and treachery. Nor was he much appreciated by his brothers, Robert and Henry. When he was not fighting one of them, he was fighting them both; and when he was not fighting either he was helping one fight the other or vice versa. His relationship with the Church was not completely harmonious, but nevertheless he was anxious to keep on the right side of this institution, even if it frowned upon his twin loves of gaming and hunting, the latter of which had by now come to be seen as a low pursuit. Yet such prejudice did not prevent the development of the royal stables, and stallions were still seen as the ultimate symbol of status and war.

Mares and geldings, however, were deemed suitable only for priests and women. It was considered unseemly for knights, not to mention kings, to ride them: one day, William Rufus, giving in to impulse and in a rush to reach the coast, was about to gallop off on a gelding when he was tactfully reminded that to ride them lacked dignity. Wild forest mares that ran freely with the stallion were seen to represent the most basic form of breeding and as a result were not interfered with, except on a yearly basis when the foals were rounded up.

As well as hunting, William II enjoyed tournaments,[20] which were still a rarity in England although they were seen as an essential sport for the preparation of war, both physically and emotionally, and during which knights could practise their skills and fight each other in jousts, melees and on foot, ensuring that they were prepared as individuals and as a group. The tournaments had to reflect the conditions of war and the participants were given plenty of time to get ready for them – perhaps two to three weeks. The actual site of the tournament, also pre-arranged, could take place over a vast area – over countryside and through villages and townships. There were usually two teams – again to reflect campaign conditions – and both sides could use whatever weapons were available, with the exception of bolts and arrows, possibly because they were too lethal in what was meant to be a mock battle. Prisoners could be taken and even held to ransom; and horses and armour could be confiscated. They were noisy, dangerous and often provided rival sides with the chance to settle old scores, but they were effective in their aim to prepare men for war and, given that royalty valued them, played a major role. The tournaments were also good preparation for the horses, which not only carried those knights taking part, but, by their rich trappings, were a visible representation of the wealth and status of their riders. Tournaments also ensured that horses became used to battle conditions and to the general noise and chaos for which the tournaments were famous.

In 1091 William and his brother Robert, the Duke of Normandy, sponsored daily tournaments in both England and France, but over time William suffered from increasing depression, which made him reclusive.[21] When his nephew Richard was killed in the New Forest during a hunting expedition he began to have unsettling dreams. However, three months later he lodged in the New Forest and planned the next hunt. It was actually his younger brother, Henry, who suggested they go hunting there and William consented – but during the course of the hunt he was struck by an arrow and killed. Whether or not this was murder is still a subject of dispute, and Henry, against whom there is no proof that he planned his brother's death, wasted no time in hanging around to find out. He took himself off and was crowned King Henry I just two days later. His brother's body, having been left in the forest, was eventually carted away by local peasants to nearby Winchester,[22] where Henry was busy ensuring the security of the royal treasury. The irony of William's death is that, having inflicted so many harsh penalties on others, no one was held accountable for his demise. The man who fired the arrow fled the country and nobody bothered to stop him.

Henry's reign (1100–35) would be remembered for his businesslike approach to making the running of his court more economical. His horses were also a part of the national economy and were growing in importance, particularly as he expanded his military and made the Royal Stud more organised. A document written towards the end of his reign details how much was paid out to his knights huntsmen, hunt servants and so on, providing a very early glimpse of how sport rated in the economics of the day. The knights huntsmen received eight pence a day; hunt servants received five pence. The huntsmen of the wolf hunt received twenty pence a day for horses, men and dogs – they had to keep 24 hounds and eight greyhounds. They were also granted £6 a year to buy horses, although, like all workers over the centuries, they complained it should have been more – £8 and not £6.[23]

Their complaints, though, were nothing to their monarch's. During the winter of 1120 Henry's only son, William, had drowned saving his sister, Matilda, as the yacht they were sailing in, the *White Ship*, sank off the Normandy coast. Six years later Henry declared that Matilda (also known as Maud to the English) would become Queen on his death. On 5 March 1133 Matilda[24] gave birth to a son, whom she called Henry. Later, both Matilda and her husband, Geoffrey Plantagenet (son of the Count of Anjou), were involved in an unsuccessful rebellion against King Henry, who died in France on 1 December 1135. Within days, his nephew Stephen, Count of Blois, Champagne and Chartres, had made a claim for the throne of England and was consecrated on 25 December. His uncle's body was returned to England at the beginning of 1136, and at Easter the royal knights swore allegiance to King Stephen.[25]

Stephen's reign proved to be the most troubled since the Conquest and much of his time and energy were spent trying to maintain an uneasy peace despite the Empress Matilda's attempts to take back the throne. Two years after Matilda began her efforts to oust Stephen, the King was taken prisoner at Lincoln. For a year Matilda had control, but England descended into civil war, which led to famine. Within the year Stephen was released and throughout the 1140s he did his best to minimise threats to his position. His ongoing struggle meant that he could not devote time to developing studs. Tournaments, in particular, were proving problematic and he was forced to break up a number of them – this was not a new thing and would be repeated in later reigns as, it was found, the competitions could be instrumental in sparking trouble or making a situation worse.[26] If knights wished to compete they had to go abroad.

By 1145 Matilda's luck was waning and Stephen was able to secure his position. Even so, a compromise was reached in 1153 when his eldest son Eustace died while marauding the abbey estates of Bury St Edmunds and Stephen was persuaded to make Matilda's son, Henry, his heir and adopt him as his son. Stephen did have a younger son, called William, who was the Count of Boulogne and would become the Count of Mortain in 1154, but it was acknowledged that Henry would succeed as King of England and not William. This may have been not only to end the fighting in England, but also because Norman kings still considered French duchies to be more important than the English kingdom. Fourteen months later, in 1154, Stephen died and Henry FitzEmpress, also known as Henry Plantagenet, became King Henry II of England – a descendant of both the Normans and Anglo-Saxons, but a born Frenchman.[27]

Notes

1. Gravett, p52
2. Davis, p18
3. Gravett, p17
4. Ibid.
5. Ibid.
6. Davis, p6, p7
7. Ibid.
8. Ibid.
9. Ibid., p21
10. Hallam, H. E. pp12–13, pp25–6
11. Bates, p94
12. Dan Beard, *Tally Ho and Other Cries* (www.inquiry.net)
13. www.genicircles.com
14. David, R H C, *The Medieval Warhorse*, p79
15. Domesday Book Online
16. Girouard, Mark, p8

17. Douglas, David C & Greenaway, George W, *English Historical Documents, Vol. II 1042–1189*, pp279–80
18. Crouch, *The Normans: The History of a Dynasty*, pp130–8
19. Lee, *This Sceptred Isle: 55 BC–1901*, p49
20. Crouch, *The Normans: The History of a Dynasty*, p136
21. Crouch, *The Normans: The History of a Dynasty*, p152
22. Crouch, *The Normans: The History of a Dynasty*, pp165–6
23. Douglas & Greenaway, *English Historical Documents: Volume II, 1042–1189*, p427
24. Lee, *This Sceptred Isle: 55 BC–1901*, pp55–9
25. Crouch, *The Reign of King Stephen: 1135–1154*, p242
26. Lee, *This Sceptred Isle: 55 BC–1901*, p154
27. Lee, *This Sceptred Isle: 55 BC–1901*, p60

2
The Plantagenets

Henry II was the first of what would be a long line of Plantagenet rulers. Possessed of boundless energy, he was constantly on the move[1] and loved outdoor pursuits, especially hunting: he would take off on horseback at dawn and stay out all day, hunting over wasteland, through forests and over mountain tops. He enjoyed the sport as much as his grandfather, Henry I, had done, and in being so energetic he had a tendency to wear everyone out.[2]

Given the nature of his chaotic life, it is ironic that, among other things, his reign was important for the strength of its administration and the meticulous records that were kept, some of which can still be viewed today at the Public Record Office in Kew. These are the Pipe Rolls – rolled-up documents that recorded details of the country's finances. They had come into existence during the reign of Henry I and so were already established when his grandson came to the throne. Over the succeeding centuries a great many of these rolls were destroyed or allowed to decay, but there are still enough to get an idea of how the Royal Household was run, and they contain details of how the royal horses were managed and what types were purchased by whom and when. The Pipe Rolls for 1164 to 1165, for instance, contain details of the horses and parks of St Thomas à Becket, the Archbishop of Canterbury: the park at Aldington in Kent was enclosed and some of his stallions and mares removed to the royal parks at Clarendon when he retreated into exile abroad. After returning to England five years later, Becket was killed in his cathedral by four knights on 29 December 1170. As his murder reverberated throughout Europe, his tomb became a centre of pilgrimage and among the many badges depicting his martyrdom there is one of him on horseback.[3]

Horses had increased in value immeasurably since the Conquest over one hundred years earlier, and the number in Henry's ownership grew steadily since he received them as payment of fines, known as immurements, or death duties. Warhorses, still the most expensive purchase at 40 shillings, were large and magnificent, especially developed to support the weight of the knights who rode them. A single knight's armour weighed no more than 70lb, but the warhorse could be expected to carry some 250–300lb. Its weight and strength added to the impact of the knight's lance, and being twice as heavy as a conventional riding horse it could be a devastating opponent in warfare. It was also equipped with sharp, nailed beads on its hooves, so that it could trample anyone and anything underfoot. Known also as the 'destrier', it was the most effective war machine of its day. But it was not fast, and nor was the 'palfrey', a short-legged, long-bodied animal used for everyday riding, and costing between 30 and 60 shillings. The horse that was relied upon for speed cost only 20 to 30 shillings, and, known as the 'courser', was essentially used to carry messengers between armies and kingdoms.[4]

Tournaments were still considered the most important preparation for war, for both men and horses, as were the rough and ready races that went on in London, as chronicled by William Fitzstephen, St Thomas à Becket's secretary and biographer. He describes how, every Sunday after dinner during Lent, young men went into the fields on warhorses skilled in combat. Equipment was provided and a mock combat, treated very seriously by the combatants, got underway with the horses champing at the bit. Then they raced, with some riders overtaking or forcing others to dismount before galloping past them.[5]

Henry II's eldest son, also called Henry, loved tournaments and understood their importance and value. As a result he spent most of his time abroad taking part in them since his father the King had banned them in England. The younger Henry was joined by some of his younger brothers and, very often, ignored summonses to return home. That was, until his untimely death on 11 June 1183. The years after young Henry's death saw King Henry fighting off his other sons in their attempts to undermine his power and if he had any doubts about the effectiveness of tournaments his arguments were justified when, in 1186, another son, Geoffrey, Duke of Brittany, died in a tournament in Paris. When the King himself died in France on 6 July 1189, he was succeeded by his third surviving son, Richard, Duke of Aquitaine, a fierce militarist who, whilst reversing his father's policy on tournaments, set about bleeding England dry in his efforts to finance his crusades in the east.[6]

In the days of William I, the mounted soldier wore a conical helmet, was clad in a hauberk (a coat of mail) and rode on an unprotected horse. The knight of Richard I's day wore a lorica (again, a coat of mail) over a gambeson which was a padded garment, mail hose and mittens and a heavy pot helmet; this indicates how dangerous the battlefield had become, involving a lot more hand-to-hand fighting. To this end the horse had to be protected too and would go into battle wearing armour under its trapper of linen or silk.[7] Richard, a keen horseman whose royal seal showed him on horseback, could be just as ruthless with his horses as he was with people and often rode them to exhaustion – being quickly supplied with others.[8]

Not surprisingly, he enjoyed hunting and appreciated the value of tournaments, but seldom took part in the latter once he became king. In fact, the one tournament in which he is known to have taken part resulted in a brawl and, because Richard was unable to get the better of his opponent, he retreated in a sulk. Even so, he encouraged tournaments in England, particularly since he and his followers had to be constantly ready for battle, but he ensured they were controlled, licensed events, arranged well in advance and in designated areas – Wiltshire and Warwickshire to name but two.[9] The aim, as in Stephen's reign, may have been to prevent insurgency, since there were plenty at home who would have liked to have seen Richard dead, and the Earls of Warenne, Gloucester and Salisbury had to form a court of control. Tournament fees were paid in advance: twenty marks for an earl, ten for a baron, four for a landed knight and two for a knight without estate. There was even a collector of fees – one Theobald Walter – and all those participating had to swear to keep the peace.[10] This not only served to keep troublemakers away, but would have helped fund Richard's crusades. He himself was seldom in England and died abroad in 1199. He was succeeded by his youngest brother, John, who was not a military man, even though one of his seals shows him as such on horseback and reveals how much this image of the soldier king had become wrapped up in the image of the monarch.

King John was the complete antithesis to the earlier monarchs and in particular his warmongering brother. He was not interested in anything chivalric and thought tournaments were pointless – particularly since they seemed to create trouble as well as prepare men for it[11] – but he did not feel the same way about hunting and was almost obsessive about it – to the point where he upset the church establishment.

John wanted to keep the Church happy, but was hardly an example of morality. Generous to the poor, but unsparing with those of a higher order, his expression of religious faith was superficial and appeared only when the occasion demanded, so much so that he was never a conscientious churchgoer and did not mind making his boredom felt while in church. For its part, the Church was not above condemning him,[12] especially as he travelled widely about the country on hunting expeditions, and had no qualms about hunting on Holy Days. This for the time would have been a huge problem for the Church trying to enforce its authority as a whole throughout the country. But when he did hunt on Holy Days, John eased his conscience somewhat by generously giving alms to the poor: for the St Mary Magdalen feast in 1209 a hundred paupers were fed at Newcastle at his expense, and 450 were fed in Eiswell in 1212. Of all monarchs, he seemed to have the most hunting lodges, the majority of which, along with his forests, were in the care of his Chief Forester, Hugh de Neville, until his death in 1203. There was a royal hunting lodge in Rockingham Forest in Northamptonshire; he made use of a hunting lodge at Axbridge in Somerset (also in use during the Saxon era); and he hunted at Cranborne Chase in Dorset,[13] Delamare Forest near Halton Castle in Cheshire, Powerstock in Dorset and St Briavels in Gloucestershire. Nor did he reserve his hunting instincts for home: huntsmen and falconers followed him overseas and this meant, inevitably, that the management of the King's horses had to be stepped up.

The key figure in the management of the Royal Stud was Thomas de Landa who, in 1207, was one of John's keepers of horses. He had a great deal of responsibility and superior status and by 1216 was spending much of his time travelling the country with the King's horses and organising crossings abroad, whether for hunting trips or not. The Pipe Roll records for March 1215 show that de Landa's brother Richard was also one of three men in charge of the King's horses in Northampton. Had John not died when he did and had he carried on with his hunting activities, the personnel would probably have expanded further.

John died on 18 October 1216 and his only son, a boy of nine, became King Henry III. He was a chip off the old block and on coming of age, Henry proceeded to spend an absolute fortune on hunting lodges, seeing them as an expression of wealth and power. In fact he took quite an interest in the royal stables, writing to the mayor and aldermen of London to ask for their assistance in acquiring three horses from Lombardy that had appeared on the London market; he had no qualms about becoming directly involved in the buying and selling of his horses, but, like his predecessors, he did have his agents and sent some abroad to buy Italian steeds. He also imported from Castile (through one of his agents called Bernard de Banares, the son of William), and from La Rochelle and Bordeaux until 1218. He also imported from Spain. French horses were good, but Spanish horses were the *crème de la crème*. Since Henry was also the Duke of Aquitaine (and monarchs would remain so until 1443), access to Spain was not difficult and any horses purchased in the Duchy of Aquitaine were probably Spanish. In 1241 two of his marshals were sent to purchase horses from a large horse fair in Lagny-sur-Marne, and in 1243 he paid the Provost of Roncesvalles 100 marks for destriers. The fact that these horses could be acquired and transported back shows how organised the royal stud was in general in making these acquisitions. It also reveals how important horse sales had become to the English market, but the King could be greedy in his acquisitions and was not above a spot of piracy if he could get away with it. In 1242 he ordered the men of Bordeaux to seize a French ship sailing from Spain to La Rochelle that contained horses among its cargo.

Part of the reason for these purchases and occasional underhand attempts to secure the very best horses was that Henry wanted to create the most sophisticated studs in England. The quality of the horses he bought was important, particularly since it was difficult to maintain breeds at home, so he continued to spend huge amounts of money on them. The studs in England would probably have ranked as some of the finest and most expensive in Europe, had not civil war broken out. As we will see in later chapters, whenever there was human conflict or disease the horse population always suffered.

Henry died in November 1272 and was succeeded by his son Edward, who became King Edward I. His coronation at Westminster Abbey on 19 August 1274 proved to be a particularly wild one when King Alexander I of Scotland showed up with a hundred knights who let loose their horses for people to chase after. The English joined in and the stampeding horses caused absolute chaos.[14]

As Edward was on a crusade when he became king, he did not return to England until August 1274, and by November 1276 he had declared war on Wales. It was then that he realised there was a dire shortage of horses and that, having become king during a civil war, he had inherited a state of disorder where the studs were concerned. Thus began a programme to import horses on a vast scale – from the King through to his barons, for he decreed that all those knights and barons in possession of £30 or more (£11,500 in today's money) should buy a horse, and preferably a warhorse. A measure of how important it was to replace those horses lost and the complexity involved can be seen by the details in the Pipe Rolls. Everything had to be accounted for and such specific records give a broad view of how the studs were being managed at this time. Between 15 November 1276 and 7 February 1277, for instance, 158 horses were brought over from Wissant and Dorset, and the barons were commissioned to import 45 more. Valuations were noted, from 1280, of those horses belonging to the King's bodyguard, and there is a schedule for those being kept at Westminster and Guildford, as well as those at Chester under the keeping of the King's servant Richard Farrier. The Royal Stud was well on its way to being replenished. By 1282 there was a second Welsh War and Edward was planning his cavalry,[15] showing that the studs were as much a part of the overall war machine as men and weapons.

When it came to horses Edward was the most organised of monarchs to date. With an eye on the wider picture, he kept horses at Macclesfield, Chertsey, St Albans and Braemore and maintained a royal stud in Wales, which made sense given the recent troubles there and also sent out the message that the monarch and his barons were at the ready should there be further trouble. Between 1282 and 1283 a stable for 200 horses was built at Clipstone, Nottinghamshire, at a cost of £108.8s.5d (£40,240 today), so the importance of the stud meant that no expense was spared. This also meant that the minutest detail was accounted for, and between 1285 and 1286 the records made over a hundred references to bridles and reins, collars, traces, girths, halters, saddles, clothes and covers, stirrups and harnesses. We are also given a glimpse of how personally the King took his horses, as some of them had quite interesting names, such as Bataro de la Tuche, Bataro de Champagne and Greyley Lyndhurst.

In fact, the King's love of horses tied in with his overall love of sports, and he took delight in hawking and hunting as well as in enjoying the spectacle of tournaments. In 1273 he took part in one such event at Chalons, and on that occasion he was grabbed around the neck by the Count of Chalons who then tried to drag him off his horse. The King was not amused, as this went against convention. A large fight ensued and a great many were injured. This violent affair had far-reaching consequences for other tournaments that took place in England, and as a result rules were put in place to reduce bloodshed and encourage restraint. Weapons had to be blunted while grooms and footmen were forbidden to carry weapons of any kind. From this point on, tournaments became less ferocious and began to lean more towards the ceremonial, a development that upset a number of the King's barons, who felt that the sport as a whole was becoming too soft.

Like Henry II, Edward killed two birds with one stone by combining business with pleasure. His hunting expeditions provided the ideal opportunity to deal with matters of state, court business, marriages, diplomacy and the planning of meetings. The monarch was not shutting himself off but, in fact, was maintaining an exhausting schedule, seldom staying in one place for long, and parliament was held at Clipstone in Nottinghamshire.[16]

Rigorous records continued to be kept of the royal studs and between 1289 and 1290 expenses were noted for the King's horses at Rayleigh, Neyland, Eastwood, Woodstock and Knoll, which not only attested to the fact that horses were being kept at many places across the country[17] but also presents a picture of Edward's life and movements at this time. In October 1289 he went to Clarendon for a fortnight, visiting his mother at Amesbury along the way. Then he went to the New Forest before travelling back to Westminster for Christmas.

He spent Lent on the upper valley of the Thames, then began a hunting tour via Winchcombe, Hailes, Feckenham (a royal manor in Worcestershire), Campden and Woodstock, where he spent Easter in April 1290. Sometime in July he travelled the forests of Whittlewood, Rockingham, Sherwood and Macclesfield. Then he stayed at Northampton and around September, as his hunting tour drew to a close, he returned to Clipstone and made plans for his next crusade. So the royal stables had not only to be well maintained, but to be constantly at the ready for any journeys the King might make. They also had to be prepared for the unexpected as in November: when Edward's wife, Eleanor of Castile, died, whatever plans he may have had would have been put on hold in order to prepare for his return to London.

The number of royal horses increased steadily, with the King's expenditure on horses reaching a peak between 1292 and 1301. It was noted that in November 1292 there were eighteen horses kept at Berwick and 164 at Norham. By May 1293 there were 269 horses held at royal residences around the country. Thirty-four of these belonged solely to the King, and the rest belonged to other members of the royal family and one of the King's keepers, John of Brabant. By 1296 and 1297 there were 30 horses at Chertsey under the keeper Richard Fohun and 50 at Hertford under Adam de Bray. The care of these horses had become a specialised and highly organised business, and not only did the royal family – which travelled from one royal residence to another throughout the year – have to be accommodated but, with war a constant threat, the management of the horses was a reminder of just how important the studs were. Between 1299 and 1301 accounts and valuations were kept of the horses the King used in the Scotch War and the supplies needed to maintain them,[18] but not everyone was convinced that so much needed to be spent on the studs and in 1301 the clergy and the barons complained so loudly about the growing expenditure that the King was compelled to economise. Nor were the stables, or those who ran them, above legal process; between 1302 and 1304, at a time when everything was strictly recorded and everybody could be held accountable for something, there were writs issued in relation to the debts of one Richard Fenn, a keeper of the King's horses, for the oats and beans acquired to feed the horses, while other records relate to the logistics of running the stables and the losses incurred through battle. An inquiry was even set up when horses were lost at the Battle of Falkirk in 1298,[19] proving that, as a commodity, their value was considerable and costs of their upkeep probably higher than that of the average soldier.

Knowing where to get the best horses was always an advantage and Edward did not always leave it to his keepers or marshals to acquire them. On 25 April

1304 he wrote a letter from Stirling to a merchant called Borgeys le Frere Pute, regarding a horse for his own use; and between 1305 and 1307 an indenture was signed for the purchase of horses for the Prince of Wales at Ripon Fair, showing that the horse fairs in England had become just as popular as those in Europe. Ripon Fair in particular was a firm favourite for many years.[20]

From 1305 the keepers of the King's stud became directly answerable to the exchequer in order to speed up the accounting process. As proof that he was still economising four years after the initial complaints about costs, Edward asked for a loan from the Archbishop of Canterbury to buy a good stallion and this was duly noted in the records. He continued the interest shown in Lombardy horses and commissioned a Lombard merchant, William Persona, to buy for him several horses and mares.[21] It was around this time that King Edward also purchased the Earl of Warenne's stud at Ditchling in Sussex, and another property to come into the possession of the Crown in 1305 was Eltham Manor which had originally belonged to Anthony Bek, Bishop of Durham. Eltham Manor was then presented to Edward, Prince of Wales because of its accessibility to London and Dover, it would, as Eltham Palace, become so important that its superiority would only be surpassed by Westminster. It was also ideal for hunting – being surrounded by vast open spaces to the north and south – and of course it housed part of the Royal Stud. In all it remained a royal favourite for the next 200 years.[22]

Two years later Edward died and was succeeded by his son, Edward II, who was tall, muscular and a good horseman, but who could be lazy and temperamental. Edward had a generous streak, however, and once paid the enormous sum of £50 to a surgeon who cured a stable boy bitten by one of the King's stallions. Edward II liked jousting and rustic pursuits and, although he was criticised for it, had four new hunting lodges built in the New Forest.

He wanted to make his mark on the studs and it was his aim to improve them. In this he commissioned his court favourite, Piers Gaveston, to help him. Gaveston was a highly competent knight who was familiar with the highs and lows of tournaments and understood horsemanship, but his role as the young King's favourite – for the King was besotted with him – aroused a great deal of resentment.[23] This resulted in Gaveston's death in June 1312 after being lured to Blacklow Hill, where he believed he was going to take part in a tournament, only to find himself beheaded instead.[24] It is interesting, therefore, that Edward II sought to restrict tournaments and, some months later, banned an event in Newmarket, Suffolk; it was due to take place on the Sabbath which would have been a good enough reason to ban it, but if the King was seeking to maintain order (especially in the wake of Gaveston's death), then restricting tournaments was one way to go about it – as his predecessors had done in the past.

It seems clear that Edward II wanted to extend upon his father's possessions, regardless of the expense. Like his father, he bought horses from Lombardy and in 1309 sent two agents there – the brothers Bynde and Philip Bonaventura – to buy twenty destriers and twelve mares. Then in 1313 he sent another agent, John de Redmere, to buy more horses abroad, and over the next two years horses were bought from Spain and Toulouse, while more were purchased in England, from York. He also acquired more keepers. In 1317 John de Redmere was made a keeper of the King's horses south of the Trent, a position he would hold for the next seven years, and his particulars and expenses appear in the Pipe Rolls alongside those of his fellow keepers Giles de Thelosa and Adam Hyde.[25]

Between 1326 and 1328 a complete assessment was made of the royal stables, with writs sent out to assessors to provide accounts for the King's and Queen's horses, including accounts for their provisions and payments to the keepers, complete with receipts. The records also reveal the change in personnel: the keepers by this time comprised Arnold Garcy, keeper of the King's horses in the south; William le Mareschal, keeper at Newnham near Bedford; John de Neusom, keeper in Northam, Lincoln, York, Lancaster and Chester; and William de Fremsworth, keeper in Risborough.[26]

The need to collate as much information as possible about the state of the studs might appear on the face of it to be business as usual within the royal household, but, in fact, Edward II had, by this time, been ousted by his wife, Queen Isabella, and her lover, Roger Mortimer, and his enforced abdication in favour of his son, also named Edward, became official on 25 January 1327. He was locked up in Berkeley Castle, where he later died, and his son, Edward III, a minor, came under the control of his mother and Roger Mortimer. Yet within three years, on 29 November 1330, Mortimer was hanged for the murder of Edward II. Queen Isabella died nearly thirty years later, in 1358.[27]

Edward III could now rule in his own right. He was bluff, brave and generous, he followed fashion and was a natural showman, but would prove to be not quite as gullible as his father. Where the Royal Stud still remained accountable to the exchequer due to the constant threat of war, the King nevertheless encouraged jousting and tournaments in general – so long as he could maintain control. Tournaments once again became very popular during Edward III's reign, as he saw them to be an excellent way of keeping up his people's morale and he enjoyed taking part himself. Tournaments also provided an opportunity for the royal family to be seen and for the King and his son, Edward, Prince of Wales, to show strength and unity which, given what had happened to his father, was extremely important to the King. Tournaments therefore became national social events used to celebrate victories or family occasions. Nor was injury a deterrent, although the first tournament in Edward III's reign, held at Cheapside in September 1331, was marred by the collapse of a scaffold. Had Edward's wife not intervened, the carpenters would have been executed.[28]

The start of Edward's reign heralded a further slump in expenditure on the royal stables that lasted until 1331, but Edward did have plans for the Royal Stud and, like his father, found it important to leave as much of a mark on the royal stables as on the country itself. The stables had become the symbol of prestige and the horses the instruments of wealth and influence. There were also political undertones as Edward made it a felony to export horses to Scotland. He made his first major purchases in Spain, buying fifty Spanish horses for 1,000 marks, while one of his agents, Arnold Garcia, bought him nineteen horses for a total cost of £649 (£172,000), the individual costs ranging from £10 (£2,650) to £60 (£15,900). Travelling from one country to the next was an expensive business, and for this trip Garcia's travel and maintenance expenses ran to £66.11s (£17,637).[29] In England, horses were bought for King Edward in York and Reading, but Edward was concerned not only with the purchasing of horses; he attached great importance to the mingling of their blood and improving the bloodlines, so breeding arrangements were made with the kings of France and Spain between 1332 and 1333.

Records provide a glimpse of how the royal stables impacted on a local level. For instance, writs were made to a sheriff in Reading for the upkeep of the King's horses there and then; to a sheriff to find fodder and litter for the King's great horses kept in Bedford, no doubt sent under the direction of the Bedford keeper, William le Mareschal; and to another sheriff to pay for oats and litter for sixteen of the King's warhorses. The involvement of sheriffs points to a need for local co-operation to keep the royal stables running smoothly, a business that would have required constant communication. Edward III also employed additional keepers: Edmund de Thedmarsh, to manage the King's horses in the north, and Manuot and John Brocas.[30]

The following years saw many elaborate tournaments take place. They were held at Reading after Christmas 1340, and then a meeting at Langley for nobles took place on 2 February 1341. They were briefly prohibited because the court was criticised for the extravagance, but exactly one year later, on 2 February 1342, the King and 230 knights took part in a tournament at Dunstable. On 14 April there was a meeting at Northampton in which a nobleman named John de Beaumont was killed, and many nobles were hurt and horses lost, but on 9 May they were competing again at Eltham. Further tournaments took place in Smithfield, Canterbury, Hereford and elsewhere; and hunting parties continued until Michaelmas. Their culmination at Windsor on 14 January 1344 was a very elaborate event that went on for a few days and saw Edward win six prizes.[31]

Between 1344 and 1346, further accounts appear for the provisions of the King's horses. By this time the records, alongside those for the rest of the household, had become a reflection of how the monarchy as a whole was being run, both on a domestic and political level, and the administration needed to ensure that it ran well. On their own, the records for the Royal Stud are detailed enough, despite the fact that a great many of the Pipe Roll records have been lost, and in the overall picture these details are just the tip of the iceberg. Those that survive give an impression of just how big the household was. The stables, in particular, seemed to have a constant turnaround of staff. Records exist that pertain to William de Pereford, who provided victuals for the horses kept at Cornbury, and William de Langley, who provided oats for those kept at Westminster, while for the years 1347–9 others involved in acquiring and providing for the King's horses include Peter de Boxstead, Guy de Seynder, Humphrey de Walden and William Bret.

Then, of course, there were the horses belonging to the Prince of Wales, a born soldier who later became known as the Black Prince and who shared his father's passion for tournaments.[32] On his return from war in Calais in 1347, he attended tournaments with his father in Bury, Reading, Windsor, Lichfield, Eltham and Canterbury. His safe return from war and numerous other English victories over the French served as an excuse to hold a further tournament at Eltham in October.

Horses had become prize possessions and not just used for war and sport. On 24 June 1348, at a tournament to celebrate the Queen's giving birth to another child, a son called William (who only lived a few months, dying on 5 September 1348), her eldest son, the Prince of Wales, gave his mother a horse called Bauzan de Burgh. The Black Prince could be generous with gifts at times like this – he even gave a warhorse to a minstrel, which gives a clear impression of what he believed constituted a valuable gift. Tournaments still continued to be highly social events, with themes and mottoes, but they were heavily criticised by the Church because of the debauchery they encouraged.[33] In the event a terrible crisis between 1348 and 1349 halted them completely as the Black Death cut a swathe through Europe, killing hundreds of thousands of people, rich and poor. Once the plague had receded jousting began again –

with some held to celebrate the marriage of Edward's younger son, John of Gaunt, to Blanche of Lancaster. But the Black Death would return intermittently over the next twenty years, although each outbreak was weaker than the last, and in the long term, tournaments as a whole were affected.[34]

On 6 December 1350 the Black Prince attended them at Norwich, but from the mid-1350s they fell into decline, possibly because of the great cost of the horses as well as the events themselves. The King was forced to sell off many of his horses, although he did seek to maintain a nucleus to keep up the Royal Stud, and some horses were kept for formal occasions. John Brocas was charged with this before being sent north to inspect the King's horses there. It was necessary to keep a careful account of the health of the horses since the days of the Black Death and a certificate was drawn up when some of the King's horses succumbed to a disease known as murrain between 1356 and 1358. In addition the King still employed a large staff to look after his horses, including nine grooms: Thomas Cassy, John de Laundels, Hugh de Chastilon, Robert de Hildcoley, Thomas de Hoo, Thomas Stok, Peter de Nutcle, Roger de Louthe and Walter Parks.[35]

Now that there were fewer tournaments they were banned altogether in Yorkshire, London, Hereford and Huntingdon in July 1354. They became rare elsewhere, although there was one at Woodstock in February 1355. The King then turned his attention to his other love – architecture – and made changes to his palaces during this decade, selling part of the stud to help pay for improvements at Windsor, where twelve of his best mares were being kept. He did not get much money for his efforts – £6 for fourteen mares and thirteen fillies – perhaps because by 1359 the cost of maintenance was on the rise, but there was no talk of cutting back; within two years King Edward was buying more horses and the studs increased once again. He bought 48 horses from the Lombard merchant Minello de Viterbo, which were housed for ten days at the Black Prince's park at Kennington at a cost of £13.9s per horse per day, including hay, oats, service and litter.

In fact, there were designated parks in the north and south, run by designated personages, who looked after the King's horses. In addition, agents were commissioned to be on the lookout for horses on land that, being under the ownership of the Church, was about to become free through the death of whichever ecclesiastical personage happened to be in charge of it. In such cases, before a replacement could be installed, the horses would be removed by these agents in a practice known as 'depasturing', which naturally did not go down too well as it affected the horses that were taken. As more parks were acquired and more horses were put in them, other problems arose; in some parks, the horses were being left too long and would not eat grass surrounded by their own droppings, and of course there were the rising costs. When one of the King's keepers, Sir John Brocas, brought this to the attention of the King in 1363, it was noted that additional fodder was required as well as vast quantities of hay, oats, beans and pease in order to ensure that all the royal horses were comfortable and well fed. This, of course, was expensive; so, instead of bargaining for goods, the King sent sheriffs to 'buy and purvey', and meant that the purchase price was fixed by the purveyor's order, and would be on the low side. Indeed, throughout the 1350s these prices were very low because the purveyors complied with the Statute of Labourers, which had attempted to fix prices and wages without reference to rapid inflation after the Black Death.

The King's horses were still unpopular however because of their numbers: they were all over the country and their management was not proving as efficient as it had been. Spread too thin across the land they were now prone to disease and were becoming a health hazard. In the end it was a change in military and economic circumstances, as well as a barrage of complaints from the King's subjects, that forced a reduction in the studs. Instead of having separate managers around the country, the northern and southern keepers were replaced with officers of knightly rank or military reputation, and overall control became central with the introduction of the office of Master of the Horse. Sir John Brocas was the first in this role, although he was not addressed as such and at that stage the term was not used as a specific title, but more as an indication of his position. King Edward, meanwhile, continued to buy horses, maintaining his belief in the importance of bloodlines, particularly with France and Spain, and from the latter country purchased fifty horses for 1,000 marks. He also received horses as gifts, in particular from the Lord of Milan, between 1368 and 1370.[36]

Edward III died in 1377. Having outlived his eldest son, the Black Prince, who had died on 8 June 1376, he was succeeded by the Prince's son, Richard, who became Richard II – a child king. By the time he was ten he could ride, but as an adult Richard never took to jousting, preferring books and cookery. As far as tournaments were concerned, he had the most curious way of thinking for a monarch and even for a horseman of the time. Conscious of his heritage, he loved ceremony and endeavoured to place the dignity of the monarchy above the competition, keeping a royal distance from the sport. This is further evidence that tournaments had become social in outlook rather than being seen as a preparation for war or a way of settling scores. Richard also found tournaments to be too violent, once witnessing an event in April 1382 when one John de Agnesford had his legs and thighs crushed.

However, Richard maintained the hunting grounds at the Forest of Needwood (near Buthfield Hall in Staffordshire), Melksham in Wiltshire, and Hatfield Forest,[37] and he liked horses enough to send four envoys to Prague to improve his stud farm, preferring to look further east for new blood and choosing not to rely on the links established with France and Spain. Essentially, horses were bought to improve the breeding horses for hunting, and chief horse-breeding districts were Lincoln, Cambridge and the north and east ridings of Yorkshire. Richard also maintained the office of Master of the Horse, and during his reign there were four: Nicholas Bonde (who held the office between 1377 and 1381), Thomas Murrieux (1381–6), Baldwin Beresford (1386–97) and Richard Redman (1397–9). The Queen's Master of the Horse was Thomas Abberbury and there is also mention of Walter Moreton, Master of the Horse of Philippa, the King's daughter.

Richard bought some expensive accessories – spending £25 (£8,750) in 1386 on a hunting knife and horn – while his wife, Anne of Bohemia, is credited with introducing the side-saddle into England. Previously, women had either sat astride horses or had travelled about in litters pulled by them. The most famous horse to be associated with Richard II is the Roan Barbary, the King's charger which, it is said, used to eat out of his hand. The horse was his particular favourite, but the popular belief is that the Roan Barbary was ridden by the King's cousin, Henry Bolingbroke (the son of Edward III's third son, John of Gaunt) at Richard's coronation, an event later immortalised by William Shakespeare in his play *Richard II*, although how much of his version of events is truth or fiction is difficult to tell. What the horse does seem to symbolise in Shakespeare's history is Henry's importance in the scheme of things as, 22 years later, in September 1399, Richard was usurped and imprisoned by Henry Bolingbroke, who then proclaimed himself King Henry IV. Since Richard's claim was greater than his, Henry's action effectively split the Plantagenet line, resulting in two houses: the House of York and Henry's House of Lancaster. Henry IV now had to work especially hard to win over the nobles and the Church in order to legitimise his claim and used jousting – a sport at which he excelled[38] – to do just that. Whereas Richard II had been indifferent, Henry IV demonstrated active participation and competitiveness, thus presenting a more traditional image of kingship that he hoped would appeal to his court. His actions served also as an expression of wealth and strength. Not everyone was convinced, and in January 1400 attempts were made to restore Richard II, who was now a prisoner in Pontefract Castle. The attempts failed, however, and Richard died there in February 1400.

The image of kingship that Henry had promoted at the start of his reign was, in the end, just an illusion and when he died in 1413 he left the country divided and in debt. It was left to his son, Henry V, to pick up the pieces and restore England's pride in itself. Henry V had been wild and undisciplined, but when he became king he adopted a more sober outlook and led many of his associates to do the same. As a way of making amends for the past, he had the body of Richard II disinterred and reburied at Westminster.

Henry V had attended jousts from the age of ten but, unlike his father, failed to see their attraction. He saw through the image his father had tried to project and went his own way in his youth, preferring hunting, which he saw as preparation for war. He was essentially a military man and took part in his first battle at the age of fifteen. Some of his biographers think it strange that he enjoyed other sports but did not like jousting, which, in the past, had been seen as an essential form of preparation for battle. There may be two reasons for this. Firstly, that when he was not in battle he preferred unrelated activities, as a way of switching off. Secondly, that he had a rather dispassionate view of jousting as a result of his father's passion for it, especially as he was rather rebellious anyway.[39] He may also have seen the sport as too time consuming and disordered when there were more important things to think about – in his case, establishing his kingship over France. In this respect he was not unlike King Richard I, who took only a vague interest in tournaments when he was not on crusades. Henry's obsession with establishing English rule over France dominated his life, resulting in the Battle of Agincourt in 1415, during which, despite his victory, the field turned into a quagmire in which horses and men alike drowned. Within a few years, Henry himself was dead, dying either on 31 August or 1 September 1422 at the Castle Bois de Vincennes in France. His body was brought back to England and he was interred in Westminster Abbey.

If anyone imagined in later years that Henry's successor, his son, Henry VI, would revive his father's desire to secure France, they were wrong. He was not of his father's mettle, had no interest in the military or anything relating to it, and set about creating a more cultural atmosphere in England. He did, however, enjoy hunting as a sport, and made use of the hunting lodges at Windsor Castle.

In 1453 Henry VI became mentally ill and many compared him with his grandfather, the insane Charles VI of France. Henry remained ill for fifteen months and in March 1454 Richard Plantagenet, Duke of York and a descendant of Edward III, was declared England's Protector. Henry made a recovery in 1455 and between May and June of that year was taken prisoner, which signalled the start of conflict between the House of York and the House of Lancaster – what has since been regarded as the Wars of the Roses (1455–85).[40] The account records for royal horses came to a stop in 1459 and it would be many years before the true impact of the civil war on the horse population would be known. Because there was now a need for warhorses, many of the studs were broken down or sold, and more horses were imported from Italy.

On 30 December 1460 Richard of York was killed in battle and his cause was immediately taken up by his son Edward. One week later, in 1461, he was ruling England as King Edward IV[41] – his foresight paid off as Henry VI failed to retrieve his crown and was executed in 1471. However, Edward's position was by no means secure and he promoted the use of tournaments to keep his men-at-arms ready for any eventuality. There is an account of one that took place at Smithfield on 11 and 12 June 1467, in his presence, between his brother-in-law, Sir Anthony Woodville, Lord Scales, who was the Queen (Elizabeth Woodville's) brother, and the so-called Sir Anthony of Burgundy, Bastard of Burgundy. It was a lavish occasion. Woodville's horse wore white cloth of gold with the cross of St George in crimson velvet, bordered with a fringe of gold about 15cm long, while Lord Scales's mount wore a trapper of velvet tawny with many bells. Others wore velvet, ermine and tassels of gold, and the pages who rode the horses were just as richly dressed, as were Burgundy's entourage.[42]

It seems that Edward did little to restore the royal studs after the wars. His reign lasted only twelve years and the studs were not fully replenished until the next century. He died on 9 April 1483 and was succeeded by his twelve-year-old son – Edward V – who was never crowned.

Since Edward V was in his minority, it was necessary to set up a regency and this at once caused conflict between the boy's mother and her family, the Woodvilles, and his father's brother Richard, Duke of Gloucester. Richard took control and at some point over the succeeding weeks managed to take control of the throne altogether. In a move that could only provoke the Woodvilles, he had both King Edward and his younger brother, Richard, Duke of York, removed from their mother's care and transferred to the Tower of London, a fortress, it must be remembered, used as a royal residence as well as a prison. Both boys disappeared soon afterwards and were believed to have been murdered – although the true circumstances may never be known – and Richard of Gloucester became King Richard III.

The supporters of the Woodvilles, prompted by revulsion at what was evidently the deaths of the 'Princes in the Tower', prepared to rise up against King Richard. They rebelled in August 1483, led by Henry Stafford, 2nd Duke of Buckingham, who until this point had supported Richard III's seizure of the throne. One of Buckingham's followers was Sir Thomas St Leger, from a family that had been linked with royalty from 1066 when William of Normandy landed at Pevensey accompanied by a knight called Sir Robert de St Leger, who became the first to settle in Kent and establish roots. By the fifteenth century the family was well known at court, in both the Lancaster and York camps, and Sir John St Leger, Sheriff of Kent, appeared in a list drawn up in 1434, during King Henry VI's reign, as one of the country's gentlemen who held the right to bear the coat of armour of his ancestors. In 1468 Edward IV had appointed Ralph St Leger of Ulcombe, Sheriff of Kent, as lifelong Constable of Leeds Castle, and thrown in an adjoining park for good measure – but life in Ralph St Leger's case meant twelve months, as he died the following year. His great-grandson, Sir Anthony, later took up residence there.[43]

Closer links with the royal family were forged when Sir Thomas St Leger, the brother of Ralph St Leger of Ulcombe, married Edward IV's sister, Anne, Duchess of Exeter. This meant that the St Legers as a family had reached the highest level of court and would have influence within it – and not just the English court, but abroad too, as Sir Thomas had discovered when he was sent as an ambassador to negotiate with Louis XI of France after Sir Thomas's brother-in-law, the King, invaded. Along with other ambassadors, Sir Thomas talked the French king into not retaliating and granting pensions to the King and his councillors. Sir Thomas was very loyal to Edward IV and protective of his interests, this prompted him to follow Buckingham in August 1483 to rise up against Edward's usurping brother Richard.[44]

Sir Thomas was a prominent rebel in the south-west of England, while the Duke of Buckingham, who initiated the rebellion, was one of the last to get actively involved. His switch of allegiance from Richard III, in particular, was a shock[45] and when the rebellion fell into trouble, Buckingham, branded a traitor, was beheaded at Salisbury on 2 November, which would also have been the thirteenth birthday of Edward V, had he lived.[46] The Buckinghams would continue to prove unlucky in the future, with all the dukes meeting violent ends (the last of them being beheaded by Henry VIII for saying that if the King died childless then he, the Duke, should succeed him) – although the title was later revived by King James I, with especial significance for the English thoroughbred.[47]

After Buckingham's execution, King Richard and his men moved on to Exeter and took up residence at the Bishop's Palace on 10 November. One of the rebels, Piers Courtenay, had already fled hours earlier, but Sir Thomas St Leger had refused to leave, knowing that if caught he would be executed. His supporters bargained for his life, but to no avail – and he, like Buckingham, was beheaded. Richard was determined to make examples of each of the rebels and his brother-in-law would have made the ultimate example, but having died a traitor's death, Sir Thomas was then accorded a burial in keeping with his rank as a member of the royal family in St George's Chapel at Windsor, next to his wife, Anne. Above his head appears the St Leger coat of arms, alongside Anne's, the Plantagenet coat of arms.

This did not signal the end of the St Legers' direct connection with the royal family. Sir Thomas's grandson, also called Thomas, achieved further distinction for the family when Edward IV's grandson, Henry VIII, created him the first Duke of Rutland. However, when the name of St Leger was immortalised two centuries later, it was not for its royal connection, but for the founding of one of England's great classic horse-races, the St Leger.[49]

Richard III was advised to keep the English nobility prepared for war – keeping the soldiers close and holding tournaments with prizes and jewels – but he failed to act on this and, in truth, from the rebellion of 1483 his days were numbered.

In April 1484 Richard III's son, Edward, Prince of Wales, died and Henry Tudor, Earl of Richmond, became a rival claimant, holding a very tenuous connection with the Plantagenet line. A Welshman, he was descended from John of Gaunt, son of Edward III, through his mother Margaret Beaufort, who was John of Gaunt's great-granddaughter. His father, Edmund Tudor, had been Earl of Richmond and was the son of Owen Tudor and Catherine de Valois, the widow of Henry V.[50]

In August 1485 Richard III was defeated and killed at the Battle of Bosworth. He was carried away to a nearby village on the back of a horse and, almost a century later, immortalised by William Shakespeare with the words 'A horse! A horse! My kingdom for a horse!'

Notes

1. Lee, *This Sceptred Isle 55 BC–1901*, p62
2. Douglas, & Greenaway, *English Historical Documents, Vol. II 1042–1189*, pp389–90
3. Lee, *This Sceptred Isle 55 BC–1901*, pp72–4
4. Davis, *The Medieval Warhorse*, pp6–7
5. www.netserf.org
6. Lee, *This Sceptred Isle 55 BC–1901*, p76
7. Powicke, p549
8. Gillingham, John, *Yale English Monarchs: Richard I*, pp18–19, p178
9. Gillingham, p140
10. Gillingham, p279
11. Painter, *The Reign of King John*, p19

11. Painter, *The Reign of King John*, p152
13. Painter, pp152–3
14. Howard, p47
15. National Archives, C47/2/7–8; C47/3/52/30; E101/97/2; E101/533/7; E101/99/1 1280–1282
16. National Archives, Sowning E101/97/4 1287–1288
17. National Archives, Rayleigh, E101/97/5 1289–1290; Memorandum, E101/97/9 1289–1290
18. National Archives, Valuation E101/9/23 1299–1301; Charges E101/98/13 1299–1301; Supplies E101/98/24 1299–1301.
19. National Archives, Debts E101/98/23 1302–1304; Debts E101/98/31 1302–1304; Wardrobe C47/22/5/53 1302–1304; Falkirk C47/22/11/74 1302–1304
20. National Archives, Ripon Fair C47/3/52/13 1305–1307
21. Hutchinson, p42
22. www.HeritageTrailGenie.co.uk
23. Hamilton, *Piers Gaveston (Earl of Cornwall, 1307–1312)*: pp11–12
24. Ibid., pp97–100
25. National Archives, John de Redmere E101/99/27 1317–1319; John de Redmere E43/675 1320–1322
26. National Archives, Assessors E43/334/I; Provisions E358/3; John de Neusom E101/100/34 1326–1328
27. Lee, *The Sceptered Isle: 55 BC–1901*, pp113–16
28. Barber, Edward, *Prince of Wales and Acquitaine: A Biography of the Black Prince*, p18
29. National Archives, Arnold Garcy E101/101/2; William le Mareschal E101/101/5–4; William de Fremsworth E101/101/7; Writ to Sheriff E43/335/I; Geoffrey Spigurnel E43/545 1329–1334
30. National Archives, Fodder and litter E43/272/I; War horses E43/371; Harnesses E101/613/26–27; Edmund de Thedmarsh E101/101/18; Manuet Brocas E101/101/18–28 1335–1337
31. Howard, p60
32. National Archives, William de Pereford E358/2; John de Forstebury E358/2 1344–1346
33. Barber, pp93–7
34. Barber, pp153–4
35. National Archives, writ to Sheriff E43/560/ii 1350–1352; John Brocas E101/105/7; Sale of horses E101/105/8; John Brocas E101/105/11; Murrain E101/105/12; William de Fremelsworth E101/105/18–19
36. Davis, pp92–3
37. Saul, *Richard II,* pp14–15
38. McFarlane, p21
39. Weir, *Lancaster and York: The Wars of the Roses*, p56
40. Lee, Christopher, *This Sceptred Isle 55 BC–1901*, p147
41. Lee, Christopher, *This Sceptred Isle 55 BC–1901*, p149
42. Myers, pp1170–4
43. St Leger, p1, p126
44. St Leger, p.4
45. St Aubyn, p186
46. Hicks, pp132–3
47. St Aubyn, *The Year of Three Kings: 1483*, p192
48. St Leger, p5
49. St Leger, p6
50. Lee, Christopher, *This Sceptred Isle 55 BC–1901*, pp153–5

3

The House of Tudor

After the Battle of Bosworth Henry Tudor, Earl of Richmond, proclaimed himself King Henry VII. He was the first monarch of the House of Tudor, which would reign over England for more than 100 years, but Henry still needed to justify his right to rule. His links with the Plantagenet line were distant, as were his links with the House of York, so in order to keep the two together he married the eldest daughter of Edward IV, Elizabeth of York, on 18 January 1486.[1] Their marriage would prove to be a happy one and would also ensure that a grandson of Edward IV would one day rule England.

Henry was not a sportsman and held tournaments to bolster the image of monarchy rather than for his own pleasure (early in his reign one disastrous event involved a competitor who had his tongue pushed back in his mouth so forcefully that he choked to death).[2] But he did love country life and was an excellent horseman, enjoying the pursuits of hunting and hawking. He was a shrewd administrator and was fully aware of how much the recent wars had drained the country's resources[3] – not least its breeds of horses. To preserve what was left and build up the numbers, he prohibited the export of horses between 1495 and 1496. His priorities did not lie in developing special breeds, but he did keep up the royal studs and his Master of the Horse was Lord John Cheney,[4] who had taken the standard for the King when its original bearer fell on the field of Bosworth.

When Henry died and his son, also named Henry, became king in April 1509,[5] the atmosphere of the court changed. Where Henry VII had sought to rebuild the prestige of the monarchy[6] and restore its finances, his son wanted to enhance its image – through pomp, ceremony, the arts and sports – and central to this was the horse. Henry VIII was an excellent and energetic horseman who enjoyed participating in tournaments and hunted to the point where he would wear out eight or ten horses at a time. Wherever he went a hunting party went with him – at Ampthill in Bedfordshire, Blewbury in Oxfordshire and Cannock Chase in Staffordshire. His Master of the Horse and Comptroller of the Household, charged with keeping up with the King's progress about the country, was Sir Henry Guildford.[7]

Sports had been regaining impetus in the years after the civil wars, and at the start of Henry's reign one particular sport to make a reappearance was horse-racing. It is recorded that races took place alongside jousts and dances[8] in May 1510. Racing was already popular in Scotland and was enjoyed by King James IV, but in England over the centuries it had been more sporadic, finding more patronage from the Romans during their occupation than in the years following their departure – although it is understood that the monks at Rievaulx Abbey, in the north of England, had bred and raced some of the finest horses in the country. Now in the early sixteenth century it was taking hold once more, though mainly in the north of the country.[9]

Some believe horse-racing was revived in Chester around 1511. Horse-racing had taken place during Roman times along a track skirting the city walls (which is still in evidence today) and for centuries there had been games and fights held on a strip of land by the River Dee outside of Chester, known as the 'Roodee' or 'Roodeye'.[10] The name derives from the Saxon word 'rood' (a cross) and the Norse suffix 'eye' (island) – the Island of the Cross. Kiplingcotes in Yorkshire is on record as being the oldest flat race in England, with the Kiplingcotes Derby,[11] essentially a local event and not on a par with today's Derby, dating back to 1519. Racing would later be re-established at another former Roman stronghold – York – where on 16 April 1530 a race took place.

But, although he loved different sports, Henry VIII is not known to have participated in horse-racing as he preferred tournaments and hunting – they demanded a greater variety of skills than simply being able to stay on a horse, and had closer connections to the image of battle: all elements that appealed to Henry. This seems typical of some of his successors: those kings who were natural huntsmen had only a passing interest in horse-racing, while those passionately fond of horse-racing were only moderate huntsmen.[12]

Even so, much had changed over time, including the image of the horse. Early in Henry's reign, in 1511, an illustration was produced for the young king of a liveried groom standing alongside a horse. It is part of the great Westminster Tournament Roll and it is interesting to see how much the dress and equipment had changed from the days of the Normans or even the Plantagenets. The horse's equipment is much heavier and more elaborate, especially the pommel and the bridle, which bears a large headdress with feathers. In contrast, the groom wears a plain, partly-coloured outfit that befits a household servant.[13] Compare that with the images displayed on the Bayeux Tapestry, where the horses' equipment was lighter, more practical and with little decoration, and one can see that the royal horse had grown in importance and was required to reflect the image of the King.

Henry was very interested in his stables and, unlike his father, looked abroad for the best horses. In 1514 he received broodmares, Barbary stallions and jennets from Francesco Gonzaga, Marchese di Mantova, and one year later Henry's father-in-law, Ferdinand of Aragon, sent two Spanish horses valued at 100,000 ducats. Money was no object and in 1517 Henry purchased horses from Italy,[14] the home of the Renaissance where new ideas in art, science and architecture were being encouraged as never before. Henry was anxious to create an English Renaissance and in 1518 he sent two agents to Italy to buy more horses. In 1519 he sent agents to both Italy and Spain. This was probably the most that an English monarch had done to strengthen the bloodlines since before the civil wars of the previous century and other European rulers were only too pleased to assist him. The King also looked closer to home for his horses and in June 1532 received a couple of Irish hobby horses from the Lord of Kyldare in Ireland.

Many of these horses were kept at Eltham Stud, which had continued to retain its importance for over 200 years. There were coursers, young horses, hunting geldings and hobby horses in addition to Barbary horses, stallions, geldings and other types. But it was the hobby horses which were specifically bred and used for racing. The word 'hobby' comes from the Middle English word 'hobi', or 'hobyn', meaning 'small horse'. The King had another stud at Thornborough which contained mares as the ground there was considered good for them. In the main, Henry had the resources to constantly breed horses and to import and export, but there was no strategy in place to breed them effectively and consequently they were crossbred without any understanding as to how this would affect the bloodlines, a fact that would not be dealt with until years after Henry's death.[15] His purchase of horses was not structured and reflects the extravagance and high expenditure that would always be the hallmark of his reign, but meticulous records were being kept of his horses' welfare and what they were being used for.[16]

Those horses that were used for racing – or running as it was known then – had their own separate establishment at Greenwich, under the watchful eye of the King's Master of the Horse, Thomas Ogle (sometimes spelt Ogull). Ogle had charge of two to four riders who were paid from the Privy Purse and classed as servants alongside pages, gardeners, gamekeepers and jesters. For January 1530 the Privy Purse Accounts show that Ogle paid for the board and lodging of three boys who ran the King's geldings and tradesmen were paid for the boys' colours.[17] One Mr Pyne was paid for a pair of quartered hosen for the 'boyes of the stabull' and John Scott provided three doublets of bruges satin and three doublets of fustian. The fact that the boys were also required to wear riding caps of black velvet and gold buttons shows that during Henry VIII's reign the elaborate image of the horse extended to the servants who rode them.

Greenwich served a dual purpose in that it prepared jousters, including the King, for tournaments; it also had an armoury and tiltyard. There was another tiltyard at Whitehall, as well as a Shield Gallery, which displayed shields presented at tournaments held in the tiltyard. Greenwich and Whitehall reflected grandeur, war and politics, while the King's other palaces reflected his image as a Renaissance prince. He had recently acquired the palace and grounds of Hampton Court from his Chancellor Cardinal Wolsey, who had originally had it built for himself in the Renaissance style, borrowing heavily from architecture in Florence, Italy. The King not only liked the place and took it over, but had it substantially renovated, so that it became one of the most impressive royal palaces anyone had ever seen.[18] It was destined to house a royal stud and would survive after many other palaces were lost. There was a trainer on hand and Henry himself had a riding master who had been the pupil of Frederico Grisone, the owner of a riding school in Naples.

More horses required more space and in 1537 Henry had some new stables built. He commissioned Christopher Dickinson to build a square courtyard stable building on Hampton Court Green at a cost of £130, providing stabling for himself and his courtiers. Above the stables were hay lofts and tack rooms while the attics housed the officers of the stable. Of course it was not just *his* horses that had to be housed. In addition to those of the court and foreign visitors, there were also the horses of his six wives: Catherine of Aragon, Anne Boleyn, Jane Seymour, Anne of Cleves, Catherine Howard and Catherine Parr. It is Catherine Howard's record that gives an idea of how extensive the queens' stables must have been. Married to Henry on 28 July 1540 and executed for high treason on 13 February 1542 when she was about seventeen years old, the accounts, in Latin, of her stables provide descriptions, details and costs of a great many horses in her household – highlighting, once again, the extravagance of Henry's court.[19]

By the 1540s horse-racing had grown in popularity. In Chester in 1539 the sport, held sporadically between 1511 and 1520, now became official under the direction of the town's mayor, Henry Gee. Sport tended to be a rough and ready affair in Chester – the justices had already banned football some six years earlier because of fights, but the running of horses, and the crowds it attracted, was nevertheless considered safe enough to be held, as always, on the 65-acre 'Roodee'. The races were to be held, officially, on St George's Day, with Henry Gee providing a silver bell to the value of 3 shillings and 3 pence for the winning horse. As the races became more popular, so the prizes increased in value.[20]

Henry Gee is considered the race's founding father, but interestingly he was also a zealous moral reformer who spent a lot of time seeking out and dealing with the sort of corrupt practices that could very easily find a place not only on a racecourse but in the wider community. He banished beggars and vagabonds, regulated markets in the city and established a school board. Perhaps he felt that by approving and organising the sport himself he could control the event and its moral tone. The expression 'gee-gee' is attributed to him and today Chester holds the Henry Gee Maiden Stakes for three-year-old maidens in the July Meeting.[21]

From the 1520s to the 1540s horses had become an important symbol of power and freedom, which the King made great use of,[22] but Henry's military campaigns in the first part of his reign had resulted in a shortage of horses and so in 1535 he introduced the first of three Acts of Parliament concerning breeding – two others followed in 1540 and 1541–2. He encouraged nobles to keep stallions and concentrate on breeding from them. He also introduced fifty Gentlemen Pensioners to keep and maintain his studs. Also known as Gentlemen of the Spears, these were the King's elite bodyguard, both during battle and at court, comprised of highly paid aristocrats who kept their own servants. Even by appearance they were formidable, and on occasion they wore cloth of gold to highlight their status.

For the King, appearance and status were everything, and the discipline he expected in this extended to his horses. He fixed a standard height – the lowest height for a stallion was fifteen hands, for a mare thirteen hands – and stallions and mares that did not measure up were to be destroyed. No stallion over two years old was allowed to feed or run in a forest or on a moor or common where there were mares.

In keeping with his Renaissance image, Henry employed Italians as officers of his stables – Alexander de Bologna and Jacques de Granado in 1526 and 1544, and Mathew de Mantua as studman in 1545 – and at Hampton Court he kept quite a large staff: a Master of the Horse, a yeoman and sixteen grooms of the stables, a sumpter man (who drove the pack horses), a saddler and a farrier.[23] Henry enjoyed jousting in the nine-acre tiltyard that he had constructed on the north side of the palace, but he was prone to injury and eventually had to give it up through increasing obesity and bad health.

When Henry VIII died on 28 January 1547, the horse's use in pomp and ceremony, and even in sport, took something of a backseat. He was succeeded by his son, Edward VI (the son of Jane Seymour), who was more of an intellectual than a sportsman. Although Edward enjoyed tournaments, hunting, hawking and playing tennis,[24] he was not as strongly built as his father had been and so would not have had the kind of stamina to participate in those sports on the same level as Henry had in his youth. Also in contrast to his father, Edward was quite happy to leave the general administration of his studs to his Master of the Horse, Viscount Lisle, and sometime during 1547 a manual of regulations, albeit incomplete, was put together for the Royal Stud. Described in the manual as the 'Studdery and Race', it contained stallions, mares and colts, although their nationality is not noted. In this fairly substantial document it was laid down that certain parks, forests and chases were to be reserved for the King's use, and that a Comptroller of the King's Stud and Race was to report on the number of horses and sales (including placing, removal and deportation of them), and to keep track of payments, charges, expenses, wages and allowances. The Comptroller also had the authority to delegate to other people who had charge of the horses, and records were delivered to auditors between Michaelmas and Christmas. The Master of the Stud had powers to name and appoint those who would keep the horses and there is reference to bailiffs, constables and king's officers regarding the requisition of wood and hay.[25]

Edward VI appreciated the value of good horses and a further account, dated 25 March 1547, by Hannibal Zynzan, Marshal Farrier to the Royal Stable, for medicines and ointments, shows how well they were being looked after. Horses were highly regarded for diplomatic purposes and, like his father, Edward exchanged many from the Royal Stud with horses from other European courts. For instance, in 1550 he sent some Spanish horses to the King of France and in return received six cortiles, three Spanish horses, one torke, one Barbary, one courser and two mules.

Horse-racing continued to flourish across the land. Prizes could be won more than once in a given year and therefore were important in identifying types of races – as at Haddington, where one Lord Seyton, winning a silver bell on 10 May 1552, presented the same bell to the provost and bailiffs of Haddington on 3 November so that the race could be run again. The prize represented continuity from one meeting to another during summer and winter, and in addition there was an element of honoured trust in returning the prize.[26]

The north of England still dominated the sport. There were meetings on Clifford Moor, near Wetherby, and Kiplingcotes, as well as spontaneous meetings, which, although extremely popular, were also extremely disorganised. In Guisborough in 1550[27] people were described as being given totally to pleasure, feasting and making matches for horse-races. There were no regulations or codes of practice, and it was the same case with racehorse breeding. Horses were still being crossbred, creating what author Roger

Longrigg describes in his book *The History of Horseracing* as a 'genetic mess'[28] that would not be resolved until much later.

Edward VI died on 6 July 1553, before any of his true promise could be realised. His sister, Queen Mary I (Mary Tudor), the daughter of Henry VIII's first wife, Catherine of Aragon, sought to consolidate her power through her Catholic religion, as her priority was to return England to Catholicism – by first despatching Lady Jane Grey, Edward's Protestant successor who was Queen for just nine days. Mary led a very secluded life once she established her authority and did not encourage feasting or festivities, so life at Hampton Court was very dull,[29] and she did little to develop the Royal Stud. However, horse-racing around the country continued regardless as its strength lay in its ability to survive the lack of royal patronage.[30] With no central control, each place organised the sport as that area saw fit and even dealt with its own disputes.

Had circumstances in Mary's life been different, the royal stables could have benefited immeasurably from a further injection of Spanish blood, but Mary's husband, King Philip II of Spain, was quickly disillusioned with his wife and had no interest in England except as a Catholic satellite. Any interest he took in the royal studs was marginal, which is a shame as Philip was a man of incredible ideas and energy. He was constantly on the move, constantly devising new schemes and always in a hurry to see them finished.[31] He approached hunting with a fervour that unnerved many about him, in particular the poachers who would have plundered his forests had it not been for the laws he imposed – and the death penalty. Fortunately, Philip did not try to impose his draconian methods on England and spent most of his time in Spain, leaving his hapless queen at home to rout out Protestants and have them burned at the stake – some 300 in all, leading her to become known as 'Bloody Mary'.

Mary believed that she was pregnant, but when this state of pregnancy continued for almost twelve months it was found that she was in fact suffering from stomach cancer. She died, much despised and feared by her subjects, on 17 November 1558, and the throne passed to her Protestant, 25-year-old sister, Elizabeth, the daughter of Henry VIII and his second wife, Anne Boleyn.

When Elizabeth came to the throne the English court was a world away from what it had been in her father's day. In an effort to enforce her authority, she sought to regain the glitter that had been the embodiment of her father's reign – to bridge their two reigns. Through this she brought about the development of the use of horses and the Royal Stud as a whole – consolidating horse-racing as a sport, albeit on a minor scale, and sparking an interest in the science of horses. The one person instrumental in this was one of very few people Elizabeth could trust in the early years of her reign: Robert Dudley.[32] During Mary's reign he had been imprisoned in the Tower at the same time as Elizabeth, so there was a common bond between them.

Robert Dudley was already acquainted with some of the duties associated with the Master of the Horse. In August 1551 he had been created Master of the Buckhounds, with the responsibility of arranging royal hunting parties and ensuring a supply of animals for the monarch to chase after. He also had to keep up the breeding standard of King Edward's hounds and was paid the princely sum of £33.6s.8d. In October 1551 he was part of a retinue of lords and gentlemen sent to welcome the Dowager Queen of Scotland and to bring her to Hampton Court.[33]

When Elizabeth came to the throne, it was recommended by her Principal Secretary of State William Cecil, partly because of Dudley's diplomatic skills, that he act as ambassador to Philip II to announce the accession, but the Queen overruled Cecil and Lord Cobham was given the ambassadorship instead. Dudley got the stables. He was created Master of the Horse on 18 November 1558.[34] At 25, the same age as the Queen, he was good-looking and tall, at just under six foot. He was also confident, which meant, since his new role was one of the busiest offices in the royal household, that he was more than ready to meet the challenge. Dudley not only had to organise transport for the Queen, he had control of the royal studs and also had to prepare warhorses (since England was under constant threat of invasion from abroad, especially Spain), organise mounts for the household, and also prepare horses for jousting tournaments – as well as taking care of the running costs and managing a large number of staff. Dudley proved to be quite capable and boosted the prestige of the office, partly through his own personality and partly through his closeness to the Queen – and very often he entertained officials in the suite of rooms allocated to him.[35]

The Queen loved him and, it seems, the title of Master of the Horse was not enough for him, for over the next few years she granted him other titles. She wished to ensure that his position at court was as secure as it could be and that he was to be a man of wealth and influence. On 24 November 1559 she granted him the office of Lieutenant of Windsor Castle and Keeper of Windsor Great Park, on the death of the former holder, William Fitzwilliam. Two months later, on 23 January 1560, she granted Dudley the site of the monastery of Walton in York, complete with church and lands.[36] Some time later a warrant was drawn up for Lord Robert Dudley, Master of the Horse, to receive £400 a year for furniture for the royal stables and provisions for the horses.[37] In 1565 he brought over to England an Italian horseman, Claudio Corte of Pavia, and made him his riding master.[38]

Dudley took his role as Master of the Horse seriously, but he did of course delegate and had managers to deal with foreign transactions. This did not always go to plan and occasionally the Queen had to intervene diplomatically, which suggests that in the main she did not interfere with Dudley's running of things. He took a great deal of interest in the progress of the royal stables and developed a keen interest in horse breeding and management. Elizabeth's reign was a time of science, exploration and openness to new ideas and since Dudley was a part of Elizabeth's interest in all things new, his efforts with the stables reflected the new aims of the court.

Elizabeth took an active interest in her horses. From 1570 the royal stables came under constant review by the Queen's surveyors, who conducted surveys between two- and four-year intervals from September to September. At Hampton Court she extended her father's stable block by adding a coach house[39] and she developed an interest in horse-racing, attending Croydon races in 1574. It was a sport which appealed to her throughout her life as she loved riding and would apparently ride so fast that she used to put the fear of God in Dudley.

Dudley was equally busy improving the royal stables and looking to outside influences to help him. In 1575 he sent for horse expert Prospero d'Osma, who lived in Naples, and commissioned him to provide a report on the royal studs at Amesbury in Wiltshire and Tutbury in Staffordshire. There had been a longstanding relationship between England and Italy since England's efforts to become more of a Renaissance court, and the exchange of horses and ideas on management continued. Italy for its part was importing horses from the Eltham Stud.

In 1576 Prospero d'Osma reported back on the royal studs. In fact, Dudley could not have chosen anyone more qualified than d'Osma, who possessed a wealth of experience that placed English experience in the shade, having an understanding not only of horse management but also of equine behaviour and environmental management. His report was clear, concise and practical, and its presentation was carefully structured. D'Osma was very meticulous in his observation and presented a detailed record of what he initially found, describing each stud in turn: the numbers and types of horses resident in them, the horses' markings and their temperaments, how the studs were and how he believed they should be. He was expert at identifying infirmities in horses and pinpointing their causes. He concluded that the studs were being mismanaged and made critical assessments of those in charge of the horses. He also noted that the crossbreeding taking place was detrimental to serious horse-breeding. He was aware of the importance of the weather on the wellbeing of the mares, comparing it with the warmer climes of Italy and his knowledge of the environment extended to soil quality and the effect of light and water upon it. He was something of a scientist in this respect, and overturned common judgements and thinking of the day. He also made some recommendations and went on to establish a riding school at Mile End outside London.[40]

The late sixteenth century was a time for new thinking on horse-management theory and many books were published, some of which were translations of books first published on the Continent. In 1580 Thomas Blundeville published *The Foure Chiefest Offices belonging to Horsemanship*, an English edition of a book published some years earlier. It made reference to the offices of the breeder, the rider, the keeper and the farrier; provided instruction on breeding and breaking in horses; looked at diseases and how to cure them; and discussed the whole art of riding. Intended as an improvement on the original edition, Blundeville's book included amendments as well as modern theories on how horses should eat and rest.[41]

Four years later, in 1584, John Astley wrote *The Art of Riding, set foorthe in a breefe treatise*. It included interpretations of pieces written by Xenophon, an Athenian born in 444 BC who had been a pupil of Socrates. Xenophon had written a treatise called *De Re Equestri*, which examined horses and horse management. Astley also looked to other writers and, recording many of the rules and ideas that he discovered, hoped that others would benefit from his discoveries.[42] That same year, Thomas Bedingfield provided a translation of a work published by Il Cava Rizzo eleven years earlier, in 1573, but by then the science of breeding went beyond horse management. There was a need to understand the horse itself and in 1585 Christopher Clifford was among the world's first to perform autopsies on horses. It became apparent to many that, due to constant importations and crossbreeding, it was difficult to keep track of and determine the parentage of many of the horses brought to or bred in this country. The forward-thinking could also see that the sport of racing horses needed proper care and discipline, and the horse breeder Gervase Markham laid down specific ideas on how this could be achieved.[43]

Different types of horses needed to be handled differently. A large horse, noted Markham, should have eight to ten weeks of strong work; a leaner horse some six weeks. Two gallops per week was enough. Just before a race the horse should be saddled within a mile or less of the starting post, and someone should be sent to the finish with the clothes. The horse should be ridden gently to the starting post, to get him acquainted with it,[44] and on commencing the race he should be put on or near three-quarters speed, but more if he could take it. The reins should be held straight but not tight, and the horse should have his head, be encouraged, and not checked unless he should begin to fail – at which he should be slowed to allow time to recover, and not be forced. Markham also recommended noting what ground the horse liked to run on. With respect to feeding, he suggested bread, dry oats, dry beans, hay, straw and short grass, and perhaps special additions such as stoned raisins and dates (boiled up), liquorice, aniseeds and sugar candy – which should be mixed up, rolled up, covered with butter and the horse given as much as it would take.

Markham always felt that the Neapolitan courser was one of the strongest horses, both in strength and courage. Also known as the 'Napoliti' because they originally hailed from Naples, they were swift, strong, lean animals, and they were also considered to be hot-blooded because they had Turkish or Barb blood in them. The Neapolitans had imported horses from the Barbary Coast in North Africa and over time had bred them with European stock to produce extremely fast horses. Markham agreed with the popular opinion that they made the best warhorses and, with their long, slender heads, sharp eyes and ears, had the appearance of hawks. Possessing long, straight legs, these coursers loved to run, but Markham preferred the English style above all other breeds and in his opinion the Neapolitan came second, with the Steppe bred Turk coming third. Where the Neapolitans provided strength, the Turks, in his view, provided grace.

Horse-racing was growing ever more popular and meetings were being established everywhere. In 1592 the 5th Earl of Derby had Leasowe Castle built on the Wirral in the north-west of England;[45] it was used as a hunting lodge and to watch Wallasey Races on Meols Sands. By 1595 races were taking place at Boroughbridge and Doncaster and were extremely popular among whole communities of all classes, but there were still no fixed racecourses and races tended to take place wherever was convenient – moorland, fields, sands. There were complaints from some quarters that racing had become too popular. The complaints of the Vicar of Boroughbridge – that the locals preferred the sport to attending church, even on Trinity Sunday – ended up in the Ecclesiastical Courts in York, where he presented a list of activities on 4 June 1595, thus providing recorded proof that horse-racing in Tudor England, at least in some areas, was taking place on the Sabbath.[46]

Guisborough had been described in 1550 as a place where the people thought of nothing but pleasure and making matches for horse races, and by 1595 it seems that little had changed. Perhaps one reason for this is the fact that with no threat of war or invasion (particularly after the Spanish Armada of 1588), people were feeling content and secure enough to enjoy amusements and sports in peace.

THE HOUSE OF TUDOR

By the close of the sixteenth century the foundation was in place for modern horse-racing. Since it appealed to all classes, the sport was beginning to overtake hunting, the domain of the upper classes, in popularity. It certainly provided the death knell for jousting tournaments, which had been on the wane for many years. Although tournaments continued to be held twice a year at Whitehall, they no longer carried the same importance and in fact seemed rather comical. Competitors wore fancy dress and the winners were presented with paper shields, which they then had to return to the Queen.[47] Dudley had been responsible for pushing forward new ideas on horse management, but he would not live to see how such ideas would develop. He died on 4 September 1588 and the Queen outlived him by fifteen years, dying on 24 March 1603. Since Elizabeth died childless, the throne passed to her cousin, James VI of Scotland, the son of Mary, Queen of Scots.[48]

Notes:
1. Weir, Alison, *Henry VIII; King and Court*, p149
2. Howard, p90
3. Ibid.
4. Nameplate on Lord John Cheney's Tomb, Worcester Cathedral
5. Weir, Alison, *Henry VIII; King and Court*, p151
6. Weir, Alison, *Henry VIII; King and Court*, pp150–1
7. Weir, Alison, *Henry VIII; King and Court*, pp106–13
8. Longrigg, pp28–32
9. Ibid.
10. Longrigg, p29
11. www.geraldsegasby.co.uk
12. Weir, Alison, *Henry VIII; King and Court*, pp99–100
13. Fraser, pp98–99
14. Longrigg, pp28–9
15. www.home.cogco.co.uk: 'A Pilgrimage to Middleham and Richard's North Country' by Hazel Goldman, October 1995
16. Weir, Alison, *Henry VIII; King and Court*,
17. Longrigg, pp28–9
18. Howard, p107
19. Longrigg, pp28–32
20. Ibid.
21. www.bwpics.co.uk: Chester Races: A Brief History
22. Weir, Alison, *Henry VIII; King and Court*, p110
23. Thurley, Simon, *Hampton Court: A Social and Architectural History*, p85
24. Weir, Alison, *Children of England: The Heirs of King Henry VIII*, p15
25. 'Manual (incomplete) of Regulations for the Royal Stud, for which Certain Parks, Forests, Chases were Reserved', C.1547, E325/1/6 (National Archives document)
26. Haddington: www.geraldsegasby.co.uk
27. Guisborough: www.geraldsegasby.co.uk
28. Longrigg, p32

29. Lee, Christopher, *This Scetred Isle: 55 BC–1901*, p175
30. Kiplingcotes: www.geraldsegasby.co.uk
31. Pierson, Peter, *Philip II of Spain*, p59
32. Loades
33. Wilson, Derek, *Sweet Robin: A Biography of Robert Dudley: Earl of Leicester 1533–88*, p45
34. Weir, Alison, *Elizabeth the Queen*, p21
35. Wilson, Derek, Sweet Robin: *A Biography of Robert Dudley: Earl of Leicester 1533–88*, pp78–102
36. www.a2a.org.uk: Longleat House, DU/BOX II/4.1559; Longleat House, DU/BOX I/B.1560
37. www.a2a.org.uk: Longleat House DU/BOX II/6.1560
38. 'Royal Stables', E351/3440.3348 (National Archives document)
39. Longrigg, pp30–1
40. 'Prospero d'Osma's Report on the Royal Studs, 1576', English translation in C M Prior, *Explanation and Account of My Sojourn at the Stud of Malmesbury and Then of Tutbury*
41. Courtesy of Mr Timothy Cox
42. Courtesy of Mr Timothy Cox
43. Davis, pp110–116
44. Longrigg, p32
45. Leasowe Castle: www.millipede.org
46. Boroughbridge: www.geraldsegasby.co.uk; Tollerton: www.geraldsegasby.co.uk
47. Howard, p109
48. Lee, Christopher, *This Sceptered Isle: 55 BC–1901,* p193

4

James I

James VI of Scotland and I of England did not have the best of beginnings and grew up not knowing his parents. His father, Henry Stuart, Lord Darnley, had been murdered soon after he was born his mother, Mary, Queen of Scots, had been forced to abdicate shortly after Darnley's death and was imprisoned in England for the next twenty years of her life before being executed in 1587 on the orders of her cousin, Queen Elizabeth I.[1] James was completely different in physique and temperament to his parents – his mother especially had been tall and graceful, while James was small and unable to walk properly or even hold himself upright without experiencing pain in his legs. However, he was constantly on the move, as if remaining still caused him more discomfort, and he did not allow his physical difficulties to stop him from learning to ride horses or hunting,[2] an activity he enjoyed with a passion. He could hunt for hours, so his body may have been weak but his constitution was not, although due to his disability he invariably fell from his horse and could not always stay the course. In this respect he compared himself with the jennet – a small Spanish horse.[3] His father had enjoyed horse-racing, which had already been established in Scotland, and although James would never take wholeheartedly to the sport there were members of his court, in particular the Scottish members, who would in England.

King James and his wife, Queen Anne (daughter of King Frederick II of Denmark), arrived in London in April 1603, a month or so after Queen Elizabeth's death. Very soon it became clear that he was content either to be alone or out hunting,[4] as he was wary of people, strangers especially, and war, weapons and loud noises. Hunting provided a form of escape and because of it he spent a great deal of time away from London. He saw the activity as 'martial' and 'noble' and always encouraged his eldest son, Henry, to take part.[5] Establishing a hunting lodge at Royston, he hunted continuously throughout December 1604 and his Council found itself having to try and catch his attention. Many remembered the days of Elizabeth, the consummate politician, and began to complain loudly. Local farmers also took offence at the King and his retinue riding through their fields and ruining their crops.[6] Almost two years into his reign, James was accused of neglecting his duties and wasting money, to which he retorted that hunting was an expression of kingship and therefore a part of that royal duty. Yet some areas where he would have been expected to hunt had become useless because of neglect – for example, Morfe in Shropshire and Pickering in North Yorkshire. On a more personal level, the Queen, who also could not understand why her husband needed to go on these trips, would not accompany him, so that by 1607 they were hardly living together.[7]

Two years after his accession, in 1605, James received from Naples twelve mares, all with foal, four horses and eleven stallions, and his wife received twelve mares from the King of Denmark. In the same year there came about the 'Order and Governance',[8] which stated what mare would be covered by what horse. Within the royal court, however, the horse would not take on the same importance it had possessed during the reigns of Henry and Elizabeth; as James did not believe in courting public approval, his reign lacked the sophistication of his predecessors, who had both concentrated on the image of the horse and its association with the monarchy. Nonetheless, he was constantly on the look out for new hunting ground, and patronised a place the moment he took a liking to it.[9]

In February 1605 he came across an area in Suffolk called Newmarket. On the 27th he hunted hare in nearby Fordham and Buckland,[10] and from that point on Newmarket became inextricably linked with the Crown. On the face of it, it was an odd choice since the then rather shabby little town had nothing to commend it, apart from the wide open spaces that surrounded it. But the King's followers responded to his enthusiasm for the hunt and Warren Hill earned its name because of the fifty or so hares that were released each year for his pleasure; while in the area, those same followers made use of the surrounding heath to race horses.[11] This was probably the first time since Edward II's reign that a monarch had taken such an interest in the place – and in Edward's case it was to stop knights from jousting there on Sundays.

James also enjoyed hunting at the grander location of Hampton Court and went there to hunt in September 1605[12] – much against Queen Anne's wishes as she thought it was too dangerous for him to be indulging in such activities while there was political turbulence building up in London.[13] Her complaints fell on deaf ears, particularly since James was taking a more than passing interest in the estate and was thinking of improvements such as repairing long-neglected buildings and demolishing others within the precincts of the stables – which would take place some two years later. James went his own way and also, curiously, was quite happy to go hunting at Tutbury, where his mother had once been held prisoner.[14]

Life continued this way and the only interruption was an event some months later, on 5 November 1605, when Guy Fawkes and his contemporaries threatened to blow up the Houses of Parliament with the King and his ministers in it. But despite the politics of his position, James carried on as before and took every chance he had to go off hunting – in particular with his young eighteen-year-old favourite, Robert Carr, who later became the Earl of Somerset and the King's advisor and who was an excellent horseman. When one day in 1607 Robert fell from his horse and broke his leg, the King sent his own doctors to him.[15] This was another side to the King's life that many found disagreeable – that, while having a wife and family, he was nevertheless attracted to men, and young men in particular.

In October 1607 a detailed survey of the King's stables was carried out by William Portenton, William Cooke, George Carleton, Thomas Baldwin and two others. It was a thorough survey giving a good impression of how extensive the stables were on the monarch's estates at Hampton Court, Oatlands, St Albans, Greenwich, Eaton, Reading and Waltham, noting the types of stables, their measurements and construction, and what needed to be amended or, if in sufficiently good repair, could be left alone. There were great horse stables, hobby stables, long stables, carriage stables and Master of the Horse stables. If the stable blocks needed to be replaced they were reconstructed in their entirety, from the floor to the roof, which makes it clear that James set great store in keeping his stables up to scratch. Their renovation was extensive, but not unreasonably so; a great deal had been neglected and work was carried out in other areas as well as the stables, such as the yards, other buildings and stone walls. Also, the survey makes no mention of individual markings or decoration, implying that the stables of James I's reign must have been simple and practical compared to those of later generations, which would be distinguished by how highly decorated they were.

In 1608, the estate at Oatlands in Surrey became the residence of the King's eldest son, Henry. Far more relaxed than his father, he did not share his love of hunting but enjoyed horseriding and would probably have appreciated the skills of a modern jockey, as he was an accomplished sportsman who loved to ride his horses hard. Since many saw Henry as pale and weak-looking, like his father he chose rigorous horsemanship to prove the critics wrong, and he kept to a strict routine. Whilst he established himself at Oatlands, his father furthered his interest in Newmarket by leasing The Griffin pub on 10 February 1608, eventually buying the place less than two years later, on 6 November 1609.[16]

While racing in England continued to gain in popularity, in Scotland the government was forced to prohibit the sport from 2 May 1608 because so much fighting took place between the spectators. Yet there is evidence that meetings were still being planned – for instance, it was announced that the annual race at Paisley in central Scotland should be run on 6 May 1608.[17] A beautiful 4oz silver bell with the burgh's arms on it had been made for the winner of the race, although the winner could only keep the bell for twelve months – and would also receive gold. Owners were instructed to have their horses at Paisley in plenty of time before the race and the riders were to be weighed. Unfortunately, however, the Earl of Abercorn objected to the races taking place and the first would not be run until 1620, two years after the Earl's death. It is possible that it was his son, Lord Paisley, who revived it.[18] The Earl was probably in a minority as racing was just as popular with the Scots as it was with the English – for instance, in 1612 Lord William Howard of Naworth Castle,[19] who also kept Barbary horses, noted that he and his family would cross the border to attend the meetings.

James not only inherited Elizabeth's crown, but an element of work left unfinished. Elizabeth's Master of the Horse, Robert Dudley, had in 1575 commissioned Prospero d'Osma to do a survey of the royal studs. D'Osma's recommendations for improvement were followed through – bar one. James I began the construction of Cole Park in 1609 at a cost of £382.16s.8d.[20]

Having been granted his own household in 1608, Prince Henry was formally declared Prince of Wales on 30 May 1610 and his investiture took place in June. Among the 25 youths who attended him during the ceremony was eighteen-year-old William Cavendish, the son of the 8th Baron Ogle. Created a Knight of the Bath along with Henry's other 24 attendants, Cavendish took lessons at the royal tiltyard in London, now Horse Guards Parade, and enjoyed hunting, but he was more interested in dressage and the fluent movement of a horse than the chase. His fascination for horsemanship and the elegance he read into it were to have a great deal of influence on how the royal family viewed the practice and equestrian sportsmanship as a whole. Over the next six decades Cavendish expanded his knowledge to such an extent that few would equal him.[21]

Prince Henry, too, was a first-class horseman and it helped that he received the very best tuition. At the start of the seventeenth century France led the way in all things equestrian. After training in Naples, Pleuvinal de la Baume had set up an academy, under royal patronage, at the Louvre in Paris. One of his pupils, called St Antoine, was selected by King Henri IV to go to England and teach King James's son the art of horsemanship with the emphasis on cavaliership and style. St Antoine proved to be quite an asset and remained in the King's service for some years.[22]

St Antoine's tuition complemented Henry's enthusiasm and his love of life – something that few princes, especially his father, had the luxury of enjoying, given the political climate of the times. Henry was handsome, cultivated, well dressed and a diligent scholar to the point of precocity. He was extremely popular as a result, establishing a kind of unofficial court which his father did not approve of and may have been slightly jealous of, but Henry was such a success within his own circle and with the general public that no one could curb him. He lived, gambled and spent lavishly, leaving his family, and in particular his shy younger brother Charles, very much in his shadow. He also liked orderliness and disliked bad language (for which his father was well known and so may explain it) and had swear boxes all over the place – the proceeds of which went to the poor, suggesting that Henry also had an awareness of his responsibility towards his future subjects.[23]

His promise, however, was shortlived. In October 1612 Henry became ill and died of typhoid fever on 6 November, leaving his brother Charles as their father's heir. Henry's death was an event that neither of his parents ever got over and James, in particular, withdrew further from the court. Nor was the potential of Charles any great comfort. He lacked his brother's poise and personality and with Henry went any dreams of a new Renaissance court to match that of Henry VIII and Elizabeth I. Charles did, however, inherit his late brother's riding tutor, St Antoine, who now had to teach the shy twelve-year-old with bad legs how to ride properly. Charles managed to learn but, to some extent, he would always be in his dead brother's shadow.

As he tended to do when times were bad, James turned to what was familiar and comfortable and in 1613 returned his attention to Newmarket, which was fast becoming his place of refuge. There he commissioned the architect Inigo Jones (who was also commissioned by the Queen) to build another palace, since the first had collapsed in 1610. Over the next few years Jones would be busy with many building projects, chief among them the Banqueting House at Whitehall, but many of those buildings which he planned for Newmarket would not be put into effect, and in fact the first architectural drawings for the palace there would take another three years to appear. In the meantime, in August 1614 the King went to Apethorpe in Northamptonshire to hunt, and while there he met George Villiers who would become his next favourite.[24]

Born in August 1592, in 1608 Villiers went to France where he learnt how to ride the 'great horse' – a horse usually reserved for tournaments and war. Italy and France had their techniques to perfection, having dominated tournaments in particular for centuries, and both horse and rider were taught to move with grace. This appealed to Villiers and he extended his skills when he travelled to

Angers in 1611.[25] He also took lessons in fencing and dancing, so that when he met King James in 1614 he presented a figure of confidence and style that may have reminded James of his late son. Since Henry had been dead for barely two years and James's loss was still painful, Villiers may have come into his life at a time when the King needed some kind of assurance and hope for the future. Villiers certainly proved to be the longest lasting of James's favourites and they shared a love of hunting that served to bind them.

On 4 January 1616 George Villiers became Master of the Horse, replacing the Earl of Worcester, who received a pension of £1,500 (£178,000 today) for handing the post over. Villiers now had control of the royal stables and coaches. He also had a staff of some 200, but was paid only six marks a year, although he, his friends and his staff were entitled to eat sixteen dishes, at two of the King's tables and at the King's pleasure and expense of £1,500.[26] As Master of the Horse Villiers had the right to take for his own use the horses, saddles, liveries and provisions that were no longer needed for the King's use – and the decision as to whether or not they were fit for the King's use rested with him. He had lodgings in the royal palace at Whitehall, which was quite resplendent, especially after Inigo Jones's changes, but knowing that if James died suddenly then he would be homeless, and that he was by no means rich, Villiers began to plan for the future. Eventually he married Katherine Manners, whose father, the Earl of Rutland, happened to be one of England's wealthiest landowners and owned an estate called Helmsley in Yorkshire. When Villiers secured this he also secured the Helmsley stock of horses, and his financial security was further improved when in August 1616 he was created Baron Whaddon, Viscount Villiers. Villiers loved horses and everything about them. His principal aim was to improve the bloodstock in England, and as he had seen enough on his travels abroad to know where to get the best horses, he began to look towards Spain, Italy and Africa, while other royal houses continued to send the King horses as gifts. A few short years later the King made him Earl of Buckingham and then the 1st Duke of Buckingham. James was besotted with Villiers and used to refer to him as 'sweet child' and 'wife' and himself as 'dad' and 'husband'.[27]

While Villiers was acquainting himself with the potential of the royal stables in 1616, Inigo Jones presented his architectural pen-and-ink drawing of Newmarket's new palace: a three-storey building with a central porch. This was not the final design, however, and for the next seven years payments were made for alterations and additions to this new royal residence – it seems that Jones attached as much importance to his work in small towns as to those in major cities. The detail had to be perfect and through his vision, Newmarket was set to become one of the most cultural towns outside of the capital – a huge leap up from just a few years earlier.[28]

Jones's work extended to the royal stables and he was one of four surveyors – along with Thomas Baldwin, George Mynors and William Portenton – who looked at those at Oatlands, St Albans, Hampton Court, Greenwich, Nonsuch in Surrey and Theobalds in Hertfordshire. Of the last residence, James enjoyed its hunting grounds and had the park enclosed with a large brick wall, $9^{1}/_{2}$ miles round, which gives an idea of his reclusiveness. Their survey contained more details than the previous survey of 1607, with some sections itemised, detailing stables, lodgings and offices, as well as the repairs, amendments and replacements.[29]

The royal stables and outbuildings may have needed constant and expensive maintenance, but at least the King and Queen could still entertain lavishly. In September 1616 they had a visit from Monsieur Bulowe, the King of Denmark's Master of the Horse and Ambassador, to whom James presented a gold chain and medal inscribed with the King's picture, weighing 3oz and worth £150 (£17,800).[30]

The King also continued to acquire horses despite the cost. On 20 December 1616 £154 (£18,200) was paid to Gervase Markham for an Arabian horse intended for King James, which became known as the Markham Arabian. A bay horse considered to be the first recorded ancestor of the thoroughbred, its own origins are obscure[31] but it may have been born in England by an imported sire out of an unknown mare of perhaps Spanish, Italian or Barbary origin. The clue is in the price, which suggests that the horse was purchased in England, as importing it from abroad would have cost considerably more. Even so, since the King appreciated good horses he was not averse to going to extreme lengths to import them. On his behalf Villiers made use of the Royal Navy and succeeded in annoying His Majesty's Admiralty; he also persuaded Count Gondomar, the Spanish Ambassador, to send four Spanish and four Barbary mares, which went a long way to improving the breed and the studs. Another member of James's court who would have a significant influence on the thoroughbred was an equerry called George Digby, who in November 1617 was given £550 (£68,300) to buy provisions for the royal horses. He was just as knowledgeable as Villiers and was sent abroad to buy several horses, which on their return to England became known as the Digby Arabians.[32]

Horse-racing, meanwhile, had moved on to become fixed social events that everybody could enjoy, taking the opportunity to make money. The sport helped to shape local identity and made places more significant, whenever possible, by royal patronage. King James had no objection to attending races if required, although his appearance tended to reflect his distance from the general public. For instance, on 3 April 1617 he saw a race in Lincoln, but stood on a specially built scaffold and the course – a quarter of a mile long – was railed and corded with ropes and hoops to prevent the local population from obscuring his view.

From Lincoln the King travelled on to Durham, which was hosting a race week that was always looked forward to because of all the additional events – assemblies, balls, theatres and dinners. Everyone, of every class, descended on the place: the city's inns were always crowded and fully booked well in advance; private houses were let as there was always someone willing to rent; and every stable was filled with private carriages and saddle horses. This was the one week of the year that everyone made time for. When James made his visit the races were already an established fixture and had been since 1613.[33]

He arrived at Durham Castle on Saturday 10 April and on the Monday travelled from there to Woodham Moor where the horses of William Salvin and Master Maddocks were to run for a gold purse. The race should have taken place on the 8th, but it was re-scheduled to the 12th so the King could watch. While there he created six new knights and then, on St George's Day, travelled to Newcastle – a hectic schedule given that he was suffering a bad back after yet another riding accident. In May he moved on to Scotland, where Sunday racing was still taking place. It is noted in the records for Clitheroe on 19 July 1617 that one Nicholas Assheton, Lord of the Manor of Downham, went there with a friend whose mare ran and lost – the two friends contented themselves with getting drunk.[34]

Back from Scotland the King resumed his hunting trips, although his wife's chaplain, Godfrey Goodman, had, the year before, described the sport as evil, and in truth, despite many years of practice, the King had not improved much as a huntsman. He once shot twice at a stag and managed only to hit its thigh bone. But his enthusiasm for the sport had grown rather than diminished and he had additional hunting lodges constructed at Newmarket and Royston. He obviously felt a greater need for privacy although he only attended these places with small hunting parties, rather than with the court – he was withdrawing more and more from that.

Over the years the King had grown increasingly distant from the Queen and they lived separate lives, so that when she died, on 2 March 1619 at Hampton Court, he was not with her. He was at Newmarket suffering from arthritis and gout, and news of his wife's death only depressed him further, despite their estrangement. Despite the Queen's death and the King's ill health, no one saw fit to suspend the race meeting at Newmarket and things continued as normal. Two weeks later the King seemed well enough to travel and was taken to the inn at Wichford Bridge in Royston, but it became obvious that he should have remained where he was.[35] He developed a high fever, diarrhoea and a host of stomach ailments, leading to ulcers on his lips and chin. He also had gallstones and was in so much pain that he suffered from violent vomiting. Everyone around him thought he was dying and there was no hope of moving him, but in April he was taken to Theobalds in Hertfordshire. The Queen had still not been buried, and the King remained too ill to attend her funeral when it eventually took place a month later on 13 May. The King did not return to London until June. It had taken him three months to get from Newmarket to London, but once fully recovered he had no intention of remaining in the capital, much to his government's exasperation, and by August he was off hunting again, this time in Sherwood in Nottingham, staying at William Cavendish's homestead, Welbeck.[36] Meanwhile, back in Newmarket, Inigo Jones's revised plans for the palace were complete – he had built a seven-bay, two-storey house with a hipped roof and dormer windows. It was simpler and less ambitious than his original plan.

James could always rely on the Duke of Buckingham (George Villiers) for company and the two of them were almost inseparable. Buckingham, though, still devoted a great deal of time to the Royal Stud and in 1620 ordered thirteen matings for the King's mares at Hampton Court. There were also six stallions there and one Spanish jennet – a small number given that at Malmesbury in the same year there were five stallions, as well as 39 mares. In August 1621 Buckingham received a further six horses from Barbary and also commissioned the construction of a new timber-framed stable at Hampton Court, which began that year and took a year to complete.

While Buckingham and William Cavendish were taking care of the practicalities of horse breeding and horsemanship, King James wrote 'Religio Regis', possibly while he was at Newmarket in November 1620, intended as instruction for his son Charles. It perhaps would have been well received across the country if it hadn't been for the fact that he was spending too much time away from the capital. In 1621, while he was visiting Newmarket yet again, twelve members of Parliament showed up with a petition, demanding that he return to London and requesting that he 'confirm their privileges' since he objected so much to their apparent meddling. James welcomed them but could not agree to their pleas, and twelve very disgruntled MPs returned to London.[37] There was a certain amount of poetic justice some days later when the King left Newmarket for Theobalds; there, while out riding, his horse stumbled and threw him head first into the frozen New River. He remained stuck fast, with only his feet visible above the water, until he was dragged out and somehow managed to ride back to Theobalds.[38] He went to bed the moment he got there and there were no ill effects from the fall, but he obviously felt he could not return to London and so took himself back to Newmarket, with Buckingham, for some more hunting. It is known that the King only spent a certain number of weeks each year at Newmarket – giving the impression it was more of a holiday place than a formal residence – but this, like the other places he stayed at, was part of his escape and allowed him to do what he wanted without interference.

While horse-racing at Newmarket was still in its early stages, elsewhere it had developed to the extent that it needed to be regulated. Even though racing had existed at Kiplingcotes in Yorkshire for more years than people could remember, in 1619 articles were drawn up and agreed upon by the 49 trustees of the course of Kiplingcotes, and a date set for the race to be held every third Thursday in March.[39] But while order and regulation marked Kiplingcotes' progress, north of the border, in Scotland, racing was getting out of control. Having been established in Paisley in 1620, the Scottish parliament now had cause to restrict it because the locals, ever fond of the sport, gambled to such an extent – or so it was believed – that a betting tax was placed on it![40] The Act stipulated that if anybody won more than a certain amount (more than was deemed good for them) then the surplus had to be handed over to the treasurer. This did not stop meetings starting up in other areas, though; records show that racing began in Cupar, Fife, in 1621.[41]

In June 1623 Buckingham directed the Commissioner of the Navy to send to Madrid a ship large and spacious enough to transport no less than 35 horses, a gift from the Spanish court to James's son Charles. Both Charles and Buckingham had travelled to Spain that summer to put into motion nego-tiations for a marriage between Charles and the Spanish Infanta, and while there, the horses were transported to England. The marriage negotiations came to nothing, however. Charles upset the Spanish court by arriving incognito and when his purpose was made clear the Spanish demanded concessions for the Catholics in England, to which it was pointed out that the English parliament would not agree. Charles and Buckingham, therefore, were soon on their way back home.[42]

Buckingham proved to be just as adept at acquiring good horses for himself as for his monarch, and by 1623, at his own stud, he possessed 22 mares – five of which were Spanish and three Barbary. He may also have had access to many more. By 1623 he had increased the number of mares at Hampton Court to 23, while at Tutbury in 1624 there were six stallions (including one Arabian – possibly the Markham Arabian – as well as one Barbary, one Spanish and one French) and 47 mares (including one Poland, six Savoys, two Barbarys, two Emperors and one jennet), so that the Royal Stud was well on the way to becoming one of the most formidable in Europe.

At the beginning of 1625 the King made his usual visits to Theobalds, Royston and Newmarket. In early March he fell ill at Theobalds, but as he was often ill and had always pulled through, there was at first no cause for alarm. But he gradually deteriorated, suffering from a slow and painful illness, and finally died on 27 March.[43]

The next day his body was taken from Theobalds to London and lay in state at Denmark House until his funeral on 7 May. The Duke of Buckingham, as Master of the Horse, took part in the procession, dressed in a long, black, hooded robe. The horse he led wore black velvet embroidered with silver and pearls.[44] Buckingham's influence at court continued into the next reign and his work at the Royal Stud would extend even further.

Notes:

1. Stewart, p1
2. Stewart, p76
3. Mortimer, *The Jockey Club*, pp3–4
4. Stewart, ix
5. Stewart, p176
6. Stewart, pp179–80
7. Stewart, p181
8. Mortimer, *The Jockey Club*, pp3–4
9. Thompson, p17
10. Ibid.
11. Thurley, p117
12. Fraser, Antonia, *King Charles II*, p292
13. Lee, Christopher, *The Sceptered Isle: 55 BC–1901*, pp196–7
14. PRO.E178/283 (National Archives document)
15. Stewart, p184
16. E214/1145, 06.11.1609 (National Archives document)
17. Paisley: www.geraldsegasby.co.uk
18. Stewart, p184
19. www.geraldsegasby.co.uk: Langwathby, Cumberland: 'Racing at Langwathby'
20. Davis, p117
21. Trease, p28
22. Trease, p27
23. Leapman, pp108–9
24. Stewart, p265
25. Lockyer, p12
26. Lockyer, p25, p53

27. Lockyer, p53
28. Lees-Milne, pp64–5
29. National Archives Document: Survey of the Stables During the Reign of James I, dated 1616... E178/283
30. www.a2adatabase: Somerset Archive and Record Office, DD/MI/19/15–1616
31. Exchequer Receipt Order Books, PROCAT
32. www.tbheritage.co.uk: Historic Sires, 'Thoroughbred Heritage'
33. www.geraldsegasby.co.uk
34. Ibid.
35. Stewart, p300
36. Trease, p47
37. Stewart, p311
38. Stewart, p313
39. www.geraldsegasby.co.uk
40. Ibid.
41. Lee, p203
42. www.bloodlines.net
43. Stewart, p346
44. Lockyer, p235

5
Charles I

Five days after King James's funeral Buckingham travelled to France to escort fifteen-year-old Henrietta Maria, the daughter of Henri IV of France, to England for her wedding to King Charles I. While there he commissioned the Flemish artist Peter Paul Rubens to paint an equestrian portrait of himself for £500. Buckingham, now in his early thirties, had made a favourable impression on the women of the French court, but Rubens found him arrogant[1] and Henrietta Maria was not totally enamoured of him either. She disliked playing second fiddle to a mere favourite, distinguished as he was, but her new husband refused to give him up. Charles depended upon Buckingham, and in the days before his father's death, had effectively ruled England with the Duke by his side, so that his transition to kingship had been as smooth as it could be. Even so, many people took it as an ill omen when in February 1626, one week after the Coronation, which took place on 2 February, Buckingham rode in state with Charles to Westminster and was unable to control his horse, finding that the bridle and feathers would not stay on properly.[2]

Within two years of Charles I's accession, regular spring and autumn meetings were established at Newmarket. Racing was confined to matches between two horses, run in heats, and gentlemen rode the horses – there were no professional jockeys. Paid riders were known as 'grooms' and boys as 'riders'. Charles also kept the palace and stables that his father had had built there, loving horses enough to take the town's potential seriously,[3] he also had a ten-mile tract between Hampton Court and Richmond turned into a deer park – just for hunting. The locals, understandably, were not impressed.[4]

His Master of the Royal Stud and Surveyor of the Royal Race was Sir John Fenwick of Northumberland, whose own horses became known as the Fenwick Breed. According to William Cavendish, now the Earl of Newcastle, he had more racehorses than anyone else in England. The King also had a Yeoman Rider of the Race at Malmesbury, Thomas Freeman, and a Yeoman of the Race, Gregory Julian. Both Freeman and Julian had worked in these capacities under James I.

Buckingham had greatly contributed to the Royal Stud but the King came under pressure from his ministers to dispense with him, and his response, one of many major breaches he would have with his government, was to seek to dissolve Parliament – but his ministers, perhaps anticipating this manoeuvre, impeached the Duke instead. In the end, the matter was solved for all concerned when, in 1628, Buckingham was assassinated, stabbed to death by one of his own soldiers.[5] Charles was devastated, and stunned and moved by his grief and loyalty to his friend, the Queen felt sorry for him and from this point relations between them began to improve. She did not object when Charles decided to keep Buckingham's two sons at court – George, now the 2nd Duke of Buckingham, and his brother, Lord Francis Villiers. Their mother was not granted custody of them because of her Catholic status, so the boys grew up with Charles's own children as playmates – the King's eldest son, also named Charles, was born on 29 May 1630.

By 1630 Newmarket had increased in extravagance and popularity and horse-racing was becoming synonymous with the town. A grandstand was built and within three years the Gold Cup was introduced. It is understood that Bay Turrall won the first Gold Cup at Newmarket in March of either 1633 or 1634.[6] Newmarket's growing importance as a cultural and administrative centre was a far cry from the small community that James I had come across 25 years before. The court physician, Dr William Harvey, completed his discovery of the circulation of the blood while in residence in the town.

The Royal Stud expressed the confidence of the court and continued to prosper under King Charles.[7] He had 97 grooms in the stables at Hampton Court, Eltham, Malmesbury and Tutbury and imported horses from Spain, Italy and North Africa, but his studs concentrated on breeding horses of quality blood, not racehorses.[8] Inigo Jones, who under James I had surveyed the royal stables and built the palace at Newmarket among other projects, maintained his position at court and in September 1631 was appointed Surveyor of the Queen's Works.[9] A few years later he ordered a survey and estimate for repairing the stables at Hampton Court, although the stables there now only served as a temporary home for those passing through and the stud was a subsidiary to the greater stud at Tutbury.

As yet no one had replaced Buckingham as Master of the Horse. Then in 1635, seven years after the Duke's death, the position was offered to James Hamilton, Marquis of Hamilton, who had married Buckingham's niece, Mary, in January. Hamilton did not like his wife and was offered the Mastership of the Horse on condition that he remained with her. He agreed and kept his new post for many years, and also grew to love Mary. In contrast, the Queen's Master of the Horse, Lord Henry Jermyn, got Mary's sister Eleanor pregnant and was subsequently banished from court for a few years.[10]

Image and morality were important to Charles and Henrietta Maria and so Charles in 1635 commissioned Anthony Van Dyck to paint two large portraits of the King, one showing him on horseback and the other standing with his horse. The King is depicted as a military leader, an image totally out of keeping with reality as events would show, but he was always anxious to make the right impression and used Newmarket to do this. In what was probably the town's first diplomatic role, the artist Peter Paul Rubens was taken there and knighted by the King.[12]

Elsewhere in England more racecourses were being established: Little Budworth, Wallasey Shore, Barnet and Hyde Park. But in 1636 people complained about the Wallasey racecourse – particularly when dirt and mud appeared to cause problems in the summer[13] – and another problem was crime. At the races in Durham on 4 December 1636, a John Trollop of the county of Durham got into a quarrel with a William Selby of Newcastle. The quarrel turned into a fight, Trollop killed Selby and immediately fled.[14] In Scotland, in attempts to keep control of the gambling that was rampant there, a betting tax was introduced on 13 April 1637. This primarily affected Jedburgh, where races had been established in 1625, running every second Tuesday in May. In addition, every horse that ran in Scotland now had to pay a fee: £10 to the treasurer, 12 shillings to the weigher and 12 shillings to the clerk.[15] Such a tax was not in place south of the border and at Newmarket it was not unusual for people to win and lose thousands.

In the spring of 1638 it was decided that eight-year-old Prince Charles should have his own household at Richmond, along with a tutor, Dr Brian Duppa, Bishop of Chichester, and a governor, William Cavendish, his grandfather James I's old friend, who was now aged 46. The Marquis of Hamilton was to act as his Master of the Horse, but within weeks of his appointment being made he had to go to Scotland.[16] Since the young Prince would be separated from his siblings, it was decided that George (the 2nd Duke of Buckingham) and Francis Villiers would be educated with him, so that he would have company of his own age. Duppa was responsible for teaching the young Prince, but it was Cavendish who would have the most impact on him. On Richmond Green he began to give Charles instruction in horsemanship.[17] Cavendish was extremely well read on the training, diet and veterinary care of horses, and was fluent in Italian, French and Latin, but he felt that it was important to balance study with activity and he tried to instil this in Charles.

It should have been a period of calm for the Prince of Wales, but the family was now living on borrowed time. In 1640 King Charles summoned Parliament – a short Parliament as it turned out that lasted three weeks – and another was called for later in the year and once more dissolved. The King had effectively burned his bridges with his parliament and intended to rule without his ministers. The situation became worse[18] and his last visit to Newmarket in peace time took place in March 1642, by which time relations with Parliament had deteriorated so much further that the course was set for the English Civil War. His nephew Prince Rupert of the Rhine, the younger son of Charles's sister, Elizabeth, had arrived at Dover Castle in February and was making preparations to raise money just in case there was a war. In April the King travelled to York and was presented with a petition by local landowner Sir Thomas Fairfax, pleading with him to come to terms with his ministers. Matters were not helped much when, as Fairfax approached Charles, the King's horse took fright and almost knocked Fairfax over.[19]

The King may have been making himself unpopular at this time, but his eldest son was proving to be the opposite and in July whilst in York he was officially presented with a white horse decorated with gold-studded velvet; the Prince wore gilt armour and proudly rode the horse, which befitted not only his rank of Prince of Wales but also his honorary command of a troop of guards comprising noblemen and gentlemen. By this time he was already something of an accomplished horseman, as was his cousin Prince Rupert, who in the same month was made General of the Horse, answerable only to the King, while Lord Henry Wilmot was placed second in command as Commissary General of the Horse, with Cavendish appointed Commander in Chief. At just 22, Prince Rupert was already a hardened soldier who had begun his military career in the Thirty Years War, and had already experienced life as a prisoner of war. There was nothing he did not know about horses and, surprisingly, for a prince of the blood, was an accomplished blacksmith, adept at hammering out horseshoes and equally at home discussing the skill with other blacksmiths.[20] But even before a shot was fired Rupert had a riding accident. Riding overnight to Nottingham his horse slipped, fell and threw him. He landed heavily and dislocated his shoulder. With no time to waste, he sought the local bonesetter and three hours later was off again.[21] He spent the next few weeks moving about the country gathering men, weapons and horses, so that by the end of September the King had 2,000 men on horse and 6,000 on foot.[22] The warhorse was much more sleek and swift than the destriers of the Middle Ages. Weeks later their numbers had doubled, but if the Royalists had Prince Rupert as their General of the Horse, the Parliamentarians had the equally fearless Sir Thomas Fairfax, who was made their General of the Horse at the age of just thirty in September 1642 – the year that war broke out.

Fairfax was a supreme horseman and a fearless rider who later earned himself the titles 'The Rider of the White Horse' and 'Black Tom'.[23] Fairfax was capable of riding his horses ruthlessly – when one of them was shot in the breast during a charge, he kept it running until it dropped down dead, then quickly found another horse and carried on. He was also capable of riding over great distances. Like Prince Rupert, he preferred a full charge rather than the German cavalry approach of riding up to the infantry line, firing a shot and then moving back. Both he and Prince Rupert were men of unstinting energy, able to deal with problems on the move while directing hundreds of men, but where Fairfax worked well with his commanders, Rupert found himself continually thwarted by his uncle the King.

In June 1644 the Royalists were defeated at Marston Moor in Yorkshire, which proved to be the turning point of the war, and that winter plans were put in place for a New Model Army, which Fairfax was considered ideal to organise. On 21 January 1645 the House of Commons voted 101 to 69 in his favour and the Lords accepted his post on 4 February. The army was formed and later, at Oliver Cromwell's request, Fairfax appointed Henry Ireton to take over his role as Commissary General of the Horse.[24]

Meanwhile, on the Royalist side, in April 1645, coded written negotiations passed between Prince Rupert and William Legge with respect to the post of Master of the Horse. The Prince was trying to persuade the reluctant Legge to accept the post,[25] but in the event it made little difference for, on 14 June, King Charles, Fairfax and Cromwell met at Naseby for the decisive battle. Fairfax cut down the King's colour bearer and the rest of the Cavaliers were beaten by the New Model Army. The King and Prince Rupert escaped to Leicester.[26]

Almost immediately after Naseby, Hampton Court was seized and the state apartments were sealed, but the King and his followers refused to surrender, although Rupert knew that the game was up – for now anyway. After escaping Leicester he had moved on to Bristol, but on the morning of 11 September he agreed to leave, escorted by Cromwell and Fairfax. Though he was a soldier first and foremost, he attached a great deal of importance to his image as a prince, and the Parliamentarians found themselves confronted with Rupert dressed in scarlet and silver and riding a black Arabian horse. He must have made an impressive sight, even to Cromwell and Fairfax, and they treated him with the utmost respect, as much, perhaps, due to his expertise as a soldier and commander as to his royal status.[27]

Others were not treated so kindly. On 14 October 1645 the army caught up with Inigo Jones, the King's architect and surveyor, who had sought refuge at Basing House in Hampshire. He had originally gone there to advise the owners about fortifying the place, but had ended up staying for what he believed was his own protection. He represented everything that the Parliamentarians had come to despise about the monarchy, and in their eyes had been the King's instrument in extravagance,[28] rather than the architect of some of the finest buildings in England. To degrade and humiliate him, he was stripped of his clothing and left with nothing but a blanket to wear while they interrogated him, but he was not executed and was allowed to live in semi-retirement, working on small projects until his death on 21 June 1652. He never lived to see the Restoration, but his work has since remained a testament to his architectural genius and style. Unfortunately, though, much of what he achieved in Newmarket has since been lost and any other plans he may have had to further enhance its cultural aspect died with him.[29]

William Cavendish, now the Marquis of Newcastle, managed to leave the country in July 1644 and lived in exile in Paris. Returning to his love of equestrianism, he bought a Barbary for £180 and acquired another horse from a friend, for which he owed £100. He intended to pay the money once back in England, believing that everyone would be returning there soon, but this was not the case and Cavendish did not return until after the Restoration.[30]

The King, meanwhile, surrendered to the Scots in 1646. He tried to conspire with them to invade England on his behalf, but this failed and he was subsequently handed over to the Parliamentarians. He was now a prisoner and, ironically, given his ministers' efforts to prise both him and his father from the place before the war, they now decided to move him to Newmarket. En route they passed through Trumpington where the people, loyal to the monarch, threw flowers and bowed low. Charles remained at Newmarket for some time, surrounded by the New Model Army, which practised daily manoeuvres on the Heath but did not interfere with his daily rides there. This seemingly peaceful existence was upset to a certain degree when Parliament announced its intention to disband the army that same year. Fearing it would do so without settling pay arrears or granting religious toleration, the army refused to leave Newmarket until the matter was resolved.[31]

In August 1647 Charles was moved from Newmarket to Hampton Court and was treated with respect by his captors. But behind the scenes efforts were in place to secure his release and in November he escaped to Carisbrooke Castle on the Isle of Wight, although he was not at liberty for long and in November 1648 the army went to Carisbrooke and brought him back. This time he was transported to the more secure confines of Windsor Castle and one of the first to meet him there was his former Master of the Horse, the Marquis of Hamilton, who paid homage to his liege by kneeling in the mud and who would eventually follow his royal master to the scaffold.[32] On 13 January 1649 Charles was taken to London and on the 20th his trial began at Westminster Hall. By the 27th he was found guilty of treason against the people and the feeling against him escalated, but the decision to put him to death split the loyalties of those Parliamentarians who had brought him to trial in the first place. Some had no qualms about signing the death warrant, but others – Sir Thomas Fairfax for one – refused to sign, an act which ultimately saved his life. It took just three days to make the preparations for Charles I's execution and on a bitterly cold morning, 30 January 1649, he was executed on a scaffold in front of Inigo Jones's Banqueting House in Whitehall. The process of dismantling the trappings of kingship began, and one of the first to be affected was the Royal Stud.

Notes:
1. Hamilton, Elizabeth, *Henrietta Maria*, p49
2. Lockyer, p308
3. Muir, p13
4. Thompson, p21
5. Hamilton, Elizabeth, *Henrietta Maria*, p91
6. Mortimer, Roger, *The Jockey Club*, p4
7. Robinson, p62
8. Hamilton, Elizabeth, *Henrietta Maria*, p107
9. Hamilton, Elizabeth, *Henrietta Maria*, pp125–6
10. Ibid.
11. Hamilton, Elizabeth, *Henrietta Maria*, p110, pp128–9
12. Hamilton, Elizabeth, *Henrietta Maria*, p135
13. www.geraldsegasby.co.uk.
14. Ibid.
15. Ibid.
16. Fraser, Antonia, *King Charles II*, pp19–20
17. Jones' Survey of Hampton Court 1637
18. Kitson, p79, p85, p87
19. Wilson-Fairfax, pp17–18
20. Kitson, pp33–5
21. Fraser, Antonia, *King Charles II*, p28
22. Kitson, p83
23. Wilson-Fairfax, p20
24. Wilson-Fairfax, p57, p63, p71
25. www.a2a.org.uk: 'Letter in Code Between Prince Rupert And William Legge, Staffordshire and Stoke on Trent', Legge family, DW 1778/I/I/37, 30.04.1644. (Also another coded letter between the above marked 'DW1778/I/I/47 18.04.1645 & DW1778/I/I/48, April 1645'.)
26. Lee, Christopher, *This Sceptered Isle: 55 BC–1901*, p223
27. Kitson, p263
28. Leapman, pp4–12
29. Leapman, p11
30. Trease, p157, p158
31. Hamilton, Elizabeth, *Henrietta Maria*, p225
32. Fraser, Antonia, *King Charles II*, p73

6
Oliver Cromwell

The late King's son was proclaimed King Charles II on 16 February 1649 in Jersey.[1] He had been there during the summer of 1646, before sailing to France and later travelling to Holland. Then, after the proclamation, he returned to the island in September 1649 before travelling to Scotland in 1650.

For months, the need to establish complete parliamentary authority in England had been gathering pace. After the execution of Charles I, a Council of State was appointed with Oliver Cromwell as Chairman and within weeks the Council had forbidden horse-racing throughout Britain, although the sport continued sporadically until 1654.[2] One month after Charles II's proclamation, on 17 March,[3] the monarchy was abolished and an inventory of royal goods was put together – primarily to value and itemise them, but also as security against embezzlement.

Many royal parks were confiscated during the Commonwealth period, but were then poached for game and the royal residence at Eltham was destroyed. It had retained its importance for the best part of 200 years since Edward, Prince of Wales, had acquired it in 1305, but then Henry VIII's residence at Greenwich had gone on to overshadow the medieval palace and throughout the Tudor period Eltham had declined, though its surrounding parkland had still been used for hunting, right up until the reign of Charles I. Now, on the order of Oliver Cromwell, the palace was burnt down. The residence at Woodstock was also destroyed.[4]

Cromwell then turned his attention to the royal studs. The Puritans believed that elegant, foreign horses were representative of royal trappings, wealth and power. What had been a symbol of status and strength was now seen as a symbol of undeserved privilege, and systematically broken down. The royal stables were not the only ones affected; William Cavendish's stud at Welbeck had been sold in 1644, soon after his retreat into exile. Cromwell had wanted to save the royal studs, to maintain a regiment of light and active cavalry, and he later encouraged the breeding of horses, but for the present the majority of the late King's horses were sold in individual lots and the studs dispersed accordingly. Fortunately, many of the horses sold were taken north where horse breeding would continue, and those bloodlines that had survived obliteration would have a chance of being re-established.

In 1649, an inventory was taken of the horses at Tutbury.[5] The stud was located near the castle and divided into six paddocks – Castlebay, The Trenches, Tockley, Rolleston, Little Park and Obholme – and was obviously one of the major studs, boasting 140 mares, colts and fillies, although there were no breeding stallions and many of the mares were descendants of Digby's and Buckingham's imports. The stud also had Morocco mares and an Arab stallion of the Villiers race, as well as two colts by the Frisell (descended from the Markham Arabian) and several horses from the Welbeck stable, plus those belonging to Sir John Fenwick,[6] which were noted as 'Fenwick's Arabian race'. The Council of State decided that these steeds were too good to be disposed of completely, although six were sent to Ireland while one of Cromwell's colleagues, Sir Arthur Hazelrigg, received six and Cromwell picked out six of the best horses for himself.

The fate of Hampton Court was not so easy to resolve. Initially it was decided that the palace and estate should be sold, and on 4 July 1649[7] there was a parliamentary Bill authorising such a move, yet nothing was actually done about the proposal. In addition, the two youngest members of the royal family, Princess Elizabeth and Prince Henry, Duke of Gloucester, were still living at the palace, effectively prisoners of the Commonwealth but treated kindly by Cromwell. The siblings were placed under the care of Lady Leicester,[8] but were not to remain there for the duration of Cromwell's reign. Instead, both were destined to die young, Elizabeth at the age of fifteen on 8 September 1650 at Carisbrooke Castle on the Isle of Wight and Henry in September 1660, soon after the Restoration of his brother.

While no firm decision was made concerning the fate of Hampton Court, the palace at Newmarket was much easier to dispense with, a state of affairs that says a lot about how the Protectorate viewed Newmarket in contrast to its attitude towards Hampton Court. While the latter was close to the nation's capital, and therefore at its political heart, Newmarket had always been the seat of entertainment, representative of the escape that Charles and his father before him had always craved, so the town was irrelevant to Cromwell's purpose and in 1650 the palace was bought by a consortium of seven for £1,772 (£140,900 in today's money), one of whom had signed Charles I's death warrant.[9] Parts of the palace were pulled down before any adequate record of how the place looked or inventory describing its contents could be taken,[10] so much has been lost as a result; what was left would house the New Model Army and be allowed to fall into disrepair. There might, however, have been another reason why Newmarket was treated with such neglect. Suffice to say that, in the prevailing political climate of the time, the town of Newmarket and its surrounding Heath posed much more of a threat than Hampton Court did, and its palace would be one of three small residences especially designed for Charles I that would be rendered useless, while the other two – those at Bagshot, near Windsor, and at Hyde Park[11] – were completely demolished. The next to go were Oatlands, Richmond, Theobalds, Nonsuch, Winchester and Woodstock, while Greenwich, like Hampton Court, was preserved. It was clear that Cromwell and his followers wanted to make a clean sweep.

The breaking-down of the old order extended into other areas, including entertainment. Having always been a favourite of kings, this pastime was affected too, ostensibly on moral grounds. However, the intention to restrict and prohibit cock-fighting, bull-baiting, theatres and horse-racing was a double-edged sword. Cromwell feared that large crowds gathered in one place could spark new support for the monarchy, which explains why the Protector chose to deal with Newmarket so swiftly. The town's Heath – most people's very reason for visiting Newmarket – was now unfit for racing and had been ploughed up, with narrow ridges replacing the smooth turf.

However, the late King's son, the new King Charles II, did not need race meetings to help rally support. In 1650 he landed at Scotland with the intention of raising an army that was loyal to the monarchy, but the New Model Army defeated his forces at Dunbar in September. He wouldn't give up, however. On 6 August 1651 he was proclaimed sovereign of England and on 22 August[12] his forces had reached Worcester. By 27 August he was in Stratford-upon-Avon, but his efforts to reclaim his throne ended in defeat. He was being hunted by the Roundheads and was at large for forty days, riding cross-country on a horse that, he complained, wasn't up to the job. He was promptly told to stop complaining since the same horse was carrying the weight of three kingdoms on its back. Eventually Charles reached Brighton, where he was able to secure a boat to France.[13]

That same year, Sir Thomas Fairfax returned to Yorkshire for good, and for his efforts during the war and in compensation for the injuries he had received he was given Helmsley Castle in Yorkshire, the former estate of George Villiers, 2nd Duke of Buckingham (now in exile with the King), and an estate that Fairfax had seized in 1644. When he first visited his new acquisition, Fairfax discovered that the castle was still in need of repair from the damage it sustained during the war, but he also found a stock of horses and, like William Cavendish – who was also still abroad – returned to the one area of his life that he truly loved and excelled at: breeding horses.[14]

Fairfax felt that the English breed of horse needed to be improved and found that horses from abroad were of better quality. He in particular liked the jennet and the Turk breeds, but loved coursers most of all, as well as Dutch mares. He looked for courage and grace in the horses that he bred and paid particular attention to their management, noting that they should be pastured with cows[15] rather than deer or sheep. At Helmsley, he was a world away from matters of state, and as he was sorting out his affairs in the north of England, at the end of October King Charles II was arriving back at the French court.

Proclaimed Lord Protector in 1653, Cromwell was still intent upon establishing a light cavalry and began importing horses from Italy and the Middle East. His agent in Livorno, a man named Longland,[16] was instructed to buy horses of Eastern blood from Naples, and he duly acquired six, paying 2,382 piastres for them.

On 5 April 1653,[17] an extensive survey was carried out on the palace and grounds at Hampton Court, including the mansion house itself, the barns, stables and outhouses. The survey ran to some 22 pages[18] and stated that the buildings situated on Hampton Court Green – which included kitchens, stables, coach-houses and gardens – were in need of repair. The surveyor described some of the buildings as being very old and marked them down as being worth £32 a year (£3,687 today), while the gross value of the estate was £10,765.19s.9d (£1,240,000 today). The plan had been to sell the property, but was stopped when Cromwell himself took up residence there in 1654, after Parliament granted him £4,000 a year (£491,430 today) for its upkeep.[19] The palace became his retreat, and he would go there on Fridays and hunt over the weekend before returning to London the following Monday. His family moved into the palace with him, and some years later his daughter Mary would be married from there to Thomas Belayse, Viscount Falconberg.

Cromwell might have relaxed his attitude to a certain degree over the purpose of Hampton Court, but he had no intention of relaxing his authority and he was watchful for anything that could threaten the establishment. On 13 November 1653, one John Topping of Tyne Castle wrote to Scoutmaster General Downing at Westminster, reporting actions between English and Dutch ships off the coast. Topping advised that horse-races be prevented from being run at the castle, a recommendation that sat happily with Cromwell's fears that large gatherings could spark insurrection. Even so, by 1654 such meetings were still taking place (despite the fact that the sport had become an offence, punishable by imprisonment),[20] or at least the means remained in place for the practice to continue, particularly in the north of England; for instance, William Blundell of Crosby noted that the work established by the

5th Earl of Derby and continued by his successor throughout the first half of the seventeenth century was still visible in Wallasey, describing the course on Crosby Marsh and the stoops around which the horses had to run. It appeared that the militia had not interfered with the practice of horse-racing, even though the races themselves had officially been stopped.[21]

The authority put in place to prevent horse-racing was a highly organised one and overseen by Cromwell, but, as in the case of Berwick, a ban wasn't necessarily for ever. Horse-racing was banned at the border town for six months in order to prevent 'tumultuous meetings', and Cromwell had every intention of sending two troops of horse there to assist Captain Charles Howard,[22] who was charged with bringing the meetings currently being held there to an end. Such an action demonstrates that the Lord Protector was aware of the sport's influence and didn't underestimate it, employing all the force he could muster to gain authority over it. Part of Captain Howard's duties in this instance was to provide reports of the goings-on at Berwick – in other words, to act as informer and receive information from other informers.[23]

Further north, in the Northumberland towns of Alnwick and Beadnell,[24] racing meetings were still taking place, regardless of the government's ban. There were even discussions about changing Hobberlaw Edge course, where a race had been planned to take place on St Mark's Day, 25 April 1654, discussions for which took place eight days earlier in the presence of Algernon, Earl of Northumberland. Nonetheless, royalist Cavaliers were barred from whatever race meetings still existed, and the Protectorate now clamped down on such events. On 5 March 1654, the mayors, bailiffs and jurats of the Cinque Ports were ordered to proclaim the Protector's order that all racing was prohibited, and on 4 July races were prohibited near Chester for six months.[25]

Over the next two years, parliamentary control over horse-racing underwent a change. In 1655 Cromwell had dismissed Parliament and divided the country into eleven districts, each of which would be governed by a major-general. Each major-general had different methods of dealing with the race meetings and was inclined to use his own discretion – for instance, Major-General Whalley allowed racing at Lincoln, but Major-General Worsley stopped it in Cheshire.[26] The individual powers of these major-generals were short-lived, however, and in 1656 Parliament abolished their rule. In September of that year, Cromwell acknowledged that he was aware of how unpopular the restrictions on horse-racing were but argued that he had prohibited it on moral grounds.

In 1657, George Villiers, 2nd Duke of Buckingham, returned to England in the hope of taking back his estates. Cromwell was quite happy to grant him passage, since he saw it as a means of luring him away from Charles II, and for this reason Buckingham was left alone. On his return, Buckingham discovered that Helmsley hadn't been left to go to rack and ruin in his absence and that his stock of horses was still intact, thanks to the expert handling of Fairfax, who was still residing on the estate with his family. Indeed, Fairfax had been quite successful with the horses there, having bred the Morocco Barbary, which had been foaled in 1655 and which might have been a descendant of one of the 1st Duke of Buckingham's imports.[27]

Buckingham was a shrewd gambler and knew that the only way for him to get his estates back was through Fairfax's daughter, Mary, whom he offered to marry. Fairfax didn't object – she would, after all, become a duchess in the process – but Cromwell frowned on the alliance, and soon after the wedding, on 7 September 1657,[28] Buckingham found himself under arrest and taken to the Tower. Fairfax pleaded on his new son-in-law's behalf, but to no avail. Cromwell had no intention of releasing Buckingham, who was left there for three years. In fact, he was in and out of the Tower on a number of occasions after the Restoration, but at least by that time Fairfax had returned his estates to him.

By this time, of course, Cromwell appeared to have taken on a higher status. 'The Protector Oliver, now affecting King-ship,' wrote the diarist Sir John Evelyn, 'is petition'd to take the Title on him, by all his new-made sycophant Lords etc, but dares not for feare of the Phanatics, not thoroughly purged out of his rebell army.'[29] Such modesty didn't stop him from living like a king, however. Image was important to Cromwell, and in imitation of the type of portraits that Van Dyck had created of Charles I[30] he had an equestrian portrait of himself produced by the engraver Peter Lombart. And despite his eradication of the Royal Stud years earlier, the Lord Protector continued to build up his own stud with his son-in-law, John Claypole, as his Master of the Horse.[31]

In 1657 Cromwell acquired a white Turk that would be known as Place's White Turk, after his stud master, Rowland Place. The horse was kept either at Tutbury or Hampton Court, and its purchase was an indication of Cromwell's plans for expanding his stud, perhaps for military reasons.

On 8 April 1658 a declaration was issued from the Palace of Westminster by 'His Royal Highness', Oliver Cromwell, that effectively prohibited horse-racing in England and Wales for eight months. There had been two previous proclamations – one in 1654 and one in February 1655 – but this new one was very cleverly written.[32] It began by alleging that secret plots were being hatched to disturb the peace, and that closed meetings – among them horse-racing meetings – were being used as a cover under which to plot new unrest. It was therefore necessary to take action, it seemed, and it was announced that Cromwell – with, it was made clear, the advice of the Privy Council – was suspending race meetings. Anyone who broke the peace would be dealt with accordingly by the law and the justices. Mayors, constables, bailiffs and other public figures had the authority to imprison anyone who disobeyed this edict, and any horses that were intended for race meetings would be confiscated. If there was any active dissent, it would be seen not as just a breach of the peace but as a contempt of the law and the army would be called in to bring about order.

It says much for the wording of this declaration of how desperate the establishment was to maintain control. Previous bans had had only a marginal effect and people were still willing to run the risk of holding race meetings. Such events remained a popular sport and had survived, despite Cromwell's efforts to control them.

In the event, Cromwell didn't have the opportunity to see his declaration through.[33] He died at Hampton Court on 3 September 1658. He was buried privately, but a state funeral, in effigy, took place on 23 November. The occasion was described by Sir John Evelyn as 'the Joyfullest funerall that I ever saw'.[34] It was indeed a sumptuous affair, completely at odds with the puritanical stance that had dominated the past nine years, and as Cromwell's effigy was taken from Somerset House in London, Sir John noted that it was carried in a velvet bed of state, drawn by six horses: 'Oliver lying in Effigie,' Sir John wrote, 'in royal robes, and Crown'd with a Crown, scepter, and Mund, like a king.'[35] He went on to describe the opulence of the procession, involving imperial banners, heralds and a knight of honour. It was an impressive sight, the diarist had to admit, but in a burst of vitriol he observed that the reason it was the best sight he had ever seen was that 'there was none that Cried'.[36]

In Oliver's absence, his son Richard became Lord Protector, but he proved to be an ineffectual leader and the following year a new Parliament was summoned, charged with the specific aim of putting negotiations in place that would ultimately lead to the Restoration of the Monarchy. General Monck, in charge of the New Model Army, liaised with the Duke of Buckingham – still living in the Tower – and across the Channel, King Charles II prepared to return to England.

Notes:

1. Fraser, Antonia, *King Charles II*, p81, p84
2. Longrigg, p44
3. Fraser, Antonia, *Cromwell Our Chief of Men*, p301
4. Thompson
5. Thompson, pp22–3
6. www.tbheritage.
7. Fraser, Antonia, *Cromwell Our Chief of Men*,
8. Fraser, Antonia, *Cromwell Our Chief of Men*, p305
9. Thompson, pp24–5
10. Robinson, p70
11. Robinson, p70, p78
12. Fraser, *King Charles II*, p119, p129, p384
13. Defeated King Leaves England via Brighton (online history resources)
14. www.highflyer.supanet.com
15. Wilson, p167
16. Longrigg, p45
17. MPD1/23 114779 (National Archives document)
18. PRO. E317/MTDDX/32 (National Archives document)
19. Fraser, Antonia, *Cromwell Our Chief of Men*, p460
20. East Sussex Record Office, Archive of Rye Corporation (RYE/45-RYE/51. Dover Castle. Thomas Wilson to the Mayors, Bailiffs and Jurats of The Cinque Ports. Ref. RYE/47/151/9. 5th March 1654. www.a2a.org.uk
21. www.geraldsegasby.co.uk
22. www.geraldsegasby.co.uk
23. Fraser, *Cromwell Our Chief of Men*, p473
24. www.geraldsegasby.co.uk
25. Mayor of Chester, ref. ZM/L/3/379, www.a2a.org.uk
26. Fraser, *Cromwell Our Chief of Men*, pp556–7
27. Fairfax, *Morocco Barb and Helmsley Turk*, www.bloodlines.net
28. Wilson-Fairfax, p169, p172
29. Evelyn, 03.09.1658, p103
30. Fraser, *Cromwell Our Chief of Men*, pp471–2
31. Fraser, *Cromwell Our Chief of Men*, p593
32. Details courtesy of Mr Timothy Cox
33. Ibid.
34. Evelyn, 22.10.1658, p104
35. Ibid.
36. Ibid.

7

Charles II

Those places across the British Isles that had formerly held races before the installation of the Protectorate wasted no time in taking up the reins again with the re-establishment of the monarchy. Cupar in Fife advertised races to be held on the second Tuesday of April, noting that there were many horses to be run and hinting that the Commonwealth hadn't entirely eradicated the top running horses. The freedom to return to racing must have been intoxicating after the draconian restrictions imposed by Cromwell, especially in those areas where the sport had been banned.[1] Despite unfounded rumours that there was an infection decimating the horse population, the prospect of attending race meetings unhindered was a welcome one. The advertisement for Cupar races expressed the hope that the event would long continue and that noblemen from abroad would attend. A fortnight after the advertisement was printed, on 30 April 1660, jockey John Hoome won a race, for which the Laird of Philiphawch received a large 18lb Sterling Silver cup. The next day, Hoome won another.

On his return, the King wasted no time in restoring the royal household, including the Master of the Horse, and for this office he chose Sir George Monck, who had already had experience of handling multiple troops of horse and had been instrumental in restoring Charles to the throne. Monck was appointed to the role on 26 May, and on 7 July he was created the Duke of Albemarle. From the beginning, Monck's office was an extensive one;[2] he would oversee the equerries (all of whom would be chosen within weeks of the King's return), the avenor and clerk martial office, surveyors of the stables and highways, clerks of the stables, pages of honour and commissioners. These appointments proved to be just the first in a long line, with many more being made over the next 25 years.

The new court also saw the return of William Cavendish (now Marquess of Newcastle), who retrieved his Welbeck estate in Northamptonshire. Cavendish's exile had been a productive one; after Paris, he had moved to Antwerp in Holland, where he had bought a house once occupied by the artist Peter Paul Rubens.[3] The two horses that he'd bought in France had since died but, despite the fact that he was short of money, he managed to scrape enough together to buy five barbs, five Spanish and a lot of Dutch animals, as well as a grey leaping horse. Later offered huge sums of money for these horses, he nevertheless refused to part with them and became renowned throughout Europe for his equitation skills.[4] He also continued his studies into horsemanship and found that, if anyone was musically inclined, they were better able to understand the graceful movements of a horse, particularly in dressage, and that to be a true horseman it was indeed necessary for one to have a head for music. He found that horses could move in musical time, especially in display, and that they could keep time perfectly.

Cavendish continued to study the French and Italian methods but felt that there were gaps in the knowledge of other experts, so he began to formulate his own theories about horsemanship. One such theory was that a horseman should show his animal who was master while treating it with the utmost respect. While in Antwerp, he decided to put his ideas into print, and in 1658 his *La Méthode Nouvelle et Invention Extraordinaire de Dresser Les Chevaux* was published.

It was clear that, on his return to England, Cavendish wouldn't be going into retirement, unlike Fairfax, who no longer bred horses. Nevertheless, Fairfax found that he still had a role to play and, on the day of Charles's coronation, lent the returning monarch his horse. (The irony here is that the horse's dam had been ridden by Fairfax at Naseby, the scene of Charles I's defeat.) Charles II's horse of state had a saddle embroidered with pearls and gold, plus a large oriental ruby donated by a jeweller named William Gem Eldon. Twelve thousand stones were encrusted in the stirrups and bosses, but these gems were borrowed.[5]

The months after the Restoration were spent building up the new court, and it wasn't long before those responsible for Charles I's regicide were brought to account. The sergeant-at-arms was ordered to seize the goods of those who had sat in judgement of the late King while they were brought to trial. Vengeance against the King's condemners was swift and each was executed. Retribution was sought against the dead, too, and Cromwell's and Ireton's corpses were dragged from their tombs and hanged for all to see.

Once King Charles I's executioners had been dealt with, there was a need to rebuild the role and trappings of kingship. Aside from re-establishing the royal household, restoration also meant rebuilding what Cromwell had destroyed, although much of what Charles II started in this regard was left incomplete at his death due to lack of money, a contentious issue all through his own reign just as it had been through his father's.

Charles also felt a need to restore order to those racecourses that had been neglected and were overgrown, and Epsom – established in around 1618 – was one of the first grounds to resume race meetings. Previously, the last race to have been held there had taken place in the 1640s, and then had been set up only to divert King Charles I at the height of the Civil War. Given that the real draw at Epsom were the mineral waters, the races were something of a sideshow, yet the first post-Restoration meeting took place there on 7 March 1661 and Charles himself attended.[6] He hadn't yet visited Newmarket by this time, but he did turn his attention to his stables.

Charles decided that the Royal Stud should not be re-established along the lines of former monarchs, but he did wish to build up a new stock of horses and appointed James D'Arcy as Master of the Royal Stud in around June 1660. D'Arcy would be one of three to serve Charles II in this capacity during the King's reign (the other two being Sir John Fenwick and Sutton Oglethorpe), and he was under instruction to assess the situation at Tutbury[7] being given, it seems, a free hand to make whatever recommendations were necessary. D'Arcy was fairly thorough and, having considered the state of the Royal Stud, duly reported back to the King. With Eltham destroyed and the stud at Tutbury vandalised, D'Arcy offered to provide colts from his own stud in Sedbury, Yorkshire, each year for a £200 annual salary and a fee of £800 for the colts. The King agreed, the Letters Patent were recorded in June 1661 and James D'Arcy's stud at Sedbury was set to become an important breeding centre.

D'Arcy was also instructed to respect those horses owned by Major-General Thomas Morgan, who had served under Fairfax in the parliamentary army but who had later supported Charles's restoration. The horses were based at Tutbury and might have fallen into Morgan's ownership after Cromwell ordered Tutbury's inventory. Nevertheless, Charles accepted Morgan's ownership out of thanks for his support.

In 1662, Symon Bazil, the Clerk of His Majesty's Works, and Arthur Hewitt, Surveyor of the Stables at Hampton Court, organised an extensive survey to determine the amount of work that needed to be done on the royal stables at Hampton Court, which had remained unoccupied since Oliver Cromwell's demise. It was decided that the stables, the barns, granaries, the esquire's lodgings and the stable-keeper's houses had to be renovated, while Charles also wanted the grounds altered to improve hunting.[8] At the Restoration, Van Dyck's portrait of Charles I on horseback with M de St Antoine was placed in the Queen's Gallery in a move that indicated his son was trying to rid the palace of Cromwell, a symbolic gesture of returning his father to his rightful place as King. However, Charles seldom visited the palace and the grounds remained unused. Earlier surveys had shown that the whole estate needed time to recover, and it wasn't until 1681–2 that substantial work was carried out on the hunting stable, guard stable and King's stable.[9]

On 20 August 1662, Charles wrote a letter to Sir John Cotton drawing attention to the state of the grounds about Newmarket and instructing the prevention of the local residents from ploughing the Heath.[10] The palace there was uninhabitable, too. Indeed, it was a veritable ruin, the only usable parts being the buildings in the front, the pantry, the tennis courts, the stabling and the outhouses, so it was necessary to begin anew.

Racing was re-established at Newmarket the following year. Charles gave one Colonel Robert Kerr £200 to take his hounds there but had thus far avoided Newmarket himself, despite having an interest in its welfare. This might have been due to his numerous commitments in London (although they hadn't stopped him from attending Epsom), or it might have been because the dilapidated state of the palace at Newmarket made it impossible to reside within the town (but then, there were other places where he and his court could stay). However, there is a third and, perhaps, more poignant reason why Charles was so reluctant to go to Newmarket, much less stay there: the town which he and his father had been so fond of visiting before the Civil War was also one of the last places at which his father was held prisoner before his execution. Indeed, there were still many reminders of the New Model Army's presence at Newmarket, and the new king probably wanted it to be fully restored before he saw it again. Whatever the excuse for his absence, there were always affairs that kept him away, such as domestic and European politics and the infighting that was going on in his own court.

Elsewhere in the country, others wished to renovate their estates immediately. On 16 March 1665, the Marquess of Newcastle became the Duke of Newcastle-upon-Tyne, and his return to England helped kickstart horse-breeding, bringing in the best mares and promoting the concept that horse-racing was the best way to stimulate horse-breeding. The Duke had a five-mile racecourse constructed at Welbeck, where meetings were held six times a year under his own rules, and instituted a silver cup. The meetings at Welbeck soon became very popular, although the Duke didn't supervise his riding school at Welbeck as much as he had before the Restoration.[11]

Charles paid his first visit to Newmarket in 1666, but because the palace was still uninhabitable, even after six years, he stayed at Audley End in Essex, a house that would always remain a particular favourite of his. Once in Newmarket, he made it his own and took control of the horse-racing scene there. He even rode in races, and is famous for having ridden a particular favourite of his named Old Rowley, after whom a course is now named at Newmarket.

The races in Newmarket weren't the most organised of events, as the King and his cohorts took up positions at the end of the course and accompanied the field to the winning post, causing a dangerous shambles, but such behaviour was an accepted practice at the time. In 1661, the King had appointed his own riders – namely Peter Alliband, George Hornbilowe, William Bungany and John Smith – and later, in 1681, he would appoint child riders – namely Charles Morgan, Thomas Robson and Robert Richardson – but according to the writer J B Muir, because these boys were on the household list, they weren't the King's jockeys and so had nothing to do with Newmarket.[12]

Charles took great pride in how his horses looked and dressed them with saddles of coloured velvet, even going so far as to place crimson silk reins on his travelling coach. The royal mews boasted 43 coursers, stallions, colts, sixty hunters, grooms and a saddler, and the costs of its upkeep were ruinous; in 1668, the Treasury paid £1,000 for hay and £700 for straw.[13]

By October 1666, royal participation had set the seal on racing and gave it the permanency it needed after effectively being driven underground by the Protectorate.[14] The Restoration had also opened the floodgates to other pleasures and entertainments that would serve to make Newmarket infamous during these years as the King attended with his followers and their mistresses. At this time, the 12st Town Plate – a race between a number of competitors – was introduced at Newmarket, the first indication that horse-racing was being regulated. Rather than being just a match between two riders, it was run in three heats, with half an hour between each, and then there was a gruelling four-mile race, so the horses that participated had to be pretty tough. Jockeys rode at 12st and were disqualified for weighing out at more than 1.5lb less than this. The event took place on the understanding that there would be no foul play – a stipulation that, of course, went for any race – but Charles was compelled to act as adjudicator in two disputes. The first was over a match between Sir Robert Carr's horse and a gelding owned by Sir Robert Geere, where there was a false start and one rider, believing that he'd won legitimately, trotted up to receive his winnings. The second was over a match between horses owned by a Mr Bellingham and a Mr Roe. The evidence of the riders was taken on oath and Charles, on due consideration, awarded the race to Mr Bellingham.[15]

At around this time, the King's former riding master, William Cavendish – the Duke of Newcastle, which he had become on 16 March 1665 – was still making headway with his new, progressive ideas on horsemanship and 1667 saw the publication of another of his books, this one titled *A New Method and Extraordinary Invention to Dress Horses and Work Them, According to Nature*. Cavendish made it clear that this publication wasn't supposed to be seen as being in addition to his first volume, although both were of equal merit. The book, he attested, was based on his own experiences, and he stated that anyone who didn't like it hadn't understood it and that, in his opinion, it was the best thing ever written on the subject.[16]

There was change all round and in that same year, Sir Christopher Wren, on visiting Newmarket, described the old palace there as a 'vacant yard'. But it was a while before anything constructive was done, possibly because Wren and other top architects were devoting their time and energy to building projects in London in the wake of the great fire of 1666.

The following year, Charles bought an old house off Lord Thomond that overlooked Newmarket High Street for £2,000 (£231,236 today), and he also bought the Greyhound Inn next door for £170.10s (£19,713 today) from a family named Piches. He then employed William Samwell, 'a gentleman architect', to construct a residence in which he could live and entertain. For now, his base continued to be Audley End, and in 1669 – despite the fact that construction work had begun in Newmarket – he offered to buy the house for £50,000, although the cost was never paid in full.[17]

While the King might not have had enough funds to purchase Audley End outright, there was always enough money to buy more horses, and in addition £2,000 and £500 were granted to the Master of the Horse and the Master of the Stud respectively in 1668. Over the coming years, the costs of Charles's preoccupation with horse-racing would escalate, as would the gambling costs associated with the court. In some quarters organisation was not as strict, and by the end of Charles's eighth year as monarch, the royal mews were stocked with coursers, stallions, colts and sixty hunters, yet there was some confusion as to who had privilege over what. On 11 July 1668, Sir William Morice wrote to Sir Edward Nicholls concerning the Master of the Horse's apparent privilege to provide warrants for transportation of horses. Morice, it seems, was seeking to find out whether or not there was a precedent on this matter.[18]

On 16 October, the King travelled back to Newmarket for hunting and horse-races.[19] While he might have been conscious of how much money was being spent on equestrianism and of the disapproval it was attracting, he was never put off by such expenditure, just as he was never put off by the danger involved in travelling from London to Newmarket. Towards Easter, at 3 a.m. on 8 March 1669, Charles, his cousin, Prince Rupert of the Rhine, his brother, James, Duke of York, and his illegitimate son, James Scott, Duke of

Monmouth, left London to travel there only to have their coach overturned at King's Gate, Holborn. Everyone inside ended up covered in mud, but they continued nevertheless.[20] Then, once they'd arrived at Newmarket, Charles and his entourage received the Abbé Pregnani, who tipped the wrong horses, believing that he could choose the winners by divine inspiration. Both he and Monmouth lost a great deal of money.[21]

By 1670, ten years after the Restoration, horse-racing around the country had recovered to the degree that meetings were once more being staged as large community events, and it was also being established in other areas. One such meeting was set up by Sir William Pennington on the sands of Drigg in Cumberland, and since the event drew many crowds from other villages, dancing and other entertainments were also provided. Across the British Isles, the sport was back to pre-Civil War levels.

King Charles also took a special interest in the grounds surrounding Windsor,[22] spending two months there in 1670, while he also organised horse-races in the water meadows in nearby Datchet, just below the castle. A painting from this time shows an interesting image of royal racing, with the King and his gentlemen standing in a simply constructed (by today's standards) stand before a course surrounded by people, carriages and horses. There is no fencing, and the weighing scales are depicted just below the royal stand. The jockeys are in their colours and wearing black caps.[23]

By contrast, Charles's new residence at Newmarket was turning out to be something of a disappointment to some people, being on a smaller scale than other royal residences in both stature and grace. On 22 July 1670, Sir John Evelyn wrote, 'Passing through Newmarket, we alighted, to see his Majesties house there now new building, the arches of the Cellars beneath, are exceedingly well turned . . . The rest meane enough, and hardly capable for a hunting house.'[24] Nor was he impressed by some of the rooms, which had chimneys placed in the angles and corners of the mews; this he believed was a new fashion introduced by the King himself. In addition, the building was located in a dirty street, with no court or avenue, inclusion of which perhaps might have lent a stately appearance. Sir John opined that such a structure should have been built on Newmarket Heath itself and bemoaned the fact that the King had been persuaded to have it built in an area that failed to complement its purposes as a house of sport.[25] He noted that the stables were far grander and the horses obviously better housed than their masters, 'with all the art and tendernesse Imaginable'.[26]

Charles, however, seemed satisfied with his new residence, although being quite tall he did complain that the ceilings were too low for him. And while

Evelyn thought the building's location in the heart of the town to be a curious one, the King might well have wanted to be a part of a bustling, ordinary, down-to-earth environment, a place where he could switch off. Of course, he didn't always stay there.

Charles II's court had a raucous, living-for-today atmosphere, and horse-racing went out of its way to reflect this attitude. In 1671, he attended Newmarket in October and brought with him his new mistress, Louise de Querouialle, whom he called 'Fubbs' and who was a former lady-in-waiting to his late sister, Henrietta-Anne (Linnette), in France. The couple stayed at Euston Hall, near Newmarket. On 12 October, the King rode a horse named Woodcock in a match against another named Flatfoot and two days later he rode the winner of the Town Plate. He would win the race again just over two years later, in March 1674.

By the time Sir John Evelyn appeared, the atmosphere had heated up, and in a diary entry dated 19 October he wrote that all the sport and entertainment was more like an 'abandon'd rout than an Christian Court'.[27] Indeed, the racing at Newmarket was a far cry from how it had been under Cromwell's directorship, although there was a reminder of those days at the end of 1671 when Lord Thomas Fairfax, former General of the Horse and more recently father-in-law to the 2nd Duke of Buckingham, died at the age of 59.[28] No horses had raced in his name, but he left behind a legacy that would help to shape the thoroughbred industry for years to come: the Fairfax Morocco Barb is attributed to him and his links with the D'Arcy stud at Sedbury contributed to the wealth of foundation mares and sires from which present-day racehorses descend.

Until this time, James D'Arcy had been Charles's stud master, but this year he too died and the contractual agreement that had been established some thirteen years earlier was not extended to his successor, Sutton Oglethorpe. This might have been because D'Arcy's service to the King ended on something of a sour note, with the King owing D'Arcy some money. The sum was later left to D'Arcy's son – also called James – in 1688 or 1689, to petition King William III, and later Queen Anne, to get it back.[29]

Charles's Master of the Horse at this time was the Duke of Buckingham, but on 5 March 1674 he decided to bestow the title upon his son, James, Duke of Monmouth. The reasons for this are not absolutely clear, but although Buckingham and the King had grown up together – indeed, almost as brothers – they didn't always get on, particularly in matters of state, and on at least one occasion Charles had had reason to send the Duke to the Tower.[30] Buckingham himself would remain close to the King at court for several more years, however, and would outlive his monarch by two years, dying in 1687 at Kirbymoorside after a fall from his horse.[31]

Charles's decision to give the title to Monmouth turned out to be a poor one, but he doted on his illegitimate son, and since this was in addition to all the other titles Charles had been heaping upon him for much of his life – possibly as a way of compensating him for the fact that he would never be king – Monmouth very probably took this new post in his stride.

Much has been written of Charles's devotion to James, born on 9 April 1649, the result of Charles's liaison with Lucy Walter. He was born in Rotterdam and from the age of two months, when he was taken to Paris, he was a special favourite, even of his grandmother, the formidable Henrietta Maria.[32] Charles, for his part, ensured that the boy lacked for nothing.

When Charles returned to England in 1660, he brought James with him, and the young boy was immediately popular. Even when Catherine of Braganza, Charles's bride, arrived at court, she didn't resent her stepson's presence there since James was a truly consistent part of her new husband's life and, in the event, proved to be a chip off the old block, enjoying horse-racing and hunting, according to the diarist Samuel Pepys, and also having mistresses. It seemed that he could do no wrong, and even when he fell into debt, his father bailed him out, although Charles made a point of having his son's finances assessed. In 1668 Monmouth survived a knife attack and, as an acknowledgement of his courage and safe delivery, the King presented him with a saddle and other trappings. Covered in green velvet and decorated with gold and silver, the saddle was used many decades later by the Duke of Buccleuch during the coronation of Queen Victoria.

Monmouth now found himself in control of arranging transportation for the monarch between the royal residences. He could always be relied upon to remind others of their duty towards their King and even of their responsibility to themselves. In October 1674, while at Newmarket, the King was offended by one Nathaniel Vincent, a fellow of Clare Hall, who it seems wore a long black periwig and Holland sleeves as he preached to the King. Charles believed that a preacher should be more soberly dressed, and it fell to Monmouth to remind Vincent of this fact.[33] Monmouth enjoyed extravagant living and the King's son loved taking part in races, too. He took part in one in Wallasey, which he won, and the celebrating throng went on the rampage in Chester, breaking the windows of Tories' houses. Indeed, being an excellent horseman and a soldier went a long way to equipping Monmouth for the role of Master of the Horse. However, it wasn't long before someone with even greater knowledge came onto the scene, even if only in an unofficial capacity.[34]

From 1675, a certain individual named William Tregonwell Frampton (1641–1727) was making himself very well known at Newmarket. Born in Dorset, Frampton belonged to a well-established family, and his mother's relations, in particular, were no strangers to horse-breeding, his maternal grandfather, Mr Tregonwell, owning the Natural Barb Mare, whose descendants are evident today. By the 1670s, Tregonwell Frampton was matching horses as well as owning them and was also interested in cockfighting and greyhounds. Nor was he a stranger to controversy, later becoming infamous for bending whatever rules existed to suit his own purposes.[35]

Meanwhile, in 1676, expenditure within the royal household was under review. Almost every aspect was taken into account, and it was decided that too much money was being invested in the running of the stables, horses and studs which collectively were costing £11,500 (£1,359,700 today) each year. This bill was reduced to £10,000[36] (£1,182,300 today). In addition, because the King also enjoyed hunting, his parks and forests were restocked, with £4,000 (£473,000 today) being spent on enlarging his hunting lodge in the New Forest and building new stables there.[37]

The year ended on a sad note when the Duke of Newcastle died on 25 December, having devoted his whole life, both at home and abroad, to horses and having developed radical new ideas on the subject. But his two far-reaching legacies would be his extended Cavendish family and the estate of Welbeck, which in the hands of his descendants would become one of the most successful centres for horse-breeding in the country for over three centuries. His family – the Hamiltons, the Portlands and the Devonshires – would not only become successful horse-breeders and racehorse-owners in their own right down the centuries but would also help to shape the professionalism of horse-racing.[38]

While horse-racing was fast becoming a sport of importance all over Britain, in some areas the horses themselves were treated cruelly. They had to be especially tough to withstand the harsh treatment they received at the hands of their masters, in addition to the gruelling races they ran, often without adequate care once the race was over. There were exceptions, of course, or we wouldn't have the thoroughbred industry that exists today, but many owners gave little thought to the welfare of their horses. Sir John Evelyn, in particular, was disgusted by the extremes that some people were willing to go to in the name of sport, and in a diary entry dated 17 August 1667 he described the sport of horse-baiting,[39] whereby a horse was baited by dogs. If the dogs couldn't get the better of it, the horse would be killed by a sword. Such cruelty must have touched a moral chord with some, however, as those who organised these events very often gave the excuse that the participating horse had killed a man and so deserved to die. Evelyn never believed this, though, and refused to watch such debased activity wherever possible.

In October 1677, Charles's nephew Prince William of Orange, son of Charles's late sister, Mary, arrived at Harwich and travelled to Newmarket to join his uncles there. His visit coincided with some important changes that were being put in place with respect to Newmarket races – namely, the laying-down of articles based on the Kiplingcotes Articles of 1619. At this time, there was still no real control or formal rules of racing, and such regulations tended to be laid down according to the circumstances and advertisements of the day – for instance, if an advertisement stipulated 'no crossing' then the riders would respect this. If nothing was laid down to this effect, such a practice could not be prevented. The codification of horse-racing regulations was an important step forward in the administration of the sport.[40]

Prince William and his uncles remained at Newmarket for a few days before returning to London, where William was introduced to his cousin, James's eldest daughter, Mary, who at first sight of him burst into tears. Unprepossessing and hunchbacked, William was the man she was expected to marry, which she did on 4 November. Fortunately, the marriage proved to be a happy one.[41]

Three years later, in 1680, Andrew Snape, the King's serjeant-farrier, whose family had been in the service of the Crown for 200 years, added to the growing literature on horses by writing a book titled *Anatomy of an Horse*. He dedicated the volume to Charles, who was appreciative of Snape's new ideas.

In the same year, there was an effort to move the royal court from Newmarket to Burford, Oxfordshire. Parliament had recently vacated London because of the troubles in the capital, so the move to Burford seemed like a good idea, but as the atmosphere relaxed in London in the autumn, so Parliament moved back, despite the King's efforts to make a success of the move. He and his retinue duly returned to Newmarket,[42] where on 22 March 1683 there was a huge fire that destroyed half the town, forcing the King to leave earlier than he had originally intended. In doing so, he foiled the plans of conspirators intent on overpowering his bodyguard and killing him as he and James travelled along the Newmarket Road, passing Rye House in Hertfordshire. The owner of said house was a former Roundhead officer named Hannibal Rumbold. Suspects among the Whigs were arrested, Lord Howard confessed and in June the Earl of Essex cut his own throat while imprisoned in the Tower. Lord Russell and one Algernon Sidney were put on trial and condemned to death. Even Monmouth, the King's son, was implicated, the Duke of York believing that, while he might not have been directly involved in the plot, he had at least been aware of it,[43] and Monmouth remained under suspicion until he was advised to leave the country.

Matters weren't helped by the fact that Monmouth, being rather gullible, had believed that one day the King would make him his successor, as the Queen had as yet been unable to provide an heir. Since this was likely to remain the case, it stood that Charles's brother, James, would be next in line, but James threw a spanner in the works by becoming a Catholic. Despite the level of intolerance against Catholics in England, James still felt justified in his decision to convert and refused to back down. The King, believing in his brother's right to succeed while at the same time despairing of his change of religion, refused to renounce James's claim, whilst Monmouth, as Charles's eldest – albeit illegitimate – Protestant son (although he was convinced that his father had been married to his mother, Lucy Walter), was persuaded that if he played his cards right, his father would make him his heir. However, Charles's mind was made up: his brother would take the throne after him, no matter what.

By this time, Monmouth had already fallen from grace and in 1679 had been stripped of his title of Master of the Horse, which was then handed over to his nine-year-old half-brother, Charles Lennox, Duke of Richmond. He wouldn't actually take up the role until he was fourteen, until which time commissioners took over the role. Monmouth eventually left the country with Lord Brandon – also under suspicion for the Rye House Plot but having escaped execution due to lack of evidence – and the two men later arrived in Holland. Charles had instructed his nephew not to receive them there, but both William and his wife, Mary, liked Monmouth and welcomed him, particularly as they did not see him as a threat.[44] Charles wasn't happy, but Monmouth seemed to settle down and travelled to France, where he rode Lord Wharton's horse in a race and won. Louis XIV offered Wharton 1,000 pistoles for the horse, but Wharton refused to sell to the King and instead offered it to him as a gift. The King graciously refused, as he would have been quite happy to pay for it like anyone else.[45]

Around the autumn of 1683, the King was considering patronising the races at Winchester instead of those at Newmarket. Sir John Evelyn believed that this vacillation was the result of the fire at Newmarket in March and in a diary entry for 23 September that year wrote that the blaze 'made the King more earnest to render Winchester the seate of his Autumnal field diversions for the future'.[46] He added that a palace was already being designed, to be built at Winchester on the site of an old castle. Indeed, a surveyor was already going over the site, which was preferable to Newmarket, said Sir John, 'for the Prospect, aire, pleasure, and provisions'.[47]

In the event, the new residence was never built, and in 1684 the King went to Newmarket for what proved to be the last time. It was a quiet visit, compared to the rambunctious atmosphere of previous years, but by now the small town and its surrounding countryside was the established seat of horse-racing and its importance as a whole for the future of the sport was due in no small measure to the patronage of King Charles II.

Unfortunately, the King didn't live to see the coming changes. In February 1685 he became ill and died at Whitehall on 6 February, oblivious to the tragedy that was about to unfold.

Notes:

1. Cupar: www.geraldsegasby.co.uk
   Online History Resources
2. Sainty, & Bucholz, p58
3. Cavendish, pp174–6
4. Ibid.
5. Ibid.
6. Longrigg, p49
7. Tutbury: www.tbheritage.com
8. Thurley, p147
9. Ibid.
10. Thompson, p25
11. Trease, p193
12. Muir, p14
13. Browning, p333
14. Thompson, pp22–23
15. Thompson, p27
16. Trease, p196
17. May, p23
18. Surrey History Centre: Bray Family of Shere, G.52/2/19/54, 11.07.1668
19. Thynne Correspondence: Correspondence of Thomas, 1st Viscount Weymouth, ref Th/Vol/XII 1665–1711, www.a2a.org.uk
20. Bevan, Bryan, *James, Duke of Monmouth*, p60
21. Ibid.
22. Drigg: www.geraldsegasby.co.uk
    Online History Resources
23. Girouard, p49, p130
24. Evelyn, 23.09.1683, pp418–19
25. Ibid.
26. Ibid.
27. Ibid.
28. Wilson-Fairfax, p187
29. www.tbheritage.com
30. Wyndham, p1, p13
31. Wyndham, p18, p28
32. Trevor, p73

33. Bevan, Bryan, *James, Duke of Monmouth*, p78

34. Ibid.

35. www.tbheritage.com

36. Browning, p334

37. Fraser, Antonia, *King Charles II*, p293

38. Trease, p211

39. Evelyn, 04.02.1685, p441

40. Van Der Kiste, *William III*, p40

41. Van Der Kiste, *William III*, p43

42. William Hayhurst to Roger Kenyon, ref DDKE/acc 7840 HMC/396, 10 February 1680–1, www.a2a.org.uk

43. Bevan, p158

44. Van Der Kiste (*William III*), p73

45. Bevan, Bryan, *James, Duke of Monmouth*, p148

46. Evelyn, John, Diary and Correspondence

47. Ibid.

8
James II to William III

Charles's brother, James, faced so much opposition to his becoming king because of his staunch Catholicism that, once he took the throne, he needed to focus entirely on what his kingship meant, and that signalled changes. As Duke of York he had accompanied his brother to the races, even if he did prefer to read his Bible during the meetings than watch the action, but once he became king his racing days were over.

Despite the objections over his accession, James wanted to assure his subjects that they would have nothing to fear from him, but a change was noticed immediately in the overall demeanour of the royal court. Charles's quiet funeral – as much to save money as anything – was a signal that the court would be more sombre from now on, with a new moral code, and the office of the Master of the Horse reflected this shift in attitude, becoming drastically reduced and with fewer appointments. George Legge, 1st Lord Dartmouth, was given the role on 13 April, and a certificate from the Board of Green Cloth dated 20 April confirms his appointment. By 1 July, the remainder of the staff were in place. There were fourteen in all, of which only two surveyors of the stables – William Banks and Ambrose Norton – were reappointed from the previous year.[1]

James's decision to restrict his interest in horse-racing was entirely personal, as the sport itself remained unaffected. Tregonwell Frampton now had a free hand at Newmarket that would last until his death 42 years later, although it would be some years before he would be made an official of the royal household.[2] Even so, James maintained an interest in horse-breeding and by royal charter created the Down Royal Corporation of Horse Breeders. He might have wished to place the monarchy above horse-racing, in direct opposition to his brother's direct participation in the sport, and so maintain a distance from the debauchery that had characterised Charles's reign for so long. Nonetheless he did attend Winchester, a move indicating that Charles's original intention to relocate the court to the cathedral town was still being considered. James, however, didn't feel inclined to have Wren's palace completed; a vast place, the residence had already cost £20,000 (£2,421,250 today). It was later turned into a barracks but burned down in 1894.[3]

James would battle for the entire span of his reign to justify his role as Catholic monarch,[4] and in June 1685, just four months after his accession and weeks after his coronation, he faced his first threat when his own nephew, James Scott, Duke of Monmouth, instigated a rebellion designed to oust him. Monmouth failed outright, however, partly because many of the new king's subjects supported and liked James and partly through bad planning. Monmouth headed an army of 7,000 untrained peasants and yeomen, and since his cavalry rode carthorses there was a fear at court that higher-bred horses would be taken by the rebels.[5] One Thomas Allen, the keeper of Lord Weymouth's horses, suggested in the middle of June that year that the Lord's stallions be moved to Kempford, noting that a great bay mare had been found dying. At that time, the Civil War and its effect on the horse population and the Royal Stud was still fresh in people's minds, and it was generally felt that the bloodlines of specially bred horses up and down the country were again in danger of being eradicated if the soldiers decided to take charge of the stocks for the duration of this current rebellion.[6]

Soon Monmouth had reached Taunton, whereupon he set about denouncing his uncle, accusing him of murdering King Charles II. It soon became obvious, however, that he had misjudged James's capabilities and found that the King was more than ready to meet the rebellion head-on. The decisive battle took place at Sedgemoor, where huge numbers of Monmouth's men were slaughtered. The rebellion was crushed and Monmouth fled the field, only to be later caught and beheaded.[7]

The politics of James's court had no effect on horse-racing, which was very much in evidence as 1685 gave way to 1686. That April, three plates were run at Berwick, one at a value of £20 and the other two between £30 and £40, and the horses had to be kept at Berwick for fourteen days before these races.[8] Then, in Lancashire on 6 May – twelve months or so after the introduction of the Ormskirk Plate – it was announced that a horse plate of £40 would be run on 1 June in Ormskirk.[9] For this event, each horse was to ride 10st weight on a four-mile course in a contest comprising three heats. It was then announced that on 2 June there would be another race run at Ormskirk for a £15 plate, again comprising three heats but this time at 8st weight and the horses could be no more than thirteen and a half hands high. This race was later scheduled to be run each year on the first Tuesday and Wednesday in June.

Meanwhile, for galloways there was to be a £5 plate, and by April 1687 there was good racing at Worthington and Windermere in the Lake District.[10] The Great Horse Plate and the Town Plate for Galloways were to be run on the second Tuesday in July, while on the Wednesday there was to be a Second Plate. Also, another £10 plate for young horses had recently been founded.

On James's accession, the number of officials handling the royal stables was reduced, but we do have an idea of how the stables were being run during his reign and the names of the people who provided their services. In May 1695 an account was put together by Sir William Villiers, relating to the years 1685–8. This account, now housed in the Petworth House Archives, refers to monies received for the purchase of horses, coaches and harnesses, as well as other goods, including 'chairs' (possibly a short term for sedan chairs), wagons and other necessities. The document is divided into three parts: Midsummer 1685 to Christmas 1686, Christmas 1686 to Christmas 1688 and services rendered during the period of mourning for the Duchess of Modena.

Meanwhile two letters under the Privy Seal – dated 17 February 1687 and 13 July 1688 and written at the Palace of Westminster – reveal that Sir William was paid £4,000, the first payment as an advance for the year commencing Christmas 1687, thereafter to continue yearly. This money was awarded for the purchase of saddles, housings, bridles, horse clothes, harnesses and reins for different types of horses, including hunters, coach horses and bottle horses. There was also money awarded to the tradesmen who provided for the stable for the buying of horses, coaches, town houses, chairs and wagons. The accounts were to be rendered for the auditors, and interestingly they were to be in English rather than the more usual Latin.

The royal stables employed a great many tradesmen – coach-makers, tailors, saddlers, bitmakers, founders, gilders, fringe- and reinmakers, glassmen, silver-smiths, beltmakers, cutters, painters, embroiderers, drapers, lacemen, harness-makers and whip-makers – and William Villiers named them all. For this period between 1685 and 1686, it appears that coach-maker Samuel Aubrey provided two town coaches, two travelling coaches and a wagon while another coach-maker, Thomas Brigham, provided two coaches, a chair and repairs.

Once constructed, the coaches then had to be maintained, and painter Peter Hall provided varnishing, colouring, gilding and repairs for twelve of the coaches built during this period as well as for a chair and a wagon, while glassman John Huogebout provided twenty large door glasses, twelve side glasses, six chair glasses and several frames. Another glassman, Isaac Taylor, provided glass for two coach doors and two side glasses while Henry Dennis provided glass for a broken coach.

Then there were the accessories to the royal coaches. William Nicholls, a mercer, provided velvet for the interiors while Thomas Price, a woollen draper, provided black, grey, crimson and blue cloths for coaches and livery for several servants. Harness-maker Nicholas Spalden provided four pairs of harness, fitting up a coach and harness and providing several necessaries for coachmen. Meanwhile, another mercer, Sir Edmond Wiseman, provided velvet, damask, serge and other materials for coaches, chairs, clothes, saddles and servants' liveries.

The needs of the servants, in fact, were much simpler. Tailor Edward Barradell provided livery for a number of them, and there are also references to their expenses being met. Coachmen and grooms received allowances for candles and brooms, while one Gabriel Glasop – a porter at the stables of St James's Palace – received one year's wages for the year ending midsummer 1686. Meanwhile, liveries were provided for the huntsmen and dog-keepers, and Postillion Extraordinary Robert Parslow received one year's wages and board wages.

The accounts also mention some of the officials involved with the upkeep of the royal stables. Henry Griffith, Yeoman of the Horse, received payment for horses bought and for repairs made to the horses' house and two stables in the mews, while Avenor Thomas Morley received payment for the housing of three of the King's wagons and Thomas Pudsey and James Beckett received monies for riding charges to the north for the purchase of horses, as did Sir William Villiers.

If anything provided a true representation of royal prestige, it was the horses themselves, which were judged as being of far greater value than were the people assigned to look after them. As well as being very well fed, both at home and abroad, their caparisons and caps were always richly embroidered while the whips used on them had lines of silk and gold and they wore numerous different types of custom-made bits. There were even metal founders, silversmiths and gilders on hand to provide the finest buckles, belts and ceremonial swords for the King's huntsmen. Whatever James might have thought of his brother's principles, it appeared that the image of kingship was just as important to him as it had been to Charles.

The royal stables' accounts from this time also provide a glimpse of the work that was done there between Christmas 1686 and Christmas 1688. During this time, coachmaker Samuel Aubrey was paid to produce six coaches and to alter and mend several others, and he also provided the King with three chairs and nine new wagons as well as repairing others. Kenneth Griffith, meanwhile, provided repairs at the saddlers' office in the Royal Mews and at Hampton Court. The equipment at both locations was kept in pristine condition and accessories were constantly being repaired or replaced, with no expense spared.

One of the royal stables' primary functions was to reflect every occasion, and it certainly played this role when the Duchess of Modena died and the court went into mourning. On this sad occasion, all of the equipment was fitted out in purple and black, from the interiors of the coaches to the accessories of the horses and the mourning clothes of the 58 servants attached to the stables. The funeral also served as a prime opportunity to purchase new equipment to replace the old – for instance, John Bignall provided fifteen saddles and new furniture for several old saddles. The costs of such refurbishment were astronomical, and yet by 13 July 1688 a further payment of £10,000 was put forward for more purchases.

By this time, James's reign was under threat again. His wife, Mary of Modena, had given birth to a long-awaited boy a month earlier, on 10 June, and it soon became clear that the people weren't about to tolerate a Catholic succession. Plans were put in place to remove James and his progeny from the throne, and his son-in-law, William of Orange, was asked to lead another rebellion, which resulted in December 1688's Glorious Revolution that saw James deposed. He and his family left England on 23 June, and by the 25th they had arrived in France to begin a life of exile.[12]

After the monarch was deposed, King James's Master of the Horse kept his position until he relinquished it to Henry Nassau D'Auverquerque, who wasn't officially to be appointed until 2 March 1689. Others, too, remained until the end, including James's riding surveyor, William Banks; avenor and clerk-martial William Ryder; and Ambrose Norton, surveyor of stables, although no one was retained by the new King and Queen. Only Bryan Fairfax, equerry during Charles's reign, was re-appointed, on 15 March 1689. Soon the offices of the royal stables were brought back up to the levels that they'd enjoyed before 1685,[13] reflecting the air of hope and confidence that had been expressed in 1660 and emphasising William's commitment to the stables, the upkeep costs of which had risen from £4,200 (£504,200) in 1686 to almost £17,000 (£2,348,450) in 1688.

Within days of the overthrowing of King James, James D'Arcy, son of the elder James D'Arcy who had been Master of the Royal Stud for King Charles II, formally requested of William III that he pay some of monies owed to him, dating back to the reign of Charles, or, in lieu, to provide him with Barbary or Arabian horses – and Mediterranean ones which had no equal in England. However, his request fell on deaf ears and he found himself having to petition Queen Anne with the same request years later in 1702.

In fact, any approach to King William at this time would have been poorly timed since he had enough on his plate without having to worry about honouring the debts of his wife's uncle. Having got rid of James II, he was now faced with the task of keeping him out, and the deposed monarch had no intention of going quietly. Nevertheless, the D'Arcy stud didn't suffer unduly because of William's non-repayment and maintained its dominant position, as did the family that had established it. Acknowledgement of royal service was later extended to James's son, also named James, who was created Lord D'Arcy of Navan, Ireland, in 1721. He died in 1731.[14]

While William did take horse-racing seriously, it was for reasons other than a love of the sport. The truth is that he suffered from asthma and felt comfortable at Newmarket and Hampton Court (the latter of which became his principal residence), which boasted much cleaner air than London. Indeed, he had an aversion to the capital, which wasn't exactly the healthiest of places to live in, and believed that his ailment was caused by an airborne disease rather than due to polluted water, the result of London's non-existent sewerage system.

William also liked Newmarket because it provided him with an escape from court life, although his absence from the court generated a great deal of criticism. In the beginning it wasn't a problem, and neither was his liking for Hampton Court, where he introduced Dutch-style parterre gardens (they reminded him of home and eased his homesickness),[15] but he also had to get used to his new people, and one way of doing this was by attending Newmarket races for ten days each autumn.

On one occasion, William arrived at Newmarket considerably hungover and not in the best of moods, and he nearly got into a fight with a nobleman who rode in his horse's way as he approached the course, prompting him to swing his cane at the errant horseman. The public was completely won over by him, and in the company of his brother-in-law, Prince George of Denmark (who was married to Princess Anne, Mary's sister), as well as the court nobility and Dutch ambassadors, William became totally relaxed, placing bets and speaking to the members of the public. Nevertheless, he did lose favour with the Catholics in the area by taking their horses off them, so that they were compelled to travel about in carts and coaches pulled by oxen.[16] This action might have been intended to prevent any ideas of insurgency in the wake of James's departure, but William's ministers were not totally enamoured of him either. He worked hard, but during his time off he liked to hunt or ride alone. Indeed, he was in London seldom enough to disconcert his advisers, who would never be able to curb the King's passion for riding.

William was an excellent horseman, a feat made more remarkable by the fact that he had a hunched back and needed a breastplate and backplate fastened together around his body in order to keep him straight and upright on his horse.[17] He understood the importance of horses and, a born soldier, probably appreciated their value better than most. Indeed, he invested a great deal in the Royal Stud, and records show that in around 1690 there were resident at Hampton Court the chestnut Arabian Pulleine (named for the stud master Thomas Pulleine) and the black barb, or 'King William's black barb without a tongue'. (Later, William would also own a fair number of barbs that would be kept at stud during the reign of his sister-in-law, Queen Anne.) There was also the Chillaby, a white barb imported at around this time from Barbary by Master of the Horse Richard Marshall, along with a white mare called Slugey that was at that time carrying a foal later named Greyhound. Arriving *in utero* at Hampton Court, Greyhound was a natural barb and would later be taken over by John Crofts. Meanwhile, the Royal African was another of William's horses in residence at Hampton Court and was a brother to one of his mares: the Moonah barb.

Besides Richard Marshall, Lord Overkirk was also Master of the Horse, and William gave him a house overlooking Horse Guards, a residence very near Downing Street.

Whilst at Newmarket, Tregonwell Frampton continued to oversee matches. Races elsewhere were still very much local affairs, overseen by local councillors and justices, and so Frampton, being neither, was unique in his position.

In January 1690, at the Quarter Sessions in Durham, the justices of the town resolved to donate their own wages towards the cost of plates to be run on Durham Moor.[18] At this time, there was no national cohesion, with each area of Britain responsible for arranging its own racing meetings and dealing with any crime that occurred at such events. Any changes to these meetings would be announced in the local newspapers, while magistrates and town councils could appoint treasurers – as in Jedburgh – to provide money for cups and prizes.

In that year, James II tried and failed to retrieve his crown, and on 12 July the Battle of the Boyne took place with King William taking active command. One of his officers, Colonel Byerley, rode what has since been called the 'Byerley Turk' – a dark brown charger of unknown parentage – into battle, having taken him from a captured Turkish officer back in 1688 at the Siege of Buda in Hungary when the horse was around eight years old. When Colonel Byerley eventually retired, the horse went to stud at his family home of Middridge Grange and then, in 1697, to Goldsborough Hall, near Knaresborough, North Yorkshire.[19] He would never be a racehorse and would remain at stud until 1701, and in the next century his descendants would dominate horse-racing, not least through the patronage of William III's successors.

On 19 April 1691, the Earl of Bristol noted in his diary that William had won a famous victory as an owner, beating a chestnut horse named Careless, bred by Edward Leedes of Great Milforth, Yorkshire. On that occasion, the King's jockey had been riding a horse named Stiff Dick, believe it or not (his sire was called Spanker!), over a five-mile course.[20] It was a popular win and served to strengthen his position and popularity at home, but William also wished to keep things on an even keel abroad.

William was a soldier, first and foremost, but used what his biographer John Van Der Kiste calls 'diplomatic warfare', presenting English horses to the leaders of countries such as Sweden, Prussia and Italy (two Protestant nations and one Catholic) as well as to the Grand Duke of Florence and Tuscany. The English stud was by this time gaining a reputation as being one of the best in Europe and William was using the Royal Stud to good effect, securing a sphere of influence for himself and protecting his defences. Significantly, he also approached France, commanding the Duke of Portland, as ambassador to Paris, to present Louis XIV with nine English horses. This move was made to keep the French king on William's side, but it seems that James II, who had sought refuge at the French court, had settled down in Paris and appeared to be enjoying the sport of horse-racing abroad, watching a race at Le Pecq, near Vesinet, in 1692.[21]

But William continued to wage diplomatic warfare[22] and in April 1698 entertained Louis XVI's envoy, the Duc de Tallard, at Newmarket. This occasion provided the town with the best event it had seen in a long while, and Tallard was guest of honour at a meeting that encompassed ten days of racing.

In March 1693, indentures for Tregonwell Frampton were drawn up that made him responsible (or, at least, meant that he would continue to be responsible) for the care and management of the King's ten running horses at Newmarket.[23] Frampton was to receive all manner of provisions in order to discharge his duties, and he was also placed in charge of servants' wages and liveries, for which £1,000 was to be paid every quarter, backdated to 1 October 1690. The document was signed by Sidney Godolphin, Richard Hampden and Stephen Fox and the warrant was entered on 30 March 1693. In taking on the role of Keeper, Frampton was replacing Robert Baynton, who was dead by 1695.[24]

So too was the Queen, who had died of smallpox on 24 December 1694. Devastated, William sought comfort in hunting and began to spend more and more time away from London.[25] On 17 October 1695 he left Kensington for

Newmarket and for four days hunted and attended the races there, before moving on to Althorp, Northamptonshire, and then Oxford by November. Wherever he went, he hunted, usually accompanied by a large retinue. The only things that stopped him were bad weather and occasional threats to his safety. Roads to and from Newmarket were dangerous and consequently rife with highwaymen, so for the King's safety there was a rotation of guards against highwaymen between Newmarket and London. Even so, no one was immune from their attacks and there were periodic raids on those attending races.[26]

The King outlived his wife by only seven years. In the early morning of 21 February 1702, although he confessed to feeling giddy, he went to Hampton Court and somehow managed to get onto his horse, Sorel, to go stag-hunting.[27] At noon the horse stumbled and the King was thrown. He broke his collar bone and was returned to Kensington by coach, a journey that served only to worsen his condition. Echoing an account of the tragedy in the *London Gazette*, Sir John Evelyn noted that, 'being himself much Indisposed before and Aguish, with his former Cough and other weaknesse, [the King] put into a Feaver'.[28]

On 4 March 1702, King William III did indeed develop a fever, and four days later, on Sunday 8 March, he died at Hampton Court at about four o'clock in the morning.[29] He was interred at Westminster Palace, quietly and without fuss, on 12 April, and in the wake of the deposed James II's death in 1701[30] King Louis XIV of France recognised the claim of his son, James Edward, as the true King of England.

Notes:

1.   Sainty & Bucholz, pp58–68
2.   Muir, p14
3.   Robinson, p88, p89
4.   Lee, Christopher, *This Sceptered Isle: 55 BC–1901*, p272
5.   Lee, Christopher, *This Sceptered Isle: 55 BC–1901*, p273
6.   Longleat House. Ref TH/Vol/XXII, Jan 1683–Sept 1686
7.   Lee, p274
8.   Berwick: www.geraldesgasby.co.uk
     Online History Resources
9.   www.geraldsegasby.co.uk
10. www.geraldsegasby.co.uk
11. 'An Abstract of the Expense of the Late James the Second by actual Payments in Money for Three Years From Lady Day 1685 to Lady Day 1688: William Villiers' Account on the Stables in King James 2nd's Reign.' May 1695. Petworth House Archives. PHA 6304. West Sussex Record Office.
12. Lee, Christopher, *This Sceptered Isle: 55 BC–1901*, pp280–4
13. Sainty & Bucholz

14. James D'Arcy: *Foundation Breeders*, www.tbheritage.com
15. Van Der Kiste, *William and Mary*, pp119–21
16. Thompson
17. Van Der Kiste *William and Mary*, p120
18. Van Der Kiste *William and Mary*, p115
19. www.tbheritage.com
20. Thompson, p60
21. Longrigg, p67
22. Van Der Kiste, *William and Mary*, pp119–21
23. Indentures for Tregonwell Frampton. 30.05.1693, LS 13/257-C201123 (National Archives document)
24. Lee, pp302–3
25. Van Der Kiste, *William and Mary*, p184
26. Van Der Kiste, *William and Mary*, p190
27. Van Der Kiste *William and Mary*, p251
28. Evelyn, 8.3.1702
29. Van Der Kiste, *William and Mary*, p256
30. Lee, pp284–6

9

Queen Anne

On Queen Mary II's death, it was widely acknowledged that her younger sister, Anne, would succeed William III, and so it was that she was crowned queen in 1702, the last of the Stuarts, who had reigned over England for the previous 29 years.

By the time of her coronation, Anne was no longer a young woman. She had endured many pregnancies that had ended in miscarriage, stillbirth or death at a very young age, so she came to the throne childless and was likely to remain so. She was crowned at Westminster Abbey on 23 April 1702,[1] having been carried into the abbey in a sedan chair due to her excessive girth, the result of years of poor health. Anne was, however, a woman of exceptional energy and interest, and she poured a great deal of that energy into hunting and horse-racing, so it's perhaps not surprising that under her reign racing would takes its next, most enduring step. Where hunting was concerned a two-wheeled carriage was specially constructed for her[2] so that she could drive herself about and follow the hunt, which she did usually at breakneck speed, while the royal buckhounds were kept at Swinley Bottom so that she could view them when the court was in residence at Windsor.

Of her household, Stephen Fox was reappointed as commissioner for the stables on 7 April 1702 along with two others on the same day and in the same capacity: Sir Benjamin Bathurst and Hugh Chudleigh. All three vacated their positions on 20 July, however, when Charles Seymour, 6th Duke of Somerset, was appointed Master of the Horse, a position he would hold until 1712. Chudleigh transferred to the office of avenor and clerk-martial and equerry on 28 June, a post he would hold until his death on 28 October 1707. Just prior to Somerset taking up his office, on 1 July, William Walsh was appointed Gentleman of the Horse, and on 6 July Michael Studholme, former surveyor of the highways, was appointed Clerk of the Stables. The Queen's riding surveyor, John Bowen, was later appointed on 20 October.[3]

Anne loved Newmarket and was as enthusiastic about racing there as her Uncle Charles had been, having been a familiar face there since her first visit in 1683. Her husband, Prince George of Denmark, had a considerable stud at Newmarket, which the Queen actively encouraged, as she did his love of horses, buying him in 1705 a racehorse for 1,000 guineas called Leeds,[4] by Leedes Arabian, who had been given to one Edward Leedes by William III. Anne didn't wish to take direct control of the management of horse-racing, however, and retained Tregonwell Frampton, who continued to act as turf arbiter and was referred to by Anne as 'Governor Frampton'.[5] She raced horses under both his name and her own, still over an average distance of four to six miles; with Frampton being an active participant his horses ran every year, although races were still essentially the preserve of the aristocracy, with the dukes of Devonshire, Bedford, Somerset, Bolton and Rutland heading the list of patronage. The Queen's groom, or trainer, at Newmarket was one Thomas Spedding, who also worked for Prince George and received £57 (£7,520) today) per annum, and until the Prince's death in 1708 there would be a royal jockey, John Hague. Also in this year, Richard Marshall was appointed Master of the Stud, based at Hampton Court.

Since the estate was more or less managing itself, the Queen concentrated on her racing interests elsewhere and began to look to the north of England, where, on Bramham Moor on 22 September 1702, the Queen's Plate was run.[6] There was also a three-heat tournament for children under six years, run at under 12st in weight, for which the Queen presented a cup worth £100.

It seems that the Queen enjoyed the larger race meetings, where there was plenty of activity (she had, after all, been attending them since she was a young girl), and liked to be surrounded by people of like mind. When the monarch was in residence there, Newmarket was the centre of court and political activities as well as those connected with sport,[7] and when Anne and Prince George travelled there on 10 April 1705, just days after attending a smaller meeting at Datchet Mead, they were present as much in a political capacity (trying to drum up support for the Whig Party) as they were to watch the races.

While Anne and George were at Newmarket on that occasion, Frampton's horse – named, somewhat ironically (given the temperament of its master), Sobriety – won a match against Mr Holloway's St Patrick, and during the same meeting Prince George's grey barb won a match against Frampton's Thiller, but the governor had a chance to break even when his colt beat the Prince's bay barb.[8] Prince George was impressed enough with Newmarket to award a gold plate of 100 guineas, to be run on the second Thursday in October, comprising one heat over the Heath's course, with mares carrying 10st. They had to be five years old last foaling time and no older.

The Queen took time to consider the future of her residence at Newmarket, and that year she decided to extend the palace overlooking the High Street, obviously planning to extend Newmarket's influence further and do more entertaining there.[9]

Anne was a popular monarch and both she and her husband drew crowds. At the beginning of October 1706, when she and the Prince attended Newmarket for a ten-day visit, people from all over the country converged on the place just to see her. Anne was gratified by their affection for her, but Newmarket, as well as being a stage for sport, was, as previously noted, also a stage for politics, and since Anne's politics didn't always sit well with public opinion, some of the local gentry weren't always pleased to see her there.[10]

Anne and George attended Newmarket for the autumn meeting the following year, but it was to be their last visit together. Twelve months later, the Prince became ill and died on 28 October.[11] The Queen would never get over his death and thenceforth isolated herself, but since Newmarket had been a particular favourite of George's Anne continued to visit the place, and the following year, it was announced that the Queen's grey Pegg would run against Lord Ryalton's mare at Newmarket in October in a race over four miles for 200 guineas. Anne also retained an interest in the welfare of Newmarket's townfolk, awarding £1,000 for the paving of the streets and, in 1710, granting £50 a year for two schools: one of twenty boys and the other of twenty girls, both held in the transept of St Mary's Church.[12]

By this time, Anne was also sending her horses to York, where racing had been established on 21 September 1709. Indeed, she was as enthusiastic about racing in the north as she was about racing in the south and in 1713 travelled to York to watch her horse, Mustard, run in a race. He finished unplaced.

From about 1710, Anne began to take an interest in Hampton Court, where general improvements were being made to the palace and the Royal Stud. Meadows adjoining the stud that had previously been let out were reclaimed and a new stable – 40ft long and 12ft wide – was built. There was also a lodge for the stud master that had been repaired during the first year of Anne's reign but wasn't occupied until 1708, when Richard Marshall assumed the role. In 1709, the lodge was rebuilt in brick at a cost of £230.[13]

Anne then began to consider a new racing interest closer to home, one that would perhaps match Newmarket for spectacle and popularity but would be more accessible to Windsor. In the summer of 1711, she began to plan a racecourse at Ascot Heath, not far from where the Royal Buckhounds were kennelled at Swinley Bottom and within shouting distance of Windsor Castle. The ground had to be prepared first, however, and the Queen's Master of the Horse – Charles, Duke of Somerset – placed Sir William Wyndham, Master of the Royal Buckhounds, in charge of this project almost as soon as the idea was proposed, in June 1711. Workmen were then employed to clear and level the course, a job that would take up the best part of several weeks, through July and August, although they were well paid for this laborious task; carpenter William Erlybrown received £15.2s.8d for his labours, while Benjamin Culchott received £2.15s. for painting posts and John Grape was paid £1.1s.6d for compiling the race articles. The Queen wanted the Ascot races set up as soon as possible,[14] and the inaugural race was being advertised in the *London Gazette* on 12 July, even before the levelling of the course was completed.

Surrounded by her courtiers, Queen Anne arrived to inaugurate the race meeting on 11 August 1711. Two days later, the main event – the £100 Queen's Plate – was run, with four horses running in three heats, each run over the entire two-mile course twice. The horses obviously needed vast reserves of stamina to do this, running the best part of twelve miles in a day, with only short breaks. Unfortunately, there's very little detail recorded concerning what took place that day, and there's no map, so we have no real idea of exactly how the course looked.[15]

The following month, there were further races on 17 and 18 September, and it was decided to repeat them the following year. And so, on 25 August 1712, the Queen's Plate was run, and that September a £50 plate was provided. Ascot was set to become one of the most popular fixtures of the year.

Then fate stepped into the way of progress and in 1714, three years after the Ascot races were inaugurated, everything changed.[16] On Thursday 29 July of that year, the Queen was taken ill at Kensington Palace. She became worse the next day, suffering two convulsive fits in the morning that left her unable to move or speak. She sank gradually and wasn't expected to survive, so the Privy Council was assembled. The Lord Mayor was also instructed to secure the peace of the city and, while all those around the Queen were bracing themselves for her death, on 31 July one of her horses, Star, won the £40 plate at Ascot.

A vigil was kept around the Queen's bedside, but just after 7 a.m. on 1 August, she died.[17] As a mark of respect, a race for the Queen's Plate that had been due to run on 13 August was cancelled. It's a sad fact that, had Anne lived longer, there would have been a valuable record of the first formative years of one of the world's most famous and influential race meetings. As it was, however, events would soon unfold that would result in Ascot taking something of a back seat.

Notes:

1.   Gregg, pp36–7; pp46–7
2.   Magee and Aird, p11
3.   Sainty & Bucholz, pp48–68
4.   www.tbheritage.
5.   Longrigg, p52
6.   www.geraldsegasby.co.uk
7.   Gregg, pp196–7
8.   Muir, pp31–2
9.   Thompson
10.   Gregg, p150, p227
11.   Gregg, pp279–80
12.   Muir, p32
13.   Thurley, p221
14.   Magee and Aird, p14
15.   Magee and Aird, p15
16.   Magee and Aird, p17
17.   Gregg, pp392–4

10
George I

Anne was the last of the Stuarts, and since she died childless the throne passed to her third cousin, Prince George, Duke and Elector of Hanover, who, as King George I of England, was the head of the House of Hanover.

The new king, a great-grandson of James I through the previous monarch's daughter, Elizabeth, didn't hurry to England from his home of Herrenhausen, near Hanover, and greeted the news that he was now monarch with very little enthusiasm.[1] He had a comfortable life in Germany and, at the age of 54 (he was born on 7 June 1660), wasn't too happy at the idea of beginning a new life abroad, particularly in a country of which he knew very little and whose citizens knew very little about him.

George couldn't leave Hanover straight away, however, and while some writers have put this down to a reluctance to leave, the truth is that he had to put his affairs in order before he could move to England, so he remained in Herrenhausen until 31 August. Six days later he reached the Hague, remained there until 16 September[2] and then travelled on to England, arriving at Greenwich two days later in the company of his two very ugly mistresses (one was very fat while the other was extremely thin). These two unfortunate women were later subjected to a barrage of heckling from the local English who turned up at Hampton Court to greet them. George's wife, meanwhile, was languishing in a castle in Germany after having conducted an affair with a Swiss army officer.

King George found himself in a country immeasurably different to the one he'd just left, and he was at first anxious to retain many of those officials who had served him in Germany. One of these was Oberstallmeister Christian Harling, who had originally been Oberhofmeister in Osnabruck, while another was his Master of the Horse, Johann Adolf Kielmansegg (1668–1717),[3] who was also his brother-in-law. According to the tradition of the time, Kielmansegg should have been treated with the respect accorded to the Master of the Horse – in London, at least – but in truth he was Vice-Master of the Horse under the overall master, Charles Seymour, 6th Duke of Somerset (1662–1748), whose letters patent reappointing him as such were drawn up on 8 October.[4]

Charles was also keeper of Hampton Court park, house and meadows, not to mention the King's coach houses in Newmarket, and he was one of the great magnates involved in politics at that time and a regent of George I. He held the office of Master of the Horse for the first few months of George's reign, from 1714 to October 1715, but resigned after his son-in-law, Sir William Wyndham,[5] was arrested for suspected Jacobite activities. In the absence of a Master of the Horse, two commissioners, Conyers Darcy (to whom the Conyers Arabian is attributed) and Francis Negus, were appointed to the stables on 13 December 1715.

Of the English members of his household, George retained Richard Marshall as Master of the Stud;[6] Henry Berkeley, who later became Gentleman of the Horse; Darcy Conyers; George Fielding; Michael Studholme, Clerk of the Stables; and Thomas Spedding, who had served Anne and her husband, George. Many of the initial appointments were made on 27 and 29 September 1714, while the rest from that year were made in November. The next four years would see even more appointments being made.

George I loved hunting (another reason why Kielmansegg was among the first of his entourage to come over), preferring it over the English sport of horse-racing, and he was a good horseman. His royal seals bore an image of the horse of Hanover and the royal arms were changed to include the same beast. In fact, King George I was a very cultured man, speaking French as well as his native German and having a passable understanding of spoken and written English,[7] while he might also have understood Latin. He also loved music, painting and gardening, but his cultural tastes and his love of hunting game didn't go down too well with his new English subjects, and accounts from this time hint at a distinct clash of personalities between the monarch and the English aristocracy, particularly since George found some English customs baffling.

Despite the reaction he provoked in English peers, George didn't shut himself off. While he would spend spring at either St James's or Kensington Palace and the summer at Hampton Court, he made regular visits to the houses of noblemen, mainly to look at their gardens. He would also visit Newmarket, although these trips were rare and usually conducted in the company of his large family.[8] To George, a very energetic man, horse-racing didn't present the same kind of challenge as hunting, and he wasn't particularly interested in the rules surrounding the sport and the technicalities of it. To him, it was essentially an English pastime without any real consistency. At that time, horses still changed hands by private treaty and colours were inconsistent.[9] Nor was there any official register, so that, although races were staged all over the British Isles, they were still ultimately localised events. George therefore had no real cause to concern himself with the sport, although he did feel that it was important to visit Newmarket, probably because it had had such a strong link with royalty in recent times. It's not known when or exactly how many times George visited Newmarket, although it's generally understood that he went there in October 1717, and by all accounts on this occasion he was very courteous and generous to his guests. According to J B Muir, writer of *Ye Olde Newmarket Calendar of Matches, Results and Programs from 1619 to 1719*, George visited Newmarket three times – in 1716, 1717 and 1718[10] – but no one knows precisely when or what he truly thought of the place. It's also understood that he didn't attend Ascot, and from the time of his accession interest in the place declined. In addition, there was no Master of the Buckhounds between 1715 and 1727.

Many think that the King's preference for hunting betrayed an indifference to horse-racing, an unwillingness to adopt the sport, but there's a difference between not being interested in it and not wanting to make it his own, as previous monarchs – in particular, Charles II – had done. George might not have wanted to patronise the sport, but nor did he want to change it. He was quite prepared to let things continue as before, and as an act of faith he retained the services of Tregonwell Frampton, who was quite happy to race the King's horses under his own name at Newmarket. At one point the course boasted eight horses, and three boys and running horses were usually retained there for a month at a time.

Nor did the King object when racing plates were created in his honour. In April 1715, at the start of the Newmarket season, His Majesty's Plate of 100 guineas was created and was won that year by a horse owned by the Marquis of Wharton. Then, on 6 October[11] of the same year, the King's Plate of 100 guineas was won by Mackerel, owned by the Duke of Devonshire.

At this latter meeting, Frampton had mixed success. His horse Lightfoot failed to beat the Duke of Rutland's Long Megg in a match and the race became a matter of dispute, although his other horse Whistle Jacket came second in a match against Rutland's Grantham Mare. Then, in a match of eight miles, Frampton's Mule came second to Rutland's Creeping Molly – an astonishing result, given that Mule had had a headstart of 260 yards.

In June 1715, Frampton's contract as Keeper of the King's Running Horses was renewed, and the new monarch was content to pay him £1,000 for one year, a sum that was to cover his salary as well as the costs of the horses' provisions of hay, oats, bread, shoeing, medicines and other materials, along with wages, liveries and other expenses. The payment was backdated to 29 September 1714 and was entered on 6 June 1715.[12]

The King loved horses, and records from this time show that he was anxious to promote horsemanship in general. In the spring of 1716 he arranged for four pages of honour to begin lessons at the Royal Riding Academy on 1 April, and the avenor was ordered to present the following allowances: £166 per annum for salary and £40 per annum for two livery on the establishment of each of the pages. The latter sum was to cover the expenses of lodging, food for him and his servant and exercises at the academy, as directed by the Master of the Horse. Board was to be paid quarterly, and the itemised accounts reveal that it cost just over £7 for each page and £4 for his servant; £2 for the room; 50s for the maid; £9.9s. for the riding; and 4s for the grooms. The pages of honour also received further lessons in academic subjects, including mathematics (£2.5s.) and French (£2.5s.), bringing the total quarterly costs for each page to £28.3s.6d, with all four pages contributing a total of £112.14s. The Master of the Horse had the responsibility of overseeing lodgings, diet, instruction and exercise.[13]

The King also took some interest in Hampton Court, and in that same year arranged the building of two new stables, each 43ft by 17ft. Paddocks were also constructed to house milky-white albino horses, with Roman noses and red eyes, that the King had brought over from Germany. These were to be state horses, and until the 1920s their descendants pulled the state coach.[14]

Since George enjoyed hunting and shooting parties, the stables at Hampton Court were well maintained, and their complement of 100 horses were managed by a staff of eighty. The stables were home to some of the King's first-rate stallions, in particular, of which there was a wide variety, as well as mares, colts and fillies. In 1718, six of the horses were weeded out and dismissed – although not the Conyers Arabian (named after Conyers Darcy), which stood at Hampton Court between 1715 and 1725.

Other horses to stand at Hampton Court from 1719 were the Cyprus Arabian (also known as the 'Hampton Court chestnut Arabian'), originally owned by John Manners, the Duke of Rutland, and previously based at Grantham, Lincolnshire, covering mares in 1719, 1720 and 1724. Then there was the Hampton Court (chestnut) Litton Arabian and the Hampton Court Arabian, the latter of which would remain at the stud until 1732. There was also His Majesty's one-eyed grey Arabian and the King's grey Arabian, which were both owned by George I and, later, George II.[15]

In fact, George I's reign was a point in history when some of the finest Arabians would be bred or imported and from which the thoroughbreds of today would descend. The Flying Childers, descended from the Darley Arabian (1700), would be bred in 1715 by Colonel Childers of Doncaster, while the

Godolphin Arabian appeared in 1724. (With the Byerley Turk, the Darley Arabian and the Godolphin Arabian are the predominant foundation sires.)[16]

Fortunately, Newmarket didn't suffer from the King's lack of patronage and the meetings from April to October 1719 were quite extensive under Frampton. On 10 April, his horse Hall won a £100 match over four miles and another on 12 October, on the same day as his steed Dangerfield won a 50 guineas match, while on 2 November his chestnut colt won a 100 guineas match over four miles. The next day, his horse Nutmeg came second in a match of 150 guineas over four miles against the Duke of Devonshire's Basto mare, and Frampton ended the season on 4 November coming second with Hobler in a match of 150 guineas, run over four miles.[17]

By 1720 Newmarket was as popular as it had been under Anne's reign, and not just for its racing. Since it was essentially a market town, it had everything that anyone could want, and it was also popular because of its location and ease of access. Nevertheless, it was the races that brought multitudes flocking throughout the year, and it was still a significant meeting place. Unfortunately, the palace fell into disrepair, indicating that the King made few visits there, if any, and it was eventually rented out to the Duke of Somerset in 1721 for £30 per annum. Nevertheless, Newmarket races were known for having a good atmosphere, and on a visit sometime in 1724 the writer Daniel Defoe compared it favourably to ancient Rome, although he was surprised at how much crime was committed in the town.[18]

In August 1720, six years after Anne's death, a two-day meeting was held at Ascot. It was a modest revival, run by hunters and staging 30 guinea plates, but it was well organised and planned in advance, with entrance fees charged at two guineas for each runner, rising to four if they were entered at the starting post. The owner of the winner would take 30 guineas while the owner of the horse in second place would receive his or her entrance money. The level of organisation behind this meeting indicates that there might well have been a view to re-establish it on a more permanent basis (if, indeed, it had stopped at all between 1715 and 1720), but it would be another two years before there was another meeting there, and that event saw the participation of horses that had hunted with the King's hounds in Epping or Windsor Forest.[19]

At this time, there was also a renewed interest in the Wallasey Stakes, in the north of England, and from 1723 the Dukes of Devonshire and Bridgewater, Lords Derby, Gower, Molyneux and Barrymore, Sir Richard Grosvenor, Mr Watham Williams Wynne, Mr Cholmondeley and Mr Buckle Mackworth subscribed twenty guineas each for ten years for the benefit of this race, scheduled to be run on the first Thursday in May each year.[20]

With so many races taking place throughout England and Wales, a new era in horse-racing began, with the publication of a calendar – 'An Historical List of All Horse-Matches Run and All Plates and Prizes Run for in England and Wales (of a Value of Ten Pounds and Upwards)' – in 1727 – of which more will be detailed in the next chapter.[21]

As one era began, however, another ended with the death of Tregonwell Frampton. His contract had been renewed not long before his death and its details and his salary were the same as when he'd first been commissioned by William III, 37 years earlier. The document isn't dated, however, suggesting that he died before it could be put into effect.[22] John Wootton (c. 1683–1764) was one of two artists to capture the image of this extraordinary personality, and his portrait *Keeper of Ye Running Horses at Newmarket* was completed in 1728, a year after its subject's death.

By this time, Newmarket seemed to be in decline again, while the Wallasey Stakes were considered to be the richest races in the kingdom, worth 280 guineas.[23]

In the summer of 1727, the King decided to pay a visit to Hanover, his third since his accession after similar trips in 1716 and 1723. (It seemed that, by this time, he had come to value his duty towards his adopted country, as he didn't escape back to his former home in Germany each and every year.) He left Greenwich on 3 June and landed at Holland four days later.[24] He did not rest there long, however, and was soon on his way again, only to be taken by a fit on 9 June as he travelled between Delden and Nordhorn. He lost consciousness, but then came around as the doctors administered the usual remedies of the period, including bloodletting, and he insisted upon continuing his journey towards Osnabruck, where his brother, the Prince Bishop (also the Duke of York), lived.[25] He arrived there at around ten o'clock that night but died two days later, on 11 June.[26] A messenger was despatched to England and the Lords of the Privy Council were assembled at Leicester House, where George's successor was proclaimed on 14 June. The next day, the new King, George II, appointed the Right Honourable Richard, Earl of Scarborough, Master of the Horse.

For the next few decades, there would never be a truly consistent picture drawn of George I, and it's only in recent years that writers have been able to place his life into context. What is known, however, is that he had a tolerance for the sport of horse-racing where many believed he was indifferent and that his reign saw the foundation of changes that would help to modernise the sport.

GEORGE I

Notes:

1. McCarthy, p36
2. McCarthy, pp36–7
3. Letters Patent: West Sussex Record Office, Petworth House, PHA/2964, 8.10.1714; Keeper: West Sussex Record Office, Petworth House, PHA/322, 1716–28
4. Hatton, p397
5. Hatton, p350
6. Hatton, p134
7. Ibid.
8. Longrigg, p69
9. Muir, p14
10. Muir, p44
11. Muir, p45
12. Tregonwell Frampton: LS 13/260-C201123. Renewals of Contract of Tregonwell Frampton, 6.6.1715
13. 'Directions Initiated by George I for Settling Pages of Honour in the Royal Riding Academy to Begin 1.4.1716', West Sussex Record Office, Goodwood Estate. Goodwood/17–1716
14. Nash
15. www.tbheritage.co.uk
16. Mortimer, Onslow & Willet, p241
17. Muir, p56
18. May, p61
19. Magee and Aird, pp20–21
20. www.geraldsegasby.co.uk
21. Tyrrel, p8
22. Tregonwell Frampton: LS 13/201 C201123. Renewal of Contract of Tregonwell Frampton, 1727
23. Wallasey: www.geraldsegasby.co.uk
24. McCarthy, p310
25. McCarthy, pp310–11
26. *London Gazette*, Tuesday, 13.6.1727–Saturday, 17.6.1727

11
George II

George Augustus, Elector of Hanover and Prince of Wales, became King George II on his father's death. Like his father before him, he saw horse-racing as an essentially English pastime, but also like his father he sought to maintain the breeding stud at Hampton Court. To this end, he retained Richard Marshall as stud groom there, although Marshall died on 19 March 1728. He was later replaced by Thomas Smith, who had been a groom at Hampton Court, along with Thomas Panton and Gilbert Todd. Meanwhile, Richard Lumley, 2nd Earl of Scarborough, was appointed the King's Master of the Horse on 27 June 1727, the first to take the post since the Duke of Somerset at the start of George I's reign.

The King himself was a stag hunter and hunted in the parks[1] each Saturday and Wednesday morning for five hours. His wife, Queen Caroline, wasn't impressed with such behaviour, however, and even George himself thought that fox-hunting was undignified.

Ironically, if George had played a more direct role in the development of horse-racing, many of the changes that came about during his reign might not have happened. Charles II had been his own authority, while William III, Anne and George I relied upon Frampton. But Frampton's death on 12 March 1727 signalled the end of that style of control, and as the years went by it became clear that the sport needed some body of authority, if not the King himself. As John Tyrrel notes, after Charles II's death there was an administrative 'vacuum'[2] that Frampton filled, but after the Keeper's death the vacuum reappeared, since there was no one around to match his personality and influence, least of all his replacement, Thomas Panton. Frampton's death signalled the fact that, if horse-racing wasn't governed, and governed well, then not only the sport but the management of horses would suffer.

Even before Frampton's demise, there was a recognition that the sport of horse-racing and its administration needed to be overhauled, since there was nothing consistent about the running of it or the people who claimed to run it, Frampton included. In the years that followed his death, as the administration of horse-racing began to drift away from royal influence, there was more of a concerted effort to consider the state of the sport, to evaluate what was wrong with it and to decide what steps should be taken to improve it.[3]

John Cheny was the first to view the problems as a whole and to provide something of a solution, identifying six key areas: meetings were rife with accidents; the conditions of running varied so much that inconsistency was blatant; articles and advertisements tended to be misleading; there was bias of interest, a sure road to corruption; disputes invariably ended up in court; and overall, because of all these issues, many involved in the sport harboured resentment. Cheny also noted that those rules that existed applied only to the King's plates, which meant that other races around the country were open to blatant mismanagement and corruption. Frampton had done nothing to extend his influence to help modernise the sport.[4]

Cheny concluded that, if the sport was to flourish, whatever governing body controlled it had to be reliable in its method and should depend upon written record and communication. He also felt it expedient to record the identities of the horses that ran and in 1727 published the book *An Historical List of all Horse-Matches Run and of all Plates and Prizes Run for in England and Wales (of a Value of Ten Pounds or upwards)*, which cost five shillings.[5]

Cheny's findings prompted a programme of reform that would continue to evolve over the years to come. Progress was slow, however, and it would be many years before anyone acted on his ideas. This inertia wasn't necessarily due to any complacency on the part of race organisers; the problem was that each district was still used to running things its own way, and the idea of the sport being run by a centralised governing body was alien to them. For a while, then, it was largely business as usual, although there were some signs of change. In 1733, for instance, the races at Wallasey came to an end, but the meeting's principal race, the Wallasey Stakes,[6] was transferred to Newmarket, and the value of it increased from the 20 guineas of ten years earlier to 100 guineas. Seven years later, on 15 January 1740, however, races were still being held on the frozen River Tees, near Barnard Castle, each comprising three heats of two miles. The pace of change was extremely slow, but it was starting to gather speed. And when change occurred, it began at the top.

On 18 January 1735 the Earl of Scarborough relinquished his post as Master of the Horse, to be replaced by a descendant of Charles II, Charles Lennox, 2nd Duke of Richmond (not to be confused with his father, 1st Duke of Richmond, who was also Master of the Horse). George II might not have been interested in horse-racing, but the Duke of Richmond was, and in 1739 he approached Cheny and asked him to revise and publish the King's Plate Rules.[7]

The following year, Parliament stepped in with legislation – the first since

Queen Anne – that was drawn up not so much to protect the sport and act as its governing body, in a directly positive sense and with an aim towards reform, but to control and limit the sport,[8] with an aim to controlling the public, and as a result many meetings were restricted. (Ironically, Parliament was at the time being run by the very people who gambled their fortunes away on the sport.) This change in the organisation of horse-racing occurred at a time when England was on the brink of the Industrial Revolution, and the demands of industry required the public wasn't unduly distracted by such leisure activities.

A parliamentary Act of 1740 entitled 'An Act to restrain and prevent the excessive increase of horse races . . .' also fixed the minimum plate value at £50 and stipulated that listed weights had to be carried and adhered to, with a fine of £200 if the correct weight wasn't drawn, authorising the imposition of fines and extensive penalties in a bid to curb corruption.

Possibly as a result of the Act and the effect it wrought, some meetings died out. Gainford and Piercebridge, near Darlington,[9] for instance, came to end, and in 1744 racing was prohibited in Durham, Newcastle, Stockton, Morpeth, Carlisle, Chester le Street and Bishop Auckland by order of the magistrates because of the interference of horned cattle.[10] This might seem to be something of a drastic reaction over a minor matter, but it hints at the sport's growing need for orderliness.

The one suggestion of Cheny's that wasn't realised before his death in 1750 was his idea of a separate stud book for pedigree horses, although he had planted a seed in the minds of many who believed that horse-racing could be controlled properly and without the intervention of Parliament or even the monarchy.

The same year saw the death of the Duke of Richmond, Master of the Horse, on 8 August, but the office remained vacant until 5 July 1751, when it was offered to William Cavendish, Marquess of Hartington. By this time, the management of horse-racing had moved onto the next stage, and the new-styled Jockey Club had been in existence for several months.[11]

The Jockey Club, in fact, was an enigma, its members a gathering of upper-class personages with nothing in common except a love of wine, food and the turf – plus the fact that they had a great deal of money to pay for it all. Nor was their meeting place very auspicious, as they convened in a coffee room and the Star and Garter pub in Pall Mall, London.[12] There was no formal recording of members' names, nor a declaration of the club's aims and purposes. In fact, the club boasted no jockeys on its list of members, and its name became the source of a great deal of curiosity. (It seems that at this time the word 'jockey' referred to the owner as much as the rider of the horse.)

Nonetheless, the English horse-racing scene finally had its governing body –
of sorts – and in 1751 another calendar, inspired by Cheny's effort, was
published by an auctioneer named John Pond who had business interests in
Covent Garden and Newmarket.[13]

While these developments were taking place and the administration of
horse-racing was gradually evolving, changes were also afoot among the ranks
of the royal family. On 31 March 1751, Frederick Lewis, Prince of Wales, died
suddenly, although his death wasn't regretted hugely by his father, the King,
with whom he'd been on hostile terms since his arrival in England in 1728.[14]
Both father and son had done their best over the years to antagonise each other
and had separated their respective households to such an extent that, when
Frederick's wife went into labour with the first of their nine children, he
hurried her to St James's Palace so that the child wouldn't be born in the
presence of his parents, the King and Queen, against the dictates of protocol.
Naturally, the King was furious, but Frederick was unmoved and brought up
his growing family in a totally separate establishment from his parents' court.
He was seen as a liar and a monster, not least by the King and Queen, but he
was nonetheless a cultured man who loved the arts, sciences and sports, with a
passion for hunting. He also had respect for his adopted country and instilled
into his eldest son the knowledge that, although he was of German origin, he
had nonetheless been born an Englishman. Until Frederick's death, King
George had taken very little interest in his grandchildren, but he did his best
for his late son's family, and a month after Frederick died, his son, George, was
created Prince of Wales and Earl of Chester.

The late Prince of Wales hadn't been a member of the newly founded Jockey
Club, and neither had he patronised the sport, although he had taken his eldest
son, George, to Ascot on one occasion. Since he enjoyed sports in general,
however, and – like his grandfather George I – would have recognised that
horse-racing was part of English culture, he might have been interested in an
advertisement that appeared on 1 April 1752 detailing 'A Contribution Free
Plate', in which unnamed horses owned by the members of the Jockey Club
competed. Moreover, the Jockey Club, now two years old, decided to set up in
Newmarket for no other reason than because they wanted premises closer to
the racecourse there. They therefore acquired land on which to build a coffee
room and, while that was being built, took over the Red Lion pub in the
town.[15] It was during this year that the existence of the Jockey Club was
mentioned for the first time in the *Sporting Kalendar*.

The following year saw the publication of Reginald Heber's *Historical List of
Horses Matches run and of Plates and Prizes run for in Great Britain and Ireland*

in 1753, a fairly detailed record of races containing such details as the heights of horses, weight carried and distance run. This volume was followed in 1758 by Heber's first general order of the Jockey Club, stipulating that 2lb overweight was the maximum permitted, unless owners declared otherwise, and that failure to do so would lead to disqualification. And so the Jockey Club was now doing what Cheny had recommended almost thirty years earlier: establishing law and order.

On 16 May 1753, Lord Gower's bay colt won the Jockey Club plates, and on 17 May[16] Captain Vernon's horse Crab won an event. Where such owners could win thousands, however, prizes elsewhere could be more wide-ranging, as in Darlington, where one could win anything from silver and gold cups or money to more everyday, practical objects such as hats, girdles, bridles, whips, pipes, tobacco, muslin aprons, ribbons, Holland smocks and caps.[17]

By this time, there was a need to look at the sport in detail and initiate further changes, and once again the royal household started the ball rolling. First of all, the Deputy Master of the Horse, John Bridger, wanted to determine the differences concerning the ages, entering or running of any horse for the King's Plate.[18] Then, in 1756, in its first recorded act of reformation, the Jockey Club abolished heats in its plates. In these events, it was decreed that, while there would be no sole judge, there would be an official on hand. A year later, a dispute at the Curragh was referred to the club, indicating just how influential it had become.[19]

These developments mattered very little to King George II, but they were of great interest to his second son, William Augustus, Duke of Cumberland, who was the first of the royals to become a Jockey Club member. Renowned for the part he'd played in the Battle of Culloden on 16 April 1746, Cumberland was later forced to resign from the army after a catastrophic defeat at the hands of the French. His reputation demolished – largely by his irate father – he took himself off to the peace and quiet of Windsor, where he was made ranger of Windsor Forest.

Soon after the move, it became clear that Cumberland wanted to establish his own stud (in fact, he was the only member of the royal family at that point to take an active interest in the breeding of horses), but he didn't have enough land for this purpose since much of the park at Windsor was open to the public. William solved this problem by moving the public out, erecting fences to keep them out and then embarking on a plan that would turn out to benefit not just him but the thoroughbred industry as a whole. As for the public, their complaints fell on deaf ears.[20]

The Duke's efforts were modest to begin with, and his first horses were bought from other owners and breeders, but one of the first that he bred himself, a horse named Muley (by Muley Ishmael, out of Young Ebony, by Crab), turned out to be his first winner. Later he acquired Muley Ishmael himself, also known as the Grey Arabian – the Duke's Arabian – which he kept at Cranbourne Lodge at Windsor Park.

By 1750, after some extensive renovations, the stables at Cranbourne Lodge had enough room for fifty horses. The stable block – resembling the Riding School later constructed at Buckingham Palace – was partially enclosed by a circle of trees separating it from an area labelled 'The Lawn' on the architect's plan (in fact, the area looks more like a deer park), while on the other side, to the east, were a house and offices and to the south there was a small stable yard. There was also a farmyard and a kitchen garden, and the stables were surrounded by vast parkland and plantations. There was even a bowling green.[21]

The Duke proved to be more successful at horse-breeding than he had been at soldiering, and by 1758 he had bred a horse at Windsor named King Herod (later truncated in the *General Stud* book to Herod), a bay by Tartar – and, as such, the great-grandson of the Byerley Turk – out of Cypron by Blaze.

Cumberland's first list of horses currently in training appeared by 1 May 1759. His father left him in peace to get on with his endeavour, but he wouldn't live to see the stud's successes, dying suddenly on 25 October 1760 at Kensington Palace.[22] As the *London Gazette* recorded, 'Yesterday in the Morning between the Hours of Seven and Eight, King George the Second was suddenly seized, at his Palace at Kensington, by a violent Disorder, and fell down speechless and soon expired.'[23]

Like his father before him, George II's contribution to horse-racing and horse-breeding had been to leave it alone for others to develop, and thanks to his lack of interference his son achieved notable progress in those fields. The results of Cumberland's work at Windsor would be seen throughout the reign of the Duke's nephew, King George III.

Notes:
1. Nash
2. Tyrrel, p7
3. Longrigg, p89
4. Longrigg, p91
5. Tyrrel, p8
6. www.geraldsegasby.co.uk
7. Tyrrel, p9
8. Tyrrel, p13

9. www.geraldsegasby.co.uk
10. Ibid,
11. Ibid.
12. Tyrrel, p11
13. Ibid.
14. Hibbert, Christopher, *George III*, pp8–20
15. Longrigg, p89
15. Mortimer, Roger, *The Jockey Club*, p10
16. www.geraldsegasby.co.uk
17. Ibid.
18. The Shiffner Archives, East Sussex Record Office, SHR/60–31.08.1753
19. Longrigg, p89
20. Hibbert, Christopher, *George III*, pp24–5
21. 'A General Plan of the Park, Gardens and Plantations of Windsor Great Park: The Seat of His Royal Highness the Duke of Cumberland', MRI/23 114779 (National Archives document)
22. Fitzgerald, pp23–5
23. *London Gazette*, Tuesday, 26.10.1760–Sunday, 31.10.1760

12
George III

George III was the first Hanoverian monarch to be born in England and, coming to the throne at the age of 22, brought with him the novelty of youth. Almost immediately on his accession, the process of organising the new king's household began, but, as in the past, the office of Master of the Horse was prone to political complications. The bestowal of such a prized appointment was something of a juggling act for the young king, one that required a certain amount of diplomacy and pacification. As Horace Walpole wrote, 'The Duke of Richmond, haughty and young, was offended that his cousin, Colonel Keppel, was removed from Gentleman of the Horse, which the King destined for one of his own servants.'[1]

The Duke demanded an audience with his monarch, and got it, but succeeded only in upsetting the King, who sent him away with a flea in his ear. Later, George regretted the outburst, and by way of making amends offered the Duke the role of Gentleman of the King's Bedchamber, which he accepted on the condition that Keppel retain his office. Walpole was of the opinion that this was an attempt by Richmond to gain further advancement for himself rather than for Keppel's benefit. Indeed, Richmond's superior attitude (he was, after all, a descendant of Charles II) annoyed a great many people, and he was obliged to resign, only to regret doing so when it was too late. Keppel, however, maintained his position in the household, having been Gentleman of the Horse since 1747, but was replaced on 22 December 1760 by Richard Berenger.[2]

A similarly short-lived Master of the Horse was the 10th Earl of Huntingdon, who kept the post for less than six months, from 18 November to 29 April 1761, when the 3rd Duke of Rutland took over. In fact, unlike under previous reigns, the positions of Master of the Horse, Gentleman of the Horse and Clerk of the Stables under George III would undergo regular turnarounds, with no one holding the office for more than a few years at a time, each post serving as a step up the ladder. Certainly, no one would keep the office of Master of the Horse for a lifetime, as Frampton had done with his post, or would so dominate racing through such an office, possibly due to the fact that horse-racing was by this time governed by an independent authority and was free from the direct influence of monarchs and politicians.

William Augustus, the Duke of Cumberland and the King's uncle, was a Jockey Club member and successful horse-breeder, and was currently reaping the rewards of his efforts with his horse Herod, which ran for the first time in a race in October 1763, when it beat the Duke of Ancaster's Roman for 500 guineas over the Beacon course at Newmarket. Herod continued to show promise into the following year and won another race on the Beacon in April 1764. This proved to be a time of special significance for Cumberland's stud, as in the same month there was a lunar eclipse and a foal bred at Windsor Forest was named for this astronomical phenomenon. Eclipse's sire was Marske, a brown horse bred in 1750 by John Hutton of Marske, near Richmond, Yorkshire, and who was by Squirt, out of the Ruby mare. Hutton had exchanged Marske as a foal for an Arabian of the Duke of Cumberland's stud, and the horse had gone on to win the Jockey Club Plate and the Round Course at Newmarket. In fact, there was some dispute over who Eclipse's sire actually was, because his dam, Spiletta, had been covered by Marske and another named Shakespeare, and at the time people were willing to believe that Shakespeare was Eclipse's sire.

It would be some time before anyone knew if Eclipse had any promise or not, but meanwhile Herod went from strength to strength and in June 1764 ran in a match of four miles at Ascot. Faith in him was growing, and in October he beat the Duke of Grafton's Antinous, again on the Beacon course.[3]

Cumberland was the only member of the House of Hanover until this time to become directly involved in horse-racing, horse-breeding and the Jockey Club, and this state of affairs was set to remain. George III was interested in riding for its own sake, and through this, combined with a deep-rooted interest in architecture, in 1764 he commissioned the building of an indoor riding school – the Royal Mews – situated at the Queen's House in Pimlico. One of George's first acts as king was to move his carriage collection and some selected horses to the Royal Mews from Charing Cross – for reasons of convenience, if nothing else – and he invited his uncle, the Duke of Cumberland, there in April 1765.

By this time, the Duke was living a quiet life in Upper Grosvenor Street, content just to concentrate on his horses, after having suffered a stroke five years earlier that left him in terrible shape, blind in one eye and half-blind in the other. He was also very overweight, an asthma sufferer and, to cap it all, had abscesses on his legs – and yet he was expected to answer his nephew's summons.

It must have come as an even greater shock when he discovered why he'd been called to the Royal Mews. The King, it seemed, wanted advice – for the first time since his accession – on how to deal with his ministers. The Duke obliged, but he didn't have much of an opportunity to enjoy his new status as the King's confidant or his membership of the Jockey Club, dying suddenly on 30 October 1765.[4]

With no intention of keeping the late Duke's horses, the King held a sale where Eclipse was bought by William Wildman for £75. Later that year Marske, Eclipse's sire, was sold to a Dorset farmer. Eclipse proved to be a rather difficult colt for Wildman, as indeed did many of his descendants, but he was rather striking in appearance: a chestnut with a white blaze, one white leg and an unusually high behind. He was also incredibly fast, as a supposedly secret trial revealed in April 1769 when Eclipse outpaced everything in sight. Touts heard of this trial through an old woman who wasn't even aware that she'd been watching a race. Word got about, and when Eclipse's first scheduled race took place, on 3 May at Epsom, he was put at 4–1. He won his first heat with no trouble at all, and one Dennis O'Kelly noted, 'Eclipse first, the rest nowhere.'

It suddenly became essential to establish Eclipse's parentage, and opinion was unanimous that his sire was Marske. Being a tall male survivor of the Darley Arabian (through Marske, Squirt and Bartlett's Childers), Eclipse was the third most important thoroughbred sire in the nation. The artist George Stubbs painted him more than once, and being an authority on the anatomy of horses (controversially so, since he used to cut up and store their corpses in order to study them) he was very impressed with Eclipse's form.

Herod was sold off to Sir John Moore and went to stud near Bury in 1768, and it's testament to his resilience that he didn't suffer much from his change of ownership after the Duke's death. Indeed, his popularity was such that £100,000 was bet on him at Newmarket, and under his new owner he secured £201,505 – a gargantuan sum for those days – and won forty hogsheads of claret, three cups and the whip. Nevertheless, he would never be a champion racehorse; having been beaten a number of times, on one occasion he ran so hard that he burst a blood vessel. He was retired to stud, becoming a champion sire, and died in May 1780. Being a descendant of the Byerley Turk he was the second most important tail male survivor after Matchem, but he was also descended from the Darley Arabian line through his dam, Cypron, making him one of the most important foundation sires, along with Matchem, bred in 1748.

The 1770s were a significant turning point in the development of horse-racing, and in 1775 the sporting calendar fell into the hands of one man. Back in 1769, William Tuting had compiled a *Sporting Kalendar*, along with Thomas Fawconer, and then conspired with James Weatherby against Fawconer over ownership of the title. Then, in 1773, Tuting died and Fawconer carried on the battle, but within two years Weatherby had the upper hand and Fawconer himself died. As Keeper of the Match Book, Weatherby received authorisation from the Jockey Club to publish a racing calendar.[5]

Meanwhile, more races were being introduced. On 24 September 1776, just months after the publication of Weatherby's calendar, a 150 guineas sweepstake for three-year-old colts and fillies was created on the suggestion of Lieutenant Colonel Anthony St Leger, run for the first time over a two-mile course on Cantley Common in Doncaster, although many of the residents of Firbeck believe that it took place on Anthony's private racecourse on the oval field near Park Hill Hall. Cantley Common *did* provide a venue for racing, and the 1776 Doncaster Race Meeting appears in the racing calendar, but the writer Moya Frenz St Leger favours the oval field as the venue for the first St Leger.[6]

The new race featured an important innovation: rather than taking the form of several heats, the horses raced for long distances in a single heat. It was also agreed that, should a dead heat occur, a run-off would be held to decide the winner. On that inaugural event in 1776, the St Leger was won by a brown filly owned by Charles Watson-Wentworth, 2nd Marquess of Rockingham, who had entered two horses in the new race. There were three other owners whose horses participated that day, including the race's founder, Anthony St Leger, who subscribed to the 25 guinea sweepstakes for each horse entered. His bay filly by Trusty came in second.[7]

Two days later, at Mansion House, the Mayor of Doncaster's official residence, the proposal was approved that the racecourse should be moved from Cantley Common on the grounds that the gentry couldn't be made comfortable there. It was resolved instead to establish a new course on Town Moor and to erect a stand in which to house spectators. A year later, Cantley Common was enclosed by an Act of Parliament and a stand and stables were built at a cost of £2,637.

It was another two years before the race was actually named, however, during a private dinner party in an upper room of the Red Lion Inn in Doncaster's market square. At first the name Rockingham was suggested, possibly because of the Marquess's win at the inaugural event, but the Marquess himself wasn't keen on the idea and suggested instead the name St Leger.

Then, in 1780, during a house party given by Edward Smith Stanley, the 12th Earl of Derby, a new kind of race was planned in which three-year-old fillies would participate over one mile and four furlongs. The race was named after a country house that the Earl had bought on the outskirts of Epsom just seven years earlier, named The Oaks, and the inaugural race was won by Lord Derby's horse Bridget.

Later that year, on 12 August, George, Prince of Wales, was granted his own establishment. Born on 12 August 1762, George was the oldest of an ever increasing brood of children; just a year after his birth, on 16 August 1763, his brother Frederick (the future Duke of York) was born, and the rest of his siblings followed in quick succession: William (the future William IV) on 21 August 1765, just weeks before the Duke of Cumberland's death, followed by no fewer than twelve other children, with the youngest, Amelia, born on 7 August 1783, just five days before the Prince of Wales's 21st birthday.[8]

Despite the fact that by this time his two younger brothers, Frederick and William, had a certain amount of freedom in their careers – Frederick a soldier and William earning a name for himself in the navy – by 1780 the Prince of Wales hadn't been given a job to do. Because of this he would always feel a need to prove himself, to make his mark, and in the coming years he would latch onto horse-racing as a vehicle for this.

By the age of eighteen, the Prince was known as a womaniser and hung around with people of whom his parents didn't approve, in particular Anthony St Leger, who was frowned upon by the King and Queen despite the fact that his family had had links with the royal family for centuries. Prince George hunted with Anthony in Northamptonshire, very often against his parents' wishes, but when they complained he always had an answer ready. Emotionally he had long since switched off from them, although he respected their positions as monarchs. Indeed, George had more of an affinity with his uncle, Henry Frederick, Duke of Cumberland, a confirmed rake living and whoring in Brighthelmstone on the south coast, and who invited the young and impressionable Prince of Wales to join him.[9] The King forbade the visit, since the Prince hadn't at that time reached the age of 21, and whatever he might or might not have known of his son's amorous activities, he certainly wasn't going to let him fall under the influence of his brother.

By 1782, however, the Prince of Wales had reached his majority and was trying to live his own life. He had taken up horse-breeding by this time, and in 1783 he bred Mufti, by Fitz-Herod, out of a mare by Infant. A grandson of Herod through his sire, Mufti was also a descendant of the Byerley Turk and would become a significant sire in his own right. He would not, however, be in the Prince of Wales's possession for long, being sold to Jockey Club member Richard Vernon at the age of three.

The first chance he got, George took himself off to Brighton, preferring the society there to that of his parents' stuffy court, and in 1784 he leased Grove House, 600 yards from the sea front. While there, he would ride on the downs and attend race meetings and shooting parties. His interest in Brighton grew and he decided to look for a permanent residence there. Fixing his sights on an old farmhouse, he commissioned architect Henry Holland (who at the time was already working on the Prince's other residence, Carlton House) to convert it into something more palatial, despite his ever-increasing debts.

Indeed, by the following year, the Prince's finances were becoming a problem. That year, while he successfully bred a foal by Highflyer, he was later forced to sell it, along with others, to cover debts totalling the best part of £250,000. He wasn't unusual in being in such a dire financial state, but unlike many young men of his age, some of whom had control of their own estates, he had no control over where his money was coming from, and he exercised little control over where it was going, too. Parliament issued his funds but also kept an eye on his spending and was growing more alarmed with each passing year, as was the Prince's father – and in the background, following the Prince's every move and providing comment and criticism, was the press. The King feared that George's brothers would be led down the same dissolute path, and ultimately he was proved right.

Meanwhile the King was leading a rather frenetic life of his own and was becoming rather eccentric. In 1786 he designed a uniform known as the 'Windsor uniform', using his father's livery colours of dark blue and gold turned up with red. The King loved it and wore it as often as possible, as did members of his household and his daughters who went hunting with him. Along with the uniform, they also wore white beaver hats and black feathers while the King would wear a black jockey's cap. He hunted ferociously and at great distance, upwards of eighty miles, and the horses he rode sometimes either were run to death or lost the impetus before the final kill.[10]

The King's equerries, who had to accompany him on all of his rides, also had a tough time of it. Although George III could be a considerate employer, he had little sympathy for any member of his household who fell ill. When he was told that one of his equerries was unwell, he would note that the man had very good colour and determined therefore that there was nothing wrong with him. His equerries had to be constantly on guard, too, as the King could decide to go riding at any time, sometimes in the severest of weather, and sometimes, by the time the long-suffering equerries were ready, he would be well ahead of them.

The King would visit his stables early in the day and would take the time to speak to the grooms, asking them how they were, what they were paid and so on. He was also aware that the grooms sometimes took themselves off to the Three Tuns public house in Windsor and turned up especially early one day to catch them there. He never missed a trick.

It was his increasingly energetic and eccentric behaviour, however, that prompted his physicians to recommend a change of scene, and in the summer of 1786 the King and Queen travelled to Cheltenham to try the waters there. During his visit, the King rode extensively, but while he took the waters, his condition didn't improve and by 16 August he was very much worse, exhibiting symptoms that doctors of today believe signified the onset of porphyria.

The King's illness, which would last on and off for the rest of his life, couldn't have come at a worse time. In 1786 his son, the Prince of Wales, was in debt again, despite receiving a stipend of £62,000 per annum granted to him by Parliament, and he was forced to close Carlton House while it was still under construction. Until that year he'd had 25 horses in training, but due to his escalating debts he had to get rid of almost all of his animals, raising £7,000 in a sale held by Tattersalls on Monday 24 and Tuesday 25 July. The *St James's Chronicle* noted that the horses were sold off so cheaply, they were almost given away.

Then, in May 1787, Henry Holland, the architect of Carlton House, was forced to revise his estimate on the place to £49,700. The Prince of Wales had been less than eager to pay for the residence's construction in the first place, and the spiralling costs spelled further bad news. In the meantime he'd taken himself off to Brighton to oversee the conversion of the farmhouse he'd purchased three years earlier and which became the Brighton Pavilion, a remarkable, eastern-styled building that was to become the focus of high society as King George retreated further and further from it.

As soon as he was financially solvent again, the Prince of Wales returned to the turf with just four or five horses. Three years later, this number had grown to 41.[11]

By contrast, George's younger brother, William, found horses boring, as nothing more than a necessary means of transportation. On a visit to his brother Frederick in Hanover, William was expected to inspect the royal stables and found it tedious. He would never understand George and Frederick's taste in horse-racing and, although he enjoyed gambling, he would never indulge in it to the same extent as Frederick, whose debts were steadily increasing. He would also never appreciate what it meant to win a race, unlike his brother George, who won the newly established Epsom Derby with a horse named Sir Thomas on 8 May 1788, one of 185 races that he would win between 1788 and 1792.

The Epsom Derby had been established back in 1780, but it might just as easily have been called the 'Epsom Bunbury'. Legend has it that, in deciding the name of the race, the Earl of Derby and Sir Charles Bunbury tossed a coin for it and Derby won. It has since turned out to be the royal family's most elusive race, with George IV just one of three royals that have actually won it. (His uncle, Henry Frederick, Duke of Cumberland, had been involved with the race since its inception but had never won it.) The Prince had been fortunate, but such luck proved illusory.

In 1789, George bought a horse for 1,500 guineas from a Mr Franco. In fact, he was buying the horse back, having been its original owner some three years earlier when it was a yearling, and it would probably have remained in the Prince's stud had it not been for his royal master's penchant for living beyond his means. The still-unnamed horse had been sold to Franco on 25 July 1786 for 95 guineas and was removed to his new home, but he'd become restless in his loose box and had kicked out at the woodwork, managing to get his fetlock stuck. 'Oh, what an escape!', Mr Franco allegedly exclaimed on hearing of the accident, and the word stuck, with the horse being named 'Escape'.

Escape proved his worth and ran five times for Mr Franco between 1788 and 1789. It helped that he was descended from the Byerley Turk through both his sire, Highflyer, and his dam, a mare by Squirrel. On 28 September 1788 he ran the Rowley Mile at Newmarket, and then on 1 October he won the Town Plate. In the following year, on 28 April, he was beaten in a match at Newmarket, but on 2 May he won a match. He seemed to have a talent for bouncing back, and by the time the Prince of Wales retrieved him some time later, he had earned a good reputation.

Escape was duly placed under the care of his racing manager, Warwick Lake, and his Newmarket trainer, Francis Neale. Neale found Escape difficult to manage and train, finding his overall performance erratic, but the Prince was undeterred, an attitude that didn't bode well for the future. Sure enough, the following year he was in debt once again, this time owing £400,000.

At around the time that the Prince bought Escape, he also expressed a wish to engage the jockey Samuel Chifney to ride for him, but Lake and Neale had reservations. 'However,' Chifney wrote later in his autobiography, 'on 14 July 1790, His Royal Highness . . . did me the honour to engage me for life to ride his running horses, at a salary of two hundred guineas a year.'[12] The Prince explained to Sam that, if he gave the jockey specific orders on how to ride a race, he was to refer to Mr Lake to finish the orders and make any alterations, where applicable, and in doing so to run as he saw fit.

These instructions would prove to be the bane of Sam's life, and from the beginning of his time racing for the Prince he found that his horses weren't being trained as well as they should have been. On one occasion, just weeks after being engaged, he informed Lake that the Prince's latest acquisition, Escape, wasn't fit to run at York. He might just win, said Sam, but he nevertheless blamed Neale for not having made the horse ready. Chifney had a high opinion of Escape's speed, having seen him run at Newmarket in April 1789, so it bothered him that the horse had been allowed to go out of condition. Lake, of course, immediately took offence,[13] but Chifney, unfazed, added that he wasn't happy with Escape's overall condition. The Prince, he stated, was putting a great deal of money on the horse. However, the stage was set, and the only person who couldn't see it was the Prince of Wales, who at the time had other priorities.

The 1790 races at Newmarket saw the appearance of the Duc d'Orléans, a friend of the Prince of Wales who was racing in England as 'the Duc de Chartres'. Also a member of the Jockey Club, the Duc was a particularly humourless man who wasn't well liked at Newmarket and probably wasn't too pleased at being pushed into a garden pond by the Prince of Wales, who recommended a closer look at the goldfish there. Nevertheless, Monsieur le Duc ran his horse, Conqueror, for a Jockey Club plate and, whatever people might have thought of the French visitor, his appearance at Newmarket – and that of the Prince – was a subject of interest for the artist John Bodger, who produced a coloured aquatint with an etched outline. The artwork was based on an original painting and drawing (artist and date unknown) titled *Trains of Running Horses, Newmarket*, a picture that provides a snapshot of the Prince of Wales's visit to the races and also highlights how central the Prince was in the racing world at the time. In the painting, Newmarket itself is visible in the background, as is Ely Cathedral, but the principal location is Warren Hill. The Prince – a central figure – stands in his phaeton, drawn by six greys, and appears to be booking a bet with the Duc d'Orléans, at his side on horseback. The Duke of York is also depicted, offering his arm to a lady (said to be Mrs FitzHerbert), while other represented personages include the politician Charles James Fox, the Duke of Bedford and other members of the social elite. Bodger's painting provides a very colourful depiction of the races, with a great deal of attention to detail.

Equally full of attention to detail is Chifney's autobiography, *Genius Genuine*, which recounts his turbulent relationship with Warwick Lake and the Escape affair. If the Prince of Wales had imagined that his racing manager and one of England's finest jockeys could co-operate with each other, he was sadly mistaken. The clash of personalities between the two, plus Chifney's lack of faith in Francis Neale's training methods, was evident from the outset of their relationship, and Chifney's book describes confrontation after confrontation over the Prince's horses and how they were being prepared, culminating in a showdown that affected the Prince's relations with the Jockey Club for over thirty years.

On 19 October 1791, Chifney noted that Escape was mentioned on a list of horses due to run for a plate at Newmarket the next day. Worried about Escape's form, he went straight to the Coffee House to see what time the race was due to start. While he was there, someone asked him if the horse could win, and he replied yes, if the horse was well. So was the horse well? 'Yes,' Chifney replied, 'he is well, or what they [Lake and Neale] are pleased to call well.' He left the Coffee House without saying another word.[14]

The next day, at the racecourse, the Prince approached Chifney, hoping the jockey would share in his confidence that Escape would win. Chifney, however, expressed reservations and advised the Prince not to back the horse. Although the Prince agreed not to place a bet, he still had faith in Escape, which put Chifney in a quandary; he was damned if he said anything and damned if he didn't. He was also becoming aware of the Prince's growing impatience with his apparent contrariness.[15]

Frustrated and angry at the position in which he found himself, he came across the Prince again some time later seated in his carriage while Lake was standing with his horse on the other side of the rails. 'Come this way, Sam Chifney,' said the Prince. 'I will give you your orders how to ride Escape.' The Prince told him to ride a strong race, then paused, perhaps waiting for Chifney to make some kind of answer. None was forthcoming, so the Prince continued, telling his jockey to do as he thought fit, depending on the conditions of the course, before driving on to the betting post.

Lake asked Chifney what orders the Prince had given, and the jockey told him. For once, they both agreed that it was better to wait with Escape, rather than make a strong race of it.

Lake then took his leave to join the Prince while Chifney went to saddle up, asking the groom if Escape had had a sweat since his last run and discovering to his dismay that he hadn't. This meant that the horse hadn't been tried – or, at least, not tried enough – since his last race.

As it turned out, Escape ran in a field of four: a 60 guinea race, two miles across the Ditch-in Course, 1–2 favourite, and as a result finished fourth behind Coriander, Skylark and Pipator.[17]

The Prince wasn't happy and told Chifney that he should have made strong play with Escape, as directed. 'And I do tell you, Sam Chifney,' he continued, 'that I am a better jockey than Mr Lake and you both, for you have lost the race by not running as I desired you.'[18]

At first, Chifney thought that the Prince was joking, perhaps unaware that he very often retreated into a world of fantasy, even imagining himself as a grand military leader and the winner of many battles. He therefore bowed and laughed, and the Prince walked away.

Chifney proceeded to the weighing house but was then summoned back to the Prince, who was over at the farther winning post of the Beacon Course with Lake. The Prince grilled Chifney as to Escape's performance and Chifney put his failure down to not being tried and not sweating. The Prince spoke to Lake, but Chifney interrupted him to ask if Escape would be running the next day, the 21st. The Prince replied yes, which suited Chifney as the horse was probably already exercised enough to win his next race. However, he did clarify his position years later when he wrote, 'I wish it to be understood that I don't mean that horses are always to run better the second day than the first.'[19]

In addition, Chifney was wary of taking orders from Lake and disappointed that sometimes the Prince wasn't satisfied with his word alone.[20] He was well aware that people thought him obstinate and opinionated, and acknowledged that such traits weren't wise for someone in his profession, but he remained convinced that, on the race on 20 October, Escape just couldn't keep up with Coriander, Skylark or Pipator.

The following day, the 21st, the Prince gave the same racing orders as the previous day, and this time Chifney advised his royal master to back Escape, then advised Lake to do the same, requesting that he put 20 guineas on the horse for him. Lake refused,[21] however, and once more Chifney was in a dilemma. If he didn't put money on the horse himself after advising the Prince to do so and Escape lost, it would look as though Chifney had deceived him. He therefore had to find someone else to place the bet for him. By the time he'd reached the starting post, he was a nervous wreck.

In the event, the race went off without a hitch and finished likewise, but once more Chifney couldn't do right for doing wrong. After Escape's desultory performance the previous day, Lake complained to the Prince about the orders he'd given for that race while Neale rode up and down the course, telling anybody who would listen that he'd been robbed of forty guineas after betting on Escape on the 20th.

'Now the appearance to me is this,' wrote Chifney of the affair. 'On the first day of Escape's running, Neale had not sufficient skill to know Escape was not in proper condition to enable him to run near his best form, and he backed him, cried and was rude.'[22]

The Prince didn't approach Chifney that day, and even the newspapers – especially *The Times* – saw little to comment about, but the following morning Chifney was called to the Prince's dressing room. They adjourned to the next room, where the Prince said, 'I am told, Sam Chifney, that you won six or seven hundred pounds upon the race on the day before yesterday, where you rode Escape and was beat upon him.'[23]

Chifney was more than a little shocked and asked the Prince how he'd come by this,[24] but the Prince ignored the question and asked Chifney if he had any objection in naming all the bets he'd had on the race of the 20th, arguing that it was in the public interest. He also asked if Chifney had any objection to submitting to an examination by the Jockey Club. Chifney agreed to do both.

Later that morning, Chifney met Sir Charles Bunbury, steward of the Jockey Club, and the Prince reminded the jockey of his willingness to be examined by the Club. Once that was agreed in the presence of Sir Charles, each went their separate ways. Chifney was told to expect a series of affidavits from Mr Weatherby, clerk of the Jockey Club.

On 23 October, *The Times* reported on the Prince's hunting activities in Newmarket, and the next day the newspaper described Escape's victory alongside the progress of another of the Prince's horses, Laurentina, in another race. (She came second in the second year of a subscription of five guineas, with Skylark coming fourth.) Even on the 25th, the paper didn't refer to any row that might have been brewing, and instead described how on the 24th the Prince of Wales had left Carlton House for Brighton, where it was believed he would remain until the middle of November while other members of the royal family would remain at Windsor Great Park for the hunting. Obviously, no one was concerned enough to change their routine and things continued as normal.[25]

Then, on 26 October, the circumstances surrounding Escape's unorthodox win finally hit the newspapers. *The Times* described what happened after the race, the Prince's reaction to the complaints and the fact that a great many people lost huge amounts of money. If anyone else doubted him, the Prince certainly had faith in himself. *The Times* was scathing, however, and saw fit to make a joke of the whole affair in its 27 October edition.

By 29 October, the argument had escalated into a public row serious enough for the Prince to cut short his stay at Brighton. That evening he was back at Carlton House with the intention of travelling to Newmarket on the 31st. On the surface, it was business as usual – the Prince had a number of engagements that he intended to honour – but it didn't help matters that this was Newmarket's busiest time of the year and that people were speculating wildly on his future in racing, enquiring of *The Times* whether or not he would sell his stud (again) and start concentrating upon more important issues.

No doubt accustomed to the barrage of public opinion, the Prince remained determined to carry on as usual, as *The Times* noted on the 31st, and that afternoon he gave an audience to the nobility back at Carlton House before leaving to attend the Houghton Meeting at Newmarket.[26]

As if fate was saying that it wasn't all doom and gloom for the Prince, he had quite a good day at Newmarket, with one of his horses coming second in a 300 guinea sweepstake and then another, Amelia, beating the Duke of Bedford's Portia in a race worth 30 guineas. Then his Don Quixote beat Sir W Aston's Anthony.

In the meantime, Chifney received his affidavits, which he swore to and then he returned to Mr Weatherby. 'I was then had up before the Stewards of the Jockey Club,' he wrote, 'who were Sir Charles Bunbury, Bart., Ralph Dutton, Esq., Thomas Panton, Esq.'[27] He was called upon to explain Escape's performance and what his orders had been on the day of the 20th. While Dutton and Panton appeared happy with his answer, Bunbury didn't, although he said nothing.[28]

Chifney was dismissed and was called almost immediately to attend Carlton House. When he got there, he discovered that the Prince had already received a visit from Sir Charles, who 'told him that if he suffered Chifney to ride his horses, that no gentlemen would start against him'.[29]

The Prince wasn't happy with this ultimatum and gave his jockey his full support, but Sir Charles had no intention of giving Chifney any quarter and had obviously decided that he was guilty even before the hearing, so he brought the whole force of the Jockey Club's authority down on Chifney and was determined to make an example of him, even if it meant alienating the Prince.

This was an interesting development in the history of the Jockey Club, as it demonstrated that the monarchy couldn't place itself above the sport and dictate terms but the Jockey Club *could* place itself above royalty and draw the line.

But why did Bunbury find it so easy to dictate terms to the Prince? He was, after all, horse-racing's greatest patron, both in the sporting and social sense. Normally, it wouldn't have done to alienate such patronage, but Bunbury appears to have acted without giving Chifney or the Prince the benefit of the doubt. It might be that, given the Prince's inveterate gambling, lifestyle and mounting debts, the Jockey Club's members – including Bunbury, whose aim as the club's first Dictator of the Turf was to improve the sport – would have received a great deal of criticism. It was therefore in Bunbury's best interests to isolate the club from any scandal. In this, he would have had the backing of the press, the Prince's greatest critic, and perhaps of the King himself. In fact, within months George III would come under increasing pressure to account for his son's expenditure, and with the French Revolution in force just across the channel the image of a prince who squandered money was not a good one.

The Prince of Wales remained loyal to Chifney, however, and cut his ties with the Jockey Club, adding insult to injury by granting his rider a £200 per annum pension for life. The business of Chifney and Lake was a case of six of one and half a dozen of the other, with Chifney doubting his superiors' ability and they resenting his familiarity with themselves and the Prince. The showdown with Escape was waiting to happen, although if it hadn't happened over that horse it would have happened over another. Indeed, given Chifney's account, one wonders why matters didn't come to a head sooner. The Prince appears to have treated all of those involved – Chifney, Lake and Neale – with equal respect and to have risen above the bickering that marked the three men's relationship, but at times he succeeded in confusing things, making communication difficult between all four of them and giving contrary orders. Lake, especially, appears to have suffered from this, unable to assert his authority over Chifney because he was wary of the jockey's confidence and of the Prince's liking for him, and in his efforts to undermine the jockey's hold over the situation he would go behind his back. Nor did it help that Chifney saw Lake as an inconvenient middle-man between himself and the Prince. None of the four acted in Escape's best interests, and the horse was later sold to Tattersalls, spending the rest of his life at stud.

If 1791 ended badly, the new year began no better when *The Times* reported that burglars had secured access to the Prince's drawing room while he was entertaining guests there. A diamond bow had been snatched from his coat and left hanging by a thread.[30]

Further to this, according to an article in *The Times* in February 1792, the Prince was back in debt. The newspaper gave its concern with the fact that the King wanted Parliament to cover the monies he owed, which had been accumulating since 1787. *The Times* didn't believe that the King would bring up the subject or approach Parliament on such a matter, since he'd tried this approach back in 1787, on which occasion parliament had kicked up a fuss, so the matter had been dropped with a compromise that the debate on a grant would be postponed. After publishing the King's declaration, *The Times* couldn't see how the Prince could now approach parliament again on the same matter. Indeed, it noted that no application had been made for Parliament to meet the debts, and nor was the Prince to get more money, particularly since the public was also paying for the lifestyles of the Duke and Duchess of York. The only additional expenditure on the royals that year went to Frederick, Duke of York (£18,000), and William, Duke of Clarence (£12,000).

While the paper expressed its doubt that the Prince had exceeded his annual stipend of £10,000, it soon became clear that he owed a massive fortune and it was announced that his entire Newmarket stud would be put up for auction, either in January or February of that year.

Not the best way for the year to start. The Prince of Wales's losses were to become the subject of a report that might have been a backlash against the debt problems of his brother, the Duke of York. He too loved the turf and had a large stud at Oatlands, his seat near Weybridge in Surrey, having also founded the Oatlands Stakes (at that time considered more important than the Derby) and having run at Ascot in 1791 and later at Newmarket.

Things began to settle down after the Chifney affair, however, and even the newspapers kept reports of the Prince's racing activities to a minimum; on 24 June 1794 when the royal family attended Ascot, there was no mention in the press that the Prince had been with them. Getting him to restrict his expenditure, however, was still proving to be difficult, and by March 1795 he was back in the red.

In addition to reporting 'with great regret' the existence of the Prince's debts, *The Times* also noted – in a tone resembling that of an obituary – how they created a rift between the Prince and the King that would later be discussed by Parliament, after the Prince's impending marriage. The newspaper wasn't about to let him get away with his exorbitant expenditure this time, and to rub salt in the wound the same column noted the potential arrival of his cousin and bride to be, Caroline of Brunswick – the ultimate price the Prince of Wales had to pay in order to clear his debts. In the meantime, the state of his finances were to be investigated by a Committee of Four Gentlemen, but this was put on hold, *The Times* observed: the King wanted to see a true state of his son's account, only to find that such a document couldn't be produced, a fact that *The Times* marked in italics.[31]

Caroline of Brunswick arrived in England on 5 April and the wedding took place on 8 April. The occasion was marked by the Prince turning up drunk, a state in which he'd been on and off since meeting his cousin for the first time, soon after her arrival. Caroline, it seemed, didn't meet with his sensibilities (she had to be told to wash), while he, in turn, was fatter than she had been led to believe. As duty dictated, he consummated the marriage and then collapsed in a drunken heap in the grate, where the new Princess of Wales left him. Nine months later, on 7 January 1796, she gave birth to what the Prince described as an 'immense girl': Charlotte, Princess of Wales, who was second in line to the throne.

Despite the fact that the marriage between George and Caroline was a disaster from day one, very few outside the royal circle were aware of the state of affairs and the papers noted several weeks after the marriage that the Prince and Princess of Wales were to attend Ascot Heath races together.[32] And so, on 9 June, the entire royal family went to the races in four coaches, presenting a united front. The Prince and Princess of Wales had previously arrived at Windsor Castle from Carlton House to be with the other members of the family, but it was noted that the Prince didn't attend the event, and on 11 June *The Times* reiterated the point, noting the presence of the King, Queen, Duke and Duchess of York and four eldest princesses on the Thursday.[33]

Throughout the 1790s, the newspapers made continual references to the presence of the royal princesses, which wouldn't be unusual in itself if it wasn't for the fact that all were their mother's permanent companions except one: Princess Charlotte, the Princess Royal, who was married. Initially, this wasn't a problem, but the Queen's advancing years and worry over her husband's health had made Queen Charlotte very selfish and she didn't encourage her daughters to think about marriage. The Prince of Wales sympathised with his sisters, who were very unhappy, but he couldn't complain to his mother for fear of worrying the King. The princesses were restricted in everything that they did, including visiting the races. They were allowed to visit Epsom and Ascot, but not Newmarket, and so they missed out on much of the social life that their brothers took for granted and for which they were heavily criticised.

It was during this year that Samuel Chifney's autobiography was published. *Genius Genuine* sold at £5 and clarified exactly where its author thought the blame lay for the events of the previous year: with Warwick Lake. The book was still in circulation almost ten years later, ensuring that no one forgot the escape affair.

Meanwhile, the Prince of Wales stayed well away from Newmarket, although he continued to pursue his horse-racing interests and had a great many winners over the next few years. Nor did he cut himself off from society, entertaining lavishly at both Carlton House and Brighton Pavilion.

By 1800, the Prince was breeding thoroughbreds again, as was his brother, the Duke of York, at Oatlands. The Prince raced his horses at Newmarket, but not in his colours; instead, they bore the colours of his new racing manager, Delmi Radcliffe.

At around this time, the Prince took on a new trainer: Frank Smallman, a relative of Sam Chifney's from Albany Grange, near Winchester, whom the

Prince employed because he liked his method of waiting and then pouncing forward at the post. He also employed Sam Chifney Jr as his jockey, paying him £8 per annum.

That year's Ascot races were busy. The Prince of Wales had a five-year-old, Speculator, in a sweepstake for ten guineas. The Prince's horse ran unplaced, though, as did the Duke of York's. To add insult to injury, a man who'd had the care of two of York's horses decided to abscond with them, and by the time the story had reached the papers the thief had well and truly vanished.[34]

As the century came to a close, King George III had been on the throne for forty years, Great Britain was still at war with France and the fact that the Prince of Wales wasn't allowed a command when most of his brothers had seen active service still rankled him constantly. To compensate for being overlooked, he began to spend more.

In 1802, the Prince met up again with Sam Chifney at Brighton, still vowing never again to set foot on the ground at Newmarket. He hadn't communicated with the Jockey Club for eleven years and had no intention of doing so in the future, but that hadn't stopped him from maintaining his interest in horse-racing, and he went into partnership with Lord Darlington of Newmarket. His trainer at this time was James Perrin, then from 1802 the post was taken up by H Smallman at Winchester and from 1806 J Acred, from Norton, near Malton in Yorkshire, trained his horses. His jockeys, meanwhile, were Delme Radcliffe, Thomas Panton Jr, William South and, from 1807, William Edwards.

But it wasn't just horse-racing that had the Prince's attention. If anyone had imagined that the Prince's withdrawal from the Jockey Club would curb his extravagance, they would have been wrong. His next construction project was the Brighton Pavilion's stables, the most elaborate and extravagant ever to have been commissioned by a prince or a monarch. Designed by William Porden, they were a magnificent architectural construction. The building housing the stables was octagonal on the outside and circular on the inside, with an immense dome crowning the central angular bay, the flanking wings surmounted with pinnacles and the whole possessing long, dignified lines. It was modelled upon the Halle au Blé ('Corn Market') in Paris, a construction that had been built in 1782, and the structure of its vast dome was rather deceptive, being just 12in thick at its base, reducing to 9in at the top, and with a diameter only 20ft less than the dome of St Paul's Cathedral in London. In all likelihood, the sheer extravagance of the place was a swipe at the Jockey Club and must have boosted the morale of the Prince no end.

The stables also contrasted sharply with those at Carlton House. A residence which didn't enjoy the same kind of secluded surroundings as other royal residences, with one side being in close proximity to three streets – Pall Mall, Little Warwick Street and Cockspur Street, which led back to Pall Mall – the stables there weren't all that far from the main thoroughfare. They could be reached passing through a wide road from the house with a garden and a park on either side. Once there, the stable block, which faced the riding house, curved around, having to accommodate an area of buildings on Red Lion Yard that also backed onto the coach house. With the riding house – 200ft long and 50ft broad, backing onto the park – the impression is one of enclosure, whilst the Pavilion, stables there suggest space and light as well as grandeur. The horses therein were housed in 44 stalls, ranged around in a circle, while in the balcony were harness rooms and quarters for the ostlers and grooms. The accommodation was reached via a light gallery, surrounding the circumference of the 250ft area, while in the centre of the floor was a fountain – entirely for the horses – which provided a cooling influence to counteract the greenhouse effect of the glass roof.

George was impressed, but the stables wouldn't do. While some of his horses were transported to the Pavilion stables from Newmarket, the accommodation was impracticable and they were moved on to Perren's stables back at Newmarket. In contrast, the Duke of York's accommodation was better and his paddocks were well constructed.

The Brighton Pavilion was seen as the height of extravagance and opulence, and the riding house, situated in the western wing, measured up to this image. The building was 178ft wide and 34ft high, with a roof that was remarkable because of its great span (it was described at one time by architect John Nash as one of the best proportioned buildings in England),[35] while the dome of the stable court dominated everything. The eastern wing was intended to house a tennis court, but William IV later installed additional stables there.

While the Pavilion occupied a great deal of the Prince's time, energy and ever-decreasing funds, he received a letter from the Jockey Club, dated 30 July 1805, in which the organisation sued for peace. The timing of the letter is curious, and its existence might have something to do with the fact that at the time of its writing the King's health was deteriorating (he'd suffered a relapse the previous year). The Prince turned down the club's pleas, and it would be many years before peace would be restored.

In 1808, the Prince stopped breeding thoroughbreds, and on 18 February of either that year or the next he ordered that the paddocks at Hampton Court be turned into a stud, under the direction of a Mr Goodwin. Meanwhile, changes were being made elsewhere in the racing world, and in 1809 a new race – the 2,000 Guineas (1 mile, colt and fillies) – was founded at Newmarket, to be raced over the Rowley Mile Course during each spring meeting. It would be followed in 1814 by the 1,000 Guineas. Today, the Derby, the Oaks, the St Leger, the 2,000 Guineas and 1,000 Guineas are seen as being major classics of the racing world.

When the King suffered his final collapse, the Prince of Wales took the oath of office as regent on 2 February 1811. The King remained at Windsor, unaware of what was going on around him[36] and, in particular, unaware that the stables at Hampton Court were being occupied by cavalry horses. A plan put together by a Thomas Hardwicke on 28 June 1811 shows just how much the stabling area at Hampton Court had changed over the centuries, as at that time it was occupied not only by stable blocks of varying sizes but also by a trash house, kitchens, gardens, a dung pit, a farrier's shop and a shoeing shop. In addition, the Mewskeeper's House had been turned into the Chequers public house – opening out onto the King's private road and occupying one corner of the largest stable block at Hampton Court – to accommodate the troops, whose horses occupied the bulk of the stables, while another, smaller public house stood next to the pig sty. Meanwhile, overlooking the King's private road was the residence of the Clerk of the Stables and, adjacent, that of Richard Ramton, the King's groom,[37] where in 1812 the Regent would establish a stud for grey thoroughbreds.[38]

The only member of the royal family to enjoy success on the turf after 1812 was Frederick, Duke of York. In 1815, just prior to the Battle of Waterloo, he was the most senior royal at the races, in the absence of the Prince Regent, and on 7 June that year his horse Scrapell came first in the 25 guinea Swinley Stakes. On the same day, his Sir Tooley Whag won the 20 guinea Sweepstakes. The following day, his horse Aladdin won the 100 guinea Gold Cup, and on 9 June the same horse came first in the Wokingham Stakes. Then, on 21 June, word reached the Duke and the Regent at St James's Palace of Napoleon's defeat at the Battle of Waterloo three days earlier. Amid the celebrations that followed, the Duke of York's Sir Tooley Whag came first in a Sweepstakes for 25 guineas on 29 August.

1816 proved to be the Duke's most successful year up to that time. On 30 May of that year, his colt Prince Leopold – one of twelve that started – won the Epsom Derby by two lengths in what *The Times* described as 'fine style'. This was only the second Derby win by a member of the royal family since 1788, yet the Duke was fairly modest about his success,[39] being something of a shy man, although he enjoyed his days at the races and the papers followed him with interest. When, on 4 June 1817, his filly by Election came third in the Swinley Stakes at Newmarket, he spent much of the day just walking about the Heath.

Attendance on that occasion wasn't as great as the previous day, but, *The Times* noted, those that were there inhabited the higher echelons of fashion.

Unbeknownst to the Duke, however, the year was about to end in disaster. On 5 November, Princess Charlotte, the Prince of Wales's daughter, who had married Prince Leopold of Saxe-Coburg-Gotha the previous year, was delivered of a stillborn son after a labour of fifty hours, and she herself died some hours later. The burial of mother and son took place on the 19th, and for the next three months the Prince Regent remained in seclusion at Brighton. He had lost not only his daughter but his heir, too, and the family line was coming perilously close to extinction, since there were no legitimate children of the next generation to succeed. Now his relatives were in a hurry to get married and produce an heir to the throne, while the Prince Regent withdrew further.

In January 1819, the late Queen's horses and carriages were sold by Tattersalls. There was a great deal of interest in the sale, and the auction yard was full to capacity well before the start of proceedings. The sale proved to be exceptional and some horses were sold above their value, with seventeen-year-old horses being sold for seventy and eighty guineas each, with other prices ranging from 115–150 guineas. The Queen's Master of the Horse, the Earl of Harcourt, bought six carriage horses and the Duke of Wellington bought one, and in the event all 55 horses went for £4,544, while eighteen carriages were sold, achieving a price of £1,077.[40]

By this time, there were two royal pregnancies, and soon the Cumberlands had a son, George, and the Kents had a girl, Alexandrine Victoria. If the Yorks and the Clarences remained childless (and in the case of the Yorks, there was no doubt that this would be the case), Alexandrine Victoria of Kent would have precedence over her cousin George and would be the heir of the next generation. Her father had no doubt that she would be Queen and told people so, but he didn't even live to see her reach her first birthday, dying of a chill at Sidmouth on 23 January 1820. Six days later, on the 29th, the King died after suffering from blindness and insanity, ignorant of almost everything that had gone on around him, including the deaths of his wife, youngest daughter and granddaughter Charlotte.

Notes:

1. Walpole, Horace, *Memoirs of the Reign of George the Third*, p19
2. www.ihr.sas.co.uk
3. Mortimer, Onslow and Willet
4. Walpole, Roger, *The Jockey Club*, p159
5. Mortimer, p34
6. St Leger, pp63–5

7. St Leger, pp64–5
8. Hibbert, Christopher, *George III*, pp239–40
9. Hibbert, Christopher, *George III*, p241
10. Hibbert, Christopher, *George III*, pp254–5
11. Robinson, p142
12. Chifney, p13
13. Chifney, p40–41
14. Chifney, p65
15. Chifney, p68
16. Chifney, p69
17. Chifney, p72
18. Chifney, pp72–3
19. Chifney p73
20. Chifney, pp79–81
21. Chifney, pp84–85
22. Chifney, p91
23. Chifney, p92
24. Chifney, p93
25. *The Times*, 23–25.10.1791
26. *The Times*, 29.10.1791
27. Chifney, p99
28. Chifney, p100
29. Chifney, p112
30. *The Times*, 21.01.1792
31. *The Times*, 16.03.1795
32. *The Times*, 12.06.1795
33. *The Times*, 11.06.1795
34. *The Times*, 20.06.1800
35. Musgrave, p47
36. Van Der Kiste, *George III's Children*, pp101–4
37. 'Ground Plan of His Majesty's Stables at Hampton Court, Shewing in What Manner and By Whom They are at Present Occupied', WORK 34/107–114779 (National Archives document)
38. Musgrave, pp43–4
39. *The Times*, 31.05.1816
40. *The Times*, 06.01.1819

13
George IV

George, the Prince Regent, became king on 29 January 1820 but wasn't proclaimed as such until the 31st because his coronation clashed with the commemorative anniversary of the death of King Charles I. Even when he was proclaimed, he was so ill that many believed that they were about to witness the shortest reign in British recorded history after living through the longest.[1] Then, within days of his accession, his former racing manager Warwick Lake died and was succeeded in his most recent role as the Duke of York's racing manager by the 27-year-old Charles Greville, who recorded in his diary (which was to become increasingly vitriolic over the coming years) that he was quite pleased to be offered the appointment on 23 February.[2]

Meanwhile, the new king, in sharp contrast to his fascination with horses as the Prince of Wales, cut down the number of broodmares at Hampton Court and sold the grey thoroughbreds. The stud was then handed over to the Duke of York, who bred racehorses there from 1822.

When racing at Ascot began, the King attended each day, being the first monarch to do so in many years. Charles Greville recorded the King's reception at Ascot: 'He generally rode on the course, and the ladies came in carriages . . . He was always cheered by the mob as he went away. One day only a man in the crowd called out, "Where's the Queen?"'[3] The new king would receive heckling of this sort for many months, and despite the fact that this should have been the honeymoon period of his reign, no one around him let him forget that he had a wife who was banned not only from his life but from his coronation too; on attending the theatre just before the event, someone in the audience shouted, 'Where's your wife, Georgy?'[4]

George still hadn't returned to Newmarket by this time, and relations between himself and the Jockey Club were still strained, even after nearly thirty years. The club's authority hadn't suffered because of this, however, and in 1821 the *Calendar* published its first warning-off order for that year when a tout named William 'Snipe' Taylor was reprimanded for watching the trials with a telescope and refusing to identify his employers. Taylor conceded to the club's decision. Meanwhile, a Mr Hawkins was also warned off for swearing at Lord Wharncliffe. He turned to the law, which upheld the Club's decision.

At this stage, the King had no intention of making peace with the Jockey Club[5] but still had horses running. Over the next few years, his jockeys would be Samuel Chifney Jr, George Nelson, James Robinson, Arthur Pavis and a G Dockeray. One of his jockeys during his time as Prince of Wales, William Edwards, became his trainer in 1828, and in the same year Emilius Henry Delme-Radcliffe was appointed Gentleman of the Horse – a position he would hold until his death in 1832 – and Stephen Pearce was appointed Clerk of the Stables. Meanwhile, Charles Sackville Germain, 5th Duke of Dorset, was appointed the King's Master of the Horse on 12 December 1821 on the resignation of James Graham, 3rd Duke of Montrose.[6]

At the start of his reign George IV had a lot to consider, not least getting used to his new role and preparing for his coronation. His wife made her return to England in June 1821 and had every intention of being crowned queen, although George had other ideas. The coronation that took place on 19 July 1821 was the most lavish ever seen, with the King wearing robes so heavy that he was almost dragged to the floor, but it is probably best remembered because of the way Queen Caroline was treated as she tried to enter Westminster Abbey. The doors were slammed in her face and the King, as an extra precaution, had employed prize fighters to act as bouncers to keep her out. She turned away, defeated, and died three weeks later, a broken woman. Aware of how it might look if he didn't at least show some regret – particularly in light of how popular his wife had been – the King gave all the appearance of being in mourning, although in truth his relief must have been great. Caroline had been a thorn in his side for over twenty years, and the timing of her death – at the start of his reign – couldn't have been better.

After a brief delay, while his deceased wife's corpse was being taken back to Brunswick, the King proceeded on a scheduled trip to Ireland. Being the first Hanoverian monarch to visit the country and, indeed, the first monarch since William III's victory at the Battle of the Boyne to set foot there, he was determined to enjoy his time in Ireland and had quite 'recovered' his spirits by the time the boat landed.[7]

The news that the King intended to visit Ireland caused a wave of excitement that seemed to put political and religious divisions in the shade. Preparations had begun in July and included co-operation with the Irish Turf Club. Funds were raised to help to pay for the visit, although it was pointed out that horse-racing would take second place to politics.

On 12 August the King arrived at Howth to a rapturous welcome. The plan was for him to attend the Curragh on the 29th, but bad weather delayed the event until the 31st, although by then the weather hadn't improved much. The heavy rain failed to dampen anyone's spirits, however, and the King presented a whip to the owner of the best horse in Ireland, based on weight for age, along with a donation of 100 guineas. The whip was first run for in October 1821, on which occasion it was won by Langar.[8]

When the King returned to England in November, he was anxious to maintain his links with Irish horse-racing, and in 1823 he subscribed to the *Irish Racing Calendar*, setting a precedent in the process. His brother William maintained the subscription when he became king, and Queen Victoria later subscribed between 1879 and 1901.

It wasn't long after his return that questions of a financial nature were being asked, but for once the King wasn't the one being criticised; this time the Duke of York was under the spotlight. Until July, 1822 had been a good year for the Duke, who won the Epsom Derby on 24 May for the second time, with Moses, winning £25,000 in the process at odds of 6–1, according to *The Times*. However, the newspaper also mentioned the Duke of York's creditors. While *The Times* sympathetically noted that the Duke's debts – unlike those of the new king – weren't considerable (which, given his history, made a change), his creditors were constantly at his heels and he was obliged to place Oatlands in the care of Colonel Stephenson and the Earl of Lauderdale, as trustees, and to honour any debts not exceeding £50. The sale of Oatlands, a residence that had been associated with the British monarchy for the best part of three centuries and had been the key location of the Duke of York's stud, took place in August at Garraway's coffee house and consisted of nineteen articles that, in total, went for £89,030 – still not enough though to clear what remained of the Duke's debts.[9]

It seems that owing large sums of money had become an occupational hazard for the royals, and his brother's perilous financial circumstances certainly didn't prevent King George from spending lavishly, particularly if it meant that the prestige of kingship was made more evident – in his own mind, at least. George felt a need to build up his position as monarch in much the same way that he'd felt a need to build up his position as Prince of Wales. He needed to make his mark, and he chose to do this via the two elements that had helped to forge his image as Prince of Wales: horse-racing and architecture.

The King turned his attention to Ascot and employed the long-suffering architect John Nash to construct the Royal Stand that now stands there. Unlike many of the projects that Nash had completed for his royal master, the stand didn't cost that much and he went only about one-tenth over budget, so the final cost of £1,100 was fairly modest, given some of the pounds, shillings and pence that had been spent over the decades. The King wasn't impressed with the stand, however, and in 1822 Nash was commissioned to plan a new one. This time the King approved Nash's designs and the stand was built in just five weeks. Soon after its construction, *The Times* gushed praise for it, describing it as light and tasteful with a noticeable Greek influence, elegant and well furnished. More importantly, of course, it provided a good view of the course, and there was also a lawn – a forerunner of the Royal Enclosure.[10]

Meanwhile, Nash was also devoting a great deal of time to the construction of the Royal Mews at Pimlico and was in close correspondence with the Office of Works. It was his intention to have a line of bricks ranged along the whole length of the north wall, next to the gardens (to be constructed in ten days), so that the garden would be enclosed and secured, and therefore ordered a gateway to be made through the wall in Arabella Row. A sketch made during this period shows the gardens, the perimeter of the wall that would also enclose the yard and, beyond it, what Nash described as the 'state stables'.[11]

Improvements were also being made to the stables at the Brighton Pavilion, completed that August. 'The King has had a subterranean passage made from the house to the stables which is said to have cost 3,000l or 5,000l, I forget which,'[12] wrote diarist Charles Greville, who had recently been appointed Clerk of the Privy Council, a position he would hold under William IV. As with the work being done at the Royal Mews, this hints at the King's increasing desire for privacy.

Relations between John Nash and the clerk of works, meanwhile, were not going smoothly. On 23 January 1823, the architect wrote that the clerk, being answerable to the Office of Works, should consult with the office in all things. Fair enough. However, Nash himself wrote that he wished to be kept informed of the progress of the contractors, as until that point the clerk had done so only occasionally, which was no good for him, as he needed to be kept constantly up to date.[13]

In the meantime, accounts and costs were being put together and assessed for the 117 six-foot-long 'King posts' framed into the beams for the roof of the Grand Stables at Pimlico, including beams and collars. In addition there were no fewer than 64 semi-circular sash frames in the stables.[14] Work continued throughout the year, with Nash providing breakdowns of expenditure while at the same time keeping in close contact with the Office of Works, particularly the surveyor general there. By September, there was concern that work on the Royal Mews was in danger of being delayed, but on the 20th Nash – whose job was becoming increasingly difficult – assured the surveyor general that this was not the case. He also itemised the costs to the final penny. Woodwork cost

£48.5s., leadwork £140.17s.3d, paintwork £5, stonework £4.1s., brickwork £5s. and ironwork £6.10. The total ran to £209.13s.3d.[15]

While Nash was dealing with the everyday trials and tribulations of his work, King George continued his tour of the British Isles by paying a thoroughly enjoyable visit to Scotland. These were indeed happy times for the King, but he was a changed man. When he wasn't travelling around and entertaining, he kept himself very much to himself and was becoming rather reclusive, even reducing his visits to London.[16] He also had ideas of turning the Stud House at Hampton Court into a private residence, but Nash told him that doing so would give him no privacy,[17] so it reverted back to its use as a residence for the Master of the Horse.

As for Hampton Court itself, the King wasn't interested in the place. Nor was he as fond of Carlton House as he had been when he'd been Prince of Wales, primarily because it overlooked a busy street but also because it had become too expensive to maintain. When it was damaged by fire in June 1824,[18] the King began to consider building another, much grander, but more private royal residence. He did nothing for the moment, though, which was probably just as well, as Nash had enough to contend with at this time.

Carlton House was still in use by Friday 10 December 1825, when the King was presented with what *The Times* described as a 'curious' pony while he was staying at Cumberland Lodge. A four-year-old mouse- or dun-coloured pony from Norway, the animal stood 32in high, and although it had a very rough coat, it was beautifully formed and docile. In fact, it behaved more like a pet dog and followed its groom everywhere. It had never been shod and ate bread, potatoes, corn, hay and beer, and it wore a neatly fitted fancy covering for the King's inspection. Rather than the King come outside to view it, however, the pony was allowed to trot up to his apartments, and *The Times* noted that George was very impressed with it.[19]

In 1825, the King finally commissioned John Nash to rebuild what had been the Queen's House (officially named Buckingham House) and convert it into a palace. Carlton House was to be demolished at the same time and the materials from that would go towards the building of this new royal residence. The cost of the venture would turn out to be ruinous.

The King did little by halves and still loved the spectacle of kingship, and in the same year he instituted the royal procession at Ascot. He and the Duke of Wellington appeared in the first coach, then there were three coaches-and-four, with a phaeton and servants on horseback following behind. The procession took place on the second day of the meeting and was met with great enthusiasm,[20] *The Times* noting that the whole stud came with the King, which put people in mind of how popular he'd been on the course years earlier. Such a procession provided an opportunity for the public actually to see the monarch – which was very important, given his father's seclusion during his lifetime – and to see him at his most relaxed, too.

Even by this time, however, people had begun to notice a change in the King. The diarist Thomas Creevey noted that he 'cut the lowest figure'.[21] Like many others outside the King's circle, Creevey might also have been unaware of the fact that, for one who had been so fastidious in his youth, George could also be the complete opposite, and what Creevey witnessed at Ascot was the first sign of the monarch's decline. Ascot served a purpose in presenting George's perceived image of monarchy, but sometimes he fell short of it himself.

By 1825 the Royal Stables at the new-styled Buckingham Palace were almost complete. Nash had excelled himself, installing a Doric archway at the entrance to the central mews and, on the west of the building, two sets of state stables with room enough for 54 horses, as well as forage- and harness rooms. A back or upper mews was also added at the north end of the quadrangle and a large house had been built for the Master of the Horse with additional accommodation for his assistant.[22]

By 12 August, it was discovered that it would cost £190.12s.6d. to spread and roll the 310 loads of gravel necessary to cover the quadrangle at the Royal Mews, and by the 15th the water pipes there were nearly completed and an estimate put together for what were described as 'sundry' materials needed to complete the job.[23] This list, however, turned out to be huge, with additions and workings-out peppering the margins, and gave a mere hint of the project's scale. Meanwhile, pipes already at the mews were to be taken up and further changes and additions were recommended throughout the month, including the construction of a large (21ft by 6ft) reservoir made of cast iron, to be completed as soon as possible.[24]

Then, on 10 September, one William Parker approached the Office of Works, on behalf of the Master of the Horse, requesting that the water pipes laid for the mews be extended to the riding house within the mews. As well as meaning that water then wouldn't have to be fetched and carried manually, it also meant that, with winter fast approaching, the porters wouldn't be able to sit in the lodge with the door open (the two middle panels could be removed and the space filled with a sliding glass shutter to be put up at night). There was also a request for a water closet on or near the farrier's house in the back mews for his wife and family's use, the Master of the Horse deeming it not right that they should have to use the public privies used by the stablemen.[25]

Two days later, the final estimate for the cast-iron reservoir was recorded at £269. Then, along with the cost of laying and cutting away brickwork for pipes (£35), there was also the cost of the gravel to be laid in the quadrangle, which had been revised to £469 to include the purchase of the material. This amounts to thousands of pounds in today's money, and the work wasn't completed until the quarter ending 5 January 1826.[26]

Meanwhile, further work was taking place at Ascot, and that year – 1825 – the Duke of York's stand was placed next to the Royal Stand. As for the Duke himself, *The Times* was following his movements with interest and on 26 May it reported that on the previous day he'd left his London residence in South Audley Street at about 12 p.m. in his carriage-and-four to attend the races at Epsom, returning to town in the afternoon. The following month he attended Ascot with the King. It would prove to be his last visit. From July through to December, the Duke of York's health began to fail.[27]

When Greville had been made racing manager to the Duke of York, it had been his task to evaluate the Duke's stock of horses, but he'd only partially completed this task when the Duke – who was King George IV's heir – died on 5 January 1827. And since no event involving the house of Hanover was ever complete without some mishap or other, the church in which the funeral service took place leaked so badly that the floor was wet. Several of his pallbearers and mourners fell ill as a result of the conditions there and died several weeks later.

During the course of attending to the late Duke's affairs, it became clear that he had literally died penniless as many of his debts still had to be accounted for, and on 5 February 1827 all of his thoroughbred stock was sold. Again, however, his financial situation had been so parlous that the sale failed to cover all that he had owed, and when the building of a tall column was commissioned in his honour with a statue of the Duke standing on top of it, some wag quipped that his long-suffering creditors wouldn't be able to reach him.[28] The Jockey Club took possession of the recently built Duke of York's Stand at Ascot and the King reassumed control of the stud at Hampton Court, expanding it and its paddocks. Thirty-three broodmares were housed in 43 walled paddocks, 17 in Home Park and 26 in Bushey Park.[29]

Greville would later manage the horses of the Duke of Portland and go into partnership with his and the Duke's mutual cousin, Lord George Bentinck, becoming increasingly disillusioned with court life, as would the King's mistress, Lady Conyngham.[30] In addition, the King, having retreated further into himself, still hadn't made his peace with the Jockey Club, which by 1828 was busy revising its rules and orders under the directorship of its second

Dictator of the Turf, Lord George Bentinck. The King was still devoting a lot of time to the fortunes of Ascot, however, and towards the end of June he instituted a second meeting there, a three-day event that included His Majesty's Plate of 100 Guineas and a Gold Cup subscription race.[31]

Then, in 1829, the King bought seven horses with the express aim of riding and winning the Ascot Gold Cup. One of these steeds, The Colonel, had been bred by a Mr Wyvill of Burton Constable and foaled in 1825, having then been bought as a yearling by the Honourable Edward Petre and later winning the St Leger before being sold to the King for £4,000. Another horse to take George's fancy that year was Zinganee, owned and trained by Sam Chifney's son, William, and rated far better than The Colonel (by William, at least).

Although reclusive as a monarch, the King succeeded in using race meetings as a forum for presenting a particular image of monarchy, and it was understood that most of those attending them, especially Ascot, were there just to view royalty rather than the racing. Sometimes, however, the image that the royals presented wasn't a positive one. At one Ascot meeting, the King became irrational on noticing the presence of the Home Secretary, Robert Peel, and shocked everyone around him by saying that he would rather see a pig in a church than Peel at Ascot.[32] It was this type of behaviour that failed to endear George to his government ministers, and he must have baffled them further when, after so many years, he at last made his peace with the Jockey Club, throwing a dinner at St James's Palace for its members. 'There were about thirty people,' wrote Sir Charles Greville of the occasion, 'several not being invited, whom he did not fancy. The Duke of Leeds told me a much greater list had been made out, but he had scratched several out of it.'[33]

The meeting took place in the throne room, and from the start there was an air of unease. After all, it had been 37 years since George and the Jockey Club had been on speaking terms, and many of those members with whom he had fallen out – most notably Sir Charles Bunbury – were dead. The King felt the tension well enough to remark to all present, 'This is more like a Quaker than a Jockey Club meeting.'[34]

Dinner was served in the supper room, with the King seated between the Dukes of Richmond and Grafton. 'I sat opposite to [the King],' recalled Greville, 'and he was particularly gracious to me, talking to me across the table and recommending all the good things; he made me . . . eat a dish of crawfish soup, till I thought I should have burst.'[35]

By this time, the ice had effectively been broken and toasts for the King followed. He thanked everyone present and said that he hoped there would be more meetings in the future. 'He then ordered paper, pens etc and they began making matches and stakes,'[36] noted Greville. The mood relaxed, the meeting was a success and the King left at 12.30 a.m.

Perhaps spurred on by his success with entertaining the Jockey Club, in July the King hosted a dinner for racehorse owners. Where the sport was concerned, he could still prove that he missed nothing and was furious when jockey James 'Jem' Robinson used 'forceful tactics' on his horse, Maria, during the Egham races. Jem tried to win from the front and, caught napping on the last bend when his rival flew past him, pulled Maria up before pushing her forward, only to win by a short head.

On 9 December the King moved into his new apartments at Windsor Castle, hoping to find something like a quiet life. Then he changed his mind, deciding that the castle was too public,[37] and moved to the Royal Lodge instead, while some believed that he would lose interest in Buckingham Palace, too. Indeed, as the months progressed, he became more and more withdrawn, although he still liked to have the race results brought to him and occasionally mustered enough energy to go out for a drive. He also enjoyed having his horses' portraits painted and employed Henry Chalon to paint those at Newmarket, along with the hounds and huntsmen on Ascot Heath. George Stubbs was also commissioned to paint the King on horseback and a number of his favourite horses and their grooms, and George Garrard also painted some of the King's horses. Such paintings and patronage were part of George's much wider interest in art – what his brother William, Duke of Clarence, referred to as 'knicknackery'.[38] The King wanted to build up an image of the monarchy in an artistic light, but he failed to live up to it. Indeed, having such pictures around him might have provided him with another excuse to withdraw, to enjoy horses and horse-racing second hand and to reminisce rather than get involved directly as he'd done as Prince of Wales.

By this time, the King was also drinking a lot more and becoming more dependant on laudanum, the liquid form of opium, which he was taking for what he believed was nothing more than a bladder complaint. In fact, he was imbibing both laudanum and alcohol in prodigious quantities, as well as eating like a horse, and consequently spent a great deal of time almost comatose, so that on numerous occasions people arriving to attend a meeting with him had to be sent away. Not everybody was sympathetic, either; in his diary entry for 17 March 1829, having formerly described the King as 'contemptible' and 'unfeeling', Charles Greville wrote, 'He leads a most extraordinary life, never gets up till six in the afternoon.'[39]

The King's servants would generally wake him – or, rather, open the curtains at 6 or 7 a.m. – whereupon he would breakfast, read his newspapers and tend to business in bed, then doze for a few hours before getting up to dress for dinner. The job of attending to his every whim, Greville noted in his diary, almost 'destroyed' his servants.

Meanwhile, although Greville had effectively removed himself from the royal court, that didn't stop him from attending another racing dinner for the Jockey Club on 10 June 1829. That affair was a large gathering, but the King, it seemed, was unwell and rather quiet, and the occasion was not an enjoyable one. The diarist noted, 'The Duke of Richmond told me that the little he did say was more about politics than the turf.'[40] The King duly thanked the club members present for their toasts and said that he was 'much gratified by our kindness, and he could assure us that in withdrawing himself as he had done from the Jockey Club he was not influenced by any unkindness to any member of it, or any indifference to the interests of the turf.'[41]

The King was less gratified, however, by the Gold Cup race at Ascot that year. Having invested in this event, he had to watch as The Colonel was beaten by Will Chifney's Zinganee, who won by two lengths. His disappointment was made worse by the fact that he'd considered this his only chance to win the race, so he bought Zinganee for over £2,000 and was intent on seeing him run the following year. His mood wasn't helped much by Jockey Club steward John Gully not raising his hat as he passed the Royal Stand. Gully would find himself barred from running a horse in the next Gold Cup for this oversight, a punishment for which the King was later heavily criticised.[42]

By this time, the King was becoming increasingly delusional, talking about horse races as if he personally had ridden in them. Greville noted on 9 November 1829, 'I hear he thinks he rode Fleur de Lis for the cup at Goodwood, which he may as well do as think (which he does) that he led the heavy dragoons at Salamanca.'[43]

Even so, the King had enough of his wits about him to move ahead with his renovation plans, and at around this time further building work commenced on the Great Park Lodges and Jeffrey Wyatville was commissioned to enlarge Henry Flitcroft's Belvedere Tower at Fort Belvedere, near Windsor. Then, on 12 August 1829,[44] the King journeyed from the fort to Windsor to lay the foundation stone for a plinth that would support the figure of his father, King George III, as a Roman emperor on horseback. Indeed, the figure does represent George III as a horseman, but no one could fathom why he was depicted as a Roman when he was always known as 'Farmer George'. Nevertheless, Richard Westmacot's 'Copper Horse' statue was duly constructed and placed at the end of the Long Walk at Windsor.[45] It had to be huge, too, since the King wanted it to be seen from the castle.

The statue still exists today and stands on a 27ft-high plinth of piled-up rocks. The King laid the plinth's foundation stone on his last birthday but wouldn't live to see it completed and the statue wouldn't be installed until October 1831. On that occasion a lunch was given inside the horse to twelve people, and later the statue was closed up for good.[46]

By now the King's health was failing by the day, and towards the end of his life he suffered considerably, although he still had enough strength to send his groom Jack Radford to Ascot to find out the result of the Ascot Cup, in which his new acquisition, Zinganee, was running. The horse ran unplaced, however, and the King died in the early hours of 26 June at 3.15 a.m. An autopsy revealed a tumour the size of an orange on his bladder and a heart surrounded by fat. He had been suffering from arteriosclerosis for years, it seemed, but what killed him was a blood vessel bursting in his stomach.[47]

Notes:

1. Smith, E A, *George IV*, pp187–97
2. Greville, Charles C F, *The Greville Memoirs*, p23
3. Greville, Charles C F, *The Greville Memoirs*, p27
4. Greville, Charles C F, *The Greville Memoirs*, p43
5. Mortimer, Roger, *The Jockey Club*, p49
6. Sainty & Bucholz
7. D'Arcy, p94
8. D'Arcy, pp96–97
9. *The Times*, 08.07.1822; 03.08.1822
10. Magee and Aird, pp52–3
11. Letter from John Nash to Robert Browne, Esq, of Office of Works, 27.07.1822, WORK 19/50 (National Archives document)
12. Greville, p54, 19.08.1822
13. John Nash to Clerk of the Works, 23.01.1823, WORK 19/50 (National Archives document)
14. Account by John Hudson, Labourer in Trust, Queen's Palace, 03.03.1823, WORK 19/50 (National Archives document)
15. From John Nash to Surveyor General of Office of Works, 20.09.1823, WORK 19/50 (National Archives document)
16. Smith, E A, *George IV*, p200
17. Thurley, p292, p347
18. *The Times*, June 1824
19. *The Times*, 18.12.1824
20. Magee and Aird, pp54–6
21. Magee and Aird, p57
22. Estimate drawn up by Mr Kidd., 08.09.1825, WORK 19/50 (National Archives Document)
23. Estimate, 12.08.1825, WORK 19/50 (National Archives document)
24. Estimate put by James Simpson of Eccleston Street, Pimlico, 15.08.1825, WORK 19/50 (National Archives document)
25. From William Parker (Master of the Horse Office) to Mr Stephenson, 10.09.1825, WORK 19/50 (National Archives document)

26. Estimate and Proposal from Mr McIntosh, 12.09.1825, WORK 19/50 (National Archives document)
27. *The Times*, May 1826
28. Fitzgerald, pp66–7
29. Thurley, p292, 347
30. Greville, Charles C F, *The Greville Memoirs, Volume I*, p31, 17.06.1827
31. Magee and Aird, p59
32. Magee and Aird, p58
33. Greville, Charles C F, *The Greville Memoirs, Volume I*, 29.06.1828. p135
34. Greville, Charles C F, *The Greville Memoirs, Volume I*, p135, 29.06.1828
35. Ibid.
36. Ibid.
37. Smith, E A, *George IV*, p266
38. Smith, E A, *George IV*, pp262–70
39. Greville, Charles C F, *The Greville Memoirs, Volume I*, p38, 17.03.1829
40. Greville, Charles C F, *The Greville Memoirs, Volume I*, pp211–12, 11.06.1829
41. Greville, Charles C F, *The Greville Memoirs, Volume I*, pp211–12, 11.06.1829
42. Magee and Aird, p62
43. Greville, Charles C F, *The Greville Memoirs, Volume I*, p241, 09.11.1829
44. Parissien, p362
45. Parissien, p363
46. Girouard, Mark, *Windsor*, pp143–4
47. Smith, E A, *George IV*, p271

14
William IV

At 6 a.m., two hours and 45 minutes after King George III's death, his doctors, Sir Henry Halford and Sir Wathen Waller, arrived at Bushey House. The King's brother William, formerly the Duke of Clarence, and his wife, Adelaide, knew immediately on being awakened what must have happened. Legend has it that, after receiving the doctors and the Duke of Wellington, who arrived shortly afterwards,[1] and on learning the circumstances of his brother's death, the King declared that he was going back to bed since he'd always wanted to sleep with a queen.

Although saddened by his eldest brother's demise, William nevertheless enjoyed the new reverence he received from his subjects. He was possibly the most unaffected of George III's fifteen children, and at the beginning of his reign he treated his new state of kingship as a novel experience, thinking nothing of walking about town and meeting people.[2] His elevation to monarch had given him a new kind of freedom, and even on the day of his brother's funeral he couldn't help but acknowledge those around him with handshakes, smiles and nods. This didn't shock people in the first days of his reign, and the populace warmed to this new affable king who genuinely liked the company of others, so different to his elder brother and father. William had led a more fulfilled life than his elder brother, too, through his successful naval career, which made him seem more ordinary and more in tune with the people. Soon enough, though, familiarity bred contempt, and when members of his court felt that his public demeanour was becoming 'unkingly', they soon put a stop to his impromptu walkabouts.

On 26 June, the King signed a warrant, along with the Duke of Wellington and others, appointing Sir William Freemantle as deputy ranger of Windsor Great Park,[3] although it wouldn't be signed officially until 16 November. William would also have three Masters of the Horse throughout his reign: the Duke of Leeds, the 4th Earl of Albemarle, the 5th Duke of Dorset and then Albemarle again from May 1835. The King's Gentleman of the Horse, meanwhile, was Frederick Fitzclarence, who was appointed on 9 December 1830, and his Clerk of the Stables was Ralph William Spearman, appointed on 26 June 1830.

William had no interest in the Royal Stud or even the horses there, for that matter, but by the same token he didn't seek to remove them from training, and when he was asked about which of them should run in scheduled races, he declared that the 'whole squadron' should be sent down.[4] As Greville noted, 'He keeps the stud, which is to be diminished, because he thinks he ought to support the turf.'[5]

Greville also observed that the new king had lived in obscurity for the past forty years, seemingly unaffected by society and the court, and possibly because of this he found that the monarch was an improvement on the previous incumbent, who many (principally his own subjects) were glad to see the back of. 'Nobody thinks any more of the late king than if he had been dead fifty years,' he wrote, 'unless it be to abuse him and to rake up all his vices and misdeeds.'[6] King William, though, was 'as dignified as the homeliness and simplicity of his character will allow him to be'.[7]

Court society bored William, and he didn't altogether understand how the court worked, having first lived the life of a seaman and then as a quiet family man well away from it. He would fall asleep during social gatherings and his wife would attend to her needlework, while on other occasions, if anyone wished to leave but couldn't do so because it was against court etiquette to leave before him, the King himself would sneak them out.[8] He was very much a family man and loved all of his children and grandchildren, even though it grated on his sons that their illegitimate status meant that they would never have the social standing that they felt they deserved as sons of a king. Indeed, all ten of the King's sons and daughters were illegitimate, their mother being a former actress named Dorothy Jordan. His own legitimate children by his wife, Adelaide, had died in infancy, the latest just weeks after King George's death, which meant that William's heir was the daughter of his late brother the Duke of Kent, Princess Victoria, who was being brought up in strict seclusion by her mother, Victoria, the Dowager Duchess of Kent, at Kensington Palace. Born in May 1819, Princess Victoria had by this time just turned eleven, and it was of paramount importance to William that he didn't die before she reached her majority.[9]

In the meantime there was much to sort out domestically, and in July 1830 King George IV's stud was sold. William hadn't been king long, however, before an argument broke out over some stabled horses belonging to another of his brothers, Ernest, who, as well as being the Duke of Cumberland, was also the King of Hanover. Ernest felt that it was his unequivocal right to keep his horses wherever he liked and had kept them in what was officially the Queen's stable,[10] as was discovered when Queen Adelaide was asked where her own horses were to be put. It was agreed that he had to move his horses out, but this could only be done with the King's order. 'The King was spoke to,' Greville noted, 'and he commanded the Duke of Leeds to order them out. The Duke of Leeds took the order to the Duke of Cumberland, who said he would be damned if they should go.'[11] The Duke of Leeds, caught in the middle of the argument, tactfully suggested that Cumberland have them moved by the following day, or else they would be forcibly removed by order of the King. 'The Duke was obliged sulkily to give way,'[12] Greville noted.

Whatever his thoughts about Ernest, Greville's first impressions of William were favourable and he found him a kind-hearted, bustling, well-meaning 'old fellow',[13] although he also noted that he was odd. 'If he doesn't go mad [he] may make a very decent King,' he observed, 'but he exhibits oddities.'[14] One such oddity was his refusal to countenance mourning for his late brother, either worn or exhibited, which shocked the court. 'All odd,' Greville noted, 'and people are frightened, but his wits will last at least 'til the new Parliament meets.'[15]

One characteristic of the Hanoverian dynasty was that each monarch was held accountable for something that another family member had or hadn't done in their own lifetime. 'I sent him a very respectful request,' wrote Greville, 'that he would pay 300l, all that remained [of] the Duke of York's debts at Newmarket.'[16] The King agreed to pay the deficit, and Greville concluded that this was very good-natured of him, given that the Duke had been dead for three years. Fortunately William wasn't like his elder brothers where gambling was concerned, and he wasn't interested enough in horse-racing to spend huge amounts on horses and stables. When he came first, second and third in the Goodwood Cup on 11 August 1830 with Fleur de Lis, Zinganee and The Colonel,[17] respectively, and had he been as enthusiastic about the turf as his late brothers had been, he would have taken it as a favourable omen. As it was, though, the King was decidedly underwhelmed by his treble victory, and his association with horse-racing in general went downhill from that point. So, too, did his popularity with his courtiers, many of whom began to view him with a mixture of disappointment and bemusement. Nor was anyone in the court particularly enamoured of his consort, Adelaide, least of all Charles Greville, who noted, 'The Queen is a prude and will not let ladies come décolletées to her parties. George IV, who liked ample expanses of that sort, would not let them be covered.'[18]

Since neither the King nor Queen Adelaide lived up to the image that George IV had tried to reinforce, their lifestyle partly resembling that which George III and Queen Charlotte had enjoyed so much, those around them couldn't take them seriously. This inability to assume the behaviour expected of them was largely due to the fact that both had come to the throne late in life

Left: Henry VIII, King of England by Samuel Rush Meyrick. The horse is seen here as representing the absolute right of kings. (1824)

Right: Oliver Cromwell on horseback. The image of the horse in representing power and authority was just as important to him as it had been to the kings of England. (c.1648)

Right: Young Edward Windsor, Prince of Wales and future King Edward VIII and Duke Of Windsor. Edward wanted to prove himself a sportsman but was restricted by court formality and criticism. (1904)

Right: Ambush II - he proved to be, to date, the royal family's one and only Grand National winner. (1900)

Left: Queen Victoria (pictured here with John Brown) loved horses and riding, but kept a distance from racecourses and after Prince Albert's death, did not attend them at all. (1863)

Below: A royal duke bred Eclipse (left), still considered to have been one of the world's best. (1820)

Left: Jockeys ride in the Royal Hunt Cup Race on the second day of the 2005 Royal Ascot Races society horseracing event at York. (2005)

Below: The queen has always been professional in her approach to the trooping of the colour and each year spends several days preparing for it. (1951)

Right: Prince Philip – as a natural sportsman he opened new doors and introduced the royal family to polo and carriage driving. (c.1970-1990)

Right: Queen Elizabeth with her son Prince Andrew and her nephew David Armstrong Jones, Viscount Linley, at the veterinary inspection during the Badminton horse trials. The queen has always taken the welfare of horses seriously. (1972)

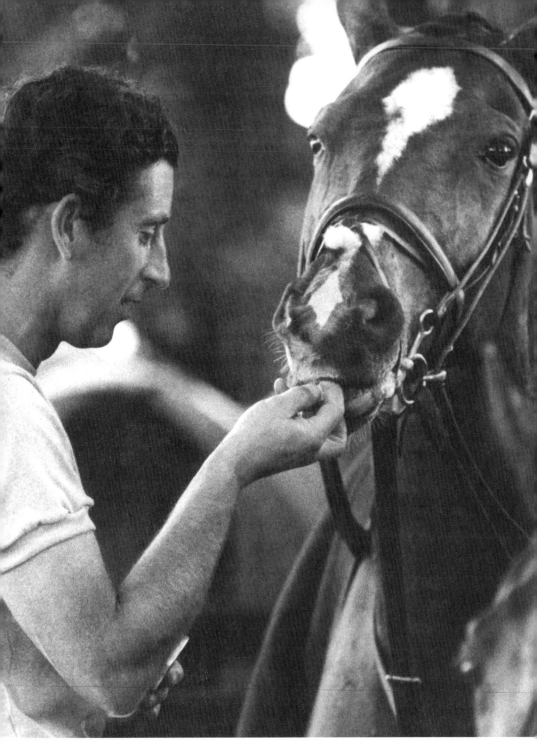

Above: Prince Charles has
proved that, whilst he is not
the most natural of horsemen,
he is the ultimate stayer when
it comes to competition.
(1978)

Top: Anne's efforts to be taken seriously as a professional horsewoman were always hampered by press attention. (1987)

Bottom: Former President Ronald Reagan, on Centennial, and queen Elizabeth, on her favourite horse, Burmese, enjoying a quiet ride and a chat in Windsor great park. (1982)

Above: Prince Philip's passion for polo has now been passed to his son and grandsons. (2001)

Left: Like mother, like daughter. Zara Philips is proving that she has as much competitive spirit as her mother Anne, the Princess Royal.
(2000)

and were too set in their ways to live up to the opulence that their positions demanded. Add this to the fact that the royal family in general was unpopular thanks to its exorbitant spending over the years and the start of King William IV's reign was less than auspicious.

Even so, the King was determined to do his duty, not only politically but socially, too, and turf appointments were made in April 1831. William felt that it was important to be seen, and Britain's racecourses were still the best venues to visit if one wanted to be visible and, indeed, find out how the public thought about one. This became clear in June when the royal family attended the first day at Ascot and were met by a stony silence from the crowd.[19] Such a bleak reception was far different to those enjoyed by the previous king, but it might have had something to do with an attempt made that year to restrict the Ascot Gold Cup to horses belonging to persons of standing, which had caused a great deal of resentment and in the end had to be dropped. In addition, as Greville wrote on 5 June, 'William was bored to death with the races, and his own horse broke down. On Wednesday he did not come; on Thursday they came again . . . The King was more cheered than the first day, for the greater number of people made a greater noise.'[20]

Nevertheless, the King's indifference to the sport was remarked upon by press and acquaintances alike. Despite the fact that Ascot was now an integral part of the image of the monarchy, he was observed turning his back on the actual running while his wife would sew or knit between races. He made no secret of the fact that he was unimpressed by the whole thing and in August there was speculation over whether he would be attending Goodwood at all on the 18th.[21] Then came the disappointing news that he would, indeed, not be attending the event. On this occasion, his absence was beyond his control, as the meeting clashed with a scheduled visit from the Duke of Saxe-Meiningen. His son Lord Augustus Fitzclarence attended in his stead.[22]

On the afternoon of 20 August, the Cup was the main attraction and there were many distinguished visitors there to see the race – although Lord Augustus Fitzclarence wasn't one of them, having left by this time. Fleur de Lis was now running at odds of 6–4, and at the close of betting stood at 5–4 against.[23] She was in excellent condition and ran a good race, but within fifty yards of the distance she was overtaken by a horse named Priam, who went on to win by two lengths.

Fleur de Lis, it transpired, had run her last race for the Cup and would be retired to Hampton Court, having won nine events in the last six years along with thirteen other races. Also retired to the stud in that year was The Colonel, who had broken down during the Oatlands Handicap. His career had been modest, having included victories at the Champagne Stakes, the Craven Stakes (twice) and the Great Park Stakes and second place at the Derby. He would remain at Hampton Court until 1837, siring Capa Pre and Chatham before being sold to Mr Tattersall.[24]

Also in 1831, King William had the royal stables at his brother's Brighton Pavilion extended, arranging for the building of extra stands, coach houses, a kitchen and a farriery, with bedrooms and lofts over them, in the east wing, in an area where George had originally intended to install a tennis court.[25] Such a venture demonstrates that William's approach to the stables was much more practical than that of his brother, whose grandiose ideas had made it almost impossible for horses to reside there.

William then turned his attention to Windsor, planning the building of a complex of stables on the edge of Windsor Park along with carriage houses and a riding school, designed by architect Jeffrey Wyatville. It was a project that would ultimately be taken up by William's niece Victoria on her accession and completed by Henry Ashton, assistant to Wyatville, who died before he could put his plans into effect.

The King's relationship with the Jockey Club, meanwhile, was fairly amicable and would never be fraught with the tensions that had marked George's association with the organisation. His detachment from the sport notwithstanding, William nevertheless appreciated the importance of the club to others and its historical value, and in the following year he presented it with a gold-plated hoof of the horse Eclipse. As a result of this gesture, a race named the Eclipse Foot was established, with the club contributing £100 to the stakes. The first winner was Lord Chesterfield's Priam, who'd bested the King's Fleur de Lis at Ascot in 1831, but the race was short-lived and was discontinued three years later.[26]

William, perhaps also aware that his attitude to horse-racing was unpopular, was anxious to court approval from his race-going subjects, and while at Ascot in 1832 he threw a coin to a gypsy woman, who was then promptly shoved out of the way as others rushed to catch it. The King gave her £5 instead and she went away happy.[27]

Not everyone, however, was so happy with the King's behaviour at the races, and a further incident at Ascot set him against attending them (or, perhaps, provided him with an excuse not to have anything more to do with them) for good. May 1832 saw the height of debate over the Reform Bill, which would eventually see a proportion of the population being given the vote. Since so many politicians were already unpopular, public revolt was inevitable, with even the statue at Welbeck of William Cavendish, 1st Duke of Newcastle, coming under attack. And nowhere was attack more likely than at Ascot.

'The event of the races,' recalled Greville, 'was the King's having his head knocked with a stone. It made very little sensation on the spot, for he was not hurt.'[28] Nevertheless, the incident provoked a sudden wave of loyalty, and 'Their Majesties were loudly cheered at Ascot'.[29] Even the Duke of Wellington, who had been mobbed and heckled over his involvement in the Reform Bill, benefited in the wave of patriotism that followed the attack on the King, but over the next few days the mood settled at the track.

Although Wednesdays at Ascot were generally quiet, the attack on the King meant that that year's was particularly sombre, and attendance was low. Unsurprisingly, the royal family decided not to attend, although according to *The Times* the attack appeared to have been forgotten. Even the races were poor, wrote the correspondent in an account that described the presence of roulette tables and the condition of the course, and ended by listing the most fashionable people of the day.[30]

The next article in the same column focused on the aftermath of the attack, most notably the defendant's appearance in a Reading court. A detailed account, it included the statements of witnesses – Captain George Smith of the Royal Navy, a Mr Benjamin Turner, Lord Frederick Fitzclarence and a Lord Brownlow – that essentially provided details of who was standing where when the stone made contact with the King's hat.[31]

The King reprieved his attacker, who was then sent into exile, but he refused to have anything more to do with the races. In addition, at the Craven meeting at Newmarket it was announced that he wouldn't have any more horses in training. In accordance with this resolve, he granted his trainer, William Edwards, a pension for his services and use of the stables and apartments at Newmarket, and he settled an annuity on his jockey, George Nelson. There was a fear that the Hampton Court stud would be sold off, but it continued to be maintained under the supervision of Colonel Wemyss, who, assisted by a Mr Worley, was left to run things as he saw fit. It was the colonel's plan to make Hampton Court stud one of the best in the country. King William kept his influence in this to a minimum, but even his wife's stables reflected Wemyss's tastes.[32]

According to a schedule of her establishment dated 16 December 1834, some of Queen Adelaide's horses had typically military style names – notably Adjutant, Dictator, Sailor (who was lame). She also owned steeds named Emerald, Diamond (who had bad feet) and Douglas, the latter of whom was a very fine kicker bought at the time of the Reform Bill – as was Adjutant – suggesting that he'd been part of the royal stable since 1832. Dictator, meanwhile, was an old horse, while others of the Queen's horses included Draysman (a fine horse with a straight neck), Dreadnought, Deceiver and one known as Anglesey or Quigley. The schedule doesn't specify whether this latter horse was male or female, but it was bought after the Reform Bill. Since all the horses were kept at London and Brighton, they were never meant to be trained for racing, and indeed some, like Douglas, Belvidere and Daniel (originally a part of the Master of the Horse's set), were destined for the posting stable.[33]

The Queen's schedule also notes the incumbent Master of the Horse's establishment, comprising three carriages made up of the state chariot, travelling coach and a phaeton, along with eight horses, one coachman, three footmen, two positions, one livery helper and three helpers. The horses had cold, forbidding names: Britton, Spex, Alarm, Contract, Clausman, Alert, Clifton and Coronation.[34]

In 1834, horse-racing was moving on. That year saw the introduction of the St James's Palace Stakes for three-year-olds and the Ascot Derby, which years later was changed to the King Edward VII Stakes for three-year-olds. The Gold Cup, meanwhile, was going from strength to strength and the sport as a whole was now receiving patronage, albeit in a limited fashion, from another member of the royal family.

On Tuesday, 11 June 1834, Princess Victoria of Kent, now aged fifteen, arrived with her mother at Windsor Castle, joining Feodora, the Duchess's eldest daughter by her first marriage, and her husband. Two days later, the company attended Ascot. Victoria, however, would never be seen attending the races with the King; even if he had been inclined to visit the races, relations between his court and Victoria's mother were so strained that such a public display of family unity was out of the question. After this season, Victoria, too, wouldn't attend Ascot until after her accession.[35]

On 8 February 1835, Greville recorded that he was 'at Stoke for the Ascot races',[36] and while riding to the course the following Wednesday he bumped into the King's son Adolphus Fitzclarence in the Park. Fitzclarence proceeded to tell Greville about his father: 'When Adolphus told him that a dinner ought to be given for the Ascot races, he said, "You know I cannot give a dinner; I cannot give any dinners without inviting the Ministers, and I would rather see the Devil than any one of them in my house."'[37]

William was nevertheless aware of the many improvements that were being made to the sport, such as transportation for the horses, which was introduced in 1836 by Lord George Bentinck.[38] Indeed, throughout the 1830s there had been calls for reform at Ascot, particularly the course, and on 4 June *The Times* published a list of eleven suggested remedies. William IV helped to instigate changes, and on 9 August *The Times* gave an update on how things were progressing. The King then assembled the members of the Jockey Club to discuss with them the state of Ascot. The management there was promptly changed and the course improved within the year.[39]

Despite such involvement, the King was still by and large unimpressed by the sport, and a commemorative picture by R G Reeve of the King's last visit to Heaton Park races on 2 June 1836 speaks volumes. In this piece, the King appears in a stand on the right, opposite the judges' box, and typically, despite the fact that the picture is supposed to be commemorating him, he is tucked away in a corner looking decidedly unenthusiastic while the horses passing the post – Touchstone, Rockingham, Lucifer, Aurelius and Valentissimo – take centre-stage. The print was later published in June 1837.[40]

Princess Victoria of Kent eventually came of age on 24 May 1837, at a time when the King's health was declining gradually. He had recently suffered an asthma attack and had liver trouble, so he was unable to attend a ball given in his niece's honour at St James's Palace. He was also absent from Ascot on 6 June (although the Queen attended), and the following day, in view of the King's illness, the house party at Ascot was abandoned. The King knew he was dying, but he wanted to see the anniversary of Waterloo on 18 June.[41]

He barely made it. At 2.20 a.m. on Tuesday, 20 June, King William IV died peacefully in the same room in which his brother George had passed away, seven years before.[42]

Notes:

1. Pocock, pp210–11
2. Ibid.
3. Centre of Buckinghamshire Studies: Freemantle Manuscripts. Correspondence D.FR/52/1
4. Pocock, pp210–11
5. Greville, Charles C F, *The Greville Memoirs, Volume II*, p2, 18.07.1830
6. Greville, Charles C F, *The Greville Memoirs, Volume II*, pp1–2. 16.07.1830
7. Greville, Charles C F, *The Greville Memoirs, Volume II*, p30, 17.11.1830
8. Ziegler, Philip, *William IV*, p157
9. Van der Kiste, John, *George III's Children*, p184
10. Van der Kiste, John, *George III's Children*
11. Greville, Charles C F, *The Greville Memoirs, Volume II*, p5, 18.07.1830
12. Greville, Charles C F, *The Greville Memoirs, Volume II*, p6, 18.07.1830
13. Ibid.
14. Ibid.
15. Greville, Charles C F, *The Greville Memoirs, Volume II*, p7, 18.07.1830
16. Greville, Charles C F, *The Greville Memoirs, Volume II*, p7, 18.07.1830
17. Longrigg
18. Greville, Charles C F, *The Greville Memoirs, Volume II*, p106, 19.01.1831

19. Greville, Charles C F, *The Greville Memoirs, Volume II*, p147, 05.06.1831
20. Ibid.
21. *The Times*, 16.08.1831
22. *The Times*, 18.08.1831
23. *The Times*, 20.08.1831
24. *The Times*, 22.08.1831
25. Musgrave, p117, p145
26. Magee and Aird, p65
27. Magee and Aird, p63
28. Greville, Charles C F, *The Greville Memoirs, Volume II*, p307
29. Ibid.
30. *The Times*, 21.06.1832
31. Ibid.
32. Fitzgerald, p87
33. 'Schedule of Establishment of Queen Adelaide's Master of the Horse and Her Horses', CR 2017/P13/1–2.1834, Warwick County Record Office
34. Ibid.
35. Magee and Aird, p73
36. Greville, Charles C F, *The Greville Memoirs*, Ed. Christopher Lloyd, p96, 08.02.1835
37. Ibid.
38. Magee and Aird, pp67–9
39. *The Times*, 09.08.1836
40. Wilder, F L, *English Sporting Prints*, p50–51
41. Pocock, p225
42. Pocock, p226

15
Victoria and Albert

Within minutes of the King's death, the Archbishop of Canterbury and Lord Conyngham left his residence and raced through deserted villages, eventually reaching Kensington Palace at around 6 a.m. Victoria was awakened and went downstairs to meet her ministers alone, without her mother. This young girl who only a month earlier had turned eighteen was now queen of England, the nation's first queen since Anne.

As Greville noted in his diary some days later, the transition between reigns was one of surprising tranquillity.[1] Her accession at the age of eighteen also came as something of a relief to Victoria, as it meant that she wouldn't be under the regency of her mother. She also wouldn't fall prey to the much-feared influence of her mother's secretary, John Conroy, who had previously been secretary to Victoria's father, the Duke of Kent. The new queen's Prime Minister, Viscount William Melbourne, wanted to ensure that, if she received guidance from anyone, it would be from him and her other ministers.

Victoria spent the next few weeks familiarising herself with her new position, but on 15 August she visited the riding house – which she found to be very large – and spent some time riding the horses there: Monarch, Duchess and an old favourite named Rosa.[2] Like most other members of her family, not only was she a natural rider but she also enjoyed riding high-spirited horses, having an innate ability to control and understand them. She also had a natural affection for them and was aware of their different temperaments, and riding was an extension of her new-found freedom as queen. During this time, she was bursting with energy and enthusiasm, having spent much of her early youth forced to live a life of tedium and quiet while being strictly chaperoned by her mother. Now, as monarch, she could live her own life, and riding provided her with the escape she'd always craved.[3]

In September, the Royal Stud held a sale, where a black Arabian horse that had been presented to William IV by the Imaum of Muscat was sold for 580 guineas to the King of Wurttemberg and would go on to prove popular in Germany.

In England, however, there were rumblings about the future of the stud, where twelve staff members had been laid off and there were now only a few horses left. For the second time in less than ten years, there were fears that the Hampton Court stud would be disbanded in its entirety, so the Duke of Sutherland wrote to the Prime Minister, Lord Melbourne, expressing his fervent hope that the stud would be allowed to continue. Unfortunately, Melbourne didn't appreciate horse-racing and thought even less of horse-breeding, and he ignored the letter, leaving it to the office of the Master of the Horse to announce that the stud would be broken up.[4]

The impact on the racing world of the dissolution of the Royal Stud was so profound that the Jockey Club sent a petition to Lord Melbourne, complete with Lord George Bentinck's and Charles Greville's names, but to no avail.[5] With the situation becoming desperate, a six-page attack against the Prime Minister appeared in the press in September. Again, nothing; the stud was to be broken up and that was that.

The situation must have been particularly annoying for Victoria. Having just turned eighteen and relying heavily upon Melbourne's guidance and direction, she was in no position to take the initiative, as her predecessors had been. In fact, Arthur Fitzgerald, author of *Royal Thoroughbreds*, believes that one of the reasons why Melbourne stood between her and the petitioners was ultimately for Victoria's own sake, to ensure that her court didn't begin to resemble that of her uncles, who'd had a deep-rooted (and expensively pursued) fascination for the turf that had made them very unpopular amongst certain folk. If Victoria's reign was to be different – if the monarchy was to survive, even – Melbourne believed that the court had to start as it meant to continue.[6]

This, however, didn't alter the fact that the stud at Hampton Court had taken a great deal of time and effort to construct and had survived where other studs had been disbanded. Disbanding it would be a travesty, its supporters argued, but Melbourne remained unconvinced and on 25 October Tattersalls advertised it as being for sale. Because it was a racing stud, it wasn't national property and didn't belong to a king or queen in office, being the private property of William IV, who inherited it from George IV and extended it. Also because it was a racing stud, it didn't contain carriage horses or horses for state occasions.[7]

What Melbourne failed to appreciate, however, was that the history of the stud was inextricably linked with the history of the monarchy. An edition of *The Times* published at around this time gave an account of the stud from the reign of King Charles I onwards and described how it was a working and viable part of the estate.

This was true. Situated on both sides of the road leading from Hampton Court to Kensington, about a quarter of a mile beyond the entrance gate of

Bushey Park on the way to Kingston, the stud consisted of 131 acres of mostly excellent grass for the horses. On the right-hand side of the road were the paddocks, sheltered by trees, and there were other paddocks elsewhere varying in size from 2–5 acres each, divided by high railings and palings, along with sheds for the tenants of the paddock. Nothing there was left to chance and the paddocks were secured against mishaps, the stallions confined and the mares and foals allowed to run loose.

The Times's account gave the impression that the Royal Stud wasn't only a working establishment but one that had been systematically developed, well maintained and organised highly efficiently.[8] At that time (1837), it was home to four stallions, 42 brood mares, thirteen colt foals and eighteen filly foals. If the sale took place, it would set the stud's development back years.[9]

All protests fell on deaf ears, however, and the sale did indeed go ahead. The biggest impact of the sell-off, however, was on the many employees who had worked at Hampton Court, in some cases for decades. These were people who had devoted their lives to the development of the stud. Out of sympathy for their plight, as well as other, more practical considerations, Lord Albemarle, Master of the Horse, gave them some money and was able to secure them either alternative employment or pensions.[10]

Meanwhile, sheltered by Melbourne's influence, Queen Victoria didn't seek to intervene. She didn't even visit any race meetings for a year, eventually attending Ascot on 14 June 1838, exactly two weeks before her coronation. On that occasion Lord Melbourne was in attendance, taking his first visit there in over fifty years, and although he enjoyed the day itself he kept very much in the background, remaining in the stand and marvelling at how much things had changed.[11] The Queen, however, was very impressed with the event and witnessed the inauguration of a new race that day over one and a half miles, introduced with a gold vase.

Charles Greville, meanwhile, wasn't impressed and was sceptical of the warm welcome Victoria received, commenting that such welcomes were well out of use.[12] The press, however, were quite enthusiastic and focused on describing the fashions on display there, including that of the Queen, dressed all in pink with lace and ribbons. Later, Victoria recorded the day in detail in her own journal, reporting people's comments and impressions, and had she continued attending races later in life she would have no doubt left an invaluable record of the sport and of the people who attended such racing events.[13]

Changes were very much afoot this coronation year, and there were plans to build a Grand Stand at Ascot between the Betting Stand and the Royal Stand, which would supposedly encourage more people to attend and raise funds with which to improve the course. Construction on the stand began in July but weren't completed until 25 May 1839, three days ahead of the start of that year's meeting.[14]

There were also changes to how the races were being run, as the Jockey Club decreed that horses couldn't be started unless their owners were trying to win with them, while the stewards, in their efforts to reduce the levels of disorderly conduct that clouded the meetings, imposed a fine of 5s[15] for those caught galloping alongside the runners, an indication of just how much of a problem such behaviour had become.

By now just two years into her reign, the Queen was about to face her first major hurdle, one whose surmounting would earn her considerable condemnation and give her an insight into the fickleness of public opinion. One of her ladies-in-waiting, Flora Hastings, was rumoured to be pregnant, and the Queen believed such gossip, particularly since Flora, with her swollen stomach, looked pregnant. On 5 July 1839, however, Flora died, whereupon it was discovered that her swollen abdomen was due to a huge malignant tumour. In fact, she died just after having received the Queen, who had been shocked to find her so ill. When Victoria attended Ascot soon afterwards, she was hissed at by the crowds at the racecourse, which once again served as a forum for scenes of public displeasure. Victoria wasn't impressed by this treatment, protesting that she'd done nothing wrong, and refused to let the episode spoil her visit.[16]

The highlight of that year's meeting occurred when a juvenile jockey called Bell won a race. When the Queen presented him with a £10 note, she asked him his weight, but he coyly replied that he wasn't allowed to say.[17]

In that same year, architect Jeffrey Wyatville carried out a comprehensive survey of the riding house and stables at Windsor Castle, including the ground. The plans that he drew up include a note indicating that the Queen's lower mews, overlooking Sheet Street and the High Street, was to be sold. Other decisions concerning the buildings hadn't yet been reached at the time the plans were made, and they contain additional notes on how they might be developed in the future. For instance, it was suggested that part of the coach houses could be 'reconverted' (into what, Wyatville doesn't say) and the smith's shop could either stay or be knocked down, although temporary coach houses on a courtyard backing onto the lower lodge, which housed the servants, were to be left alone. Wyatville was not very impressed with the ground, however, finding it very 'irregular' and judging that it would need to be levelled for the riding house and stables (part of it, in fact, already had been); he also intended to make use of the workshops for rebuilding work and a yard set aside for masons' workshops and plasterers for working on the stables.[18]

It was at around this time that other, more personal changes were about to happen in Queen Victoria's life. Since her accession, she'd enjoyed her new-found independence and had no plans to marry, but in truth this decision wasn't ultimately her own, since she was still viewed as being a child. It had always been hoped and planned that she would marry her first cousin, Prince Albert of Saxe-Coburg-Gotha, three months her junior, whom she'd first met in 1835. However, although she liked both Albert and his brother, Ernest, she had no great desire to marry. Nevertheless, on their second meeting,[19] in February 1840, she fell in love with him and they were soon married, settling down to a life of domesticity at which some of Victoria's Hanoverian uncles would have been amazed.

Prince Albert, however, soon found himself forced into the background, shut out from his wife's confidence in matters of state and not taken seriously by her ministers or her surviving uncles, who, protecting their interests and those of the Queen as members of the house of Hanover, regarded Albert – a member of a rival German house – with suspicion.[20] Others took an interest in him, however, such as the Marquis of Westminster, who in April 1840 presented him a black charger, Conductor, a five-year-old bred at Eaton Hall and standing fifteen and a half hands high.[21] It was a gift of which the Prince – a lover of horsemanship – would have approved, having that year been made ranger of Windsor Great Park, while the next year he would establish a riding school to the southwest of the Castle. What he wasn't interested in, however, was horse-racing, although he was often enough the subject of the popular pastime of royalty-spotting at the races.[22]

In 1840, the Coronation Stakes were introduced at Ascot, a race for fillies run over one mile, although Gold Cup day was still the highlight of the event. Both were of little interest to Albert, however, who had little patience for any such form of entertainment. Nevertheless, he did attend the Derby in June of that year with his wife, and on that visit they both received a warm welcome, particularly since the young Queen had recently survived an attack on her life on Constitution Hill, which had brought home to all how fragile the monarchy still was in England.[23]

The changes that were subsequently put in place over the next twenty years would transform not only the monarchy's image but also the nature of its involvement with horse-racing. These changes didn't come about overnight, however. Domestic strife, an attempt on the Queen's life and constant pregnancies had resulted in the Queen relinquishing much of her authority to

Albert. They worked together, side by side, but she was quite happy to follow her husband's lead and take his advice in all things. Through his influence, the court evolved into something that former monarchs wouldn't have recognised, and the ideal of monarchy was placed above the machinations of politics.

It was also placed above society. After the attempt on the Queen's life, her and Albert's attendance at Ascot in June was as much to present a reassuring sight as to attend the races. In later years, however, although they attended Ascot each year, they did so only on the Tuesday and Thursday of each meeting. The days of royalty being a constant presence on the racecourse were gone – for now, at any rate – and gambling was being stamped on hard.[24]

These changes also had an effect on the Royal Stud. While the Prince was largely indifferent to horse-racing, he did see the value in bloodlines and in August 1842 had been presented with the welcome gift of an Arabian mare who, it was intended, would be used to raise a stock of horses of the purest Arabian blood.[25] She would eventually be sent to Cumberland Lodge, but she was first housed at Hampton Court, where her shoes – designed for sandy areas – had to be changed to something more appropriate for the firm ground. Her original shoes were something of a curiosity, being heart-shaped and made of a single piece of iron. They were set deep in the hoof, too, a sign of neglect by her previous owners.[26]

Just three weeks after the mare's delivery, Queen Isabella II of Spain sent four more horses as a gift, complete with Spanish grooms. The Queen and Prince chose two each, and all four were put through their paces by the Prince's riding master. They were larger and heavier horses than the English breed, similar to those from Flanders and the Low Countries.[27]

Prince Albert's desire to distance the monarchy from the actual sport of horse-racing and the debts resulting from the gambling associated with it had much to do with the corruption that still pervaded the sport. The attack on Constitution Hill had brought home to him not only the Queen's vulnerability but also that of the monarchy itself. At that time, the unpopularity of Victoria's uncles was still fresh in the public mind, and the last thing she needed was to be attached to a sport that was capable of generating negative publicity and scandal.

Meanwhile, Lord George Bentinck and the Jockey Club were also trying to reform horse-racing. This was the time of the 'filthy forties' and the Jockey Club was doing all it could to improve the sport, particularly under the guidance of Bentinck, who was instrumental in exposing the Running Rein scandal of 1844, when a three-year-old horse of that name substituted a four-year-old at the last minute and subsequently won the Derby. There was corruption within the administration of the sport itself, however, and in 1845 the bestowing of gifts to the stewards and judges was replaced with set payments for the major races on an authorised basis.[28]

Prince Albert was determined to isolate the monarchy from the influence of corruption at a time when Europe was experiencing political unrest. It was a time to introduce structure and discipline, and for the royal family there was a need not only to distance itself from corruption and scandal but also to place itself above the sport, just as it was placing itself above party politics. So, while the Queen and Prince Albert might attend Ascot for two days, they would never become the focus of the meeting as George IV had been or their descendants would be. While they might thus have distanced themselves from high society, they maintained their popularity by adopting middle-class views, in contrast to the Hanoverians.

Nevertheless, a day at the races still had diplomatic value for the monarchy, and in 1844 Tsar Nicholas I of Russia paid a visit to Ascot. Nicholas enjoyed the races and made a point of looking at the winners,[29] a purpose for which the Royal Enclosure was rapidly coming into its own. The Tsar was a fan of English thoroughbred horses and in the previous year had arranged to have one hundred of them sent to Russia in the care of one seventeen-year-old named William Archer, father of the famous flat-race jockey Fred. That year, the Tsar gave £500 towards the Gold Cup in the form of plate, proving himself something of a popular figure. In fact, Ascot was starting to attract more and more foreign royalty, including one visit from the King of Oude, who was amazed at the notice he attracted from the ladies.[30]

In March and October 1845, the Queen was the recipient of several Arabian horses, and two years later, in July 1847, part of her stud was moved to Scotland. In the intervening time, both she and Prince Albert had leased Balmoral in Scotland, a place they both loved, reminding the Prince of his former home in Germany. So much did they love it, in fact, that they bought the place in 1852. It soon became the couple's principal residence, so it made sense to move part of the Queen's stud there.[31]

Such changes went on regardless of what was happening elsewhere, but the outbreak of revolutionary activity in Europe and another attempt on the Queen's life in March 1849 – this time in Hyde Park – sharpened the imperative to change the monarchy's image and to distance it from anything that could invite condemnation. At that time, King Louis Philippe of France was deposed and he and his family sought refuge in England, staying with the royal family until their future could be decided, while in Paris in February 1849 the horses from the former king's royal stables were sold.[32] In fact, by the early summer there was still a certain amount of unease after the troubles in Europe and Chartist demonstrations in London, and this concern was realised by a marked police presence during the Queen's visit to Ascot that year.

One of the highlights of the summer race meetings was the introduction of three silver cups, described in detail in *The Times* on 29 May and modelled by a Mr Cotterill. The first was the Emperor of Russia's Ascot Vase, representing the fate of Hippolytus, adorned with sea monsters entwined about the stem, while the dropping of the water from the mouth of the cup was introduced to give a marine character. The second cup was the Queen's Ascot Cup, representing a fight between a Spanish picador and a bull, while the third was the Goodwood Cup, representing the chase of the bison by Native Americans. All three cups were exhibited in Messrs Gerrards' shop.[33]

While Prince Albert was less than enthusiastic about horse-racing, he was an enthusiastic huntsman, as he demonstrated in the Belvoir Hunt of 1849. He tended to ride aggressively and put as much energy into his sport as he did his work, but his understanding of the breeding industry and the potential value of the Royal Stud persuaded him to re-establish the stud at Hampton Court, which had been disbanded and sold in 1837.[34] Racing thoroughbreds was one thing, he reasoned, but breeding them was something else, and being possessed of a mind fascinated by science and method he might well have been attracted to that behind the breeding of top-quality thoroughbreds. He certainly saw the importance of the Hampton Court stud and placed one John Ransom in charge of getting it up and running again.

Then, in 1850 General Peel relinquished his lease on the paddocks at Bushey Park. The stables there had deteriorated through lack of use over the years and had to be renovated and restocked, but each June for decades to come there would be a yearling sale at Hampton Court, visited by hundreds of people from all over Europe.[35]

Sir Michael Oswald, former stud manager of Queen Elizabeth II, once noted that 'Queen Victoria owned the second largest stud in the society, which also proved to be the most influential.'[36] Exactly how influential, however, no one back in 1850 would have guessed.

At some point during 1855, the Royal Stud extended its interest by acquiring a seventeen-year-old horse that had once belonged to William Palmer, who had recently been hanged for poisoning a large number of people, including his own family. Shortly after this, the Queen established at her own expense the Buckingham Palace Royal Mews School, for the education of children of the servants attached to the Royal Mews. The school would remain in service for over twenty years, and in 1859 new accommodation would be built for the 198 staff and their families.[37]

Meanwhile the royal children were growing up, and in February 1857 the Prince of Wales – christened Albert Edward but known to his family as Bertie – took to the field for the first time as a sportsman. On the whole, the sixteen-year-old Prince led a very strict, secluded life regulated closely by his parents. Every minute of every day was accounted for, so this opportunity to attend the sports field must have come as a welcome change to the Prince, a naturally sociable young man who craved the company of people other than his family and the royal household.[38] In this he wasn't much different from his mother, who still enjoyed her occasional visits to the races. Indeed, during the 1857 Derby, she insisted that Derby and Oaks winner Blink Bonny be brought to the Royal Stand so that she could inspect it.[39]

In 1860, at the age of nineteen the Prince of Wales was a better horseman than he was a cricketer or tennis player, despite the fact that the only horse he was permitted to ride was an old animal named Comus, and even then he had a tendency to fall off.[40]

Then, in June, after he'd pleaded to be allowed to go into the army, the Prince was sent to the Curragh Camp in Kildare, Ireland, for intensive military training, arriving there on the 29th. He enjoyed his time there, but some months after his return – when, much to his annoyance, he was sent back to Cambridge to continue his studies – it came to the attention of the Queen and the Prince Consort that their son had had an affair with an actress while in Ireland. Albert, not in the best of health, went to see his son in Cambridge to have it out with him, but when he returned it was obvious that his health had deteriorated even further and on 14 December 1861 he died of typhoid fever.[41]

Although it was never fully appreciated at the time, Prince Albert achieved a great deal in the 21 years he spent in his adopted country. For instance, he changed the whole outlook of monarchy, probably stopping it from going the way of other European houses, and he also changed people's perception of it. He restored respect for the monarchy, too, largely by making it aware of its responsibility, of its image and of the example it needed to set to its subjects. Nowhere was this change more important than with horse-racing, and for the first time the royal family distanced itself from the sport while maintaining its responsibility towards the thoroughbred industry.

It would be left to the next generation to achieve a balance between this responsibility and that towards a public that was becoming increasingly involved in horse-racing.

Notes:

1. Greville, Charles, *The Greville Memoirs*, Ed. Christopher Lloyd, p110, 25.06.1837
2. 'Queen Victoria's Journal', 15.08.1837, courtesy of Her Majesty, Queen Elizabeth II, Windsor Castle
3. Woodham-Smith, pp148–9
4. *The Times*, 18.09.1837
5. Fitzgerald, p95
6. Fitzgerald, pp95–8
7. Fitzgerald, p98
8. *The Times*, 18.09.1837
9. Thurley, p292, pp354–5
10. Fitzgerald, p100
11. Magee and Aird, pp74–5
12. Greville, *The Greville Memoirs*, Ed. Christopher Lloyd, 14.06.1838
13. Victoria's journal, courtesy of Royal Archives, Windsor Castle
14. Magee and Aird, p78
15. Tyrrel, p33
16. Woodham-Smith, p180
17. Magee and Aird, pp80–81
18. 'Windsor Castle. New Riding House and Stables Shewing the Principle on which they have been made to suit the ground', Jeffrey Wyatville, Architect, 1839, WORK 34/266–114779 (National Archives document)
19. Van Der Kiste, *Queen Victoria's Children*
20. Van Der Kiste, *George III's Children*, p194
21. *The Times*, 10.04.1840
22. Magee and Aird, p82
23. Magee and Aird, pp80–1
24. Magee and Aird, p83
25. *The Times*, 27.08.1842
26. *The Times*, 01.09.1842
27. *The Times*, 23.09.1842
28. Tyrrel, p33
29. Magee and Aird, p85
30. Magee and Aird, pp86–7
31. www.balmoralcastle.com
32. *The Times*, Feb. 1849
33. *The Times*, 29.05.1849
34. Woodham-Smith, p244
35. Fitzgerald, p103
36. Courtesy of Sir Michael Oswald
37. Royal Mews Works, WORK 19/50 (National Archives document)
38. Van Der Kiste, *Queen Victoria's Children*, p26
39. Fitzgerald, p110
40. Mortimer, p108
41. Weintraub, pp89–90

16

Albert Edward, Prince of Wales

Hearing of his father's illness while still at Cambridge, the Prince of Wales hurried home but was too late to see his father before he died. His mother, inconsolable, blamed him for her husband's death, and while relations between them would eventually improve, the Queen would always feel that he was too irresponsible to be trusted. Bertie would therefore spend the next forty years trying to compensate for this lack of trust and faith in him. For the world of horse-racing, this might have been a blessing in disguise.

The Queen withdrew from the court, but in the royal household business continued as normal. As Victoria isolated herself at Osborne, on the Isle of Wight, sales of yearlings took place at Hampton Court in the summer of 1862; she had allowed the re-establishment of the Royal Stud as long as all the horses were sold as yearlings (i.e. as long as the stud wasn't contaminated by the presence of racehorses for longer than necessary).

Meanwhile, work continued on the Royal Mews. A document dated 21 August 1862 refers to a tender for the construction of a new granary over the farrier's shop and over the coach houses in the lower mews. Then, some months later a tender was put out for the construction of a covered shed for the front of the large coach houses in the lower mews as well as a glass roof for the covered shed. It wasn't a case of no expense being spared, though; it was usually the cheapest quotes that were accepted, as long as the contractor in each case could adhere to the plans and specifications, and if a firm had already done work at the mews, this was no guarantee that it would be chosen again. Days, weeks and even, in some cases, months would be spent on deciding the best quote.[1] Even though the Royal Mews was constantly being improved and updated, gone were the days of extravagant expense, and anyone involved in such improvements had their work cut out for them, including such personages as the Master of the Horse (who had to approve proposed plans), the clerks at the Office of Works (who had to make good any alterations to the plans and liaise with the Office of the Master of the Horse over cost estimates) and the builders (who had to construct the proposed building or buildings and deal with any requested alterations in the time allocated and at the lowest possible price). The negotiations over the construction of two washing sheds for the royal carriages at the mews, for instance, took almost three months to complete, between the first week of September 1864 and the end of November, and tenders for the job didn't come in until January 1865.

By this time, Bertie had been married to Princess Alexandra of Denmark for two years and the couple had taken up residence at Marlborough House. However, despite the fact that his mother wasn't expecting to live long and kept telling her daughter, the Princess Royal, that she would soon be joining her husband, Bertie still wasn't allowed to help his mother or to have anything constructive to do. He felt that it was important to be seen, however, and to this end travelled about the country with his new wife, but even then he was criticised by his mother, who was in fact quite jealous of the popularity of her son's family.

Frustrated at being unable to please his mother, Bertie began to attend the horse races more frequently even though he knew he was being scrutinised and judged when he was there. In June 1863 he first attended Ascot, where the Prince of Wales Stakes had been established the previous year. The following year, the Alexandra Plate was established there and a wooden construction down the course from the grandstand was designated the Alexandra Stand. Still, the Queen was unhappy at her son's and daughter-in-law's interest in the races and felt that they led a frivolous lifestyle. It did not help matters, either, when in March 1865 the Prince was robbed of his watch at Chertsey Steeplechase. The theft failed to put him off, though, as did the latest scandal to hit the sport and society.[2]

It transpired that Henry Chaplin, a friend of the Prince's and a popular personality at Ascot, became involved with a certain Lady Florence Paget, although in June 1864 she attended the opening day at Ascot with Henry, Marquis of Hastings. She later became engaged to Chaplin but eloped with Hastings. Chaplin, it seems, never got over being cuckolded and swore eternal rivalry against Hastings, both on and off the racecourse. Hastings, meanwhile, quickly accumulated debts that would eventually ruin him. It was the type of scandal in which the Queen dreaded to see her son involved.[3]

By this time, the Prince of Wales had become a regular feature at the race meetings and took as much pleasure in attending steeplechases as he did flat racing. On 15 February 1867, he was seen at Windsor races while his wife was at home, expecting their third child. In fact, she became very ill, having contracted rheumatic fever, and yet it took three telegrams to draw the Prince of Wales away from the races, and even then he didn't turn up until the early hours of the next day. Such irresponsible behaviour earned him a great deal of criticism from all sides, particularly since his wife had refused sleeping draughts so that she could be awake when he returned.

Eventually, though, Princess Alexandra gave birth to a daughter, Louise, on the 20th, remarkably – considering the pain she must have been in – without the aid of chloroform. Over the next two years, the baby would be joined by two sisters, Victoria in 1868 and Maud in 1869, while she also had two older brothers: Albert Victor (known as Eddy), born in 1864, and George, born in 1865. Alexandra's final child, a boy, was later born in 1871, but little John Alexander would live for only a few hours.

Towards the end of the 1860s, the Prince of Wales was still hankering for something to do and in March 1868 appealed to his mother to let him go to Ireland to do some work there, arguing that even going to the races there would be a good opportunity for people to see him. While the Queen allowed him to go, however, not even the Prime Minister could persuade her to allow him any responsibility while he was over there. The Prince and Princess of Wales duly travelled to Ireland some weeks later on a goodwill visit and attended Punchestown races, where they were greeted by 50,000 spectators. Alexandra proved to be especially popular and was praised in the Irish newspapers.

On his return to the UK, riding on his success in Ireland, the Prince approved the revival of the royal procession[4] at Ascot, although nothing could have induced the participation of the Queen, who forbade the use of Windsor Castle for these meetings. Then, in July she complained about the Prince attending Goodwood, while her son argued that it was important for the royal family to be seen by its subjects. Even so, Victoria was becoming increasingly concerned and even tried to compromise. On 1 June she asked Bertie to attend only two days of the event, hoping that this would set a good example.

In fact, it appears that the Queen and the Prince of Wales had this argument each year: Victoria worried about the shiftless lifestyle such attendance represented and Bertie protested that he was trying to raise the sport's national profile. He felt that to stop going would damage the image of the sport and would appear uncivil. And besides, he pointed out, at the age of 28 he was old enough to make up his own mind about such matters. Nevertheless, Victoria was concerned that her son's lifestyle would leave him vulnerable to scandal. Her fears were realised the following year, when Bertie became embroiled in a divorce case concerning the legitimacy of a child and was required to give evidence in court. His mother felt that, guilty of fathering Lady Mordaunt's baby or not, it was his lifestyle that had got him involved in the case in the first place.

The Prince had no intention of changing his social life, but he did attend only the big races: Ascot, Epsom, Newmarket and Goodwood – a concession, perhaps, although it was true that such large-scale events provided a greater opportunity for him to prove that they had their diplomatic uses. In 1875, for instance, the Prince used Ascot to entertain the Sultan of Zanzibar, as well as other foreign dignitaries. Plus, the Prince's brothers and sisters were marrying foreign royalty, so royalty at the races was as much a family affair as it was a public one. In the same year, too, the Prince introduced his two sons – Princes Albert Victor and George, aged thirteen and twelve, respectively – to the sport, taking them both to Ascot. While his own father, the Prince Consort, might have balked at such an act, the Queen remained aloof. Soon, the racecourses – particularly those at Newmarket, Epsom and Ascot – would become extensions of what was essentially the Prince of Wales's alternative court.

The Prince of Wales was still unable to race horses himself, but in 1875 he finally registered his colours of purple, gold braid, scarlet sleeves and black cap with a gold fringe. His new career as a racehorse owner, however, was less than auspicious. In July 1877, his first horse to run in his colours – an Arab – failed to win its race, beaten literally out of sight by thirty lengths. For some years after this débâcle it looked as if the Prince's contribution to the world of horse-racing would be a mediocre one.

By 1880 the Prince had a number of horses in training at Newmarket, but the horse-breeding side of the business was proving very difficult to get off the ground. The foundation mare he bought – a daughter to Hermit – died of heart disease, and it would be another few years before the Prince's fortunes changed.

In the meantime, the races that he and other members of the royal family continued to attend were being won by other people admitted to the Royal circle. By 1881 it was clear that a certain element of decorum was expected at these race meetings, as the Honourable George Lambton discovered at Ascot, writing, 'I stayed for the first time at Ascot for the week. That meeting was chiefly memorable for Peter's Hunt Cup.' (Peter was owned by Jockey Club member Sir John Astley.) 'I don't know if it was in this particular year that Peter's gallant owner . . . appeared in the Royal Enclosure in a short white coat without any tails to it. The Prince of Wales took exception to this and told him he should come properly dressed. So the "Mate" [as Sir John Astley was nicknamed] got a pair of large buttons and wore them sewn onto the back of his coat next day. He showed himself to the Prince, saying that he hoped His Royal Highness was satisfied. The latter was too amused to be angry.'[5]

The Prince had set a new standard, one that was complemented by the Jockey Club, the trainers and the jockeys, helping to create a new golden age of horse-racing. Soon, though, scandal once again clouded the scene, although this time it did not involve the Prince. 1881 was the year of the Bend Or libel case, in which the Duke of Westminster's groom claimed that Derby winner Bend Or had in fact not been that horse at all but another of the Duke's horses, named Tadcaster. The whole business ended up in court. The case highlighted the fact that horse-racing still had a long way to go to improve its image, and in October it was announced that new racing rules were to be introduced. In addition, in 1883 the Jockey Club decided to put a check on the number of race meetings throughout the country so that the calendar wasn't crowded with fixtures.

Security, too was an issue. As with the 1884 Grand National when the security had to be stepped up. One house was already being kept under surveillance and Chief Constable Fenwick was keeping a close eye on several individuals who had been seen loitering in the city about a week before the event. Given the attempt on the Queen's life two years earlier, the police were taking no chances. On the Thursday instructions were issued to detectives to watch the passengers arriving at Chester railway station while the railway officials there were told to be vigilant and check parcels and boxes.

That night, police surrounded the house that had been under surveillance and apprehended a group of people referred to as 'dynamitards'. Whatever information they'd received came to nothing, however, and nor could they locate the original source of the information on which they'd acted.[6]

The attendance at that year's Grand National was huge. The Prince of Wales was there, having driven into the enclosure leading to the Steward's Stand with Lord Sefton and others soon after 1 p.m. on the Thursday. The weather was fine, although there was a mist over the track that made many of the events difficult to see. That year, the Prince was represented by a horse named The Scot. Just as the horses got past the post for one race, however, news reached the Prince that his brother, Prince Leopold, Duke of Albany, was dead. He left immediately and as a mark of respect all the gentlemen removed their hats and the track fell silent. Racing resumed later with the Spring Nursery, and later the fifteen competitors for the National – including The Scot – were weighed out.[7]

Despite starting out as a favourite and being admired by all, The Scot's performance failed about a mile from the finish, when he jumped into a fence and lost ground. The race was ultimately won by Voluptuary, although this victory wasn't altogether lost on the royal stables, since Voluptuary – an Ascot winner as well as a Grand National winner – had originally been bred at Hampton Court. The Scot was also scratched from the Sefton Steeplechase.[8]

The *Liverpool Daily Post* covered the details of Prince Leopold's death and how the rest of the family found out the news, which came as a total shock as, despite the fact that the Prince was delicate, there was no real warning that he would die. The coverage overshadowed that of the Grand National.[9]

Prince Leopold, Duke of Albany and youngest son of Queen Victoria, had suffered from haemophilia and was 31 years old when he died, leaving behind him a pregnant wife and a two-year-old daughter. As well as losing a son, the Queen had also lost a personal secretary, as for some time Leopold had been privy to the contents of the despatch boxes, a role that the Prince of Wales would have appreciated but was denied. Leopold's death changed nothing, however, and the Prince was soon back to his old routine.

The Princess of Wales, too, enjoyed attending race meetings and wasn't above visiting the Newmarket stables, which Queen Victoria never did, even when Prince Albert was alive. The Princess enjoyed riding and was quite a horsewoman, but during the early years of her marriage the Queen hadn't let her ride in the park. She did, however, share her husband's interest in racing and, since she was a setter of fashion, her example may have encouraged other women of high status to take an active interest in horse-racing and stud management. Other ladies with an interest in horses included Caroline, Duchess of Montrose, who ran her own stud as well as that of her husband and was at that time trying to secure jockey Fred Archer's services. Then there was the Prince of Wales's mistress, Lillie Langtry, who within a few years was not only a horse owner but also a member of the Jockey Club under the male pseudonym 'Mr Jersey'. Alexandra didn't seek to go as far as these women, but she did enjoy horse-racing enough to visit the stables at Newmarket.

'I remember one or two visits made by the Princess of Wales,' recalled the 6th Duke of Portland in his memoirs before going on to mention one such visit to trainer Mat Dawson's domain, Heath House: 'The old man was extremely courtly in his reception of her.' Indeed, it was well known at the time that Dawson was impeccable in his manners, although he wasn't greatly impressed when a huge parrot, perched on the Duke of Portland's wrist, suddenly gave vent and started swearing at everyone present.[10] 'After the Princess had gone, Mat's indignation with me and the parrot was extreme,' the Duke continued. '"I don't know which is the worst: Your Grace or the parrot."'[11]

In 1885, the Prince of Wales attended yearlings sales at Newmarket to buy bloodstock with which to form a new breeding stud in the town. By this time he had acquired the services of trainer John Porter, who owned a training establishment named Kingsclere and was registering results by the following year.

Also in 1886, Fred Archer, the best jockey of his day, won two races for the Prince: on Counterpane in a maiden two-year-old plate at Sandown on 4 June, and on Lady Peggy in a maiden plate on 26 October. Out of over eight thousand races, these were the only two that Fred would take part in while wearing the royal colours, and on 8 November of the same year he shot himself at his Newmarket home, Falmouth House. He'd been suffering from typhoid fever and had been in a state of delirium when he took his own life.

The racing fraternity and, indeed, much of the country grieved for the 29-year-old jockey, who had been one of the outstanding horsemen of his generation. The Prince of Wales sent a wreath to the funeral and later in the month employed Fred's stud manager, Edmund Walker, to work as a stud groom at Sandringham. Fred's stock of horses was sold on 17 December at Newmarket, where John Porter bought the broodmare Hazy for 440 guineas. A former friend of Fred Archer's, Captain George Machell, who owned a stud at Newmarket, succeeded Edward Stevens as stud groom at Hampton Court, where the Queen always maintained an interest and was kept informed of the horses' progress by her secretary, Sir Frederick Ponsonby.

The following year, 1887, was Golden Jubilee year, marking the fact that the Queen had been on the throne for fifty years. In addition, she was Empress of India, and the British Empire – upon which the sun never set – was at its height in power, wealth and influence. Indeed, by the end of the century most of Victoria's children and grandchildren would be heads of ruling houses across Europe and the Queen herself would be heralded as the Grandmother of Europe. But the Prince of Wales – the Uncle of Europe – still didn't have a specific role in life, and his horse-racing career could be pretty hit and miss, as he discovered at the 1888 Grand National. That year there was disappointment when Magic, the Prince's horse participating in the event, wasn't saddled in the enclosure, and it had been thought that the Prince wouldn't make it to see his horse run. He eventually got to Aintree before the first race. Magic, however, ran unplaced, the race being won by a horse named Playfair.[12]

The Prince wasn't put off by such a poor result, however, and in the following year's Grand National he entered two horses: Magic and Hettie. Although Hettie performed well, the race was won by Frigate,[13] while Magic came first in the Ninth Champion Steeplechase.

The Prince's sporting luck changed for the better again when he hired a friend of his, Lord Marcus (de la Poer) Beresford, as his racing manager. Beresford appealed to the Prince because of his sense of humour; if the Prince of Wales loved anything, it was being entertained.

Life continued to tick over until January 1892, when the Prince's son Albert Victor ('Eddy') – recently created the Duke of Clarence – became ill. At first his illness wasn't taken seriously, as everyone around him was under the weather, too, but he grew progressively worse and was diagnosed with influenza, succumbing to the virus several days after his birthday. His younger brother, George, himself recovering from typhoid, now found himself second in line to the throne and was forced to give up all ambitions of a naval career. Later, the Queen bestowed the title of Duke of York upon him.

As the months progressed, it became obvious that, if George was to marry, it should be to Princess Victoria May of Teck, known as May, originally Eddy's intended. George and May had become close in the months following Eddy's death, and both families approved of the match, although some among George's extended family objected on the grounds that May was only minor royalty, despite the fact that she was a great-granddaughter of King George III through his son Adolphus. Even so, the engagement was announced and the wedding was scheduled to take place on 6 July 1893, in the Chapel Royal at St James's Palace.[14]

Meanwhile, in the autumn of 1892 it was decided to move the Prince of Wales's horses from Kingsclere and to find another trainer to replace John Porter. The next was Richard Marsh, who wrote in his 1925 autobiography, 'I like to think that the honour accorded me of being selected to train for the Prince of Wales was largely the outcome of my record and proven ability up to that time.'[15] Marsh did indeed have an outstanding reputation as a trainer, but the incentive behind the change in circumstances was that the Prince wanted to find somewhere closer to Sandringham in which to house the horses. Marsh's newly built Egerton House at Newmarket was perfect for the job, having the best of everything and the most up-to-date accessories for the 'breeding, rearing and education of the thoroughbred', according to Marsh.

Initially, Lord Beresford, the Prince's racing manager, wrote to Marsh on behalf of the Prince and then met him at Challis's Hotel in London, where, when asked if he would train the Prince's horses, Marsh confessed that he was currently training for the Duke of Hamilton.[16] 'Lord Marcus knew his business,' wrote Marsh. 'There was no finer judge of a horse and of racing. He understood the breed of the thoroughbred.'[17]

Beresford explained to Marsh that the Prince wanted closer contact with his horses. For any trainer, this was an opportunity not to be missed. 'Stupidly, I suppose, I told Lord Marcus I had better consult the Duke of Hamilton,' Marsh remembered.[18]

Beresford was dumbfounded and told the trainer dryly that monarchs of old would have had his head for saying something like that, but he was too amused to argue Marsh into submission. He went off to report to the Prince while Marsh talked to the Duke, who reportedly declared, 'For goodness' sake, wire off at once your grateful acceptance. You ought not to have said what you did.'[19] In fact, the Prince was impressed with Marsh's loyalty and respect for the Duke, although it would be many years before he confessed as much to the trainer.

On 1 January 1893, Marsh travelled with Beresford to Overton, the entraining station for the horses at Kingsclere, where he inspected the initial eight animals – Versailles, Turidda, Downey, The Virgil, Florizel II, St Valerie, Laissez-Aller and Barracouta – that were to leave John Porter's care before being prepared for transfer to Newmarket. Marsh was unimpressed with almost all of them, except Florizel II, who looked promising. Twenty more horses would follow these eight.[20]

John Porter was relieved to see the back of the horses, saying to Marsh, 'I am glad, as they are leaving me, you get them. They will help fill up and pay the expenses of the new establishment. You and I are not foolish enough to fall out with each other over other people's quarrels.'[21] Marsh didn't know what quarrels John was referring to, but Porter's words made him suspect that there might have been some friction between him and Beresford.

Marsh would never forget his first visit to Sandringham, which took place in June of that year. On that occasion, he was given lunch and then the Prince sent for him to join him out on the lawn. 'There gathered about him were many of the distinguished guests who were representing the other nations at the royal wedding, including the King of Denmark,'[22] recalled Marsh, referring to the Prince of Wales's father-in-law and the marriage of George and May. Marsh became nervous as everyone present turned to look at him, but the Prince put his new trainer at ease, introducing him to the King. They then went to inspect the horses at the stud, which was divided into two: Sandringham and then Wolferton, the latter situated near the sea.

With his horses safely installed at Egerton, the Prince of Wales had more direct contact with them and began to visit Newmarket more regularly, often staying at the Jockey Club, where he had rooms and a private entrance at the back of the building, leading from Station Avenue. He also introduced Sandringham time and put the clocks back an hour to allow for more shooting and to accommodate his wife's lack of punctuality.

During Marsh's first year as the Prince's trainer there were only two small wins, although he hoped that Florizel II would fare better as a three-year-old in 1894.[23] Marsh found the horse plain and backward, although his quiet and sober temperament was in his favour, so unlike that of his sire and dam, the temperamental, skittish and unpredictable St Simon and Perdita II. Marsh described Florizel II as 'nice-tempered' and was justified in his faith in the horse, who as a three-year-old won five races, totalling £3,499.[24] He reached a peak as a four-year-old and won many significant races for the Prince of Wales, namely the Ascot Gold Vase, the Manchester Cup, the Goodwood Cup and the Jockey Club Cup. He continued training as a five-year-old, but in 1896 he developed suspensory trouble.

Florizel II's full brother, Persimmon, born in 1893, would fare better. Also trained by Marsh, the horse was doing well in 1895 as a two-year-old. His first race was the Coventry Stakes at Ascot.

While things appeared to be ticking over at Newmarket, the Prince of Wales's son, George, Duke of York was having to deal with the horse-racing debts of his brother-in-law, Prince Francis of Teck, his wife's younger brother, known in the family as 'Frank'. Frank was a reckless gambler and in the early years of his sister's marriage was very often in debt. On 25 June he found himself owing £11,000 after betting on a horse called Bellevin at the Curragh. On that occasion, George agreed to help to avoid a scandal and Frank – who referred to George and his sister May as 'Master and Mistress of York' – found himself packed off to India with the army. He wasn't sorry for the trouble he'd caused, however, quipping that he'd send his pregnant sister a betting book for Christmas.

On 14 December, the anniversary of the Prince Consort's death, Princess May gave birth to her second son, Albert Frederick Arthur George (her first son being Prince Edward, born in 1894). By all accounts, the Queen was rather put out by the birth taking place on such a date.

At least Persimmon had had a good year, winning the Richmond Stakes at Goodwood in July, although in the Middle Park Plate he finished third behind St Frusquin. In 1896, as a three-year-old, he proved to be rather sluggish and had to be removed from the 2,000 Guineas. The problem, it appeared, was that he was temperamental, very much like his sire, St Simon.

Then, on 26 May 1896 the Prince and Princess of Wales, the Duke and Duchess of York, Princess Victoria, Princess Maud and her husband, Prince Carl of Denmark, Miss Blanche Forbes, Sir Dighton Probyn, Beresford and Sir Derek Keppel attended a Derby trial. In the presence of such distinguished company, Marsh was anxious for Persimmon to do well, and indeed he wasn't disappointed: the horse won by three lengths. Marsh was confident that they had a Derby winner on their hands.[25] The Prince, too, was pleased and Alexandra asked Marsh if Persimmon stood a good chance of winning. Marsh didn't want to tempt fate, although he did tell the Princess of Wales that if Persimmon kept well he stood a tremendous chance. Satisfied, the royal party returned to Sandringham.

Marsh, meanwhile, was having domestic problems. Having been forced to dismiss his cook, he was hunting high and low for a chef while at the same time continuing with Persimmon's preparations for the Derby at Epsom. He arranged for the horse to be boxed from Dullingham Station the day before the race that year, intending to travel with him. Once they arrived at the station, however, Persimmon had other ideas.

'Never shall I forget it,' wrote Marsh. 'The devil seemed to be lurking within him that morning . . . I nearly had a fit . . . He positively refused under any sort of pressure to go into his box.'[26]

Marsh and another man joined hands at Persimmon's rear and tried pushing him in the box, but the horse kicked out. Then matters were made worse by a gathering group of onlookers. 'I turned to the crowd,' related Marsh, '[and said], "Now this horse has to go to Epsom and he has to go into this box. To every man that helps me to get him in I will give a sovereign."'[27]

There wasn't exactly a mad rush to assist which did little for Marsh's nerves, although in hindsight he was also relieved as paying the crowd would have meant parting with half of the Derby stakes. Not that he was concerned about that at the time; getting the horse aboard the train was his main priority.

'Finally,' wrote Marsh, 'at about the time I must have been approaching an apoplectic state, I got about a dozen volunteers . . . We practically lifted him in.'[28] To Marsh's exasperation, Persimmon entered his box with little protest and very leisurely began to munch his corn. It was a long time before the trainer could forgive his charge.

On the journey to Epsom, Persimmon had a sweating fit. He eventually settled down, but as if things weren't bad enough Marsh reached Epsom to the sound of rumours that the horse was unfit. He now had the additional worry of having to reassure the Prince and Beresford that the rumours weren't true.

Then there was the jockey, Jack Watts.[29] Having spent a great deal of time and energy wasting for this event, Jack was now in depressed spirits. Marsh could only sympathise; he knew how devastating the effects of wasting could be, but he managed to persuade Jack to carry on. The trainer believed that it was the thought of riding this particular race for the Prince that kept the jockey going.[30]

On the morning of the race, Watts cantered Persimmon onto the course, and Marsh later accompanied him on a walk around Ashtead Park. 'He had a sweater on,' the trainer recalled, 'and, believe me, I had no occasion to lose any weight at that time, but I went through with it, chiefly to keep him company and his mind occupied.'[31] Marsh, meanwhile, was preoccupied enough for both of them and could not relax until he had seen Jack safely into the saddle. Only then could he feel that everyone had done everything they could to prepare for the race. Even so, he felt that he needed to watch as Jack led Persimmon to the starting post.

A large royal party had gathered, but Marsh was unaware of this and stayed at the starting post until it was almost time for the race to begin, so it took him a while to thread his way back through the dense crowd. In addition, the police, who had cleared the course, blocked his path and wouldn't let him through. By this time the race was well under way, so he stood on the steps of the public house[32] and watched from there. All he had was a blurred view of the race until Tattenham Corner, and then all the horses and riders were out of sight.

With the race over, Marsh followed the crowd back, bumping into Morny Cannon,[33] who had also ridden in the race on Knight of the Thistle but was unplaced. 'He must have spotted me,' remembered Marsh, 'for he exclaimed, "You've won!"'[34] Persimmon, it seemed, had beaten St Frusquin – the favourite – by a neck.

Once this piece of news had sunk in, Marsh, elated, hurried off to find Watts, forcing his way through hundreds of people. 'No rugby forward pushed harder than I did during the next minute or two to get to Persimmon,' he later recalled.[35]

When Marsh found him, Watts looked miserable, drained utterly by his efforts in the race, but the trainer knew that the jockey was inwardly pleased, having achieved what many jockeys could only dream of achieving. Marsh also recalled the Prince's delight at the result, which represented the culmination of all he'd hoped for and, what's more, justified his involvement in the sport, in the face of his mother's opposition over the years.

By 1897, four-year-old Persimmon had grown up to become a large, impressive-looking horse and was Marsh's pride and joy. He was booked to enter the Ascot Gold Cup, and before the race Beresford told Marsh that if he thought Persimmon was likely to win, Queen Victoria would attend the races to see him run.[36] A challenge indeed. Persimmon did well in his trials, so Marsh contacted Beresford and told him to bring the Queen to see Persimmon run in the Ascot Gold Cup, which the horse won. The Queen, though, did not attend. 'I believe,' recalled Marsh, 'that same day she was only arriving at Buckingham Palace from Balmoral for the Jubilee celebrations.'[37]

In Persimmon's next race, the Eclipse Stakes, the ground was much harder, so Marsh worked him on the tan. He remembered that the day of the race was very hot and the crowds suffered under the sun.

Minutes before the race, Princess Alexandra sent word that she wanted a photograph taken of Persimmon. Marsh tried to refuse, as he didn't want Persimmon to be distracted, but he was overruled and the photograph was taken. In the event, however, Persimmon went on to win the race.

Hard ground prevented Persimmon from entering the Champion Stakes at Newmarket, and then he threw out two Jack Spavins, one in each hock, effectively putting an end to his racing career. He was retired to stud.

Persimmon's retirement wasn't the end of the St Simon/Perdita II connection, however. In 1897, Persimmon and Florizel II's full brother Diamond Jubilee was foaled, named after the celebrations held that year in honour of the Queen's longevity. 'Possibly because of his relationship to Persimmon,' Marsh noted, 'Diamond Jubilee as a foal and then as a yearling was made too much of.'[38] But Marsh had other things to occupy him and the world of horse-racing moved further into a new era.

In 1898, a series of articles appeared in *The Times*: one concerning Lord Durham and the starting gate in April; one reporting on a royal Windsor meeting in May; and one about American jockeys. One such American jockey, Tod Sloan, had been in England for about a year when he was introduced to the Prince of Wales. He'd arrived at a time when the popularity of both the Prince and horse-racing was at its height, the latter being overseen by the Jockey Club, one of the most revered institutions in the world and one that had the power to overrule royalty when required.[39]

Tod Sloan was the latest American to conquer English racing at that time. The first American horses had been brought over years earlier by Richard ten Broeck, who, despite encountering some difficulties, won some top races with them: the Cesarewitch at Newmarket with Prioress in 1857, the Goodwood Stakes with Umpire in 1859 and the Goodwood Cup with Starke in 1861. He was followed in the 1870s by Milton Sanford, but until Sloan's time Pierre Lorillard had been the most successful, with Parole and Isonomy, primarily because of his severe but far-reaching training methods. So, although Sloan wasn't the first American horse-racing import, he represented what his biographer described as the 'second American Invasion' and also inspired the expression to be 'on one's tod' (i.e. alone).[40]

So, after being called to meet the Prince of Wales while at Newmarket, Sloan hurriedly put on a coat over his riding clothes and was taken to him. Writing about the meeting years later in his autobiography, he described how impressed he was by the fact that the Prince smiled at him as he approached and shook his hand warmly, how much he was put at his ease and how well he was treated. He hadn't believed that a jockey – and a visiting American jockey, at that – would be welcomed so generously. The Prince asked him if he was happy and if he liked riding on grass, and Tod felt that he could have talked to him all afternoon.

Before he left, the Prince asked Tod if he would ride for him, and Tod replied that it would be an honour to do so. However, the American jockey proved to be something of a loose cannon. At Ascot the following year, while he won three races in one day, he also got into a fight with a waiter on the same day, and it was left to Beresford to smooth things over, giving the offended waiter several hundred pounds.

Equally problematic was Diamond Jubilee, who was proving to be of a rather different temperament to his two brothers, Persimmon and Florizel II. Horses, as Marsh discovered, could be like children, if spoilt. 'He had cultivated a taste for succulent carrots and other titbits,' the trainer recalled, 'sure evidence that consideration and kindness in his case had been accepted in the wrong spirit.'[41] Even so, Marsh referred to the horse as a gentleman and found him a flawless and fearless physical specimen, while he exuded strength and character, standing at fifteen and a half hands on his arrival at Egerton. 'Again, though, let me say that during the period of breaking in . . . there was no harm in him, but he seemed to know quite enough – in fact, too much for a racehorse.'[42]

Marsh was, however, satisfied with Diamond Jubilee's progress (the horse won his trial) as well as his behaviour. He seemed to be a model horse, and when Sir Dighton Probyn came to the stable one day to look over Diamond Jubilee the trainer remarked upon this. 'Really, I sometimes think [the horse] must have understood what I said,' wrote Marsh, 'for no sooner were the words out of my mouth than he lashed out and kicked a man nearby on his hand . . . Sir Dighton looked at me and fled back to the royal box.'[43] Rather as an understatement, Marsh added, 'For myself, I was not unduly disturbed at the time . . . nothing like so much, I imagine, as the man who was kicked.'[44]

Marsh attributed Diamond Jubilee's skittishness to being unfamiliar with his surroundings, but the incident proved to be the shape of things to come. At Ascot, of all places, the horse showed his true colours, rearing up and down at the starting post and then walking about on his hind legs, before trying to turn his head about and snatch Jack Watts' foot in his mouth. That was enough for Watts;[45] it was obvious that the horse couldn't win while in this state, and Marsh remembered how his behaviour depressed everyone around him.

On the last Grand National meeting of the century, the weather was beautiful. Although the Prince himself didn't attend, the authorities of the Jockey Club were represented, attendance was very good all round and Ambush II was one of the race's four favourites. All his competitors started at near enough the same price, but Ambush II was described as being one of the 'gamest' and 'stoutest' of chasers and at one point commanded the field, although he was later overtaken and finished unplaced.[46]

In 1899, Marsh's priority was to control and subdue what he termed Diamond Jubilee's 'excessively high courage and proneness to temper'. He put the horse's 'ticklish' behaviour down to the fact that the two-year-old was young and at no time felt the need to discipline him forcefully.

Diamond Jubilee was entered for the July Stakes at Newmarket, for which he stood as favourite, but on the day of the event he wouldn't behave himself and even unseated the jockey before trotting onto the course regardless. One of the lads from Egerton hauled him back to the starting post, where Watts was waiting.[47] Then, as the race began, instead of running with the rest of the horses Diamond Jubilee chose to run all over the course. Not surprisingly, he finished last.

After the race, the Prince, Beresford and some of the Prince's friends turned up at Egerton House for tea. Some of the friends suggested various unorthodox remedies for bringing Diamond Jubilee to order – for instance, whipping him into submission. Marsh, however, knew that if he, or the stud in general, began to adopt such measures then the colt would be driven completely mad. He begged the Prince to be allowed to deal with it in his own way.

'Very well, Marsh,' the Prince replied, 'you shall go on trying what you like and think best. But I'm afraid he is a bad case. I very much hope not, but it looks like it. Try your best.'[48]

Marsh believed that part of the problem lay in the fact that Diamond Jubilee really didn't like his jockey, although if this was the case then his feelings were nothing compared to the dislike Watts felt for Diamond Jubilee.[49] For this reason, Marsh allowed Morny Cannon the dubious honour of riding the horse in the Prince of Wales Stakes at Goodwood that year. On that occasion Diamond Jubilee behaved himself and ran well, although he was beaten by half a length by Epsom Lad.

When Watts later rode Diamond Jubilee in the Middle Park Plate, the horse behaved himself again. At last, Marsh had found some kind of middle ground in the colt's training, and over time the horse's behaviour began to improve. 'It was necessary that he should be kept tractable and that feeding and steady exercise should in the smallest detail be suited to him,'[50] the trainer wrote. He would watch the horse's progress carefully.

In 1900 there had been several withdrawals from the National, reducing the field to seventeen, and at the last minute a list of the probable runners was posted, citing Ambush II third. The horse wasn't seen in as favourable a light as he had been the previous year, and he was half expected to be beaten by Manifesto – the horse's principal threat – and Hidden Mystery (although the *Sporting Life* correspondent hoped that he would win). Even so, many backed the Prince's horse to add some interest, so the contest was still open. In the event, Ambush II won.[51]

Then Diamond Jubilee was due to run in the 2,000 Guineas, but to Marsh's dismay, with the race just days away, the three-year-old was showing signs of returning to his 'monkey tricks' – and at a time when the Prince of Wales was due to visit, too. Two days before the royal visit, Morny Cannon decided to put the horse through his paces, taking him for a private gallop around Egerton, and everything was going well until the end of the gallop, when Cannon pulled him up, got down and began to lead him in by his rein. 'Instantly,' recalled Marsh, 'the horse seized him and rolled him over.'[52] Help was at hand, so Cannon was rescued before his charge could do too much damage, but the colt's participation in the forthcoming event was immediately thrown into doubt. 'Again,' lamented Marsh, 'I was confronted with the possibility that his unquestioned racing merit was going to be lost because of a temper which might become a danger and ungovernable.'[53] Months of progress was in danger of unravelling and Marsh sympathised with Cannon, who was fast losing faith in the horse.

With the return of his temper, Diamond Jubilee lost his impetus to race. Cannon suggested that Marsh should find another jockey, and the trainer agreed. This left the stud with a serious problem, however, as Diamond Jubilee had seen off the very best in Watts and Cannon.

Finally, Marsh looked to Herbert Jones, who might not have had the artistic skill of Watts or the finesse of Cannon but was still one of the finest horsemen Marsh had ever come across; the trainer couldn't praise him enough. Most importantly, he could handle extremely difficult horses, those who wouldn't work for anyone else. Marsh therefore approached Beresford and Beresford approached the Prince, who ultimately agreed to let Herbert ride Diamond Jubilee.

Jones turned out to be a godsend for the stable, and Marsh described the jockey's influence over Diamond Jubilee as 'mesmeric'.[54] The horse trusted him, although he could still be contrary, doing as he was told one minute and then refusing to do anything the next. 'He was so intelligent,' observed Marsh, 'that I sometimes used to think he plotted mischief.'[55] Nevertheless, he did well in his preparatory work for the Derby that year.

On the day of the race, the Princess of Wales requested that Diamond Jubilee enter the royal procession. Marsh wasn't sure that inflicting a parade on a high-strung horse was such a good idea – nor, indeed, was it wise to inflict a high-strung horse on a parade. 'However,' he wrote, 'I discussed the point with Jones, and it was arranged that Diamond Jubilee should parade in front of the stands.'[56]

As they approached the starting post, the horse began to play up. Jones secured a good place, but at Tattenham Corner Diamond Jubilee was jostled by Disguise II (ridden by Tod Sloan) and unbalanced. He resumed his pace, however, and won by half a length. Jones was awarded £1,000 – to be invested by Beresford – and the Prince was lavish in his thanks to all.

Diamond Jubilee had now won the 2,000 Guineas and the Derby and needed only to win the St Leger to secure the Triple Crown. However, on one wild, wet morning before the race, as Marsh anxiously got the horses back into their stables before they caught chills, Diamond Jubilee refused to enter his box. 'Did he do so?' demanded Marsh. 'Not he. There he took up his stand, and neither cajoling nor threats could bring him to any other frame of mind.'[57] Everyone there – including the horse – was soaked, and the longer he stayed outside, the worse his chances were of even reaching the St Leger, never mind running in it. It got to the stage where Marsh himself didn't know whether to walk away or risk pneumonia by staying. He decided that he couldn't leave him.

Then, just as the stablehands were beginning to despair of ever getting him into his box, Diamond Jubilee trotted quietly into it and began eating his hay.

The problems didn't end there, however. On the day of the race, he was in an even more devilish mood. 'A rare old battle we had in a corner of the paddock, which I generally used for saddling my horses at Doncaster,' Marsh later recalled. 'Every time I went near him with the saddle he would shoot straight up in the air and stand on his hind legs.'[58] Once the saddle was in place, Jones literally had to jump at him to get into it.

Despite these problems Diamond Jubilee and Herbert Jones went on to win the St Leger by a length, thus securing the Triple Crown and placing the Prince of Wales at the head of the list of winning owners.

In contrast with his success on the racecourse in 1900, on a domestic level the year was one of the worst for the Prince, with both his brother, Alfred, Duke of Edinburgh, and his sister, Vicky, Dowager Empress of Germany, dying of cancer.

For Tod Sloan, too, the year ended on a sour note after the Jockey Club launched an investigation into betting on the Cambridgeshire and found against him. He was instructed not to apply for another licence and drifted away from the racing scene altogether before being deported from England in 1915. He died in 1933.

Then, at the beginning of 1901, Queen Victoria's health began to fail, and at the age of 82, having reigned for over sixty years, she died at Osborne at 6.30 p.m. on 22 January. Her body was transported back to London for a state funeral attended by many ruling heads of Europe, most of whom were members of her own family.

Notes:

1.   'Royal Mews', WORK 19/50 1861–1868, 21.08.1862 (National Archives document)
2.   Magee and Aird, pp99–100
3.   Magee and Aird, pp100–2
4.   Magee and Aird, p100
5.   Lambton, p47
6.   *Liverpool Daily Post*, 29.03.1884
7.   Ibid.
8.   Ibid.
9.   Ibid.
10. Portland, p88
11. Portland, pp88–9
12. *Liverpool Daily Post*, 24.03.1888
13. *Liverpool Daily Post*, 30.03.1889
14. Van Der Kiste, *Queen Victoria's Children*, p62
15. Marsh, p92
16. Ibid.
17. Marsh, p100
18. Marsh, p103
19. Marsh, p104
20. Ibid.
21. Marsh, p105
22. Marsh
23. Marsh, p109
24. Ibid.
25. Marsh, pp150–1
26. Marsh, pp152–3
27. Marsh, p154
28. Ibid.
29. Marsh, p155
30. Ibid.
31. Marsh, pp156–7
32. Marsh, p159
33. Ibid.
34. Marsh, p160
35. Ibid.
36. Marsh, pp171–2
37. Marsh, pp174–6
38. Marsh, p198
39. Dizikes, p102
40. Dizikes, pp104–5

41. Marsh, p199
42. Ibid.
43. Marsh, p200
44. Ibid.
45. Marsh, p201
46. *Liverpool Daily Post*, 25.03.1899
47. Marsh, p202
48. Marsh, p203
49. Ibid.
50. Marsh, p206
51. *The Sporting Life*, 30.03.1900
52. Marsh, p211
53. Ibid.
54. Marsh, p214
55. Marsh, p216
56. Marsh, p215
57. Marsh, p107
58. Ibid.

17
Edward VII

Queen Victoria's death had left a huge void in more ways than one, as very few people could remember a time when there wasn't a queen on the throne. Even those in the royal household had to research the protocol required for Victoria's state funeral. And then, of course, there was the daunting prospect of arranging the coronation, the first since 1838. In addition, the transition from the erstwhile Prince Edward's old residence, Marlborough House, to his new home as king, Buckingham Palace, wasn't going to be easy for anyone, and from the very beginning it was made clear that the Royal Mews would be one of those departments within the royal household that would come under extreme pressure.[1]

In a letter dated 8 February, Edward's Master of the Horse, the 6th Duke of Portland, expressed his concern about the poor accommodation available for the state and other royal carriages. There wasn't enough cover for them, he complained, and the recently erected temporary coach houses were inadequate, particularly considering that there were one or two more 'dress carriages' to be added to the inventory. Portland wanted to know if a new, permanent coach house could be built to replace the temporary ones.[2]

Meanwhile, a letter from the Crown Equerry, Henry Ewart, on 15 February highlights the fact that there was no money to deal with the interior of the coach house's accommodation. A great deal of money had already been spent throughout the 1890s on sanitation and the married men's quarters, and by the turn of the century there was even more pressure to accommodate the new king and queen's own modes of transportation.[3]

Matters grew worse as it became clear, at the end of May, that there was also a need to cut back on the amount of water being used to clean the carriages, water the quadrangle and hose down the stable windows, since the water was now being supplied by the Chelsea Water Company, rather than being drawn directly from the Serpentine. However, the clerk of works didn't have the authority to ask the Master of the Horse to instruct his staff to save water.[4]

In fact, the amount of water used at the Royal Mews had been reduced of late because members of the royal family no longer used the royal carriages as often as they had used to.[5] The reasons for this – in particular with respect to the King – would become clear in time, and would present a whole new set of challenges. In the meantime, the wrangling over water usage continued, the row heightened by the Master of the Horse requesting that the windows of the Riding School, too, be cleaned on a monthly basis. It was a hectic time, and on top of everything else the Master of the Horse had to think about the preparations for the coming coronation.[6]

Things were quieter at Newmarket, however, because the court had entered a period of mourning. King Edward's horses ran under the Duke of Devonshire's name and in his straw colours, including Lauzan, who'd won the St James's Palace Stakes at Ascot. Diamond Jubilee ran there too, although as usual he was being difficult. The King always had sympathy for Marsh, knowing what it took for him to get the horse to run well.[7] Indeed, it was taking all of Marsh's efforts just to make the horse behave, and in July 1901 the horse reached new levels of aggressiveness by biting off a stablelad's finger as he was fixing the horse's bridle for the Princess of Wales's Stakes. Even Marsh was finding himself a target, as every time he approached Diamond Jubilee in his stable the horse would kick up a fuss and scream at him.[8] 'He tried his best to put years on my life,' Marsh recalled, amazed that he'd managed to remain so patient with him over the years. Even Herbert Jones' patience was sorely tested. Diamond Jubilee's most loyal jockey became a bag of nerves and unable to sleep at night, which in turn began to affect his health.[9]

As Diamond Jubilee eyed him suspiciously from his box, Marsh decided to keep his distance, not wanting to upset the horse further, and would approach him only when he really had to. It was obvious, however, that matters couldn't go on like this, and it was decided that the horse would be retired after the Jockey Club Stakes that autumn. The decision saddened the King, but he nevertheless congratulated Marsh on his efforts.

One day, the King turned up unannounced at Egerton House. 'I should like to speak to you privately, Marsh,' he informed the trainer. 'Have you a room where I can do so?'[10]

Marsh led his employer into his own private sitting room, feeling somewhat apprehensive. As he later wrote, 'Not having the slightest idea of what was to follow, I was wondering what was the matter.'[11]

The King came straight to the point. 'I want to present this Coronation medal to you,' he told the trainer, 'because now I consider you are one of the household. There is a miniature of it, and you should wear it with your evening clothes.'[12]

Marsh was dumbfounded and stammered his thanks. The award represented the culmination of all his work, the ultimate reward for his efforts and a measure of the faith that the King had in him. With it, however, came the sense that the best years had now come and gone. Indeed, with the retirement of Persimmon and Diamond Jubilee, and with no other horses to match their calibre, Marsh could see 'a lean time' ahead, partly reflected in the fact that the Duke of Devonshire took over the King's horses during the period of mourning. Marsh liked the Duke but found him too quiet, and the trainer didn't have the same easy rapport with him as he did with the King.

Marsh could also foresee a change in the development of the bloodlines at the Royal Mews, noting that there was too much of a dependency on Galopin blood, from which St Simon, Persimmon and Diamond Jubilee were descended. He feared that over-breeding would cause the strain to deteriorate.[13]

At this time, changes were taking place at Ascot, too. First of all, the Royal Buckhounds were disbanded, the Master of the Buckhounds' title being transformed into the King's Representative at Ascot, a post whose first incumbent was Viscount Churchill, an absolute stickler for form and etiquette. There were also structural changes taking place at Ascot of interest to the new king, such as the demolition in August 1901 of the three stands in the Royal Enclosure and the stabling for the royal carriages and horses, along with that of the old police barracks, although the Metropolitan Police office and the post office would remain.[14]

In September 1901, Messrs John Allen and Sons of Kilburn were commissioned to build two stands and a new weighing room at a total cost of £28,350, plus a further £7,950 if the work was completed by 1 May of the following year. There were also plans to build a third stand, costing £27,636, and in keeping with the need to modernise the Otis Elevator Company were paid £5,740 to install lifts. The work being done at Ascot seemed to be constant, the authorities apparently determined to have the site completed before the King's coronation so that the races could provide an additional focus for celebration. By April 1902, the renovations were largely completed, with the three new stands – the Jockey Club Stand, the Royal Stand and the Royal Enclosure Stand – in place, each providing a better view of the course.[15]

By the time of the coronation, however, the King's move from Marlborough House to Buckingham Palace still wasn't totally complete – at least, as far as the King's carriages were concerned. Back in December 1901,[16] the Crown Equerry, Henry Ewart, had requested the building of a temporary coach house at the palace as soon as possible, as seventeen carriages were expected to be arriving there in the following February and would need accommodation. To add to his woes, the King's medical officers had condemned the current quarters for the single men. Ewart appealed to Viscount Esher at the Master of the Horse's Office and asked if there was any money available and, if so, would he consider handing it over? Esher replied that he'd do what he could. Then, in the new year, Ewart wrote a short letter back, thanking him but reiterating the urgency of the single men's quarters. Thus began the usual round of queries as to who should pay for what and when.[17]

Soon preparations were in place for the King's coronation, scheduled to take place in July 1902. In his determination that everyone would enjoy it, the King had special cards made inviting members of the public to a street party on Coronation Day. He'd even come up with the wording on the cards so that everyone would know that they'd come from him personally.[18]

Then, just days before the coronation, the King fell ill. He remained determined to go ahead with the coronation ceremony, however, as the Duke of Portland discovered on a visit to Windsor Castle, the King having requested his presence in order to wish him luck in the Gold Cup, due to take place that afternoon. 'Everyone in the Castle knew that King Edward was unwell,' the Duke wrote, 'but I was dismayed . . . to find His Majesty in a chair, his face as white as a sheet, and beads of perspiration on his forehead . . . I added how extremely sorry I was to see him so unwell and in such pain. "Yes, I feel rather bad," His Majesty replied, "but don't for one moment think I shall not be crowned next week. I have made up my mind to go through with it, and nothing will induce me to disappoint my people."'[19]

After Portland's horse, William the Third, won the Gold Cup, the Duke returned to the castle to find the King in a worse state, and by the time Edward returned to London the following Monday it was obvious that he had appendicitis and needed an operation. So desperate was he to attend his own coronation,[20] however, that he refused to admit that he was seriously ill and was literally hours from death before he agreed to go under the knife.

The coronation was postponed and the operation went ahead. It proved to be a success and *The Times* was soon reporting that the King was doing well, due to his robust constitution.[21] Part of the coronation celebrations went ahead in celebration of the King's recovery, and the government granted a half-day holiday.[22]

Less of a cause for celebration, however, was the news in the same month that the King's one-time jockey, Jack Watts, having continued racing for five more years after Persimmon's Derby win, was taken ill at Sandown Park. It proved to be a short illness and the jockey died ten days later.[23]

The coronation eventually took place on 9 August. Once it was over and out of the way, however, the Royal Mews found itself facing yet another dilemma.

On 12 August 1902, Henry Ewart wrote to the Secretary of the Office of Works expressing his concern at the cost of first putting up and then taking down the temporary stalls at the Riding School. Was the Master of the Horse Department expected to pay for it, or were the costs to be included in the Office of Works' coronation expenses? In the same letter he pointed out that the floor of the Riding School had been made unsafe by the holes made by posts and would have to be relaid, so if the cost was to be met by the Master of the Horse then the account would need to be sent quickly.[24]

Back came the reply that the Office of the Master of the Horse would meet the costs. Everything was in hand with the Riding School's floor and the account would be sent.

By 11 September, however, work on the school's floor had still yet to begin. The Office of the Master of the Horse sent out an urgent request to fix the problem post haste, as horses were scheduled to be trained there throughout the autumn and winter. It also needed to be in good order for the royal family on their return from Scotland. A week later, the office received a reply to the effect that the work would be completed as soon as possible.[25]

As 1902 rolled into 1903, the King's horse Ambush II was being prepared to participate in the Grand National at Aintree on 27 March. This was Edward's first National as monarch and his reception at Liverpool was reminiscent of the coronation celebrations. Proceeding from Knowsley Hall to Aintree in the company of Lord and Lady Derby and Lord Roberts, the company was preceded by outriders and piloted by postillions,[26] while the *Liverpool Echo* noted the presence of other dignitaries, too, including the Russian Ambassador. Such a glamorous event compensated for the weather, which had been very bad the previous day,[27] along with the fact that, although Ambush II was heading a list of promising runners, the horse wasn't enjoying the same form with which he'd secured the 1900 Grand National. *The Sporting Life* magazine described his recent performances as disappointing, although the publication affirmed that its faith in his ability to win the National was still strong, pointing out that once again Manifesto was really the only threat to his chances. In the event, Ambush II ran a fairly good race until he stumbled and fell, although he was just one of a number of fallers. The race was eventually won by a horse named Drumcree, while Manifesto came third.

Back in London, several months later, the Royal Mews was having to deal with another of the King's loves: collecting motor cars. The present motor house was inadequate to house his collection as what little lighting and heating it boasted were run on gas, thereby making the building dangerous for the storing of motor vehicles. The Master of the Horse therefore requested that two small coach houses in the back mews be converted as soon as possible and fitted with roofs, as well as being provided with hot water, heating and electric lighting.[28]

At that time the King's collection comprised five cars, and there was every likelihood that he'd obtain more, so Ewart didn't think that even these changes went far enough. The Office of Works therefore suggested the construction of a new building in the back mews behind the coach house, which would cost around £600. However, lack of sufficient funds compelled the Office of Works to inform the Office of the Master of the Horse that the project would have to wait, since others took priority.[29]

At the Grand National of 25 March 1904, the King led another royal procession as he left Knowsley Hall, complete with an escort of police and outriders. Security that year, under Superintendent Baxendale's vigilant eye, was tight, so there was no trouble en route. Even so, crowds lined the streets and a huge cheer was heard when the monarch reached Aintree. The procession entered the racecourse from the Melling Road entrance, and once the King had reached the royal box, he stayed there for the rest of the afternoon.[30]

That year, Ambush II again headed the list of probable runners, just above Manifesto. The weather also complemented the occasion and was crisp, clear and sunny. Once again, despite his performance the previous year, faith was strong in the King's horse and even the ground was in his favour. However, he failed once more, falling, losing his rider and galloping off before getting in the way of Detail at the Canal Turn. The race was won by the New Zealand horse Moifa, while Manifesto – Ambush II's greatest rival – came eighth.[31] Despite his poor performance, however, it was decided that Ambush II would race again at Aintree.

By April 1904, the stables at the Royal Mews had made further inroads to modernity, growing into a vast area. In addition to the Riding School, stables and coach houses, there were adjacent engine- and boiler rooms; the Office of Works premises, which stood adjacent to the stores, across the way from the Riding School; one of three switch rooms, sandwiched between the Riding School and the coach house; a small racquet court; and further office areas.[32] The administration of the place, too, was clearly in evidence, with both the superintendent of the mews and the Secretary of the Privy Purse having residences on site. Horse management, too, had been modernised at the mews; two of the stable blocks had additional sick boxes, and there was also an onsite surgery.[33]

While the royal household, too, might have felt the effects of modernisation, certain traditions remained. When the King's horse Mead – ridden by Herbert Jones – won the Prince of Wales's Stakes at Ascot (a victory that saw a rendition of 'God Save The King' being drowned out by 'For He's A Jolly Good Fellow), the Royal Enclosure was kept for the exclusive use of the elite, thanks to the tyrannical efforts of Viscount Churchill. The King was also strict, although he did allow distinguished actors to attend – much to Churchill's chagrin, since acting was still regarded by some to be a lowly profession. Divorced people were, however, most certainly not allowed in the enclosure.[34]

Then, on 18 February 1905, tragedy hit the royal stable when Ambush II, in preparation for that year's Grand National, was taken for a strong gallop at the Curragh and promptly dropped down dead after only two miles. With the National just weeks away, it was vital that a replacement be found and trained quickly – no mean feat. Nevertheless, before the end of the month the King had bought Moifa,[35] winner of the 1904 Grand National.

On 31 March at Aintree, the market price for the New Zealander remained steady and he was a firm favourite, with one correspondent describing him as a born fencer.[36] The weather had been favourable, too, and the King's presence seemed to make the day complete, although there had been a panic that morning when Moifa's jockey, George Williamson, broke his arm and had to be replaced.[37] The royal party were sympathetic and Lord Marcus sent a letter on behalf of the King, conveying his thanks for all he'd done to assist Moifa in his training. Moifa did not win (in fact, he ran unplaced, the title going to a horse named Kirkland),[38] but as he made his way back to Huyton Station the King was congratulated as if he had won. The following Saturday, George Williamson received a cheque from the King.

Then, in October 1905, King Edward attended Newmarket. As the Honourable George Lambton commented, 'There was no place where the King was happier than at Newmarket, riding out in the morning to see his horses work, going to tea at Egerton House after the races to see them in the stable: he, for the moment, was free from the cares of state, for, greatly as he appreciated the lighter side of life, his capacity for hard work was even greater, and no man in any station of life fulfilled his duties with greater ability or more conscientiously than King Edward.'[39]

Unlike those at Newmarket, the paddocks at Hampton Court Park didn't suit the King's purpose, and so the stud there was reduced, the grazing let to dairy farmers.[40]

At the end of the year, Diamond Jubilee was sold to the Argentine breeder Señor Ignatio Correas for an as yet undisclosed sum.[41] The horse had made such an impression on the racing world – for good or bad – that he's still remembered today as one of the world's best racehorses, the only monarch's horse to date to have achieved the Triple Crown and therefore an extremely hard act to follow.

Meanwhile, Marsh was right in thinking that nothing would ever be the same again in the racing world, and by 1907 the stables' fortunes were so low that the King leased six yearlings from the Royal Stud.

The following year, 1908, didn't begin well. In January, Lord Marcus informed the King by telegram that Persimmon had broken his pelvis,[42] and then by February the 1896 Derby winner was dead. Such was the affection and esteem that people had for Persimmon that the famous Russian jeweller Carl Fabergé made a silver statue of him. Later, in February 1910, the King presented Persimmon's skeleton to the British Natural History Museum, where the skeleton of Eclipse was also housed.

Then, on the morning of 2 April, further tragedy struck at the Duke of Portland's Welbeck Stud when Persimmon's sire, St Simon, suddenly fell over on his way back from exercise. Five minutes later, he was dead, at the grand old age of 27. The cause of his death was unclear – either from heart disease or senile decay – but he was given a lengthy obituary in *The Times*. A very spirited racehorse, with a temperament to match, he'd been almost as bad as his son, Diamond Jubilee, and had seen off so many stablehands that no one would approach him unless he was wearing a muzzle. He was afraid of nothing but horse boxes and, oddly, open umbrellas.[43]

In June the King attended Ascot, where a new stand that he'd suggested – the Five Shilling Stand (later known as the Silver Ring Stand) – had been constructed at a cost of £30,000. Perhaps more so then than at any other time in its history, Ascot was the epitome of style and elegance, highlighting the wealth, prestige and confidence not just of the Edwardian era but of the entire British Empire.[44]

At the end of August, the stables at Egerton Stud took delivery of six colts – LaLa, Moorcock, Calderstone, Oakmere, Prince Pippin and Minoru – from the Tully Stud, just outside Kildare in Ireland. 'All apparently were regarded as promising,' wrote Marsh, whose eye was nonetheless caught by Minoru, who he described as 'the gentleman of that little party from Ireland'.[45] Minoru's limbs were light but well shaped, wrote Marsh, who believed that he looked every inch the racehorse. 'I was just the slightest bit afraid that he might not be robust enough to stand training.'[46]

These fears were groundless, however, and the colt thrived and was found to have a gentle disposition. He also became something of a pet at Egerton, and

Marsh's small daughter would feed him carrots.[47] Unfortunately Minoru proved to be a disappointing runner as a two-year-old, although he won the Great Surrey Foal Stakes at Epsom. Marsh gave him a gallop and realised that he had Derby potential, but in this the trainer had more faith in the horse's abilities than Beresford did and bad weather was hindering any progress that might have been made. By now Minoru was proving to be quite easy to train, being possessed of an easygoing nature, and Marsh, having considered pulling him out of the Classics, changed his mind and entered him for the Greenham Stakes at Newbury and the 2,000 Guineas at Newmarket, both of which the horse won, under Herbert Jones.[48]

As time passed, Marsh refrained from training Minoru too hard for the Derby. 'He had not been overdone for the 2,000 Guineas,' he recalled, 'and the last thing he wanted was a severe or even orthodox preparation for the Derby.'[49]

Meanwhile, the King wanted to be kept fully informed of Minoru's progress, and Marsh was confident enough to provide glowing reports, unlike those of previous years with Persimmon and Diamond Jubilee. Even though Bayard (the original favourite for the 2,000 Guineas) was making great progress and was Minoru's chief opposition, this didn't concern him too much. However, perhaps because of Persimmon and Diamond Jubilee, he was always wary.[50] 'No one can understand what tense moments these are for a trainer,' he confessed.[51]

As Derby day approached, Marsh began to feel the strain with Minoru, particularly since, at the same time, the future of Egerton Stud was in doubt. Around two weeks before the event, there was talk of the King removing his horses from Egerton because keeping them there was so expensive. 'One felt,' wrote Marsh, 'that certain people behind the scenes were pressing His Majesty to take the course of leaving.'[52]

The trainer was in a quandary. What should he do? Train privately elsewhere for the King or stay where he was and have to start all over again with new owners? The prospect of running Egerton Stud without the patronage of King Edward after almost twenty years was a depressing one. When Beresford (who liked the idea of the King leaving Egerton no less than Marsh did) finally announced that the King did intend to leave, Marsh took the only course of action left open to him and approached one of his neighbours who was also a particularly close friend of the King's: Lillie Langtry.[53] 'I almost at once encountered her out at the sale paddocks at Newmarket,' he wrote, 'and asked her, should an opportunity present itself, whether she would put before His Majesty the case of Lord Marcus and myself for staying on at Egerton.'[54]

Lillie agreed to approach the King. In fact, she did so twice, and once she had the answer she wanted, contacted Marsh and told him that the King had changed his mind. As it turned out, the King had reversed his decision only reluctantly, and when he appeared at Egerton for a group photograph with Minoru he peevishly informed Marsh of his intention to stay. Marsh didn't care; the King's continued patronage meant that he could now concentrate on the Derby.

On the day of the event, Marsh reported, '[Herbert] Jones . . . was smartly away, and he rode the horse in the first three or four furlongs most judiciously.'[55] Another of the King's horses, Sir Martin, fell and Marsh later noted in his autobiography that if Minoru had done the same he'd have had the shock of his life. Minoru secured the rails, however, and swept the remainder of the course, with Jones keeping him perfectly balanced. Nonetheless, the finish was an extremely close one and Marsh, watching from the trainers' stand, had to wait like everyone else for the numbers to come up. 'In my heart I felt Minoru had just won,' he later wrote, 'but I could not be sure . . . There was that awful pause and then I knew.'[56]

When Minoru's number came up first, the course erupted, the crowd surging around Jones as he walked Minoru back to the weighing-in enclosure. The King and the Prince of Wales came down to receive the reins, but the thronging crowd pushed them back. 'In vain did I try to force my way through to the horse,' Marsh remembered, 'until at last I shouted to the crowd to let me through.'[57] Finally he had the reins and was able to lead Minoru back to King Edward, who was jubilant at the horse's success. 'Though I recall now,' added Marsh, 'how the excitement seemed almost too much for him. Certainly during those minutes he must have undergone a most severe mental strain from what I might describe as the shock of victory.'[58]

Soon the crowd were raising a lusty chorus of 'God Save the King'. As George Lambton wrote later, 'I think . . . when Minoru won for [Edward] as King of England that the enthusiasm was even greater. The police were then quite unable to cope with the crowd, who patted the King on the back, and shook him by the hand with cries of: "Good old Teddie."'[59]

Later that year, on 17 June 1909, the King saw Minoru run in the St James's Palace Stakes. At first the pace was set by a horse named The Story, but after a quarter of a mile Minoru overtook him and won by two lengths. The King and Queen were delighted, the former raising his hat several times to the crowd's applause.[60]

Minoru went on to win the Sussex Stakes at Goodwood and then came fourth in the St Leger. He ended the season winning a free handicap with

Danny Maher (Jones had taken a fall) by a neck, and after the race Danny was delighted when the King sought him out in the weighing-in room to shake his hand.[61]

Unfortunately, Minoru's run of successes was short-lived. In 1910 he developed eye trouble and ran unplaced in the City and Suburban races. He was later sold in 1913 and was taken to Russia, where he subsequently disappeared.

King Edward, meanwhile, continued with his busy schedule, giving a Jockey Club dinner at the end of May and, in June, attending Ascot before going on to Newmarket. Then it was off to Goodwood and Ascot once more, before Doncaster in September and Newmarket in October.

Over the years, King Edward's horse-racing career had been quite successful, unlike that of his mother's uncles, the Hanoverians. He won £20,000 in 1909, was never in arrears with Weatherbys' and earned £270,000 in stallion fees during his whole race career.[62]

By this time, however, his health was deteriorating, and although at the beginning of May 1910 no one thought that his condition was too serious, on Friday 6 May he took a turn for the worse.

'On my way through London to Kempton Park,' wrote Marsh, 'I called at Buckingham Palace to make personal inquiry regarding the King's condition, and at the same time ascertain what the wishes were about [the horse] Witch of the Air keeping her engagement to run.'[63] Sir Francis Knollys came down to meet Marsh and confirmed that the King was very ill but would not go to bed and was, in fact, seated in his armchair, fully dressed. 'I suggested,' Marsh continued, 'that it might be unwise to run Witch of the Air in the circumstances, but Sir Francis at once assured me that the King had ordered her to run.'[64] She was, indeed, expected to win at Kempton Park, as she'd done well in a trial with her three-year-old sister, Vain Air, so Marsh continued on to Kempton Park.

As if fate intended to crown the King's racing career, Witch of the Air won her race. 'The crowd on the racecourse, realising something of the gravity of His Majesty's illness, did not know whether to cheer, as they were accustomed to do on the occasion of a royal win, or be silent,'[65] noted Marsh, who felt a bit unnerved by the atmosphere at the course and wanted to leave as quickly as possible.

The news of Witch of the Air's victory was relayed immediately to Buckingham Palace by telegraph, and the King – by now at last having been persuaded to go to bed – conveyed his pleasure at the result. Six hours later, just before midnight, he was dead.[66]

Much later, Lord Marcus would make sure that Marsh knew of the King's delight at his horse's win, and the following morning people awoke to the news that their king of nine years was dead. The first his grandson, Prince Albert ('Bertie'), knew about it was when he looked out of a window at Marlborough House and saw the royal standard flying at half mast over Buckingham Palace.

As expected, *The Sporting Life* magazine devoted a great deal of coverage to the King as an all-round sportsman – a hunter, a dog lover and racehorse owner. No other king before him had received such a tribute, especially by the press, and on 11 May *The Times* described how he had excelled as a huntsman and a yachtsman, while he'd also been at the top of his league in shooting and, of course, racing. He is still, to date, the only monarch to have secured the Derby – not once but twice – and the Grand National.

Although Edward VII was a first-class competitor in all of the sports he engaged in and devoted equal energy to all, he was also very shrewd and had a good understanding of those about him. On 16 May, the *Daily Mirror* ran the headline 'EDWARD THE PEACEMAKER AT REST'[67] above a photograph of the late king that dominated the rest of the front page, while much of the rest of the paper was devoted to coverage of the King's life, picking up on the fact that he'd ended it on a high note with Witch of the Air's success. The sporting world, too, paid homage to such a celebrated patron who had taken the prestige of horse-racing to new heights, and as a mark of respect many race meetings were cancelled (even though the King himself would probably have wanted them to continue) while some – the Whitsuntide meeting at Hurst Park, scheduled for 16–17 May and the Ayr Meeting for 18–19 May – were postponed.

'As a sportsman,' wrote George Lambton, 'he was by far the most popular man in England . . . It is when you get the rivalry of such men and horses . . . that racing deserves the title of "The Sport of Kings".'[68]

Notes:

1. 'The Royal Mews', WORK 19/50 1901–1905 (National Archives document)
2. Henry Ewart (Crown Equerry) to the Viscount Esher, KCVO, 08.02.1901, WORK 19/50 (National Archives document)
3. 'The Royal Mews', WORK 19/50 15.02.1901 (the Crown Equerry, Royal Mews) (National Archives document)
4. 'Memoranda: The Royal Mews, Supply of Water for Washing Carriages', 25.05.1901, WORK 19/50 (National Archives document)
5. Letter from Henry Ewart, Crown Equerry, to Viscount Esher 17.06.1901, WORK 19/50 (National Archives Document)
6. 'Memoranda: W Westcott', 03.07.1901, WORK 19/50 (National Archives document)
7. Marsh, p226
8. Marsh, p227
9. Marsh, pp224–8

10. Marsh, p229
11. Ibid.
12. Ibid.
13. Ibid.
14. Magee and Aird, p128
15. Magee and Aird, pp128–9
16. Black bordered letter from Henry Ewart to Viscount Esher, 05.12.1901, WORK 19/50 (National Archives document)
17. Reply to above
18. Van Der Kiste, *Queen Victoria's Children*
19. Portland, pp66–7
20. Ibid.
21. Ibid.
22. *The Times*, 02.07.1902
23. Van Der Kiste, *Queen Victoria's Children*, p95
24. Letter from Henry Ewart to the Secretary of the Office of Works, 12.08.1902, WORK 19/50 (National Archives document)
25. Letter to the Secretary of the Office of Works, 11.09.1902, WORK 19/50 (National Archives document)
26. *The Liverpool Echo*, 28.03.1903
27. *The Sporting Life*, 27.03.1903
28. Letter from Henry Ewart to the Secretary of the Office of Works, 09.03.1904, WORK 19/50 (National Archives document)
29. Letter from J B Westcott to the Secretary of the Office of Works, 10.03.1904; reply letter to the Crown Equerry, 14.04.1904, WORK 19/50 (National Archives document)
30. *The Liverpool Echo*, 26.03.1904
31. *The Sporting Life*, 25.03.1904
32. WORK 19/50 April 1904 (National Archives document)
33. WORK 19/50 1904 (National Archives document)
34. Magee and Aird, pp132–3
35. *The Times*, 20.02.1905
36. *The Sporting Life*, 31.03.1905
37. Marsh, p22
38. *The Liverpool Echo*, 01.04.1905
39. Lambton, p236
40. Thurley, pp380–1
41. *The Times*, 11.12.1905
42. Mortimer, Onslow, Willet, p425
43. Portland, p35
44. Magee and Aird, p129
45. Marsh, p242
46. Marsh, p243
47. Ibid.
48. Marsh, p49
49. Marsh, p247
50. Marsh, p248
51. Marsh, p249
52. Marsh, p260
53. Marsh, p261

54. Ibid.
55. Marsh, p262
56. Marsh, p250
57. Marsh, p251
58. Ibid.
59. Lambton, p226
60. *The Times*, 18.06.1909
61. Tanner and Cranham, p119
62. Van Der Kiste, *Queen Victoria's Children*
63. Marsh, p263
64. Marsh, pp263–4
65. Marsh, p264
66. Rose
67. *The Times*, 11.05.1910; *Daily Mirror*, 16.05.1910
68. Lambton, p224

18
George V

By 23 May 1910 there was still some speculation about what was going to happen to King Edward's horses, since nothing had been made public. *The Times* wondered if the new king, George V, would adopt his father's colours, but it would become increasingly obvious over time that King George V had come to the throne very much in his father's shadow, at least as far as horse-racing was concerned. This posed a problem as his subjects expected him not only to follow in King Edward's footsteps[1] but also to measure up to his father's example as a sportsman. King Edward, after all, had helped to set new standards and had raised the sport of horse-racing to new heights of professionalism.

On George's accession, Sandringham Stud boasted eighteen broodmares, which the King intended to maintain both there and at Newmarket, putting paid to rumours that he intended to disperse or reduce the royal stable. Since he wasn't as amenable to change as his father had been, he wanted to keep things as they were, in all aspects of his life, and Lord Beresford and Richard Marsh found themselves part of this new traditionalism. King George relied upon Marsh to keep things running as he saw fit and gave the trainer total authority. From the beginning there was a mutual respect between the two; King George was very plain speaking – largely as a result of his time in the navy – and at times could be impatient and intolerant, but with Marsh he appeared to have all the time in the world.[2] As Marsh later wrote, 'If I may be permitted to say so with greatest respect, I at all times found King George a most human and kindly man.'[3]

However, the trainer hadn't realised that the new monarch's interest in horses was so deep-rooted and was somewhat surprised to note that 'King George is a better judge of a horse than was his father.'[4] When Marsh apologised for not having a two-year-old ready, 'His Majesty observed in reply, "Never hurry a horse for me, Marsh. When you tell me it is ready to run, I shall be quite satisfied. I would much sooner have a nice three-year-old than a two-year-old."'[5]

King George also intended to carry on hosting Jockey Club dinners, which is to his credit. He'd never enjoyed London society and was shy by nature, so events of this sort tended to be more of an ordeal than a pleasure for him. Nevertheless, whenever one of his horses won a race he would enter into the spirit by presenting each female guest at the dinner with a brooch bearing his racing colours of purple, scarlet and gold.

Throughout the summer of 1911, the King was set for a great many engagements and in May *The Times* announced that he would have to miss certain race meetings on account of them. One of those that he wouldn't be able to attend was at Newmarket, although he did attend a meeting there on 8 May, staying overnight at the same Jockey Club rooms[6] as those occupied by his father. That evening he dined at Palace House with his hosts, the Rothschilds,[7] the Earl and Countess of Derby and Lord Beresford. The public had waited a long time to see the King and the crowds at Newmarket cheered him as he was driven along the High Street towards Palace House. Another crowd there gave him an enthusiastic welcome and the King acknowledged them from the doorway of Leopold de Rothschild's residence by raising his hat three or four times before entering. The next day, he enjoyed his first race win when his horse Pintadeau won at the course.

The King enjoyed only modest success on the racecourse between 1910 and 1914, but he didn't mind this as he generally enjoyed the race meetings more than the racing itself and would always be more interested in breeding horses than racing them. Those first four years of his reign, however, were representative of British confidence, a time when the royal family was more popular than it had ever been and headed one of the greatest empires ever seen. At that time, more than any other in the sport's history, horse-racing reflected patriotism and the confidence that the public had in its monarchy.

At Ascot on 13 June 1911, a beautifully warm day, the atmosphere was exuberant, attendance was huge and *The Times* described the meeting as 'cosmopolitan'.[8] Indeed, more and more people sought admission to the royal box, including distinguished visitors from abroad who wouldn't normally be seen at Ascot.

That day, the King and Queen Mary attended in state, driving from Windsor Castle and coming within sight of the New Mile just after one o'clock. The crowds were hugely enthusiastic, delighting the royal couple, who arrived to the sounds of the Royal Marines band (Portsmouth Division) playing the National Anthem.

A week later, on 22 June, King George V and Queen Mary were crowned, and in December they travelled to India for their coronation as emperor and empress.

ALL THE KINGS' HORSES

At this time, just before World War One, horse-racing was still central to the international stage, and we're provided with one of the final glimpses of the extent of the sport in European society before the war began. On the night of 5 June 1912, while the King was entertaining the Jockey Club, the Duchess of Devonshire was hosting the Derby-night ball. Among her guests were the German, Russian and Austro-Hungarian Ambassadors and, among the royal guests, the Queen's family, the Tecks, and members of the King's family: the Schleswig-Holsteins and the Battenbergs.

The old traditions that still persisted around this time were complemented by new, modern ideas, and nowhere was this more evident than at Ascot. On 18 June 1912, the King and Queen drove there in state from Windsor, arriving just after 1 p.m., their landau being drawn by four bay horses with postillions in Ascot livery. Scarlet-coated outriders preceded the royal carriage, and beside them rode two equerries while seven other landaus – drawn by two bays – transported their guests. On the entourage's arrival, they were warmly received and the Royal Marines played the National Anthem. *The Times* described the scene as the most picturesque in the world, and for the very first time a motorised omnibus was seen on the Heath, complying with a new regulation allowing motor vehicles to be parked behind the rails opposite the grandstand. New gates had also been erected, linking up the Royal Enclosure with the paddock, which provided a continuous expanse of lawn along the rails – a welcome change, as the paddock had always been a favourite meeting place for the royal guests between the races.

The Queen, however, didn't always attend the races. On 31 October, for instance, she abstained from visiting Newmarket to make a surprise visit to the Disabled Soldiers' and Sailors' Workshop at Brompton Road, London, laden with Christmas presents, whilst at Newmarket the King presented his jockey – a man named F. Foy – with a gold-mounted riding whip for having ridden three winners in the royal colours. He also contributing £5 to a pension fund for 'Old Kate', a race-card and button-hole seller. On the whole, though, it was a mixed day with appalling weather of cold winds and driving rain.

One race that stands out even today as being the most significant of George V's reign was the Epsom Derby of 4 June 1913. On this occasion the King's horse Anmer (named after a village on the Sandringham estate) was due to run, with Herbert Jones up. Although not many rated the horse's chances, he ran a good race until a woman ran onto the course, possibly to grab his reins. She was knocked to the ground and Anmer was subsequently brought down with her, rolling onto his jockey. Fortunately, Jones escaped serious injury, despite having a foot in the stirrup and being dragged some yards. He was carried unconscious to the weighing-in room while the woman was taken to Epsom Cottage Hospital. Jones later recovered consciousness, with slight concussion and cuts and bruises, but the woman was less fortunate and later died of 'concussion of the brain'. The labelling in her clothing identified her as 'E. Davison', and further enquiry led to her being identified as the suffragette Emily Davison. While the Queen inquired after her, the King made inquiries after Jones, Marsh and Anmer. The incident was caught both on film and by camera.

Then, as a final dramatic note on what had already been a shocking day, it was announced that the favourite, Craganour, had been disqualified and the stewards declared that Aboyeur had won the race.

The fact that Emily Davison chose the King's horse as a vehicle with which to turn a social event into a political one demonstrates Epsom's enduring importance as a social event. Davison achieved unprecedented national status for her cause, placing the suffragette movement on a new, extremist level, although even today it's still not clear whether or not she meant to kill herself. Every now and again the film and photographs are re-examined. As she comes onto the course, she raises her hands, and it's unclear at this point whether she intended to throw herself in front of the horse or whether she meant only to try to stop it. Either way, 4 June 1913 is a Derby day that's still remembered over ninety years later.

At this time, evidence of social change was all around. At Ascot on 17 June 1913 there were 120 motor cars – 119 more than had been there the previous year – and the vehicle now seemed to be an essential requirement at the racecourse. However, it was a mixed blessing, heralding progress but lacking the air of dignity possessed by carriages.

At that year's event at Ascot, there were fewer people in the Royal Enclosure than had been there the previous year. Although a fair number of royalty were present, *The Times* groused that the fashions, although beautiful, didn't have one colour that stood out as unusual. The newspaper also noted with disapproval that some men went against tradition by wearing white duck trousers, morning coat and tall hat.[9]

That year, the King had many horses lined up for many races, but one steed that showed great potential was Friar Marcus, listed in *The Times* on 20 January 1914. He had developed well and had responded to training, and Marsh wrote that 'at all times he was very much a favourite. Perhaps it was due to the fact that he was so very kind and good-tempered.'[10] He was an excellent sprinter and, being very strong, was never beaten as a two-year-old, and on 16 April he won the Maiden Plate with ease. He would then go on to win all five races in which he participated in 1914, despite becoming ill just before Ascot.

Just after Friar Marcus's Ascot win in 1914, the King and Queen travelled to France. While Mary enjoyed travelling abroad, particularly if she had the opportunity to take in the cultural delights of the country she was visiting, George did not and had never taken the trouble to master French or German. On this occasion, however, he was compelled to go. Having visited the British Hospital and the Exhibition of Decorative Art at the Louvre on 23 May, the royal couple were among the luncheon guests at the Marquis de Breteuil's house, situated in the Avenue du Bois de Boulogne in Paris. At 2.20 p.m. they left the residence, whereupon they were greeted by a large crowd standing outside the house. They then entered the royal carriage – drawn by four horses and preceded by outriders – and proceeded slowly to allow people time to see them.[11]

Their next stop was the Auteuil race meeting, which, given the beautiful weather, promised to be a successful one. In the spirit of Anglo-French relations, the principal races were named in the King and Queen's honour, dubbed 'York Cottage', 'Balmoral', 'Windsor Castle', 'Buckingham Palace' and 'Sandringham', and there were English as well as French competitors. In the event, however, the French horses proved to be superior.[12]

Within days of arriving back in England, the King journeyed over to Newmarket, where he again stayed overnight, arriving at his private rooms at the Jockey Club just after 1.30 p.m. After lunch he attended the races and watched Friar Marcus in his preparations for the maiden two-year-old race. The horse was fully fit now, having recovered from his illness, and went on to win the race. Later the King travelled to Egerton House to inspect his horses at the stables there and returned to his rooms at 7 p.m.[13]

The following day the King watched from the Jockey Club's stand as his filly Symbolism won the first race of the day, the Wilbraham Plate, by a head. This success was something of a surprise, as Symbolism hadn't been expected to win, but nevertheless she'd had the lead for some two hundred yards before the finish to eventually beat Premiere. Her victory augured well for the 2,000 Guineas, for which Friar Marcus had trained well but couldn't gain the mile, losing to Sir John Thursby's Kennymore. It was decided then not to force the horse for fear of damaging his speed, so he wasn't prepared for the Derby, either, although he did go on to win the Middle Park Plate.[14]

On 27 May – Derby day – both the King and Queen were present at Epsom along with members of the British, German and Russian royal families. *The Times* reported that the crowd attendance ranged from 350,000 to 400,000 and a great many were brought by a large number of omnibuses.

That year's event wasn't the most auspicious occasion for the King, however, as his horse Brakespear, with Herbert Jones up, ran unplaced. The race was won by Durbar II.[15]

That evening the King gave his usual dinner to members of the Jockey Club at Buckingham Palace, the meal being served to the 56 guests in the state dining room. The Queen, meanwhile, attended the Derby-night ball, hosted by the Duchess of Devonshire at Devonshire House, where the guests included the Russian, Austro-Hungarian, American, Spanish, French, Italian, Turkish and German Ambassadors as well as other ministers from Greece, China, Denmark, the Netherlands, Belgium, Argentina and Chile – representatives of millions of people, all under the one roof.[16]

Two days later, Friar Marcus won the Great Surrey Foal Stakes at Epsom by three lengths after keeping and maintaining a strong lead. Before the month closed, this victory on behalf of the King was followed by Vervaine's narrow success in the Redfern Two-Year-Old Plate, where, running under Richard Marsh's name, he won by a head. Then Sunni's success in the Red Rose Stakes provided the King with his seventh stakes win that season and put him at sixth place in the list of winning owners. Despite her success, however, Sunni was still considered moderate, although she had four more engagements booked the following week at Ascot,[17] which the King and Queen attended in the company of a great many guests, including foreign dignitaries.

On 22 June 1914, the Trooping of the Colour provided the public with a procession as the King led the guards along the Mall to the Victoria Memorial instead of having them dismissed at Horse Guards. This change from the normal routine was witnessed by other members of the royal family – the King's mother, Queen Alexandra; her sister, Empress Marie of Russia; the Battenbergs; and the Connaughts[18] – from the Levee Room at Horse Guards. Little did the public realise that, behind the scenes, a storm was looming and that what they were witnessing was the calm before it.

On 28 June 1914, Archduke Franz Ferdinand of Austria and his wife were assassinated in Sarajevo by the Serbian Gavrilo Princip. As the ensuing crisis in Europe escalated, the King cancelled his 26 July visit to Goodwood, where Friar Marcus won the first race on Cup day as well as the Prince of Wales Stakes by a head. Two days later, Austria declared war on Serbia, and by 1 August Russia (Serbia's ally) and Germany (Austria's ally) were at war. Since both Russia and France were allies of Great Britain, the British government had no option but to make an ultimatum to Germany, but when Germany failed to respond to this war between the two countries was declared on Monday 4 August (a bank holiday in England).

When World War One first broke out, the majority of the British population saw it as one big adventure and few feared that their lives would change to any great degree. Almost immediately, however, the racing world was affected when, 24 hours after war was declared, *The Times* reported that the government was requisitioning all horse boxes, although it also announced that the Brighton meeting would still go ahead. Nevertheless, with the government seizing the boxes, the paper concluded that meetings all over the country would be severely affected, particularly since there had been no statement from the Jockey Club on the matter.[19]

In fact, the Jockey Club was anxious to preserve normality as far as possible, largely because none of its members could agree on what course of action to take. Meetings arranged months earlier were still scheduled to take place and horses and race meetings were still being prepared for the following year. The hiatus in racing, however, was costing owners and trainers dearly, while manpower was being drained as huge numbers of men enlisted to fight. It was an unprecedented situation in racing history; never before had it been suggested that meetings should be suspended or abandoned for an indefinite period of time because of war. Up to 1914, the greatest events of the turf had continued to take place while many British subjects were fighting abroad, preserving the Empire. Now the Jockey Club was daunted to find itself discussing the black-and-white scenario of continuing with or abandoning these events, and its members found themselves split on an issue that could effectively destroy the sport.

The minutes from a Jockey Club meeting held on 16 September 1914 reveal that the stewards were compelled to call a further meeting, not only to explain their reasons for allowing racing to continue but also to find out whether or not they should let it continue in the first place. The stewards felt that, if Newmarket was abandoned, the rest of the meetings would follow. They were wary of the future and the progress of the war but equally wary of the effects of a complete suspension of racing, both in the short and long term, and convinced that a total cessation of horse-racing would result in high unemployment. Horse-racing was, after all, a national industry, and there were thousands of stablemen and helpers employed by some 290 trainers across the country, most of whom were fighting overseas at that time but who had nevertheless been guaranteed before leaving that their jobs were safe. In addition there were 190 licensed jockeys and 210 apprentices currently employed, while 54 licensed racecourse companies employed gatekeepers, groundsmen and caterers. A full suspension, the Jockey Club concluded, would be ruinous. However, many considered that continuing with the sport was disrespectful to those fighting.

A compromise was eventually reached whereby it was recommended that racing should continue where local conditions would allow. Even here, though, the stewards were divided, and over the next few months they debated whether or not it should continue at all.

While the arguments were rolling back and forth, Buckingham Palace found itself having to adapt to the new situation. On 7 October the King gave the army permission to train in the Riding School, but the floor there was a problem in that the clay beneath it was still wet, a situation that was unlikely to change as the sawdust that needed to be scattered upon it had to be kept moist. The whole floor was therefore taken up, down to the original clay bed, on which was deposited a layer of broken brick followed by six inches of coarse sand. Then the old sawdust was relaid, followed by more sand and more sawdust.

To complicate matters further, the war was by this time affecting the costs and timescales of other works being done at the Royal Mews, and it was uncertain whether or not work could continue into 1915 or how much it would cost. The best option, it was decided, was to plan ahead and try to carry on as normally as possible, and to bring current plans to maturity so as not to waste money later.[20]

The following year, one of the national newspapers ran an article describing how wounded soldiers were being turned out of Epsom Grand Stand (which had been turned into a makeshift hospital) in order to make way for the running of the Derby. On reading this, the Duke of Portland wrote a letter to *The Times* expressing his belief that horse-racing should be suspended. In the letter, which appeared in the paper on 1 March, Portland observed that the French couldn't understand what role horse-racing had in the lives of fighting soldiers (the sport had come to a standstill in France), and neither could they understand why the soldiers were being turned out nor why their relatives were attending the race.[21]

The allegation that soldiers were being evicted from their hospital beds was vehemently denied by the senior steward, Lord Durham, who was incensed to think that anyone would believe that soldiers would be treated in a such a way. Nevertheless, Portland now believed that racing during wartime should be stopped – and he wasn't the only one who believed this.[22] The Jockey Club had been sent so many letters expressing similar sentiments that they resolved to hold a meeting to discuss the issue.

Meanwhile, *The Times* provided a balanced view, noting pleas for suspension and the difficulties that the horse-breeders were facing. Lord Derby, however, expressed his opinion that the sport should continue and a Mr Kemball Cook wrote that the French would think morale was extremely low if the Derby was stopped.[23]

In a letter published on 10 March in *The Times*, George Lambton explained not only how the races were a morale boost, particularly for wounded soldiers, but also how the top owners – even the Duke of Portland – had no intention of removing their horses from top events. Shortly after this, another letter was published giving reasons why it should be stopped (the railways were dislocated, there was too much pressure on police and the races would interfere with military training, although shopkeepers wouldn't suffer without them). Then yet another letter noted that, in those perilous times, most people were more concerned with taking care of the wounded. One Bernard Alderson wrote a letter to the newspaper condemning those who called for racing to continue when they themselves were attacking those striking for a fair wage. This was followed by quite a long letter criticising those taking luncheon at Epsom Grand Stand.

It seemed that horse-racing was a subject about which feelings ran extremely high, veering from seeing it banned altogether to calling for the troops' opinions on the matter.

Then, on 12 March *The Times* noted that racing had been suspended completely in France. The meeting at Thirsk in Yorkshire had also been abandoned, it reported.[24]

In the next day's edition of *The Times* there were calls for a compromise and articles arguing for keeping racing (e.g. for reasons of amusement) along with an article from Lord Curzon.

Three days later, at a special meeting held by the Jockey Club, Portland argued that, with the war having escalated, all energies should be concentrated on fighting, and racing was a distraction. The larger race meetings, he believed, should be stopped, leaving the smaller meetings to follow their example – or not. The breeding of horses would come to no harm if the sport was suspended for one or two seasons. Racing, too, could survive the ban, and the horses might even benefit from the rest. Employment would be unaffected, said Portland; stablehands could just take up other jobs to help with the war effort, returning to their former occupations once hostilities had ended.[25]

Lord Durham, meanwhile, argued in favour of continuing with horse-racing during wartime and convinced the Jockey Club's members that it should be kept going where conditions were more favourable. In fact, Lord Crewe expressed doubts that it was worth stopping all race meetings if the war was going to come to an end within the next twelve months, as the Duke of Portland had predicted. Lord Ilchester, however, believed that to continue to hold the meetings – particularly Ascot – would be misunderstood by the Allies.

At the special meeting, the only person even to hint that horse-racing might be used to raise morale was Sir Hedworth Meux. He pointed out that soldiers would be disappointed at being denied the chance of cheering on the King's horse Friar Marcus, for example, who had been unbeaten as a two-year-old in 1914 and in that year – 1915 – had won twice. No one should listen to scaremongering and agitation, he urged, and racing should continue.

The clerks of the courses then made their feelings known, and the general consensus at the meeting was that racing should continue on the grounds of business and morale. But, opinions would continue to veer between abandonment (for practical reasons) and continuance (in order to boost morale).

After the meeting, the Jockey Club was still wrestling with the question of whether or not racing should continue, and for once its members decided that they needed a higher authority to decide for them. That authority came in the shape of Walter Runciman, who wrote a letter dated 19 May 1915 to Captain Sir Henry Greer, a Jockey Club senior steward, informing him that, for practical reasons, the organisation would argue for the suspension of all meetings for the duration of the war, with the exception of Newmarket. This letter was published in *The Times* on the 20th, while a following article explained the decision and how it had been reached.[26]

The next day, the Jockey Club's reply appeared in the paper, in which the organisation pointed out that such a suspension would result in financial losses. Nevertheless, the meetings were generally opposed in the House of Commons. The stewards seemed happy to comply and responded with relief, saying that the government had only to say the word and racing would be stopped. The next day they gave official notice of fixture cancellations.

However, uncertainty over the progress of the war still created an air of insecurity. In addition, the burghers of Doncaster refused to have the St Leger run anywhere other than Town Moor, so the following year the government would be compelled to establish a September Stakes.[27]

In June 1915, the emergency powers of the Jockey Club were modified. And then at Ascot the races on the Tuesday were cancelled. The fixture, it was decreed, would now last only three days and the Gold Cup and Coventry Stakes would be moved to Newmarket. Meanwhile, part of the Grand Stand at Ascot would be used as an army recruitment office and another part would be used as a hospital, while King Edward's Five Shilling Stand would store medical supplies.

On 19 November the government announced that a limited number of meetings could take place across the country, under certain restrictions and as long as the railway services weren't compromised. Once again, the government was having to play a balancing act, seeking to keep the crowds to a minimum and gambling holiday-makers at bay in an attempt to maintain the races as a business venture rather than as a source of amusement. Entrance fees were therefore set at a minimum of 5s.

Then there was the Grand National to consider. At that stage, there was every hope that it would take place, especially among those trainers, who were working their horses in preparation for the great steeplechase the following spring.[28]

In January 1916, the Jockey Club's stewards requested to approach the government, and by the end of the month communication between them appeared to have reached a balance, although public opinion still veered sharply between all-out bans and saving the industry. Even so, on 11 February 1916 a new racing programme was published in *The Times*.[29]

On 3 May, *The Times* published complaints about those attending race meetings wasting valuable petrol. Soon after this, a new regulation was introduced: racing could not impede the progress of munitions, and the Minister of Munitions was given the authority to prevent meetings if it could be proved that holding them might do so. Anyone ignoring such a regulation would be in breach of the Defence of the Realm Regulations.[30]

On 8 December, plans were put forward for converting the Riding School into a dormitory for soldiers, with a new floor laid, partitions erected, sanitary arrangements in place and hoardings installed to shut off the palace grounds. The £350 it would cost to renovate the school was to be paid by the army. By the 14th the plans were approved and work began immediately.[31]

On 20 January 1917, washing facilities outside the dormitory were urgently requested, since the soldiers couldn't use the facilities at the Buckingham Palace Hotel before leaving for the front as they had to quit the premises very early in the morning. The project was approved by the 29th, and later a boiler would be added to heat water for cleaning purposes.[32]

That year, the Jockey Club held another meeting, this one to discuss facilities for racing. The same conditions for racing as the previous year still applied, and steeplechases would take place in January, February and March, but the same old arguments continued.

An article that appeared in *The Times* on 29 March gave details about which race meetings were still running at home and abroad, appearing alongside the casualty lists.

By 30 April, the government was calling for a complete cessation of horse-racing, officials in the War Cabinet arguing that it wasn't in the nation's best interests to allow it to carry on. This failed to impress many of the stewards, even though they were given two months' warning before all racing activities had to be suspended. They argued that racing had resumed in France back in May, albeit on a limited basis. Nevertheless, the government's intention was published in *The Times*, along with a list of all cancelled fixtures from 15 May to 2 November.

Over the next few weeks, fears that the racing and horse-breeding industries would never recover escalated, and on 31 May the War Emergency Committee of the Royal Agricultural Society urged the government to reconsider its position. By 19 June, a compromise of sorts had been reached, whereby the government allowed eight days of racing at Newmarket – the absolute minimum required to preserve the industry. Races resumed on 17 July and fixtures were made. At Ascot, however, the hospital was shut down and the building was taken over by the Royal Flying Corps, while a cinema opened on the Heath.[33]

In the midst of all this furore, it was felt that the interests of the horse breeders had to be protected, and so the Thoroughbred Breeders' Association was created, led by Lord D'Abernon.

By 1918, the progress of the war was changing. While matters were by no means certain, on 22 March *The Times* cheerfully provided details of that year's Gatwick races, announcing that special trains had been laid on and that an increased number of motor cars were present. Despite this success, however, there were more suspensions and restrictions in the months ahead. In that year, too, the Master of the Horse sought to reclaim the former stud lands at Hampton Court – an unpopular move as land was at a premium for the growing of food.

At the close of the season on 2 November, the Jockey Club was still trying to resolve the questions of what to do about the next season. But then fate lent a hand and on 11 November, after just over four years, the war came to an end. Racing had survived the war to end all wars, but half of Europe's royal families had either been deposed or were dead.

On 16 November *The Newmarket Journal* published extensive reports on the celebrations held in Newmarket, describing jubilant people carrying flags, rosettes and ribbons, while in the High Street lamps were lit for the first time since the war had begun.

Less than two weeks later, on 29 November, an article in *The Times* argued that racing in wartime was indispensable, that it was an important national asset. *The Sporting Life* magazine, meanwhile, focused on getting the sport back to normal in peacetime, while a deputation appointed by the Parliamentary Horse Breeding Committee was now in a position to request a reintroduction of fixtures, a request that the War Cabinet no longer had any grounds to refuse. The prevailing mood, indeed, was one of optimism for the future.[34]

With the war over, the King felt it necessary to return to what had been familiar, and he also wanted to see and be seen by the public in order to present a reassuring image of the monarchy.

After the cessation of hostilities, it seemed to be a time for reflection in Britain. On 4 June 1919 *The Times* published a lengthy article detailing the history of the Derby, from its inception in 1780 right up to the present day, recalling the highs and lows of the race over the years, reminding people of its heyday and of its place in society. That year's Derby, attended by thousands, was dubbed the 'Peace Derby', and on the same day as the *Times* article appeared the King's horse Viceroy won the Steward's Handicap, a minor race that nonetheless won popular applause. It was the only highlight of the day, however, the other events appearing rather lacklustre, largely due to the weather, which, according to *The Times*'s correspondent, was 'sulky'. Later it rained and humidity soared.[35]

On 17 June 1919 – the day that racing resumed at Ascot – *The Times* took steps to revive national pride by publishing an article detailing the history of horse-racing there and reminiscing on the larger meetings. Then as now, Ascot was a great society event, demonstrating an outward and visible sign of the King's interest in the sport of his people, and in this regard it was and is unique. The article then described Ascot's history, including the attack on William IV in 1832. There would be more articles like this, but none with as much significance. A foreign politician had once said that as long as Britain had its horse-racing it would never have a revolution, but nevertheless the wounds inflicted by the war on all the classes ran deep. For the aristocracy, the conflict precipitated a sudden shift in their fortunes, forcing some to sell their London properties to help pay a communal tax bill. The knock-on effect of this was that racing lost the financial confidence that had helped to build and sustain it, although in the long run this proved not to be detrimental. A new, golden age of racing was about to begin, proving once again that it was as much a sport of the people as a sport of kings.[36]

The *Times* article went on to describe the fashions present at that year's Ascot, taking an almost surprised note when it reported that the styles were reminiscent of those worn before the war, although the ladies' dresses were a little more sombre. For gentlemen, top hats were back in vogue.

That year, when the royal family arrived in carriages with outriders, *The Times*'s correspondent was given to remark that he hoped the royal procession would never take place in motor cars. The royals were later joined by other members of the British royal family and guests, but extended royalty was lacking. This would be the first year that Ascot wasn't attended by the royal houses of Hohenzollern and Romanov, as the head of the former, Kaiser Wilhelm II, had left Germany and was living in exile in Holland, while Tsar Nicholas II of Russia and his family were all dead, having been shot in July 1918 at Ekaterinburg in the wake of the Russian Revolution.[37]

That year, however, patriotism and support of the British royal family was higher than it had ever been before the war, and the King himself paid tribute to one of the conflict's biggest naval battles by naming one of his racehorses Jutland. (This was also something of a personal gesture, as his second son, Prince Albert – 'Bertie' – had taken part in this battle.) When the horse appeared before running in the Royal Hunt Cup, the Prince was cheered, but Jutland failed to secure the race. Pesaro, another of the King's horses, was narrowly beaten in the Ascot Derby, however, while another, Viceroy, won the last race, which left the crowds in a very upbeat mood at the end of the day's racing.

On 1 July 1919 the King was driven down to the July course at Newmarket just in time to witness the first race of the event. It was his first visit since 1914 and he was enthusiastically welcomed. Then, after watching the races, he travelled on to Egerton House to inspect his horses there before being driven to his Jockey Club rooms, where he arrived just after six in the evening. Again, he took the suite formerly occupied by his father – resuming his former routine – and dined at the club.[38]

Two and a half months later, on 15 October, the King, Queen, Princess Mary and the King's sister, Princess Victoria, drove down to Newmarket from Sandringham, arriving before the last race of the day, while Princes Albert and Henry came over from Cambridge and met them later. Despite a strong wind that day, Newmarket was very well attended. After the second race, the royal party went to the paddock, where the King's filly Sunny Princess was being saddled for the next race, and the Queen spoke to Richard Marsh and Herbert Jones. Sunny Princess failed in her attempts to secure the Cheveley Park Stakes, but the Écija filly won the Two-Year-Old Plate to the delight of the King and Queen, who were especially pleased at the public's approval of her triumph. *The Times*'s correspondent noted that he didn't believe Queen Mary had ever attended Newmarket and interpreted her presence there that day as a compliment.[39]

Five days later, on 20 October, an article followed in *The Times* detailing the King's successes at Newmarket. He'd had three in the Second October Meeting with Sunny Princess, who won the Two-Year-Old Plate on the afternoon of the Cesarewitch, beating Prince Herod by three-quarters of a length; Lemonade, who won the Bretby Stakes by three lengths; and Viceroy, who secured the Royal Stakes. The first race earned the King £261, the second £1,000 and the third £800.[40]

Not everything was getting back to normal quite so easily, however. On 23 October there was a railway strike, and the Jockey Club made a bad mistake in deciding to hold a meeting at Newmarket on that day. After the first day, the meeting was cancelled and the government appealed to the people to be sparing in the use of petrol if they intended to drive to Newmarket in the future.

By the time Derby day came around again the following May, things had settled down a bit and there was a record number of people there to watch Spion Kop's triumph – including the King, who telegrammed the result to the Prince of Wales in Canada at 3.16 p.m. The message was sent to London, then forwarded on to Halifax, Nova Scotia, where it arrived at 3.19 p.m., and then telegraphed across the country and by Pacific cable to Australia, where it arrived just 23 minutes after the race was completed, demonstrating the cutting edge of contemporary technology.[41]

Unlike Epsom, where women were seen driving each other around without chaperones, Ascot provided proof that not everything had changed in the racing world. Racegoers there didn't approve of photographers and King George made it clear that he didn't want them in the Royal Enclosure, a landmark decision that would be enshrined in the regulations in 1920 and a stipulation still in force today.

By this time, interest in equine sports had moved on to the next generation of the royal family, and in 1921 Prince Albert, Duke of York, was elected a member of the Jockey Club. Meanwhile, his elder brother, Edward, Prince of Wales (known to his family as 'David'), was developing an interest in point-to-point, participating in a race at the Grenadier and Coldstream Guards' point-to-point meeting at Warden Hill, London, held by permission of Major Heywood Lonsdale, Master of the Bicester and Warden Hill Hunt. This was the Prince's first experience of point-to-point and he was understandably apprehensive, arriving on the course before noon and walking it over with the clerk of the scales, Mr Percy Flick. Later that day, while riding the Grenadier Guards' race, he fell at the second fence but recovered to come third. He later made light of his fall,[42] and it didn't put him off attending the Grand National with his family that March.

At Epsom that year, on 31 May, the King didn't have any runners and his arrival was quiet – as was the meeting in general, in fact, because of the lack of local rail facilities. The roads, however, were quite crowded with cars, *The Times* estimating that some 100,000 vehicles tried to reach the downs. King George didn't mind the presence of motor cars at the course, in fact, as people could view the races from them, but the authorities were concerned and launched an R33 airship to fly overhead and monitor the traffic. Despite this rather unusual sight, however, the racing still dominated.[43]

The following day, the King, Queen, Prince of Wales, Duke of York, Princess Mary and Prince Henry arrived at Epsom by motor car at 12.45 p.m., receiving a great welcome. The King and Queen lunched between the first and second races in the salon of the royal box and later in the day their children visited the paddock while the airship flew overhead, providing reports of the traffic situation to and from the course. Indeed, the airship was proving to be so invaluable that a request was made for it to continue flying until 5 p.m.[44]

As summer rolled into autumn, on 27 October it was announced that, while the King wouldn't be giving up racing, he would be curtailing royal expenditure in the sport, and in 1922 he planned to remove his horses from Egerton House to a smaller, as yet unknown establishment. Richard Marsh would continue to act as trainer, just as Beresford would continue to act as manager, and there would be no change to the Sandringham stud.[45]

Later that year, Beresford asked Steve Donoghue to ride for the King. Not for the first time, Donoghue turned him down, telling the manager that his horses just weren't good enough. Nor did the year end on a good note.

On Saturday, 16 December, Lord Beresford, extra equerry and racing manager to two kings, was found dead at his St James's Street flat. It was believed that his heart had failed him, as he'd previously suffered from cardiac trouble that had prevented him from attending that year's Derby. Just the previous day he'd seemed to be in his usual spirits, having been seen at the Turf Club for much of the day, returning home just after 11 p.m., and he'd expressed his intent to go to Hurst Park on the 16th to watch his horse Rory O'Neill in the 3.30. He would have been 74 that Christmas Day.[46]

Lord Beresford's funeral took place at the Church of St Jude, Englefield Green, London, on 21 December 1922. There was a huge turn-out, with Richard Marsh and Herbert Jones among the mourners, while the King was represented by Sir Derek Keppel. Queen Alexandra sent a wreath and a memorial service was held in the Chapel Royal at St James's Palace, where the Dowager Queen was represented by General Sir Dighton Probyn, VC, and Queen Mary by Sir Edward Wallington.[47]

Beresford was succeeded by Major F H Featherstonhaugh, who took a somewhat different attitude to how the King's horses should run. Where Lord Marcus felt that they should run in the big races, Featherstonhaugh felt they should be placed according to ability and, with this in mind, secured nineteen winners for the King that first season, with one horse, Weathervane, winning eight times.

On 15 March 1923, Prince Edward rode in the army's point-to-point race at Arborfield Cross, near Wokingham, while his brother Henry was taking part in a nomination race on Rathgaroque. When Henry's horse refused the second fence, swerved and clashed with a spectator and his bicycle, the horse fell, cutting his legs, and brought Henry down with him. The Prince escaped with no more than scratched hands.

That day, too, Edward was thrown by his horse, Little Favourite (inappropriately numbered thirteen), who also fell. Less fortunate than his brother, however, the Prince of Wales landed heavily, incurring concussion and facial abrasions. His brother Bertie was one of the first to reach him, dazed and insisting that he was capable of walking, but he was carried off and taken to the house of the clerk of the course, Major H F Tanner, where once again Edward made light of his accident and, indeed, was well enough to drink tea. Later he was taken to Aldershot, where he passed a good night, but he spent the next day in bed and some of his engagements had to be cancelled. Within a couple of days, he'd returned to London.

It was unfortunate that both Edward and Henry should have had accidents, as they'd ridden well just previously, Edward on Passport II in the lightweight race for the Prince of Wales Challenge Cup and Henry on Ocean III in the welterweight steeplechase for Lord Beatty's Cup.

Edward was well enough a few days later to accompany his father and Prince George to Liverpool to attend the Grand National, and on 4 April[48] the Prince of Wales rode Little Favourite in the Welsh Guards' Challenge Cup, the main feature of the Household Brigade meeting at Hawthorn Hill. The King and Queen arrived shortly after two o'clock on that beautiful summer's day, and before the race Prince George wandered about with Edward, greeting people.

As her name implied, Little Favourite was indeed one of the favourites. Many of her fellow competitors came to grief early, so it didn't take long for the Prince of Wales to take the lead. He won by many lengths and was mobbed as he passed the post. This was the second time he had won this race, the first being in 1921, on Pet Dog. *The Times* was of the opinion that he had improved as a horseman, and indeed a few days later, on 6 April, he attended the Beaufort Hunt point-to-point meeting at Alderton, where he won on Kinlark.

Later in the month, Prince Albert – now Duke of York – married 23-year-old Lady Elizabeth Bowes-Lyon. From the beginning of their union, Elizabeth was a popular member of the royal family who took to people straight away. How she would fare as Duchess of York, however, only time would tell.

At that time, the Prince of Wales was proving to be one of the most popular royals yet. He was still taking part in point-to-point meetings, and at first the King supported his son's sporting endeavours, but when Edward started to have accidents King George and government ministers tried to persuade him to stop. While Edward was less than happy at their interference and failed to see what all the fuss was about, the King confided to his mother, the Dowager Queen Alexandra, that Edward was taking 'unnecessary risks', and it also bothered him that his eldest son didn't ride like a gentleman. Edward's feelings as Prince of Wales and his need to prove himself in competitive sport might have been a response to the live-for-the-moment atmosphere of the 1920s and also a way of compensating for being unable to prove himself during the war while his younger brother, Bertie, had seen active service during the Battle of Jutland. In fact, Bertie had proved to be something of an all-round sportsman, being excellent at cricket and golf (he rivalled Edward at the latter with a handicap of nine to Edward's eleven), so, despite their closeness, there was a certain amount of competitiveness between the two. Bertie was also the better horseman and outdid his brother time and time again, particularly in his handling of skittish horses.

As 1923 rolled into 1924, King George found himself with another problem, this one in the shape of Derby hopeful Knight of the Garter, who had recently won the Coventry Stakes. While the horse had been doing well, Marsh suspected that he was a non-stayer, having a tendency to rush forward too soon and burn himself out. After the trainer had worked on him, Knight of the Garter improved enough to be considered for the Derby, but such hopes proved to be premature.[49]

'One evening,' Marsh recalled, 'on going round stables, I found one of [Knight of the Garter's] joints was a bit flushed. Outside the joint were one or two pimples.'[50] He was greatly alarmed, especially since the leg was flushed up almost to the knee. What he had discovered was a condition known as heel bug, which can be contracted through contact with certain weedy flowers. It was necessary to tackle the affliction immediately and the horse was worked on around the clock, and to Marsh's relief Knight of the Garter finally began to improve – enough, at least, for him to be cantered twice. Just when it looked as though he could go to Epsom after all – indeed, minutes before he was installed in a horse box bound for Epsom – Knight of the Garter had a relapse.[51]

'I have never known or heard of such a stubborn case,' wrote Marsh. 'I have noticed that this heel bug is prevalent about the end of April and the beginning of May . . . The annoying thing is that the poison does not necessarily attack the horse which is unhealthy and low in condition. No horse could have been healthier and fitter than Knight of the Garter was.'[52] Knight of the Garter was ruled out of the Derby and would be replaced by Resinato.

Epsom, too, at the beginning of June, was something of a washout, taking place under a deluge of constant rain. It was won that year by Lord Derby's Sansovino, while Resinato ran unplaced, so once again the Derby eluded the royals. However, there was some consolation to be found when Weathervane won the Royal Hunt Cup.

When the King's son-in-law, Lascelles, expressed an interest in buying Egerton House for his wife, Princess Mary, so that she could have a Newmarket residence, it was suggested to Marsh, who leased Egerton House from the Ellesmere family, that he might like to retire. Marsh dutifully did so, having been a trainer for two kings and serving for 31 years. And so, on 9 January 1925, a presentation was made for him at the Newmarket Masonic Club, where George Lambton proposed a toast and presented Marsh with a silver cup, provided by his fellow trainers, along with a cabinet fashioned from oak and silver and filled with cigars.[53] Marsh would have a productive retirement and that year would produce his autobiography, *Trainer to Two Kings*, detailing not only his life and work but also the golden age of racing, and following that of fellow trainer Lambton, titled *Men and Horses I Have Known*, which was first published in 1924. In later years, the 6th Duke of Portland, too, would write a book, his a set of memoirs titled *Memories of Racing and Hunting*, published in 1935. All three works paid tribute not just to horse-racing but to the contributions made by Edward VII and George V as patrons of the sport.

After Lascelles bought Egerton House, Marsh was replaced by William Rose Jarvis, who came from a distinguished family of trainers and who would help to turn the King's stables' fortunes around. Jarvis took over the entrance lodge at Egerton House, which was then renovated, a programme of works that included the installation of a staircase that had originally come from Charles II's Newmarket abode. This new addition generated quite a lot of interest, with many people wondering how many times Nell Gwyn had climbed them.

That year, Ascot was held on 16 June, a pleasant day, although attendance was moderate and not all the races ended as expected. One of the day's most popular wins was in the Queen Mary Stakes, won by the King's Aloysia, a good-looking, well formed filly by Lemberg out of Veryaine. She had run only once before, in a minor race at Doncaster, and had arrived at Ascot fully prepared, although she wasn't tipped as a favourite. At the start of the race she began in front and maintained her position, winning by a length, with Moti Mahal second and Sweet Cicely third. The *Times* reporter attributed her success to her trainer, Jarvis, and noted that she was the best two-year-old of the season so far.

Royal racing might have become more modest than in recent years, but people still enjoyed the spectacle of the royal procession. The sight of carriages, beautiful horses and liveried gentlemen never failed to impress the crowds, and *The Times*'s correspondent was fascinated by people's response to it. The Queen, meanwhile, commissioned Sir Alfred Munnings to paint the cavalcade, and each morning the artist was chauffeured to Windsor Castle to watch the horses as they were being harnessed and then transported to watch the procession. The painting he produced, titled *Their Majesties' Return from Ascot*, was very lifelike and detailed, conveying the impressive array of colour and spectacle for which Ascot was and still is known.[54]

Meanwhile the Prince of Wales was still under pressure to give up competitive riding. In the middle of March 1926, however, he rode Passport II in the Bicester point-to-point, and succeeded in losing a leather.

Then, on 23 March – an extremely cold day – Edward, as a Welsh Guards colonel, competed in the Grafton Hunt point-to-point in Pattishall, near Northampton, participating in the Brigade of Guards' inter-regimental race. One of 24 starters, he again rode Passport II, but he failed to win, compounding his disappointing performance of the previous week.

Despite efforts to persuade him to give up point-to-point racing, on 16 March 1927 a defiant Prince of Wales took part in the Bicester and Warden Hill Hunt steeplechase meeting, which took place at Hillesden, near Buckingham. On that occasion he improved on his performance of the previous year, when he'd won the Lord Manners Cup on Cark Courtier in the Grenadier Guards point-to-point race. *The Times* described his jumping as faultless, but it was nevertheless a close finish, even though he'd dominated much of the race.[55]

Edward's brother Henry also enjoyed competing, and on the same day he was attending the 1st Cavalry Brigade's point-to-point steeplechases at Dippenhall, near Farnham, Surrey, although he was there only as a spectator, and Princess Mary – whose interest in equine sports matched that of the rest of her family – was attending a hunt meeting at Wetherby racecourse on Bramham Moor.

Then, on 22 March, the Prince of Wales participated in the Pytchley Hunt and army point-to-point steeplechases at Holdenby, near Northampton. On that occasion he spent so much time inspecting the course before the race that he was the last to weigh out. The clerk of the scales, a hurried man named Mr Over, was so intent on his job that he asked the Prince his name without looking up first to see who he was addressing.

Later that day, the Prince rode in the Prince of Wales' Cup in the Grand Military lightweight steeplechase, but after a good start Cark Courtier failed to clear the first fence safely and fell, throwing the Prince, and then galloped off. Although the Prince was never put off by this accident and others, the rest of his family were becoming increasingly worried.

The next day, it was announced that the Prince had nominated his eight-year-old brown mare Lady Doon for the lightweight race at the Belvoir Hunt point-to-point Steeplechase, scheduled to take place the next day at Barrowby, some two miles from Grantham. In fact, he rode two races that day, coming second in the nomination race on Cark Courtier and fourth in the Belvoir Hunt lightweight race for the Duchess of Rutland's Cup.[56]

Six days later, the Prince was back in the saddle in the Heythrop Hunt and Brigade of Guards point-to-point races near Chipping Norton for the Welsh Guards, once again on Cark Courtier, but he finished behind three riders for the Scots Guards. Later, on 7 April, he took part in and won the Adjacent Hunts Race on Lady Doon, and in another event he came third in the Master's Nomination Race on Cark Courtier.[57]

As 1927 rolled into 1928, the Prince was still competing. On 1 March he took part in the Duke of Beaufort's Hunt point-to-point, which was held at Hazelton, near Tetbury, and rode Degomme in the Welsh Guards' Race. Degomme stumbled but recovered and went on to win by ten lengths.[58] He rode the same horse in the Brigade of Guards inter-regimental race in the middle of March but fell at the water jump, although he was well enough by the 22nd to ride in the Belvoir Hunt. Then, on 24 March – a particularly miserable day – he competed in the Blankney Hunt point-to-point at Boothby Graffoe, riding Degomme in the Adjacent Hunts' Race and coming second, being beaten by Miss Gris.[59]

Five days later, the Prince was taking part in the Highland Brigade annual point-to-point races at Dockenfield, again in bad weather. This time he rode Miss Moffitt in the Highlanders' Cup Race, fell off, remounted and won by 300 yards. He also rode Lady Doon, but she failed to win anything.[60] Nevertheless, the Prince was determined to continue – much to his father's annoyance – and attended other point-to-point events and steeplechases throughout April.

That June, the entire royal family attended Epsom and Ascot, where the

King met and began chatting with a young jockey named Gordon Richards. After the King had left, Gordon was asked what he thought of 'the guvnor' by Joe Childs, the King's first jockey, who believed that the King was a gentleman and would toast his health with champagne every time he won a race for him.

That year, there was cause to celebrate when the 1,000 Guineas was won by the King's horse Scuttle, who had had been bred in 1925, a bay by Captain Cuttle out of Stained Glass and one of the first horses that Jarvis trained for the King. As a two-year-old in 1927, she'd been extremely good, winning the Cheveley Park Stakes at Newmarket, but her 1,000 Guineas win in 1928 established her place in history, since this was King George's only Classic win of his reign. Scuttle was later beaten in the Oaks and came third in the Coronation Stakes at Ascot, and again finished third in the Nassau Stakes at Goodwood, but these defeats would never override her Classic win.

If anything, the King had proved himself to be the ultimate stayer as an owner and had learned to take the rough with the smooth, watching the progress of his horses with interest. His favourite had always been Friar Marcus, but he discussed the merits of all of his horses on a regular basis with his trainer and manager and always liked to be kept informed of what was happening. If his horses didn't win, though, he wasn't a poor loser; instead, he just enjoyed the sport of horse-racing – a sport that was increasingly subject to the technological changes that marked his reign, including the introduction of radio broadcasting, bringing racing to those unable to attend in person.

Between 1928 and 1929, the King became quite ill. He convalesced at Bognor (despite protesting, 'Bugger Bognor!' when the doctor had the temerity to advise a recuperative trip there) in the company of his granddaughter Elizabeth, daughter of the Duke and Duchess of York. Known as 'Lilibet', because of her early attempts at pronouncing her name, Elizabeth was the King's favourite grandchild and George was fully appreciative of her interest in horses (he later gave her a Shetland pony named Peggy as a Christmas present). She was also an avid collector of toy horses on wheels and would ride around the house on them, treating them as if they were real horses, changing their saddles and harnessing them up at night. She had the King wrapped around her little finger, and he would willingly go on his hands and knees to act as an impromptu horse for her to ride, as the Archbishop of Canterbury discovered one day on a visit.[61]

Elizabeth would also accompany her grandfather on his visits to the stables to inspect the horses, and the two became a regular feature there. She began riding lessons early and was given her first lesson in the Riding School at the

Royal Mews, with Crown Equerry A E Erskine supervising. She also received lessons from her parents and the stud groom at the mews.[62]

By May 1930, the King had recovered sufficiently to attend Newmarket, accompanied by his daughter Princess Mary (now the Countess of Harewood), who had brought her house party over from Egerton House in time for the first race.

The King soon resumed his old routine,[63] and after attending Ascot and the Derby in June he was back at Newmarket on 2 July. The following day he arrived at the track just before the first race and spent much of the day walking around the enclosure, making the most of another beautiful day, while his daughter and son-in-law visited the paddock.[64]

On the whole, these were pleasant times, although the Wall Street Crash of 1929 and the start of the Great Depression, which would dominate the 1930s, cast a very dark shadow. Amid this turmoil, on 21 August 1930, the Duchess of York gave birth to her second child, a little girl named Margaret Rose, whose arrival meant that the line of succession to the throne was secure for the next generation. The Prince of Wales, however, was still showing no signs of marrying and continued to lead a life of bachelorhood with no apparent thought of settling down, and was criticised by the American press for being a playboy.

The King and the Prince of Wales were like chalk and cheese in temperament. The King still held onto traditional Victorian values, which he believed brought stability, while Edward was a prince for the modern era who had his own ideas on how a monarch should behave in an ever-changing world. Ultimately, neither of them would be reconciled on this fundamental difference or fully understand each other's approach, but at least they agreed that attending race meetings was a family affair. Even so, *The Times* observed that, where the King and Queen would attend each of the four days at Ascot (which in 1931 was due to begin on Tuesday 16 June, depending upon the weather), the Prince of Wales would instead be entertaining guests at his recently acquired Fort Belvedere,[65] some three miles from the course.

Throughout 1932, life continued much the same for the royal family, but the following year another link with the past was lost when, on Saturday, 20 May, Richard Marsh died at his home in Shelford, Cambridgeshire, at the age of 81, after having been ill for some time and nursed at home by his wife. A message of condolence was sent from Buckingham Palace that also acknowledged his service to both King Edward VII and King George V, and the funeral service was held on 23 May at Great Shelford Church, with the burial taking place at Little Shelford, the King being represented by Brigadier Tomkinson. There were a great many mourners that day, including Somerville Tattersall,[66] and in the eulogy Marsh was described as courteous, charming and a great trainer who was always ready to talk graciously about racing. Among the wreaths were those from the Princess Royal and the Earl of Harewood. Richard Marsh is still remembered today, not only as a trainer to two kings but as a gentleman who never tired of sharing his knowledge about horse-racing with others.

Towards the end of July 1933, the King attended Goodwood, where his horse, The Abbot, won the Sussex Stakes – the first race of the second afternoon – by a head. Although the King wasn't there at the time, the win was nonetheless well received. On that occasion, The Abbot was ridden by Joe Childs, who was given a run for his money by a horse named Gino, ridden by M Beary.[67]

Later in the year, on 14 December, the King presented silver cups to both Joe Childs and trainer Jack Jarvis.

Then, in March of the following year, it was announced that F Fox would ride for the King and that the Right Honourable Gavin George – Baron Hamilton of Dalzell, KT, CVO, MC – would become the King's representative at Ascot, succeeding Viscount Churchill, who had died earlier that year. Hamilton, a close friend of the King, would prove to be a turf reformer, and one of the first tasks that he supervised was the redevelopment of the Royal Stand to include masks of all the Empire's dominions months ahead of the King's Silver Jubilee.[68]

Meanwhile, the Duke and Duchess of York's children, Princesses Elizabeth and Margaret, were becoming familiar figures at public events, and on 26 June they attended an international horse-show tournament at Olympia with their parents, arriving just before 3 p.m. at the Hammersmith Road entrance, where they were received by the show's president, the Duke of Beaufort. The show presented a varied performance, and the children loved both the displays and the judging. On that occasion, their distant cousin Prince Gustav Adolf of Sweden took the place of Captain Claes de Kroenig in the final.[69]

On 8 November 1934, Gordon Richards beat Fred Archer's record for the highest number of wins in a season 48 years after the famous jockey's death at the age of 29. The King sent him a congratulatory telegram and also presented him with a gold cigarette case and a pair of racing pigeons from his own loft at Sandringham. These birds would form the foundation of Gordon's own loft and he would go on to win many races with them. Breaking Archer's record turned Gordon Richards into a celebrity and the newspapers were full of his victory for weeks, comparing him with the great jockey and prompting others to write in with their own personal reminiscences of Archer.

The fact that the King didn't have any outstanding runners wasn't too much of a problem for the royals were cresting a wave of popularity. At a thanksgiving service held at St Paul's Cathedral in London on 6 May 1935, given to celebrate the Jubilee, the King was overwhelmed by the affection shown by the public, and when the Yorks attended the Royal Tournament later in June the welcome they received was so enthusiastic that police had to cordon people off at the entrance.[70]

On 16 November, the King enjoyed his final flat-race victory with Curraghmore, son of his all-time favourite horse, Friar Marcus. The horse that marked the end of King George's reign, however, was Marconi (by St Jerome, out of Wireless), who came fourth in the Rosehill maiden three-year-old hurdle race at Cheltenham but later improved his position when he came second in the three-year-old hurdle race at Birmingham on 25 November. Unfortunately, as with a number of the King's horses in the past, Marconi was unable to improve, coming fifth twice in December: in the Boveney hurdle race on the 25th and in the Berkshire hurdle race on the 30th.[71] While such dubious results failed to put a dampener on a family party the royals held that Christmas, they proved to be the King's last.

On the evening of 20 January 1936, the King died. That same night, his coffin was taken to Sandringham Church, preceding a procession of estate workers, a piper playing a lament and the King's favourite white cob, Jock.[72]

King George V would be remembered for a great many things in the future, although sporting success wouldn't be one of them, as he had never received the wealth of accolades that his father had. Rather, he would be remembered as the king who saw his country through the dark years of war after the golden years of the Edwardian era and who, along with his queen, had a high sense of duty. Where horse-racing and horse-breeding were concerned, his contribution was an enduring one. As Sir Michael Oswald affirms, 'Although he enjoyed less success than his father, George V laid the foundations for the success achieved by George VI and our present queen.'[73]

Notes:

1.   *The Times*, 03.06.1910
2.   Fitzgerald, p183
3.   Marsh, p285
4.   Marsh, p286
5.   Ibid.
6.   *The Times*, 04.05.1911
7.   *The Times*, 09.05.1911
8.   *The Times*, 31.05.1911; 01.06.1911

9. *The Times*, 18.06.1913
10. Marsh, p288
11. *The Times*, 24.04.1914
12. Ibid.
13. *The Times*, 29.04.1914
14. *The Times*, 29.04.1914; 30.04.1914
15. *The Times*, 28.05.1914
16. Ibid.
17. *The Times*, 01.06.1914
18. *The Times*, 23.06.1914
19. *The Times*, 05.08.1914
20. Memoranda: Buckingham Palace Riding School 07.10.1914
21. *The Times*, 01.03.1915
22. Ibid.
23. *The Times*, 09.03.1915
24. *The Times*, 10.03.1915; 12.03.1915
25. *The Times*, 13.03.1915
26. *The Times*, 19.05.1915; 20.05.1915
27. *The Times*, 21.05.1915
28. *The Times*, 19.11.1915
29. *The Times*, 11.02.1916
30. *The Times*, 03.05.1916
31. Lionel Earle to the Master of the Horse Office, 08.12.1916 (National Archives document)
32. Valentine Matthews, Inspector of Rest Houses for London District, 20.01.1917; 23.01.1917; 29.01.1917; 21.03.1917 (National Archives document)
33. *The Times*, 29.03.1917; 30.04.1917; 19.06.1917
34. *The Newmarket Journal*, 16.11.1918; *The Times*, 29.11.1918
35. *The Times*, 04.06.1919; 05.06.1919
36. *The Times*, 17.06.1919
37. *The Times*, 18.06.1919
38. *The Times*, 02.07.1919
39. *The Times*, 16.10.1919
40. *The Times*, 24.10.1919
41. *The Times*, 03.06.1920
42. *The Times*, 05.03.1921
43. *The Times*, 01.06.1921
44. *The Times*, 02.06.1922
45. *The Times*, 27.10.1921
46. *The Times*, 18.12.1922
47. *The Times*, 22.12.1922
48. *The Times*, 05.04.1923
49. Marsh, pp291–2
50. Marsh, p292
51. Marsh, pp292–3
52. Ibid.
53. *The Times*, 10.01.1925
54. *The Times*, 17.06.1925
55. *The Times*, 17.03.1927
56. *The Times*, 23.03.1927

57. *The Times*, 31.03.1927
58. *The Times*, 02.03.1928
59. *The Times*, 24.03.1928
60. *The Times*, 30.03.1928
61. Judd, p116
62. Pimlott, p16, p27
63. *The Times*, 03.07.1930
64. *The Times*, 04.07.1930; Pimlott, p17
65. *The Times*, 06.06.1931
66. *The Times*, 22.05.1933; 24.05.1933
67. *The Times*, 27.07.1933
68. *The Times*, 03.05.1934
69. *The Times*, 27.06.1934
70. *The Times*, 15.06.1935
71. Weatherbys 1935, p149, p212, p234
72. Lee, Christopher, *This Sceptered Isle: Twentieth Century*, p191
73. Sir Michael Oswald

19
Edward VIII

As tradition dictated, King Edward VIII's accession to the throne was officially announced on the morning after his predecessor's death. At the age of 42, he was the youngest monarch to ascend the throne since his great-grandmother, Queen Victoria, had become monarch back in 1837 at the age of eighteen. As discussed in the previous chapter, he wasn't cast from his late father's mould and had always presented the modern face of royalty, having been an energetic and competitive sportsman in his youth. However, he had been restricted by his position as heir to the throne. Now, as king, he wanted to move away from the Victorian values of his father's reign and to modernise the monarchy.

For now, though, the proprieties had to be observed, and as a mark of respect for the late king the Windsor meeting was cancelled some days after the funeral. It was later discovered that King George had bequeathed Egerton House to his daughter Mary, the Princess Royal, while the Sandringham estate passed directly to the new king.

On 1 February 1936 *The Times* announced that Lord Derby would lease King George's horses until the end of the year, and that morning both Lord Derby and King Edward met to discuss the details.[1] The horses, it was decided, would remain at Egerton House under William Jarvis, they would be managed by Tomkinson and they would be run separately. One of the horses was Marconi, who, having failed to achieve a win under his late master's colours, came first in the Saltley Steeplechase on 25 February and also at Cheltenham on 11 March, when he came first in the National Hunt Juvenile Steeplechase. Unfortunately, such luck didn't last. On 4 April he came third in the Stratford-on-Avon Steeplechase, under Fulke Walwyn, and on the 15th he came third in the Stroud Novices Steeplechase at Cheltenham.[2]

During his discussion with Derby on 1 February, Edward confirmed that he would be maintaining the royal connection with the turf, in relation to both the stables and the stud, but hinted – as *The Times* related – that, while things would continue much as before, he would implement such changes as he would 'find necessary'. Exactly what changes he was considering, no one knew.

One of the first such changes, however, was announced in *The Times* on 21 February:[3] spectators attending Ascot would not be expected to wear mourning clothes to commemorate the death of the late king. Of course, George V had decreed the same in 1910 on the death of Edward VII, but people had dressed in black anyway. This time, however, Edward's decision was rooted entirely in reasons of practicality. It came as a result of the King's visit on the 20th to the British Industries Fair at White City, where he'd met representatives of the textiles industry and discussed the effect that court mourning could have on the industry, which was still suffering from the effects of the Great Depression. The King's decision to ask the public not to wear mourning dress – as reported in *The Times*[4] – provided a boost for the textile trade and continued in the same tradition initiated by his predecessor.

Another, less settling development applied to the royal horses. On 26 March, *The Times* announced that the Sandringham stud was to be closed[5] and the broodmares sent to Hampton Court, where the King could enjoy better access, not just to them but also to the foals and yearlings. The Sandringham stud, the newspaper reported, needed 'a rest'. Some horses – Wolferton, for instance, as well as Friar Marcus and Limelight – would stay, but the others would be moved. It was also reported that the King had decided to sell some two-year-olds currently stabled at Egerton House: Polonaise, Pretty Spark and Felstone.

The decision to close the Sandringham stud – established under Edward VII as Prince of Wales, the most successful royal owner to date – signalled the end of one of the most important racing establishments in the country and came as a terrible shock to the horse-breeding and -racing industries, as it meant that all of those who had loyally served both Edward VII and George V for decades would be out of work at a time when work was hard to come by. And then, to make matters worse in the middle of the year, it was announced that the whole Sandringham estate would be put on the market.

The Royal Stud wasn't the only cause for worry. With his coronation scheduled for May 1937, it was becoming increasingly clear that Edward VIII was still maintaining a close relationship with an American divorcée named Wallis Simpson, who was all but separated from her second husband, Ernest Simpson. Just as worryingly, the King was cancelling a number of engagements in order to spend more time with her. While the Prime Minister anxiously tried to establish the true state of play behind the scenes, on the surface it was business as usual and the public remained ignorant of the young King's colourful love life, watching with pride as he participated in the Trooping of the Colour that June.

The public also took delight in the King's nieces, the Princesses Elizabeth and Margaret of York, aged ten and six respectively, and on 4 June, when they and their parents visited the International Horse Show, a crowd of onlookers had to be held back by police.

That year the royals didn't attend Ascot because they were still officially in mourning for the late King George, but on 15 June Edward visited the racecourse – where he was received by Lord Hamilton of Dalzell and Lieutenant-Colonel Sir Gordon Carter, the clerk of the course – to inspect the improvements that had been carried out there, including improvements to the lawn in the Royal Enclosure and new unsaddling arrangements.[6] The King then visited the royal stables, where his horses (as leased by Lord Derby) were located. Shortly afterwards, he returned to his nearby home of Fort Belvedere. The Ascot meeting that year promised to be one of the best in a long while, but this was as much as the King would see of it.

As the summer rolled on, the royal court speculated about whether or not the King would give up Mrs Simpson, whilst the royal family continued to act as normal, finding enjoyment and no doubt relief from the stress of Edward's dalliance in the various horse shows and race meetings that were taking place. On 9 September, for instance, the Princess Royal attended the St Leger[7] while he was trying to negotiate a settlement to secure Wallis Simpson's place at his side after his coronation. The current bone of contention was her divorce hearing with Ernest Simpson. Those who feared that the King would seek to marry her before his coronation asked him to persuade her to delay the hearing, but he refused, arguing that he couldn't interfere with the proceedings. His intentions at this time were still vague, and over the next few weeks many would try to find out exactly what they were. Meanwhile, the public were still none the wiser about the relationship between Edward and Mrs Simpson, largely because by now a full news blackout had been imposed.

King Edward enjoyed great popularity and had a strong rapport with his people, as demonstrated when Salford City Council Watch Committee presented him with a chestnut gelding named Cherry Grove on 14 September. Standing at over sixteen hands high, the horse had previously been with the mounted police for two years since April 1934. The King, delighted with him, nevertheless refused to accept the horse as a gift and later bought him for £150.[8]

On 28 October the King appointed a new jockey, a man named J Crouch, who it was hoped would remain in the saddle for a long time. By this time, however, Wallis Simpson's divorce hearing had taken place in Ipswich and it was becoming more and more evident that the King intended to marry her.

Then, on 30 November, an event happened that, ever since, has been considered a dark omen for Edward's reign: the Crystal Palace – an inspiration of King Edward's great-grandfather, Prince Albert – caught fire. The conflagration was so great that it could be seen from Brighton. The King's brother George, Duke of Kent, and his equerry, Lord Herbert, drove down to watch as the structure was consumed.[9] The blaze made headline news and has been compared since with the fire at Windsor Castle in 1996.

On the same day, the *Daily Mirror* announced that King Edward's horse Marconi, who had failed at the hurdles at Wolverhampton, had been removed from the race programmes at Newbury and Kempton and would instead run in the New Windsor Steeplechase on 16 December. However, this news was overshadowed by the news of the true nature of the King's relationship with Wallis Simpson. The British public were outraged by the revelation that their king had been conducting a relationship with the American divorcée, so much so that Wallis was forced to leave the country (for many decades, as it turned out), travelling to France to await the King there.

Edward VIII was king for less than twelve months. As his father had predicted, he ruined himself. The only direct effect he had on racing was when his abdication speech of 11 December 1936 caused problems for people trying to return home from race meetings, getting caught up in traffic as other members of the public rushed home to hear the speech on the radio.

That evening, Edward (now Duke of Windsor) and his brother, 'Albert' (now King George VI), dined at Royal Lodge, Windsor, along with other members of the royal family. In the early hours of the following morning, the ex-monarch left Portsmouth aboard a destroyer bound for France, where he arrived at 2 p.m.[10] It would be many years before he would see his family again.

Notes:

1. *The Times* 01.02.1936
2. Weatherby, 1935/1936, p319, p385, p490, p551
3. *The Times*, 21.02.1936
4. *The Times*, 22.02.1936
5   *The Times*, 26.03.1936
6. *The Times*, 16.06.1936
7. *The Times*, 10.09.1936
8. *The Times*, 29.09.1936
9. *Daily Mirror*, 01.12.1936
10 Donaldson, Frances, Edward VIII, p296

20
George VI

After King Edward VIII's abdication, an unsettling twelve months followed, and it is to King George VI's credit that, despite his lack of confidence in his own fitness to rule, he presented a reassuring figure to the public. With his wife and children beside him, he represented stability and hope for the future, and the public warmed to him.

George's first priority was to reassure not only his people but his staff, too. On 15 December 1936, therefore, it was announced that he would maintain the Royal Stable and Stud just as his father had maintained it, and in a reversal of his brother's plans he bought back Sandringham stud, completing the contracts that had been drawn up to this effect when Edward abdicated. As well as maintaining this particular link between his family and the horse-breeding industry, the King also wanted to build on his limited knowledge of the sport – particularly since his father and grandfather had been experts – and so he employed Brigadier Tomkinson to act as stud manager. Tragically, Tomkinson died on 20 January 1937, twelve months to the day after the death of King George V, at the age of 56. He was replaced by Captain Charles Moore, a highly experienced trainer who owned his own stud at Mooresfoot, County Tipperary.

As Moore joined the Royal Stud, he found the place to be at a particularly low ebb, with just 21 horses in training – of whom four would win minor races – out of the stud's twenty broodmares, fourteen yearlings and thirteen foals.

On 12 January, the King enjoyed his first victory when five-year-old Marconi – who had previously won for George V on the flat and Edward VIII over fences at Birmingham – won the Smethwick Steeplechase by eight lengths, making history in the process as the first horse to win races for three different kings. On that occasion he was ridden by D Morgan and they passed the post to rapturous applause. However, another of the King's horses, Fairlead – a good, well-trained jumper with a good record – lost her race that day.[1]

That same morning, the King and Queen left their home at 145 Piccadilly to visit Buckingham Palace, where they were taken on a tour of the various apartments by the master of the household, Brigadier-General Sir Hill Child, and planned new decorations and refurbishments, while the Queen decided who would stay where during the coronation.

That afternoon, the King received Lord Cromer, the Lord Chamberlain, at the Palace to discuss such matters as levees, investitures and courts before he and the Queen visited the Duke and Duchess of Kent's residence at 3 Belgrave Square. Then, in the evening, they were paid a visit by Queen Marie of Yugoslavia.[2]

When the King and Queen eventually moved into Buckingham Palace, their children brought with them their collection of toy horses, which would remain outside their bedroom doors until Princess Elizabeth married, a little over ten years later.

On 18 January 1937, the King and Queen visited Egerton House with Queen Mary and then had lunch at the Severals House with a Mrs Edward Clayton before returning to the centre of Newmarket and making a tour of the King's apartments at the Jockey Club. Then they made their way back to Sandringham, intending to remain there until the end of the month before going back to London. It was also announced that they would be attending the Grand National in March and would be staying at Knowsley Hall from 18 March as guests of the Earl of Derby.

That year at Aintree, the King had two entries: Jubilee in the Molyneux Stakes and Fairlead in the Coronation Hurdle.[3] Jubilee's race opened the meeting, but because he and the Queen were still en route at the time the King missed his horse winning. The victory was so popular with the crowd, in fact, that it made the headlines in *The Sporting Life*.

A few days after the event, on 12 March, Princesses Elizabeth and Margaret attended the National Pony Show at the Royal Agricultural Hall, Islington, with their grandmother, the Countess of Strathmore and Kinghorne. They were there for two hours, watching the children's riding classes and, later, the judging of them.[4] It was considered that getting them to attend events such as these and to be seen by the public was good experience for them, and indeed it demonstrated how far they'd come in acknowledging their royal duty. In this regard, they also had the example of their grandmother, Queen Mary, who that summer presented a vase for the winner of a charity race at Northolt Park, the proceeds of which would go to the City of London Maternity Hospital, of which she was a patron.[5]

Meanwhile, Princess Elizabeth was determined to learn everything she could about horsemanship and was tutored in this by Horace Smith. He had replaced Henry Owen and gave her and his own daughter twice-weekly lessons together at Buckingham Palace, while Elizabeth also received lessons from

Cybil Smith. Horace taught her from scratch and found the Princess to be an apt pupil who listened and learned well. Of course, her love of horses and the role-playing games she'd played as a child had provided invaluable preparation for this, but her biographer Ben Pimlott has looked into the possibility that this role play was a way of compensating for lack of children her own age with whom to play. Nevertheless, Elizabeth was conscientious about horsemanship and Smith found her to be fascinated about stable management and training. She also developed an interest in carriage driving that she would pursue further at Windsor.[6]

On 4 March 1938 both Princess Elizabeth and her sister, Margaret, were back at Islington for the National Pony Show, arriving just before three in the afternoon in the wake of their Uncle Henry, the Duke of Gloucester, who had been there earlier, presenting rosettes and touring the stables. They were escorted around the arena by Major H F Faudel Phillips, the show's president, and stayed for two and a half hours, following the proceedings intently, watching the competitions and tests and marking up their catalogues. Both princesses presented rosettes to the winners.

Newmarket heralded the start of a busy summer of racing, and the King travelled there on 26 April 1938, staying overnight at Egerton House with his sister, Mary, and Lord Harewood. The following day he was driven around Newmarket's racecourse and was met at the stands by William Bass and Lord Ilchester. That year, the King's horse Foxbrush was scheduled to run in the Somersham Stakes, but he finished unplaced.

This was the honeymoon period of the King's reign. Less than three years after his accession, England found itself once again at war with Germany and the future looked grim. The racing world, too, was experiencing a time of instability. Shortly after the Prime Minister issued a statement that England was at war, *The Times* issued another statement to the effect that sports gatherings would be stopped for the foreseeable future, while the *Daily Sketch* announced that the Jockey Club would shortly be making its own statement, as would the National Hunt Committee. In the UK, three days after the announcement of hostilities, trainers were carrying on as usual, still waiting for instructions from their owners, while in Ireland it was decreed that racing would continue as normal unless the government said otherwise.[7]

Generally, the racing world was optimistic that the sport would be resumed, but as with the previous global conflict objections to its continuance abounded on the grounds that it was unpatriotic and a waste of resources. These arguments encouraged more protests, while an article in *The Times* predicted further public resentment if racing continued. The Jockey Club found itself facing the same dilemma as it had been up against during World War One.

Then, on 25 September, an article appeared in *The Times* discussing the fate of racing and how the owners and trainers were coping. At Doncaster, it was reported, the St Leger had been abandoned, leaving the owners and trainers there wondering what would become of their horses. It was felt that many of the poorer class of animals would have to be shot, as trainers and owners couldn't afford to keep them, although those with stud value were safe.

As time passed, it became clear that the War Department would be requisitioning training land at Newmarket, Berkshire and other racecourses throughout the country for the use of army training exercises, something to which many trainers were opposed.

The following January, 1940, the Jockey Club sent a circular letter to racecourses inquiring if they would be available for flat racing, the season for which was scheduled to begin on 24 March. As yet, there was no decision about where to host the substitute Grand National, but Cheltenham was favourite for 19 and 20 March, the second day signalling the end of the jump meetings. There was also the possibility that there would be other jump meetings; Plumpton, for instance, was granted an additional fixture on 22 February.[8]

Although confidence in holding fixtures increased, Ascot was nonetheless abandoned in February 1940, while in April of that year it was announced that the Gold Cup and the Wokingham Stakes – both usually held at Ascot – would be transferred to Newmarket. Indeed, throughout World War Two Newmarket would host all of the Classics bar the St Leger of 1940 and 1941, which would be held at Thirsk and Manchester respectively. In all there would be 65 meetings, constituting 89 days of racing on 28 courses.

Throughout May and June 1940, just as the country was about to enter its most testing time of the war to date with the Blitz and the Battle of Britain, the Jockey Club engaged in talks with the Home Office, who were considering banning the broadcasting of racing results and then, indeed, racing altogether. Eventually, racing was officially stopped on 18 June. In that same month, a bomb fell at Newmarket, bringing home to all the fact that the British population wasn't immune from danger.

The time had come for the racing world – and, in particular, the Royal Stud – to adapt and implement the lessons learned in the previous war. The King's racing manager, Charles Moore, followed the course set by Lord Marcus Beresford during World War One and leased yearlings from the National Stud. These 'hirelings', as he called them, would be trained by Fred Darling of Beckhampton – a man who understood the workings of the National Stud –

and then be returned to the stud at the end of their racing days. In addition, Sandringham had been closed, its paddocks and the golf course used for agriculture, in contribution to the war effort.

Meanwhile, articles still appeared in the press debating the justification for racing, such as that which appeared in *The Times* on 27 August in which the sport was discussed as being an industry. The response was swift; on the 29th letters appeared in the paper calling for the racing and breeding industries not to be underrated.

The following day, the paper published an article that cited the problems of resuming horse-racing. The fact was that people still appreciated the spectacle of the sport, and indeed on 14 September the meeting at Ripon was re-established, one of the first since June, possibly as a litmus test for public opinion. With no wave of public condemnation sweeping the nation after Ripon opened for business, Newmarket followed in October. Ascot, however, stayed closed, having been commandeered by the army once again, its Grand Stand being used to house the Royal Artillery.

Further confirmation that running race meetings was a good idea came on 28 October, when King George enjoyed his first win of the season at Nottingham with his colt Merry Wanderer, who won the Bestwood Nursery to great acclaim.

The new year of 1941 opened with more bombing at Newmarket – an especially easy target due to the surrounding open fields – but there was a determination to carry on as normal. As if to emphasise this resolve, details soon appeared in the press concerning the King's turf entries.

However, on 31 January *The Times* published a short parliamentary statement from 'H Morrison' concerning the Grand National. The Home Secretary, it appeared, had refused to grant permission for a substitute race to take place at Cheltenham. Allowing the event to go ahead, said Morrison, would be 'undesirable'. Not everyone was convinced that it would be, however, and on 10 March the same newspaper published a letter from a member of the public who had listed his reasons for exactly why racing had to be resumed. At around the same time, Newmarket suffered its worst bombardment to date when the White Hart Hotel in the High Street received a direct hit. Twenty-seven people were killed and 248 were injured.

The ferocity of the arguments concerning horse-racing increased over the next three weeks, and on 1 April, with the question of racing becoming more prominent, the King's brother-in-law, Lord Harewood, announced that the Jockey Club and the government were in close touch. Two days later it was announced that flat-racing fixtures would continue as planned, while a decision would be made later about the other races.[9] In all, 65 race meetings took place that year, on thirteen different racecourses: Edinburgh, Lanark, Lincoln, Manchester, Newbury, Newmarket, Nottingham, Pontefract, Ripon, Salisbury, Stockton, Thirsk and Worcester. Racing in Ireland hadn't been affected by the British government's interdictions, of course, although by 1941 it had nevertheless been reduced by one-sixth.

As far as the Royal Stud was concerned, scheduled races for the King's horses were well on track, and in April Big Game, one of the hirelings, made his first appearance at Salisbury, winning the Hurstbourne Plate, with Gordon Richards up.[10] The horse later won the Cranbourne Stakes, the Salisbury Plate and the Coventry Stakes at Newmarket, on these occasions with Harry Wragg up, as Gordon was injured after an accident. Big Game's final race of the year was the Champagne Stakes at Newbury, which he won. Unsurprisingly, there were great hopes for him for the future.[11]

By September 1941, racing in the UK had been confined to five racecourses and meetings were effectively being cut to the bone. Then, the following February, the government ordered that horses couldn't be accepted for race meetings as transporting them was interfering with the running of the railways. Each year, it seemed that the government presented the sport with more and more challenges and a greater need to adapt, but there was also a need to assess progress – or, indeed, the lack thereof.

On 12 March it was announced in a White Paper detailing accounts of commercial services run by government departments that the National Stud in Ireland had suffered losses of £5,579 in the previous year.[12] Considering that the stud's net profits amounted to £86,498, the loss was a moderate one, yet it was clear that the war had taken its toll. Then an article in *The Times* listing the average prices of horses sold since 1936 revealed that in that year nine horses cost on average £1,684, while twelve horses cost £1,740 in 1937 and £1,127 in 1938, sixteen would fetch on average £835 in 1939 and six would fetch £367 in 1940. In addition, receipts by the Ministry of Agriculture from third-share stakes won by horses leased for racing amounted to £25 in 1940 – a huge drop from £1,888 in 1939.[13]

On 26 March the Jockey Club denied trainers permission to go to Newmarket, despite the need for a balance to be reached if horse-racing was to continue.

Back at the Royal Stud, meanwhile, the number of broodmares was further reduced from nine to eight, but another horse was leased from the National Stud, a filly named Sun Chariot, who had been bred in 1939 by Hypericum, out of Clarence. Like Big Game before her, she was trained by Fred Darling at

Beckhampton, although she was a lot more temperamental than her predecessor. Indeed, by 1942, at three years old, her temper was deteriorating, causing problems for her jockey, Gordon Richards, who noted in his autobiography that she was temperamental and obstinate, wanting to run her races her own way, without any interference from him. Richards had always had faith in the National Stud, but Sun Chariot unnerved him, particularly at the starting gate, when she would turn her head about to glare at him. She did, however, like many thoroughbreds before her, have the quirky trait of behaving herself for just one individual – in this case, her head lad, G Warren, to whom she was absolutely devoted.[14]

One day, the King and Queen visited Beckhampton to watch Sun Chariot and Big Game at work. After arriving on the dot of eleven, they followed Richards and Fred Darling onto the downs, where they found Sun Chariot behaving particularly badly – so badly, in fact, that she was almost violent.[15]

Nevertheless, Sun Chariot's behaviour didn't prevent her from running in the Oaks that year, even though she spoiled three starts before the race got under way. Then she seemed to get into her stride and went on to win. With all her sins forgiven, a delighted King led her off the course.[16]

Meanwhile, three-year-old Big Game – Sun Chariot's fellow 'hireling', who'd won a seven-furlong event at Salisbury that year – was of a completely different nature, with a tendency to become nervous. Then, on 12 May, he won the 2,000 Guineas by four lengths from Watling Street after running a strong race, and he and Gordon Richards were enthusiastically cheered by the crowd. Big Game had shown himself to be a stayer, and *The Times* judged him to be one of the best three-year-olds of the season, ridden with confidence by Richards and securing the winning post 'in truly regal style'. News of Big Game's victory soon reached the King and Queen, who were spending a quiet day at Buckingham Palace.

Sun Chariot was then scheduled to run on the afternoon of the next day, 13 May 1942, in the 1,000 Guineas. The *Times* correspondent observed that she would do so only 'if she is willing', adding that she'd been behaving 'like a very naughty young lady' of late, which was something of an understatement. He believed that she could win, but only if she was in the right mood. As it turned out, the newspaper later announced that Sun Chariot had won the race with 'ease and elegance' by four lengths from Perfect Peace, owned by Lord Glanely (who, tragically, would be killed in a bombing raid just a few weeks later), with Lord Rosebery's Afterthought coming third. Sun Chariot wasn't put out by her win and she behaved herself impeccably. Newmarket, the *Times* reporter noted, seemed to suit her temperament.

Both Big Game and Sun Chariot were now clear favourites for the Derby and the Oaks, which this year Princesses Elizabeth and Margaret were permitted to attend, along with the rest of the royal family. Knowledge that the royal family would be in attendance that year, combined with restricted rail access throughout June, meant that the roads around Newmarket (both races' new wartime home) were horribly congested. The girls, in particular, were remembered for their presence, and Fred Darling noted that Elizabeth had a good eye for a horse. In fact, by this time Elizabeth was an accomplished horsewoman and, on being made an honorary colonel in February 1942, had even ridden side-saddle in order to receive a salute at Horse Guards. Now she was developing a knowledge that impressed seasoned trainers like Darling.

Sun Chariot won the Oaks at Newmarket that year to thunderous applause for both her and the King. The next day was Derby day, and all hopes were pinned on Big Game to win. Unfortunately, before the race, he became hyperventilated and fought against being settled. Eventually he did calm down, but he never recovered his stride and came in sixth. This disappointing result didn't detract from Sun Chariot's victory, however, which even today is considered to be one of the more memorable Classic races, particularly as it was run at a time when the nation was at war. Indeed, the image of the King in his RAF uniform leading Sun Chariot off after her win seemed to establish horse-racing's place at such a volatile time and justified the efforts of all those trying to keep the sport going.[17]

The King went on to have further successes in July, and on the 29th a filly named Open Warfare, ridden by Gordon Richards, won the Balsham Stakes at the Third July Meeting. If she continued at such a pace, it was judged, she would do well the following season. Meanwhile, another of the King's horses, Garter Stitch, came third in the Hadstock Stakes, only just beaten in a very close finish.

Then, on 23 August, tragedy struck when the King's brother George, Duke of Kent, was killed in an air crash. Again, though, there was no period of mourning, as the royals recognised the nation's need to maintain normality, and just two days later Big Game – again, under Gordon Richards – took part in and won the Champion Stakes at Newmarket, beating Afterthought – who'd come third in the 1,000 Guineas – by a length and a half. Richards had kept Big Game back for part of the race but came forward towards the finish and gained the advantage with ease. Again, the horse showed that he possessed great stamina.[18]

On 7 September, *The Times* published an article on the King's horses, in particular Sun Chariot, who at that time was being prepared for the St Leger, scheduled for the 12th. She went on to win the race, beating Derby winner Watling Street – a piece of poetic justice for Big Game – by three lengths, again under Gordon Richards. She was now classed as one of the great fillies of the day, ranked alongside Sceptre, Pretty Polly and Rockfel. The race took a great deal out of those horses who came in second and third, but soon after her win Sun Chariot was nibbling grass in the unsaddling enclosure and seemed unperturbed.[19] Her behaviour days afterwards, though, was less than pleasant and indeed became so bad at one stage that she was sent back to Ireland, although she got only as far as Swindon railway station, where it was discovered that she didn't have the right papers and so was taken back to Beckhampton.

Later that month, William Jarvis retired after twenty years of royal service, but his retirement was a tragically short one as he died at the start of 1943. He was replaced by one of the country's top trainers, Cecil Boyd-Rochfort, trainer of Freemason Lodge, who took over at a time when the King became the first reigning monarch to head the list of winners. King George had done quite well with his National Stud horses, having won four of his five races – all Classics – but, disappointingly, didn't enjoy the same degree of success with his own.

On 15 May 1943 racing resumed at Ascot, where there would be nine days of racing between then and October. At Newmarket huts were constructed to accommodate the aircrews based there, while beds had also been set up in the Rowley Mile grandstand, on the covered steps and the long bar. The saddling rooms became Station Headquarters and the Armouries' workshop was installed in the Jockey Club bar. 161 Squadron bunked at Sefton Lodge, in the stablelads' quarters above the horse boxes, while the WAAFs got the house itself. The RAF, meanwhile, shared the Heath with the training establishment, while clerk of the course Cecil Marriott worried about whether or not the RAF had permission from the Jockey Club to land their planes on it. Such a manoeuvre was risky business, after all, as demonstrated when an RAF plane crashed onto the July course at around this time, killing the pilots. As a mark of respect, the Guineas race was postponed for a week.

On 26 May, the King's horse Knight's Daughter won the Pampisford Stakes at Newmarket under Doug Smith, who had only recently joined Boyd-Rochfort's stable. Smith later wrote of how Knight's Daughter could be temperamental and obstinate, noting that at times she 'behaved like a little cat'. On the day of the Pampisford Stakes, however, she behaved impeccably and won the race with ease. She was a horse blessed with first-class speed and was later retired to the Royal Stud with a good record, although she was later sold to a stud in America.

On 2 August the King and Queen visited Ascot, and both were acknowledged warmly by the thousands of people there, the King wearing his field-marshal's uniform. That year the King's horse Sun Blind was due to run in the Eton Stakes, where he finished second. Later, the King presented a portrait of the horse by A J Munnings to Gordon Richards, who hung it proudly on his dining-room wall.

On 9 August it was announced that the Egerton establishment – horses, stables, trainer's house, gallops and stud farm – had been sold to the Honourable Mrs Macdonald-Buchanan, the sale handled by Mr Norman J Hodgkinson of Messrs Bidwell and Sons, Cambridge. The stud farm was then leased to the Aga Khan. The sale signalled the end of an era, but as one era ended, another began.

In the autumn of 1943, seventeen-year-old Princess Elizabeth went hunting with the Garth foxhounds and, later, with the Duke of Beaufort's Hounds in Gloucester. In this year, too, she met Henry George Reginald Molyneux Herbert, Lord Porchester, the grandson of the 5th Earl of Carnarvon (of Tutenkhamen fame), whom she would call 'Porchie'. Lord Porchester would become very important to the Royal Stud in later years.

Meanwhile, Elizabeth and her sister, Margaret, continued to enjoy attending horseshows, and just days before D Day, on 27 May 1944, the royal family attended Windsor Horse Show, in which both girls competed for the first time, winning prizes in two classes. The King presented Margaret with a silver cup for her performance in the utility single driving class, while in the non-hackney section of the private driving class the two girls rode a phaeton that had once belonged to Queen Victoria, pulled by a Norwegian pony named Hans. The Duke of Beaufort handed the cup to them and later the Princesses handed out prizes to other winners.[20]

The following year, in the middle of March 1945, Princess Elizabeth became patroness of the National Horse Association of Great Britain, of which her father, the King, was already a patron.

Then, on 10 April, with the end of the war almost in sight, large crowds attended the July course at Newmarket. The King's horse Rising Light ran early that afternoon in the Column Stakes, which it won by a length. It was a very well-received win, particularly by the King, since Rising Light was one of his own horses, rather than one of those he'd leased from the National Stud.

By the time victory in Europe had been celebrated in May, the Royal Stud was in need of a shake-up. The King was committed to its role in the horse-breeding industry and understood the importance of horse-racing, and he decided that from that point on the Sandringham stud would be a stallion stud as well as one for broodmares. As a thank you for his efforts to keep things going, the King received a pair of race glasses from the stablelads, who'd each contributed sixpence towards the gift.[21]

Throughout the war, the King and Queen had been reassuring figures on the racecourse, and now their daughters were providing hope for the future. On 26 April the two girls attended the Royal Windsor Horse Show in Windsor Home Park with their parents; their aunt Marina, Duchess of Kent; and her daughter, Princess Alexandra of Kent. On that occasion, Elizabeth won first prize in the private driving class with Margaret as passenger in a cream and red phaeton, drawn by a black pony owned by the King, while Alexandra also competed in pony riding but didn't win anything. There was also a parade of Arab horses and the Duke of Beaufort presented Elizabeth with a picture of her driving a phaeton at the previous year's event.

In the days immediately after the end of the war, which ended on 9 June 1945, the King enjoyed some success on the flat, although in the Derby Rising Light – Princess Elizabeth's favourite – came fifth. This didn't cause him to go down in the Princess's estimation, however, and she would continue to photograph him for the rest of his life. In fact, the royal family were lucky to be at the Derby at all; they'd had some difficulty in reaching the course since petrol was still rationed. In addition, at Epsom in June that year, the grounds were still occupied by troops, encamped at Tattenham Corner, not far from the buildings that had suffered bomb damage.

The wartime ban on racing was lifted on 6 July, and soon afterwards it was announced that the King had leased four yearlings from the National Stud. While Charles Moore, the King's racing manager, could now concentrate on building up the numbers of broodmares for the Royal Stud, he also introduced a policy of sending foals to Ireland, with fillies going to Mooresfoot and colts to the Mondellihy Stud, County Limerick, owned by Peter Fitzgerald.

By this time, there was a sense of things in the world of horse-racing getting back to normal. The impact of the war was still very much in evidence, however, and nowhere more so than at the Buckingham Palace Riding School. The scene of so much change for the best part of 150 years, towards the end of July 1945 it saw itself playing host once more to wounded soldiers visiting the King and Queen.[22]

On Saturday, 4 August, the Princesses and their parents attended Ascot, Gordon Richards rode five winners that day, while Doug Smith rode the King's horse Rising Light in the Burghfield Stakes. The going was very hard and the field was quite small, so competition was neither strong nor fast. A horse named Stirling Castle began well and was two lengths in front of

Rising Light, but the King's horse had tremendous staying power and forced the pace, wearing Stirling Castle down to pass the finishing post almost neck and neck with Stirling Castle and a horse named Hobo. Rising Light had won.[23]

Then, on Monday, 6 August, the King enjoyed further success when a horse of his named Kingstone won the Sulhampstead Handicap. The horse later repeated his success on 1 September when, with Doug Smith, he won the Maple Durham Handicap at Ascot, his third win, bringing the total of successes for the King that year to seven. In the latter race, Smith rode Kingstone steadily and then, some three furlongs from the finish, pushed him forward.

Kingstone's win augured well for Rising Light,[24] who ran in the St Leger on 4 October and won, beating Lord Astor's High Stakes. This was a great success, considering that Rising Light had been beaten at York in the previous month, and he was starting to be recognised as a better class of colt. The victory was the King's tenth that year.[25]

In the same month, Smith had his first success on Hypericum, sister of Knight's Daughter, who, foaled at Hampton Court, had gone into training at Freemason Lodge in 1944. She showed a lot of speed but was difficult (Smith described her as 'temperamental'), although that was seen as a positive attribute, indicating that she had spirit. Even so, Smith suffered a nasty fall while riding her and was forced to stop riding her thereafter. The general consensus was that a rider of especial skill, above and beyond that of most experienced riders, was needed to handle her, and Ray Burrows was brought in to help break her in. Describing her as a 'brain box', he also thought her scatty – quiet one moment and jumpy the next – and noted her tendency to fly-kick. He rode her at Ascot in the Swallowfield Stakes on Saturday, 6 October, where she at first tried to take the gates on. Once the race was under way, however, she proved perfectly manageable and won easily, before going on to win the Dewhurst Stakes.[26]

Next on the racing calendar was the Houghton meeting at Newmarket, attended by Princess Elizabeth and a number of her guests, including Lord Porchester. Since the end of the war she had become a much more familiar figure on the racecourse, and on 30 October she was present in the unsaddling enclosure after Doug Smith's strong finish on Hypericum in the Dewhurst Stakes.

In 1945, Doug Smith was poached by the Earl of Derby. At the time, King George hadn't been best pleased about the business, but the fact remained that the stables at Stanley House were far more established than the royal stables, which had been affected adversely by the war. Captain Moore told Smith that, if he had a better offer, he should take it and not feel obliged to ride for the King. Smith even approached the King's brother-in-law, Lord Harewood, for advice on the move. In later years he would write that he had few regrets concerning his decision to move, despite the fact that the Royal Stable went into decline after his departure, and he no doubt felt guilty about leaving the King's service. As Smith worked off his notice, however, the King himself quickly forgave him, particularly since his final season would prove more successful than that of the previous year.

On 20 April 1946, at Hurst Park, Princess Elizabeth and her father looked on as Hypericum came second in the Kathryn Howard Stakes. Such an unpredictable horse, she always had to have horses on either side of her to stop her from darting out, but she was seen as a promising entrant to the 1,000 Guineas.

In preparation for the race, she was put through her paces with other horses and seemed fine to run, but on the day itself, 3 May, it seemed that she had other ideas. Before the race had begun, she unseated her jockey, Doug Smith, and took off along the course, disappearing into a car park, where she was retrieved by stablehand Johnny Grimes. By the time they'd returned to the gate, there had already been a fifteen minute delay and Gordon Richards was furious. To add insult to injury – to Richards, at least – Hypericum went on to win[27] the race (although it was later discovered that she could well have lost it on a technicality, as she'd still been wearing a neck strap). The King was delighted, however, and presented Smith with a gold-mounted whip.

In June 1946, Hypericum ran in the Oaks at Epsom while the King, Queen and Princess Elizabeth looked on, but again she ran into trouble, coming in fourth. She later injured herself but gamely took her chances at Ascot, where the Royal Meeting had been resumed on 18 June, but ran badly in the Coronation Stakes and was later retired to stud.

Despite the resurrection of the Royal Meeting at Ascot, that year post-war austerity meant that there was little in the way of high fashion on display, and while the royal family was in attendance, the Royal Procession was reserved for only two of the four days: Tuesday and Thursday. On the Wednesday, however, a new race was introduced, the Princess Elizabeth Stakes for two-year-old fillies, which was won in its inaugural year by Neocracy. Many felt that this new development indicated a burgeoning confidence and hope for the future.

Four years earlier, in 1942, the King and the Jockey Club had approved extra meetings at Ascot to take place in July, September and October. Now at last, this plan had become a reality, and on 19 July a six-race programme was transferred there from Sandown Park (although this was done more for reasons of practicality than anything else, since post-war Sandown still wasn't ready to hold meetings). That year saw the introduction of the Princess Margaret Stakes, for two-year-old fillies, followed in September by the Princess Royal Stakes.

Following Ascot's lead, Epsom too introduced a new race, the King George VI and Queen Elizabeth Stakes. That year's Derby – watched by 31,000 people, including the King, the Queen and Princess Elizabeth – was won by a horse named Dante. In the north, meanwhile, the King had success with Kingstone, who won the Great Yorkshire Stakes.

The royal family were regular visitors to the races and were now inextricably linked to the sport and industry of horse-racing and its image. Throughout the war, both horse-racing and the monarchy had served to boost the morale of the people, and now the royals found themselves actively participating in the reconstruction of the sport, which the King noted was a vital tool with which to pull the country back together. Where there was continuity, however, there was also change.

Throughout the summer of 1947, preparations were being made for the wedding of Princess Elizabeth and Prince Philip of Greece – also known as Lieutenant Philip Mountbatten, His Royal Highness the Duke of Edinburgh, Earl of Merioneth and Baron Greenwich – who had recently been nationalised as a British citizen. The wedding, scheduled for 20 November in Westminster Abbey, was just what the country needed after years of war. Amongst the royal couple's many wedding presents was a filly from the Aga Khan, by Turkhan out of Hastra. Elizabeth named her Astrakhan.

In 1949, the King's filly Avila won the Coronation Stakes at Ascot, and that evening, over dinner, former steeplechase jockey Lord Mildmay suggested that Queen Elizabeth branch out and have a horse trained for jumping. And so it was decided that she and Princess Elizabeth would share a horse, and that Lord Mildmay would act as their racing manager, with Peter Cazalet acting as their trainer.

Later in the year, Peter spotted an Irish-bred eight-year-old steeplechaser named Monaveen who had won three steeplechases and had come second and fourth in a couple of other races. Currently being trained by Peter Thrale at Epsom, he looked like he could also handle the Aintree course, so Cazalet and the King's racing manager, Charles Moore, visited Epsom to give him the once-over. They liked what they saw and negotiated to buy him, whereupon he was stabled at Peter Cazalet's Fairlawne property in June and scheduled to participate in the autumn meeting at Fontwell Park on 10 October.

At this time, Prince Philip, the Duke of Edinburgh and Princess Elizabeth's husband, was also considering a change in direction. Until he'd married Elizabeth, he'd no real idea of the depth of her love of horses. He himself was a natural sportsman and enjoyed playing cricket, sailing and horsemanship (although the last of these had never been a real passion in his life), but when he found that Elizabeth preferred to watch his uncle, Lord Louis Mountbatten, play polo rather than watch him play cricket, he decided to take up the sport himself. He discovered that Lord Mountbatten had even written a book about polo, under the pseudonym 'Marco', and decided that, if anyone could teach him the rudiments of the sport, it was his uncle. He approached his uncle and soon lessons were under way at the Marsa Club, where Philip discovered that the best conditions for playing polo were on hard ground under a hot sun (which is why Argentina is such a favoured place for the sport), while the worst conditions were in soggy weather or with a bad pony or both. Prince Philip took to the sport quite quickly and became so enthusiastic while playing it that he tended to shout a lot, not instructing or encouraging, but simply an animalistic response produced by sheer terror. It was, he agreed, a form of abuse.

After a visit to Malta with his wife, Prince Philip joined Cowdray Park Polo Club, where he and fellow naval officers formed a team, dubbed 'the Mariners'. Their captain was a marine general named Sir Robert Neville, who before the war had been part of Lord Mountbatten's blue-jacket polo team. Unfortunately, Neville suffered an accident before the start of the season, so a replacement was recruited who had once been a member of the Indian Army.

When Cowdray Park proved to be difficult to get to, Prince Philip moved to a club at Smith's Lawn, Windsor Great Park, and hence the Household Division or Guards' Polo Club was established.

The high point of the polo calendar was the International Polo Day in August, and when he attended in 1949 Philip produced his own colours for the sport: the red and green livery of Windsor Park.

On 29 September, the partnership between Queen Elizabeth and the Princess Elizabeth was registered under National Hunt rules and then announced the next day in *The Times*, while Princess Elizabeth had also registered her colours: scarlet with purple hooped sleeves and black cap with gold tassel. These colours had been debuted with Monaveen on his first royal run, at Fontwell Park, Chichester, on Monday, 10 October. That day, Elizabeth was accompanied by Lord Mildmay, a steward of the National Hunt Committee and a patron of Peter Cazalet's stable, where Monaveen was being trained. Monaveen was ridden in the Chichester Handicap Steeplechase over three and a quarter miles by Tony Grantham, beginning at 100–30, and won by fifteen lengths. Peter Cazalet later judged that the next challenge for such a sound horse was the Grand Sefton Steeplechase at Liverpool.

By this time, the King wasn't in the best of health and Queen Elizabeth was taking on more and more of the couple's public duties. She was therefore unable to watch Monaveen run as often as she would have wished, but her daughter did when she was able to. She was watching with her sister, Margaret, when he came second in the Grand Sefton Steeplechase, again ridden by Tony Grantham. In that race, Monaveen had a good run but was beaten by Freebooter, who later went on to win the 1950 Grand National. There was consolation, however, in Monaveen's comfortable winning of a new three-mile handicap – the Queen Elizabeth Chase – followed by similar victories at the Walton Green Steeplechase and a race on the Sussex Steeplechase course at Fontwell Park.

Monaveen ended 1949 by winning the Queen Elizabeth Chase on New Year's Eve. Then, on the first Saturday in January 1950, he won the Queen Elizabeth Steeplechase at Hurst Park, giving what *The Times* called a 'sparkling performance'[28] and raising hopes for his participation in the Grand National. While he later demonstrated – again, at Hurst Park – that he didn't like heavy ground, preparations continued nonetheless and he was entered into the Grand National, which took place on 25 March in the presence of the King and Queen. He was doing well until the fourteenth fence, where he fell back, effectively putting paid to any further aspirations of him achieving a victory at the National, although he did manage to finish fifth.

At around this time, Peter Cazalet developed pneumonia and spent two months abroad to convalesce. During this time, Monaveen was placed in the care of Cazalet's friend and colleague Anthony Mildmay, head man Jim Fairgreave and travelling head lad Bill Bradden.

In April, in something of a change of fortune for Princess Elizabeth, her horse Astrakhan won the Merry Maiden Stakes at Hurst Park, but tragedy followed victory and on 12 May Lord Anthony Mildmay drowned while out swimming that morning, possibly as a result of the crippling neck cramps that had brought his career as a jockey to an end. His death came as a terrible shock to those who knew him, and in his will it was found that he'd left all of his horses to Peter Cazalet.

Later that month, the King's two-year-old Northern Hope won the Fillies Plate at Leicester. Then on 3 July she won the Savile Plate by two lengths and another two-year-old, Norwester, won the Fillies Plate by a head for the King, before going on to win the Great Kingston Plate at Sandown Park later in July. In the same month, the Queen purchased a horse named Manicou, who had been left to Peter Cazalet in Lord Mildmay's will. Princess Elizabeth didn't take a share in this horse, and so he would later appear under the Queen's own colours: blue with buff stripes, blue sleeves and black cap with a gold tassel – the same colours, in fact, as those of her great-uncle Lord Strathmore, which she would register in October.

On 19 October, Queen Elizabeth watched Monaveen run under her colours for the first time at Hurst Park in the Grand Sefton Trial. There were twenty runners that day and Monaveen finished fifth, having jumped well. Then, less than a month later, on 11 November he ran at Aintree in the Grand Sefton Steeplechase, but he lost the lead at Valentine's Brook and the other horses swept past him.

Later that month, on 24 November, Manicou won the Wimbledon Handicap Steeplechase at Kempton Park with Tony Grantham up. On that occasion Queen Elizabeth saw him run in her colours, even though she had been up late the previous night, dancing at a ball held at Buckingham Palace in honour of Queen Juliana and Prince Bernhard of the Netherlands. Manicou, taking the race in his stride, jumped very well and won by eight lengths.[29] However, having enjoyed the highs of racing, the Queen was about to experience some of its lows.

On 2 December, Monaveen took part in the Queen Elizabeth Steeplechase, ridden once more by Tony Grantham, but while he was negotiating the water jump, he broke his leg. Grantham escaped with cuts, bruises and concussion, but tragically Monaveen had to be put down.[30] Hopes for the Grand National now rested on Manicou.

On 14 December, under his new jockey, Bryan Marshall, Manicou ran in the Ewell Steeplechase at Sandown Park and performed well, again demonstrating a good measure of staying power – essential for the Grand National. He was challenged only once, by Freddy Fox, but eventually secured the race from Lucky Number. Marshall recalled later how the Queen talked about his mother, who had ridden at the Richmond Horse Show years before, describing the Queen as 'frightfully nice' and extremely knowledgeable.[31]

On Boxing Day 1950, Manicou proved himself once again by winning the King George VI Chase at Kempton Park. Ridden by Bryan Marshall, on that occasion he beat Silver Fame by three lengths.

The King, too, enjoyed success in 1950 with Above Board, bred by him in 1947 and trained by Cecil Boyd-Rochfort. As a three-year-old, the horse was a good stayer and in that year won the Yorkshire Oaks and Cesarewitch.

By this time, however, the King wasn't at all well, having undergone a lumbar sympathectomy the previous year. While he was determined to continue with his duties, his health was deteriorating further, although he was well enough to attend Kempton Park with the Queen in March 1951.

That April, the Queen attended Newmarket, and she and Princess Elizabeth were present on the 25th to watch Manicou finish last of six in the Gold Cup. Nonetheless, it was an impressive run, as he finished just 21 yards behind the winner, Silver Frame.

That summer proved to be a busy one. On 4 May the King's two-year-old horse Lyon King was scheduled to run in the Littleport Two-Year-Old Stakes on Newmarket Heath, and meanwhile Princess Elizabeth attended Hurst Park. The family came together to attend Ascot, but there was an upset in August when Manicou injured his leg. A horse named Devon Loch – a recent addition to Fairlawne – was recommended as a replacement. He would run that autumn.[32]

Before that time, however, on 31 August, while the King was recovering from an operation,[33] his two-year-old Deuce, under Gordon Richards, won the Taplow Plate – the opening event at Ascot – after Richards drew steadily away from the pack after taking the lead halfway through the race.

In October, Deuce won the Newmarket Foal Stakes by a comfortable margin, making up for his failure at Goodwood earlier that year, and later in the same month another of the King's horses (though leased from the National Stud), Good Shot, won a five-furlong nursery race under Gordon Richards, maintaining a strong race from start to finish and winning by half a length. The King watched the race from his sickbed on television.[34]

Also in October, Devon Loch, running in the Queen's colours, ran sixth in a race at Nottingham and three weeks later was running at Kempton, where again he couldn't keep up. He returned to form towards the end of the year, though, and was in good form by the time he ran at Newbury, where he finished second. Indeed, his form was improving day by day. On 17 January 1952 he ran at Hurst Park and came second once more, but he later damaged a tendon and had to be rested.

By that time, the King had been at Sandringham for almost a month, having been there since 21 December. He was recovering from another operation, this one to remove a malignant tumour, along with his left lung, on 29 September. While he was there, he spent a lot of time shooting, and his doctors judged that he was making good progress.

In February 1952, George saw Elizabeth and Philip off on a tour of Australia via Africa, and then visited his mother in London before returning to Sandringham. In the early hours of 6 February, he died peacefully in his sleep.

On the morning of 7 February, as the circumstances of King George's life and death were published, the newspapers were able to give details of what was to happen to horse-racing. *The Times* announced that the cancellation of fixtures would come into effect immediately, while future fixtures were still being considered. (This applied particularly to the Grand National, where entries had dropped from 84 to 67.)[35] Haydock, however, was stopped straight away and the *Daily Mail* had it from the National Hunt stewards that there would be no more racing until after the King's funeral, which took place on 15 February.[36]

Notes:

1. *The Times*, 13.01.1937
2. Ibid.
3. *The Times*, 19.01.1937
4. *The Times*, 13.03.1937
5. *The Times*, 01.07.1937
6. Smith, Doug, *Five Times Champion*, p26
7. *The Sporting Life*, 04.09.1939
8. *The Times*, 25.09.1939
9. *The Times*, 17.01.1940
10. *The Times*, 01.04.1941; 03.04.1941
11. *The Times*, 19.09.1941
12. *The Times*, 06.02.1942
13. *The Times*, 12.03.1942
14. Richards, pp136–7
15. Richards, p137
16. Richards, p138
17. *The Times*, 30.07.1942
18. *The Times*, 26.08.1942
19. *The Times*, 07.09.1942
20. *The Times*, 22.10.1943; 22.12.1943
21. Thompson
22. *The Times*, 06.07.1945
23. *The Times*, 06.08.1945
24. *The Times*, 07.08.1945
25. *The Times*, 05.10.1945
26. *The Times*, 31.10.1945
27. *The Times*, 03.05.1946
28. *The Times*, 02.01.1950
29. *The Times*, 25.11.1950
30. *The Times*, 04.12.1950
31. *The Times*, 15.12.1950
32. *News Chronicle*, 04.05.1951
33. *The Times*, 01.09.1951
34. *The Times*, 15.10.1951
35. *The Times*, 07.02.1952
36. *Daily Mail*, 07.02.1952

21
Elizabeth II

From the start of the second Elizabethan era in 1953 to the present day, the world of horse-racing and the monarchy have undergone sweeping changes and have been forced to adapt, not just to the changes themselves but also to the pace of them. In this regard, the monarchy has been more successful than most people might think, but at the same time it has held onto those principles of duty that have characterised the institution of monarchy over the centuries. Queen Elizabeth II has always seen her involvement in horse-breeding and horse-racing as being part of her role as a landowner and a monarch, and it's true that under her patronage and that of her mother, the late Queen Elizabeth, the Queen Mother, the profile of horse-racing has been raised immeasurably. In addition, the Queen's reign has seen many characters in the royal household, both human and equine, take on a previously unheard-of status via television and the internet.

Back in February 1952, such developments would have been unthinkable for a populace who had recently endured a world war and lost a king who had gone to great lengths to see them through it. Horse-racing, too, had lifted their morale during that time of crisis, but the sport was still recovering from the impact of the war. To make things worse, on the King's death, the world of horse-racing was also about to lose the patronage of one of its most dedicated supporters, Queen Elizabeth (now the Queen Mother), at least for a while.

Between 1952 and 1953, although she supported her eldest daughter in her new role as queen, the Queen Mother withdrew from the public eye and sport. During her husband's illness, she'd had little time to patronise horse-racing and after his death spent the next twelve months or so coming to terms with her loss, dividing her time between her homes in England and Scotland.

Meanwhile, Queen Elizabeth II continued where her father had left off and announced that she would not only maintain the royal studs but would also continue racing the royal horses along the same lines as her father. She had inherited nearly twenty mares from King George, including Feola and her daughters, Hypericum, Angelola and Above Board. Cecil Boyd-Rochfort, meanwhile, would remain as trainer, as the Queen liked him and understood his way of doing things.[1] She would also continue to lease horses from the National Stud, and these would be trained by Noel Murless, who had succeeded Fred Darling, having trained first at Beckhampton and then at Warren Place, Newmarket. Meanwhile, Captain Charles Moore would remain as racing manager and would also run the Hampton Court stud, although the Queen wouldn't continue with racing under National Hunt rules, leaving that side of the sport to her mother in the years to come. And from March, during the period of mourning following her father's death, her horses would run in the Duke of Norfolk's name.

Until that time, however, there was much to come to terms with, and in February the Queen extended a message of thanks to the public in response to their reaction to the King's death.

In 1953, the newspapers followed the progress of the Queen's horses with interest, including one named Choir Boy, who provided her with her first win as monarch in a handicap at Newmarket. However, they seemed most interested in a horse named Aureole, who was seen as a Derby hopeful for that year. Originally bred by George VI in 1950, Aureole was by Hyperion, out of Angelola. Trained by Boyd-Rochfort, he could be temperamental but had potential for the Classics. His first appearance had been at York on 19 August the previous year,[2] and since then he'd won the Acomb Stakes, but there was nevertheless some concern that, although he was down for the major Classics the following year, he wasn't good at the gate and hadn't been sufficiently trained. And his sixth-place performance in the Middle Park Stakes did little to increase confidence.

At the start of 1953, much was written about Aureole's chances in the Derby. On 2 February, for instance, it was announced that he'd been backed to win £30,000 in it, although Victor Sassoon's Pinza was the undoubted favourite, not only because of his past performance but also due to the fact that Gordon Richards was riding him, making them the perfect combination of horse and rider. If Aureole won, however, sporting history would be made, as he would be the first Derby winner owned by a monarch since 1909 and the first for a reigning monarch in their coronation year.

The Queen was anxious about both events: her coronation and the forthcoming Derby, particularly Aureole's preparation for it. The competition was fierce, with Pinza's owner, Victor Sassoon, stating his belief that his horse was suited to Gordon's 'riding genius'.[3]

Before the Derby, though, both the Queen and the Queen Mother were present for the Cheltenham Gold Cup, for which Peter Cazalet had trained Statecraft, owned by Mrs White, sister of the late Lord Mildmay. When

Statecraft's original jockey, Tony Grantham, was hurt in an accident, Cazalet approached a jockey named Dick Francis, who agreed to ride in his stead.

On the day of the event, Dick got ready and entered the parade ring, where Cazalet told him that he was about to meet the Queen. (As he recalled in his autobiography years later, at this point he was very conscious of the fact that he wouldn't be able to remove his cap, as it had been fixed firmly to his head so that it wouldn't fall off during the race.) When the Queen approached him, they talked about Statecraft for a few minutes and then Cazalet helped Dick into the saddle.

That year's Gold Cup wasn't the best of races, as Statecraft pulled a tendon during the running, but Dick had made a favourable impression on Peter Cazalet. Six weeks later, as the two men stood on the veranda outside the weighing-in room at Sandown Park, the trainer asked him if he would ride on a regular basis for him the following season – which meant riding the royal horses. Dick was delighted but confessed that he was still under contract to ride Lord Bicester's horses and said he'd have to check with his employer, but there turned out to be no problem and Dick began the 1953–4 racing season at Cazalet's stable at Fairlawne.

Just a few weeks later, on 1 June, Gordon Richards received a letter from Sir Winston Churchill, the current prime minister, informing him that he would be knighted. Overwhelmed by the honour, he had no idea how to answer Sir Winston's letter, feeling that whatever reply he made would be an inadequate representation of his feelings, but he did reply.

The following day – the day of the coronation – Richards met Churchill at Lingfield races and the two men discussed the importance of the knighthood. Sir Winston pointed out that it was an honour for the sport as a whole, elevating both it and the riders connected with it in a social context. Such an honour confirmed the notion that jockeys had moved on from being servants to being professionals in their own right. While appreciation of their services had always been recognised, Richards' knighthood conveyed respect of the highest level.

On 3 June 1953, the list of runners in that year's Derby was released. Pinza, Aureole and Aureole's stable companion Premonition had done well at Newmarket in their trials for the event, Pinza running with an easy grace over eleven furlongs and currently approaching his peak, according to the *Daily Telegraph and Morning Post*. Aureole, meanwhile, had shown energy over seven furlongs and Premonition too had run well.[4]

The Queen continued to follow Aureole's progress, even asking how he was doing on the day of her coronation, broadcast live on television. Among the congregation at Westminster Abbey that day was the Queen's trainer, Cecil Boyd-Rochfort, who later described the Queen as 'magnificent'.

Four days later, the Queen attended Epsom for the long-awaited Derby. That year, Harry Carr had the honour of riding the Queen's horse Aureole, but when he saw how fit Pinza looked his heart sank. Indeed, the race did eventually go to Pinza, with Sir Gordon Richards riding, and the Queen was so impressed by the performance of Victor Sassoon's horse that in December both she and the Princess Royal would become part owners of him.

Aureole, however, was proving to be very excitable and temperamental – so much so, in fact, that neurologist Dr Charles Brook was consulted in an attempt to calm him down. Brook's method involved the laying on of hands and had been successful on other horses, most notably those that had pulled the coach during the Queen's coronation, and indeed he was successful with Aureole – for a while, at least.

Then, at the beginning of July, the horse suffered a troubling cough. Although it cleared up well enough, it was doubtful that he would run in the Eclipse Stakes. Instead, he was booked to run in the King George VI and Queen Elizabeth Stakes at Ascot. In the event, he did run in the Eclipse Stakes, where he came third, and then came second in the latter race.

Following such a promising result, he was entered to run in the St Leger in September, but on that occasion he played up so much that it cost him the race and he came third. The relaxation treatment he'd received earlier in the year appeared to have failed, but at least there was hope for the following season.

Also in the autumn, the Queen Mother bought a dark-brown gelding named M'as-tu-vu, a recent acquisition of Peter Cazalet's who first appeared in the Queen Mother's colours at Kempton, where he enjoyed a comfortable win. Two days later, he won the Blindley Heath Handicap Chase at Lingfield while the Queen Mother looked on, and he would go on to enjoy five more wins. The following year the Queen Mother's horses would increase to four with the acquisition of Gypsy Love, from Major Eldred Wilson's farm at Hillington, King's Lynn, who would join Devon Loch, Manicou and M'as-tu-vu at Fairlawne. In the future Major Wilson would provide the Queen Mother with a number of young horses, and she would keep an eye on all of them, showing a keen interest in their development and progress.

1953, meanwhile, ended on a high note, and in the new year Devon Loch was proving to be a stayer. He'd beaten some good horses in novice chases, so much was expected of him – which was more than could be said for the Queen's Aureole, who had mixed fortunes that year. After winning the Coronation Cup for the Queen, he was beaten in the Coronation Stakes at Sandown, where he was almost brought down. He did, however, go on to win the Victor Wild Stakes at Kempton.

On 18 June, Aureole participated in the Hardwicke Stakes under Eph Smith, who was deaf and was the only jockey there that day with a hearing aid, the batteries for which he kept in a little holster beneath his silks. A wire connected them to the earpiece, which was kept in place with a headband. The hearing aid worked, to a certain extent; people would shout to him and he'd shout back. Sometimes, though, he wouldn't realise how loudly he was shouting and horse owners would shrink back as he announced for all to hear that their horses were rubbish. A quiet word with Smith would quickly turn into a shouting match. On one occasion he got into trouble with stewards when he reprimanded Lester Piggott, effing and blinding all over the course, loud enough for television crews to pick up, and was warned about his language.

The problem was that Smith frequently misunderstood what was said to him. Even the Queen didn't escape this when, a few days before the Hardwicke Stakes were due to run, she asked Eph about Aureole's eye, which he had knocked. Eph loudly replied that Aureole's leg was fine. When he was corrected (something he was quite used to), he added that, with him being half deaf and Aureole being half blind, they made a good team.

Aureole's last race was the King George VI and Queen Elizabeth Stakes on 17 July 1954, and on that occasion the Queen came to watch him run. To begin with, Aureole, who had at first seemed calm and relaxed, suddenly threw his jockey, and, while Smith was picking himself up, quietly began cropping grass. Undeterred, Smith remounted, whereupon both horse and rider took command of the race and won it comfortably from Vamos, proving that Aureole could run when he wanted to. In fact, he'd won seven of his fourteen races, coming either second or third in the Derby and St Leger. Nevertheless, he was soon retired to stud, where he proved to be a great success as a sire.[5]

While Aureole and Landau had dominated horse-racing in July, at the end of the month the Queen had beaten all others to become leading owner, and her run of success continued in September, when on the 21st the Sterling Handicap was secured by her horse Opera Score in a thrilling finish. A few weeks later, on 8 October, her newcomer Alexander was successful in the Duke of Edinburgh's Stakes. A good horse who was improving steadily, he was soon entered in the Dewhurst Stakes.[6]

Meanwhile, the Queen Mother was steadfastly supporting her horse Manicou. When he ran the Eridge Steeplechase at Lingfield on 26 November, the weather was atrocious, but nevertheless she watched him run.

By the time he completed the course with Bryan Marshall up, he was caked with mud.

The following month, Manicou seemed to weaken,[7] and after he'd blundered in a Boxing Day event he would never run again. The Queen Mother was disappointed but had learned to take the rough with the smooth where this sport was concerned and looked forward to the following season.

On 5 February 1955, the Queen and Queen Mother attended Hurst Park, where Bryan Marshall rode Devon Loch to victory in the New Century Chase, despite Peter Cazalet's opinion before the race that he wouldn't win and should instead concentrate on simply completing the race safely. When the horse did win, therefore, the royal party were delighted. After the race, Marshall was invited to meet the Queen and her mother to explain the progress of the race, but when he opened his mouth to speak the royal women suddenly dissolved into fits of laughter. Bryan, it appeared, wasn't wearing his false teeth, having removed them before the race, and the two women couldn't understand a word he said.

The next month, on 16 March, the Queen Mother's horse M'as-tu-vu did well at Lingfield, where he jumped in perfect, confident style, despite competition from Colonel Bagwash and Atom Bomb. He was proving to be an all-weathers horse, excelling on both dry and heavy ground, while Devon Loch suited firm ground. This preference was noted in a two-mile steeplechase in which he ran well and jumped confidently, winning comfortably after Bryan Marshall took him to the front early on and kept him there.[8]

Throughout November and December 1955, there had been a number of articles in the press about the Queen Mother's horses, and on 15 March the following year it was announced that both Devon Loch and M'as-tu-vu would run in the Grand National. Of the two horses, Devon Loch was the favourite, having won at Lingfield Park the previous day. Overall, he was a short-priced favourite, and it was noted that he usually worked best late in the season. M'as-tu-vu, meanwhile, was considered to be one of the most dominant horses among the many hopefuls, particularly after the form he'd demonstrated at Sandown Park, but he'd also run an unsatisfactory race at Cheltenham.

One person who had a great deal of affection for Devon Loch was Dick Francis, who was scheduled to ride him in the Grand National. Francis had first noticed the horse in October 1951, when Devon Loch had run in his first race, a maiden hurdles event at Nottingham, and had seen a big, intelligent-looking horse with signs of developing strength. The jockey had actually requested of Peter Cazalet that he be allowed to ride him in the National, despite the fact that Devon Loch hadn't had much experience in the novice and handicap races that ultimately led to Aintree. A while later, with Bryan Marshall up, Devon Loch had won the New Century Novices Steeplechase at Hurst Park, while Francis had been riding Lochroe. He later partnered Devon Loch in November 1955, although they lost the race. Nevertheless, hopes were still high for the Grand National the following year.[9]

Dick was excited at the prospect of competing in the National but was still aware of the responsibility participation in the event placed on him. Fifteen days before the race, he cracked his collarbone – for the ninth time – but decided not to tell anyone about the injury because he knew he'd be all right on the day. Indeed, by the time he got to Aintree, he was fine.[10]

Dick always believed that it was best to approach any race with a plan rather than rely on luck, and the Grand National was certainly no exception. The plan was for Devon Loch to lie towards the back of the field during the first mile – an unusual tactic because most jockeys took their horses to the front, enabling them to get out of trouble as fast as possible. The first quarter of a mile was too long, so after much deliberation Dick decided to keep Devon Loch's progress steady. So deeply wrapped up was he in plans for the race that he remembers hardly speaking to anyone at Aintree before it began.[11]

He also remembers seeing the Queen, the Queen Mother and Princess Margaret watching Devon Loch and M'as-tu-vu walking around the parade ring, commenting to Dick on how well the horses looked. When Devon Loch had been what he later described as 'kindly handicapped', Cazalet helped both Dick and M'as-tu-vu's jockey, Arthur Freeman, into their saddles before they went onto the course to join the other 27 runners.

Although there were some falls, the start of that year's Grand National was a good one. Devon Loch strode forward and continued to press. He made the National a delight for Dick, who felt that the horse knew what he was doing where other horses had to be coaxed. They jumped Becher's Brook, the Canal Turn and Valentine's Brook with ease.

Then, two fences later, Devon Loch sidestepped a sprawling horse named Donnato, almost in mid-air, and continued on what was turning out to be a dream run. In fact, his running got better and better as he cleared the Chair and the Water Jump. By this time he was lying in sixth place, with M'as-tu-vu behind him, but by the time he approached the Canal Turn he was lying second, behind Armorial III. He still had a great deal of energy at this stage, but Dick held him back. They had plenty of time.

It was a sound tactic. Armorial III fell at the fence after Valentine's Brook and Eagle Lodge took his place, but Dick still held Devon Loch back with energy in reserve. Nothing could stop them. They jumped the final fence with ease and headed for the finish – but then, just one hundred yards from the line, Devon Loch sprawled and his race was over.[12] Nevertheless, as Dick would write years later in his autobiography, *The Sport of Queens: A Champion Jockey's Personal Story*, it was better to have run and lost than not to have run at all. *The Sporting Life* described the race at the time as the most amazing Grand National ever run.

A minute after Devon Loch had fallen, Dick stood forlornly on the course, searching for his whip, which he'd foolishly thrown away in anger and anguish, unable to believe his bad luck. Devon Loch was being led back to his stable, so Dick took his time about returning to the weighing-in room, wanting to be alone to come to terms with what had just happened[13] before having to face the sympathy of his colleagues. An ambulance came to his rescue, though, and he was driven back to the paddock.[14]

As Dick was finishing getting dressed, Cazalet came into the changing room and told him to come up to the royal box. Dick followed him, feeling as bad for the trainer as he did for himself. When he got there, the box was hushed, in what the jockey later described as a 'shadow of silence'. As Dick apologised, the Queen and Queen Mother tried to comfort him, telling him that, at the end of the day, he'd ridden a great race. 'That's racing, I suppose,' the Queen Mother told him, although Dick could tell that she and the Queen were upset.[15]

On leaving the royal box, Dick and Cazalet visited Devon Loch at the stables, where, oblivious to his ignominious defeat, he was quite calmly munching hay and being groomed. Dick patted him and Cazalet checked his legs but could not find anything wrong.[16]

Devon Loch was later taken to the horse's hospital to be checked over, and the Queen Mother and Princess Margaret visited him there. 'What a tragedy,' observed the Queen Mother, and indeed both women were deeply disappointed, remaining for fifteen minutes. It later transpired that Devon Loch was uninjured, and the winning jockey, Dave Dick, paid tribute to him by saying that he hadn't expected to catch up.

After collecting his wife, Mary, Dick and his family returned to Bangor, hardly saying a word, although his children demanded to know why Devon Loch had 'sat down'. One said he'd lost money and another asked if the Queen was cross. When they got back, the youngest, aged three, made matters worse by imitating Devon Loch's sprawl, hurling himself across the carpet, limbs outspread.

That evening, the phone rang off the hook and was answered by Dick's friend Douglas while Dick and Mary walked off their disappointment. The next day, the family returned to Berkshire, and throughout the following week

Dick received hundreds of letters although, notably, none from what he described as the 'cruelty of Aintree' brigade.

Four days after the race, the Queen Mother visited Devon Loch at Fairlawne with Dick, who, on riding him in the park, found him well and not suffering from any after-effects of the fall. The Queen Mother still wanted to hear what Dick had to say about the race, however, and soon afterwards the jockey found himself at Windsor, discussing what had happened. It was agreed that no one was at fault, least of all Dick, and he left with a cheque and a cigarette case.[17]

The 26 March edition of *The Times* described that year's Grand National as 'infamous' and tried to make some sense of Devon Loch's fall before eventually concluding that the exact cause of his tumble would probably never be known. There was then an account of the race, including the winning time, which, at 9 minutes and 21 seconds, came very close to breaking Golden Miller's record of 9 minutes 20.4 seconds. Given that he'd run well, there was hope that Devon Loch would run the following year, but sadly he never did, although he did go on to participate in other races before he eventually became trainer Noel Murless's hack.[18]

In 1956, three-year-old talent proved somewhat thin on the ground, although the Queen had some highly promising two-year-olds, including one named Carozza, a filly with whom the Queen enjoyed some success that May when she won the Rosemary Plate at Hurst Park. Carozza was by Dante, the winner of the 1945 Derby, who was leased to the Queen by the National Stud and trained by Noel Murless. Shortly after her triumph at Hurst Park, however, she suffered an injury after rearing backwards in her box and was out of action for some time. There was consolation for the Queen that year, though, when another of her horses, Alexander, won the Royal Hunt Cup at Ascot.

The following year's season was the Queen's most exciting to date, and at the start of 1957 she had thirty horses in training: 21 with Cecil Boyd-Rochfort and nine with Noel Murless. That year, she also had three top-class fillies – Almeria, bred at Sandringham; Mulberry Harbour, also bred at Sandringham; and a now fully recovered Carozza, who was from the National Stud – as well as two colts: Doutelle and Agreement.

On 7 May, Mulberry Harbour won the Cheshire Oaks at Chester and on the 24th Doutelle won the Derby Trial Stakes at Lingfield. *The Times*, however, was of the opinion that the Queen would win the Oaks with Mulberry Harbour rather than the Derby with Doutelle, since the latter horse had won the Trial Stakes by only a neck against an undersized horse. In the event, Victor Sassoon's Crepello won the 1957 Derby and Doutelle went on to win the Granville Stakes at Ascot.

In the Oaks that June, the Queen had two horses running: Mulberry Harbour (ridden by Harry Carr in the Queen's colours) and Carozza (ridden by Lester Piggott in the second colours with a white cap). Piggott later wrote in his autobiography that to him the Oaks was one of the most exciting contests in horse-racing ('pulsating' was the word he described it as) and he always tried to ride it like a Derby. The Oaks fields are smaller, however, and it's easier to hold fifth or sixth position when coming into the straight – and this is where Lester and Carozza found themselves as they reached Tattenham Corner. Lester pushed Carozza into the lead with a quarter of a mile still left to run and had to ride her hard, fighting to maintain position and eventually winning by only a short head. He recalled that being led in by the Queen was the proudest moment of his life. She gave him some cufflinks to mark the event – his sole Classic success in royal colours.

Mulbery Harbour, meanwhile, came last, causing many to believe that she'd been doped. Indeed, her eyes were glazed and her heartbeat was very irregular. After a series of tests, it was decided to give her a rest.[19]

Elsewhere, further success was achieved by another royal favourite, a two-year-old named Pall Mall – by Palatine out of Malapert – who won the Maiden Plate at Haydock Park before going on to win the New Stakes at Ascot and coming second in the July Stakes at Newmarket. For Carozza, meanwhile, things weren't going quite so well. At around the same time she came fourth in the Nassau Stakes and, sadly, became lame, whereupon she was retired to stud.

That year, the Queen didn't attend the St Leger. It was won easily by her horse Agreement, who didn't seem even to be breathing heavily after triumphing on one of the toughest races on the flat. And, to add to the Queen's achievements, Almeria won the Yorkshire Oaks and was soon after rated the best three-year-old trained in England in 1957, with Carozza second and Mulberry Harbour third.

At this time, there was fierce competition between the Queen and Victor Sassoon for the coveted title of leading owner. At one point, the *Daily Herald* announced that the Queen was in front by just over £500 but added that, if Sassoon's Boccaccio won at Newbury, he would gain the advantage. Ultimately, though, the Queen headed the list, primarily – but not solely – thanks to Agreement's achievement; in the final analysis, 21 horses from the Sandringham stud won 23 races while nine from the National Stud won seven.[20]

That autumn, the Queen Mother was present at Newbury to watch her horse Double Star – who'd been her best of the previous season – run in the Tote Investors' Cup. When he won the race, the Queen Mother had the unusual distinction of receiving the cup that she should have been presenting, immediately showing it off to her nine-year-old grandson, Prince Charles. Double Star would prove to be one of the Queen Mother's most indomitable horses, participating in fifty races over eight years.

The 1957–8 season also saw the Queen Mother enjoy 45 racing wins – her highest to date – with eight of her horses in training. One of these, named Queen of the Isle, wasn't a particularly good racehorse, and later went to stud. She proved to be an outstanding broodmare, becoming the dam of Inch Arran, Colonious, Isle of Man and Queen's College, who between them would go on to win forty races over jumps.

The next three years saw the Queen and her mother on something of a roll, with the Queen's Pall Mall winning both the 2,000 Guineas on 30 April 1958 and the Royal Hunt Cup in 1959. To her list of wins, she could also add the Cumberland Lodge Stakes, Limekiln Stakes, Lockinge Stakes, Coventry Stakes, the Doncaster Cup and the King Edward VII Stakes, amongst numerous others.

The Queen Mother, meanwhile, achieved a double victory on 8 January 1959 at Lingfield with Double Star and Sparkling Knight, although on this occasion Double Star appeared to be the more natural runner, full of confidence and ability.

Then, on Saturday 8 February 1959, during a tour of New Zealand, the Queen Mother took time out to attend the Trentham Royal Meeting. When Sir Ernest Davis, former Mayor of Auckland, won the St James's Gold Cup with Bali Ha'i, he presented the horse to her, promising to have it shipped back to England. On reaching England, Bali Ha'i was trained by Cecil Boyd-Rochfort. He was Her Majesty's only horse on the flat, appearing for the first time at Chester and then in the Coombe Stakes at Sandown, where he won £1,200 for the Queen Mother, who promptly cabled the news to Sir Ernest. Bali Ha'i then went on to win the Queen Alexandra Stakes at Ascot.

Also in 1959, the Queen Mother acquired The Rip, by Manicou and bred by the landlord of the Red Cat pub at Wootton Marskes in Norfolk. The Queen Mother had originally seen the horse on the lawn of the pub and had asked the landlord for first refusal, paying 400 guineas for him and changing his name from Spoilt Union. The task of breaking him in was given to Major Eldred Wilson, who thought him clumsy, as did jockey Bill Rees – but then, the horse didn't have much of an opinion of Rees, either, and used to throw him.

Although he quickly became one of the Queen Mother's favourites, The Rip was a late developer, arriving at Fairlawne in the spring of 1959 as a four-year-old and not appearing on the racecourse until six months later.

The close of 1959 signalled the end of an extraordinary decade in which the Queen had proven herself to be as successful an owner as her father and great-grandfather, King Edward VII, had been. She and her mother were also having to adapt to the television age as her successes and failures were scrutinised in a much more public way than those of her predecessors in previous decades. Indeed, the 1950s were a kind of golden age for both the Royal Stud and the Queen. They saw her probably at her best as an owner, developing her knowledge in the world of horse-breeding so that her working relationship with stud managers and trainers began on an even keel, and balancing her commitment to the stud with her responsibilities as monarch.

The Queen Mother, meanwhile, became the first mother of a monarch to be a racehorse owner and the first to take a direct interest in the world of steeplechasing as well as flat racing.

Both mother and daughter became directly involved with horse-racing, and in this they'd started as they meant to go on. The Queen Mother, in particular, proved that she wasn't going to be like her predecessors, and she and her daughter's enthusiasm for the sport reflected the prevailing optimism of the post-war decade.

This enthusiasm for horse-racing seemed to have been passed on to the next generation of the royal family, too, with the Queen's children Prince Charles and Princess Anne developing their riding skills at this time, at the age of eleven and nine, respectively. Anne was the more confident rider of the two, less nervous than Charles, having first encountered horses when a pony was brought to the Royal Mews for herself and Charles, then aged three and five respectively. Anne learned quickly, being taught initially by her mother – who also taught them how to look after their ponies – and then by Sybil Smith of Horace Smith's riding school, who with her husband had originally helped their mother and Princess Margaret.

Charles and Anne also received lessons from their father and great-uncle, Lord Louis Mountbatten, and shared a cream-coloured pony named Bandit, on loan from the Crown Equerry's sister. Anne was the more adventurous rider and learned jumping with Bandit before progressing on to a pony named William, while Charles moved on to one named Greensleeves, both eventually being succeeded by a horse named Mayflower. Anne later had her own miniature cross-country course, built by the Crown Equerry, Lieutenant-Colonel Sir John Miller, and demonstrated an interest in show jumping, while Charles received extra tuition from Sir John, whose encouragement helped him to overcome his nervousness. Although he was growing up surrounded by horses, however, he settled into the riding of them later than his sister, who by this time had moved on to riding a horse named High Jinks and was teaching herself the rudiments of competition.

The next decade would prove something of a testing time for the Royal Stud. This wasn't the stud's first period of disquiet, but as the world and society were changing like never before, the monarchy had to fight to adapt with it and so, by extension, did the Royal Stud. Unfortunately, it was under pressure to adapt not just from social development but from problems within itself, which signalled a decline in fortune for the Queen.

Given that the previous years had been so successful there was no reason to suppose that the start of the 1960s would be any different, but 1960 was a terrible year for the Royal Stud. In that year, the stud had twelve horses in training, none of whom won a race and some of whom succumbed to coughing and viruses. Both the Freemason and National Studs were affected by such failure. One solution was to send some of the horses to Tom Masson of the Lewes Stable.

The Queen Mother fared better that year, however, enjoying a double act with her horse Double Star and jockey Arthur Freeman, who took part in the Champion Chase and would go on to win together ten times. Freeman, however, would always have problems with his weight, eventually resorting to a diet of what he referred to as 'pee pills'[21] (diuretics, taken to help with weight loss).

By the 1960s, advances in air travel meant that jockeys could now fly to exotic locations to race, acting as ambassadors for British horse-racing abroad, and when the Queen and Prince Philip paid a state visit to India in February 1961, Lester Piggott was invited to take part in cup races there. Staying at the Taj Mahal Hotel, he took a hot bath in order to lose some weight before the race, and was promptly attacked by ants, escaping only after he'd eventually raised the water level so high that they went back to their nests. At least, staying in the tub so long, he was able to lose the weight.

The Queen and the Duke of Edinburgh arrived back in England in time for the start of the flat-racing season and Badminton horse trials. Then, on 29 May, the Duke attended a special race meeting at Newbury racecourse in aid of the Playing Fields Association. Despite his lack of interest in horse-racing, he appreciated the importance of equine sports in general and in the middle of June that year became patron of the Sports Turf Research Institute. Over the years he would successfully combine his responsibilities as patron of this establishment with his interest in competing, and that July he participated in a polo match watched by his wife.[22]

The summer of 1961, unlike that of 1960, was a fairly productive one for the Queen, whose horse Aiming High had won the Coronation Stakes at Ascot.

She also enjoyed two further wins at Kempton Park, with Highlight in the Ash Stakes and Augustine in the William Hill Diamond Handicap.

The Queen also had entries for events in September. On the 24th, Joe Mercer rode Height of Fashion in the Hoover Fillies Mile at Ascot while her colts by Aureole did well in the St Leger. Five days later, on the 29th, she combined her royal responsibilities with her interest in horse-racing by opening the Gladys Yule surgical wing of the Animal Health Trust's Equine Research Station at Newmarket.[23]

1962 began promisingly for the Queen, as she leased Polhampton Stud near Kingsclere, on the Hampshire downs. The year began well for her mother, too, as in the final week of January The Rip won at Lingfield Park, beating Domstar by eight lengths. The Rip proved to be the Queen Mother's best that season, winning five races, while her second-best horse was Laffy, who secured four wins, contributing to the Queen Mother's overall success rate of 29 wins out of 69 races. The rest of the season wasn't such a good one for her, though, and she enjoyed only five successes out of 51 races, with Super Fox securing two and Double Star, Gay Record and Silver Dome winning one each.

1962 proved to be a very busy year for the Queen, as she tried to fit in her equestrian interests around her royal duties. After attending the Badminton Horse Trials in April, she attended the Windsor Horse Show on 11 May, during which she made a presentation to Ann Davy, who had been riding Free as Air. Then, two days later she presented the Challenge Cup to RASC at the Royal Windsor Horse Show for the inter-services team show-jumping event. Also present that day were Princess Anne – whose fascination with horse shows was as strong as ever – and Prince Richard of Gloucester, second son of the Queen's uncle Henry, Duke of Gloucester.[24]

That year was also a busy one for the Duke of Edinburgh, who on 22 June took part in a semi-final match of the Royal Windsor Polo Cup in Windsor Great Park. During the game, however, while trying to avoid a collision with another pony, he was thrown from his own and landed heavily, although he dusted himself down, unhurt. But then, in July, he suffered another fall in another polo match. Nevertheless, he was fit enough to attend the Royal International Horse Show later in the month and, undaunted by the danger of the sport, took part in another match that August.[25]

1962 was also a year of changes. In December it was announced that Peter Hastings-Bass would become the Queen's second trainer at Kingsclere, and then Captain Charles Moore retired at the end of the year at the age of 81, turning down the offer of a knighthood. It had always been his objective to breed middle-distance three-year-olds for the Classics, and he advised the

Queen to send no more than one or two mares a season to sprinting sires, stressing the importance of having a stallion or outstanding broodmare in the top and bottom half of a horse's pedigree and confiding his faith in the blood of St Simon, Blandford, Gay Crusader and Hyperion. Noel Murless looked up to Moore as a genius and the former manager would remain close throughout his retirement, residing at the Pavilion – a grace-and-favour house – at Hampton Court. His final purchase for the Queen before his retirement, Amicable, won two races the following year: the Lingfield Oaks Trial at Lingfield Park and the Nell Gwynn Stakes at Newmarket.[26]

Moore was succeeded by his second-in-command, Brigadier A. D. R. Wingfield, and throughout the 1960s the Queen's horses would be sent either to him or to Ireland, most of the latter going to Captain Peter Fitzgerald's stud at Mondellihy, with just one or two each year going to Mooresfoot. Eight out of eleven two-year-olds trained at Freemason Lodge in 1963 would go on to win twelve races.[27]

The year ended on a high note when, on 23 November, Peter Cazalet was listed as that year's leading trainer over jumps, ahead of W. Marshall and Fulke Walwyn in second and third place respectively. However, the Queen Mother enjoyed only moderate wins that season; the sixteen horses she had in training covered 87 races between them that year yet won only eighteen, with Makaldar achieving six and Super Fox securing four.

Even so, the only real downside for royal racing that year was the resignation of Brigadier Wingfield, who left in order to run his own stud at Brownstown, County Meath, Ireland, to be replaced by Major Richard Shelley. The following year, most of the Queen's horses would be sent to Freemason Lodge, Kingsclere, while six would go to Major W. R. Hern at West Ilsley.

In 1964, horses owned by the Queen secured the Wood Ditton Stakes and the Glasgow Maiden Stakes, and she enjoyed further wins in the summer. Then, after the Trooping of the Colour in June, at which she showed off her new baby, Prince Edward, she attended Epsom, where her horse Gold Aura won the Great Metropolitan. This was followed by a further win at Sandown Park, where Golden Oriole won the Crockford Handicap. But then, just as the year seemed to be going well, tragedy struck.

In June 1964, Captain Peter Hastings-Bass, the Queen's trainer at Kingsclere, succumbed to cancer and died. He'd succeeded in training just one winner for Her Majesty: Planta Genista, who won the Horne Maiden Stakes at Lingfield in April, just two months earlier. It was hoped that his assistant Ian Balding would stay on at the stud, and the Jockey Club granted him a temporary training licence in order to persuade him to do so. However, as he later wrote in his autobiography, *Making the Running: A Racing Life*, he wasn't sure if he wanted to continue as a trainer on a permanent basis. Having just secured two very good wins at Ascot, he knew he could do the job, but staying on would mean giving up his own steeplechase career and any hopes of riding in the Grand National, and his family commitments were making the decision even harder to make.

Then, at Arundel in July, during the annual Goodwood meeting, Balding met the Queen and the Duke for the first time and found that they were aware of his dilemma. In a roundabout sort of way, the Duke indicated that he should stay on at Kingsclere, noting that it would be a shame if bright young men didn't take up the challenges they came across. Abashed, Balding stayed. After all, if anyone knew about challenge, it was the Duke of Edinburgh, who met with yet another fall while playing polo later that month. Despite his steady stream of mishaps, however, his interest in the sport was rubbing off on his son Charles, who found that he preferred polo to jumps.

In fact, once he'd started at Gordonstoun School, Charles had stopped competing in equestrian sports altogether, but he continued to develop an interest in polo and that year his father loaned him a polo pony named San Quinina, a small but compact Argentinian mare. While he got used to riding her Charles practised the techniques of the sport on a wooden horse until, during Easter, he was ready to play in a friendly or two at Smith's Lawn. By this time he'd acquired another pony, this one named Sombra, a gift from Lord Cowdray, while he received additional coaching from his Uncle Louis, Lord Mountbatten.

Meanwhile Charles's sister, Princess Anne, competed at Benenden School in Kent, helping the school's A team to victory in the Combined Training Cup, a tournament that involved dressage and show jumping. She then came second in the individual Junior (fourteen years and under) Combined Training Cup and third in dressage. She would continue to practise during the holidays and entered minor Pony Club competitions at around this time.

At around the same time, there was speculation about the Queen Mother's horse Gay Record, whom her trainer found to be erratic and over-excitable and was often referred to as 'a ruddy nuisance'. Some felt that the horse was neurotic, while Major Wilson found him highly strung and always fretting. He wasn't a very good traveller, either, and was sent to Sandringham to have this worked out of him, returning for training as a six-year-old. However, he proved to be still unmanageable and so was sent away again, this time to Priory Stables at Reigate, where he spent some time under trainer Jack O'Donoghue, a specialist with difficult horses. Jack did everything he could to relax Gay Record – hunting with him, giving him the company of donkeys, taking him to racecourses to enable him to get the feel of the meetings, even talking to him – and the Queen Mother would track his progress, making suggestions but ultimately acquiescing to his advice. In fact, O'Donoghue found her knowledge about horses to be very accurate and found too that she had a good understanding of veterinary knowledge; if a horse wasn't right, she would recommend that it didn't run.

Eventually, Gay Record improved and won eight races for the Queen Mother, including the Sevenoaks Chase at Folkestone by three lengths in October 1964 when he was twelve years old, becoming her 100th winner in the process.

The season continued and in March 1965 the Queen Mother attended the Grand National to watch The Rip, after the press had run headline details concerning his prospects for the race. There were hopes that he would accomplish what Devon Loch had failed to do in the previous decade, but in the event he came seventh.

Disappointment turned to grief the following day when Mary, the Princess Royal, collapsed and died at her home, Harewood House in Yorkshire, while out walking with her son. Reporting the details of her death, the newspapers paid tribute not only to her life and public service but also to her knowledge of sport and racing. She'd always been a popular figure at York races, was an excellent horsewoman[28] and had a solid understanding of the sport as a whole.

The same was true of the Princess Royal's niece, the Queen, as Ian Balding discovered when she and the Duke paid their first visit to Kingsclere one evening in the early summer. Straight away, the trainer was struck by her knowledge of the sport, which surpassed that of the Duke, who wanted to know why the Queen's horses were thinner than others. That, replied the Queen rather pointedly, was how racehorses were supposed to look. After that, the Duke didn't ask any more questions and, indeed, didn't visit the stable again.

The Queen, however, visited Kingsclere regularly, sometimes in the company of Lord Porchester. Each year, she would visit one morning in spring to view all the horses there, not just her own, spending a few minutes with each one, discussing their welfare with Balding and feeding them carrots. The trainer believed that she had a sixth sense about horses, as she could immediately spot those who had a tendency to kick and bite. She also had no fear of horses, knowing to stand still if some of the colts decided to gallop and turn while everyone else got out of the way. Her interest, he believed, was based on more than just a love of horses; she understood how the environment could affect them and was even on hand to solve a respiratory problem that the horses had been suffering from. Like many other trainers before and since, he was left with the impression that she would have liked to have been one herself.

In June 1965, the Queen's horse Skerry won the Westminster Stakes at Epsom, although at Ascot Crest of the Wave was trounced in the Hardwicke Stakes while Canisbay came third in the Winston Churchill Stakes and ran unplaced in the Champion Stakes. Nevertheless, the Queen had confidence that he could secure the Eclipse Stakes at Sandown, which he did. The Queen also went on to secure the Goodwood Cup with Agreement, while Gold Aura won the Goodwood Stakes and Apprentice went on to win the Yorkshire Cup at York.

The Queen enjoyed a run of luck at Goodwood, securing the Goodwood Cup again in 1966 with Gaulois, but if the royal trainers believed that their employer was going to follow on from the success of 1965, they were sadly mistaken, as the Goodwood Cup proved to be the only major win of the year. However, Castle Yard won the Slaley Stakes at Newcastle and Gaulois won the Falmouth Handicap at York, although Aureole's son Hopeful Venture, trained by Noel Murless, wasn't considered good enough to race as a two-year-old and didn't run until 1967.

By contrast, for the Queen Mother the 1966–7 season would be her best since that of 1961–2, bringing her 22 wins, her horse Ballykine securing four.

Both the Queen and Queen Mother took an active interest in the studs abroad and in May 1966 the Queen Mother, while on a visit to New Zealand, visited Sir Woolf Fisher's 177-acre stud near Auckland to view the racing stock there. Twelve months later, in May 1967, the Queen spent three days in Normandy, where she visited the best studs of the region: Madame Elisabeth Couterie's stud at Le Mesnil, the Duc d'Audrifret-Pasquier's Château de Sassy, Comte François de Brignac's Haras de Verrerie, Marcel Boussac's Haras de Fresnay le Buffard stud, Madame Stern's Haras de Saint Pair du Mont, Baron Guy de Rothschild's Haras de Meautry and Alec Head's Haras de Quesnay. This busy tour helped to extend the Queen's knowledge of stud management.

On her return, the Queen was soon preparing assiduously for that year's Trooping of the Colour, something she did each year so that nothing would go wrong on the day. Unfortunately not everything worked out as well as she'd hoped and, during the procession, a guard's horse backed into a four-year-old boy from Hertfordshire named David Payne. He was rushed to Great Ormond Street Hospital, while his brother, John, had minor grazes and a five-year-old girl from Muswell Hill named Jennifer Williamson also received slight injuries. The Queen asked to be kept informed of David's progress and was relieved to be informed soon afterwards that he'd been discharged from hospital. She invited him to visit the Household Cavalry at Wellington Barracks, where he was offered a ride on a trooper's horse.[29]

It seemed that each year was proving to be an improvement on the last. At Epsom in 1968, for instance, Gold Aura won the Rosebery Memorial race, while later at York Zaloba won the Lonsdale Handicap. However, the year belonged to Hopeful Venture, who justified all hopes that he would perform well as a three-year-old by winning the Grosvenor Stakes at Chester, the Oxfordshire Stakes at Newbury and the Princess of Wales Stakes and Wood Ditton Stakes, both at Newmarket, also coming second in the King Edward VII Stakes and the St Leger. His only disappointments were in France, where, having initially won the Prix Henri Delamarre at Longchamps, he was relegated to second place by the stewards before running unplaced in the Prix du Conseil Municipal in October, again at Longchamps.

1968 was an interesting year for the Duke of Edinburgh, too – at least, as far as polo playing was concerned. In May, on a visit to Quirindi, New South Wales, and participating in a polo match with an Australian club, he was stood in a line-up of players receiving commemorative whips, handed out by the club's president, and kisses, bestowed by his wife, Elizabeth Carter – who missed out the Duke. He insisted that he get what his teammates got, and Mrs Carter duly obliged by giving him a kiss.

On his return to England, the Duke triumphed in the final of the Combermere Cup and his handicap went from minus two to zero at the end of the season, rising to one the following year.[30] Meanwhile, his son Charles had had his first success in a tournament at Windsor Park and was proving to be quite a proficient player.

The last important win for the Queen in 1968 was achieved by Castle Yard, who won the Zetland Gold Cup at Redcar and the Falmouth Handicap at York. In the future, the Queen would stand syndicated stallions in which she had shares, although this would mean that the range of the stud manager's responsibility would be increased. Even so, such a decision demonstrated that the Royal Stud was flexible and could respond to change.

By 1969, Princess Anne was nineteen years old and thinking about pursuing eventing as a career. Having left school in July the previous year, she was learning the rudiments of the sport from scratch under the care of eventing champion Alison Oliver. Her horse at this time was six-year-old Purple Star, whom she liked because he challenged her riding skills. In that year she rode as many novice horse trials as she could and made a good start by winning the senior individual event at the South Oxfordshire Pony Club Horse Trials, but later she came eighth at Windsor in a one-day event.

At this time, in competitions Anne was also riding a horse from Ireland named Royal Ocean, who was more reliable than sparky, and it was with him and Purple Star, respectively, that she came second and first in a novice combined-training event, later winning with Royal Ocean at the Windsor Horse Trials. Her favourite horse, however, was a beast named Doublet, with whom she competed for the first time at Basingstoke on 26 June. In the following month, she enjoyed another win at a horse trial – again, in the novice class – to qualify Doublet for the Midland Bank Novice Event Championships, scheduled to take place at Chatsworth on 18 October. In the meantime, she participated in numerous other events.

By the close of the 1960s, it was clear that the racing world that had existed in the 1950s had not been recaptured. The Queen hadn't achieved Derby success and her horses had achieved mostly only moderate wins. The stud couldn't just tick along; it needed to change with the times, and the 1970s would see unprecedented developments not only in its infrastructure but also in the outlook of the people running it.

This change began with the stud's management. When Richard Shelley retired as manager of the royal studs through ill health in 1969, two posts were created and came into effect on 1 January 1970: those of stud manager and racing manager. The first incumbent of the former position was Michael (later Sir Michael) Oswald, while the Queen's friend 'Porchie' (Lord Porchester), who would succeed his father as the 7th Earl of Carnarvon in 1987, became her racing manager. 'I became manager of the royal studs at Hampton Court, at Sandringham and Wolferton in Norfolk and at Polhampton in Berkshire,'[31] Sir Michael later recalled, adding, 'I also became the Queen Mother's racing manager.'[32] Oswald also had the responsibility of the Queen's syndicated stallions and provided advice on the management of the mares, although the Queen would always have the final say on their mating, after hearing his advice and that of Lord Porchester. Oswald proved himself more than ready to meet the challenge of his new post, bringing with him a wealth of experience, having previously managed the Lordship and Egerton studs at Newmarket.

Meanwhile, Lord Porchester's role as the Queen's racing manager was to represent her at race meetings, liaise with trainers, make decisions about bloodstock when she was abroad and advise on the buying and selling of horses. Having been an owner/breeder himself since the age of nineteen, he too brought a wealth of experience to his post.

At around the same time, as a reflection of the generally optimistic view of the future displayed by those employed by the royal studs, the Queen Mother acquired her 200th winner as a racehorse owner.

Meanwhile, Anne was becoming increasingly optimistic that she could carve out a career for herself in eventing and at first light would get up and ride for three hours before fulfilling her royal duties and attending official engagements.

On 24 May Anne competed at the Tidworth three-day army horse trials. She was doing well until she fell at the last fence. Both she and her horse were unhurt, however, and undeterred the Princess jumped back on and carried on to complete her round.[33] She was still going strong four days later, when she came third in the *Daily Express* Foxhunter Competition at Aldershot, riding the Queen's horse Doublet.

In January 1971, the Queen, her husband and her daughter, Anne, made an official visit to Singapore, along with jockey Lester Piggott, who was scheduled to ride in the Queen Elizabeth II Cup there on Jumbo Jet, trained by Ivan Allan. Piggott paced the Queen's five-year-old along the eleven-furlong course and won the race, and the Queen presented him with the eponymous trophy. The race would henceforth be run annually, carrying a stake of £4,700.

Singapore's Turf Club had been established in 1842. Situated in lush countryside, at that time it was one of the finest racecourses in the world, with 350 acres of grounds including stabling for more than 650 horses, training tracks, a swimming pool for the horses, an equine hospital complete with operating theatres, recuperation stables and a laboratory. However, no horses were actually bred in the country; instead, they were imported from Europe, Australia and New Zealand, while the jockeys who participated in the racing there came from either Malaysia, Singapore or Australia.

Back in England, Princess Anne participated in her first ride in a three-day event in March at Badminton, where she rode Doublet. After the first day of the event she was leading the field with a fellow named Mark Phillips in second place, while on the second day she came fourth on a course made dangerous by bad weather. Overall, she finished fifth out of 47, the event being won by Phillips, riding Great Ovation.

By now very much into the highs and lows of her new sporting career, the one thing she couldn't come to terms with was the attention of the press, who scrutinised her every move – and fall – on the course. This intrusion was particularly galling since she was still learning at the time and Doublet wasn't an easy horse to handle. Since he had a tendency to stop quicker than other horses Anne had ridden, she was thrown often, and the cameras were there to catch it every time.

Although she'd finished fifth at Badminton, her performance had been sufficiently impressive for the European Championship selectors to invite her to participate at the event, scheduled to be held at Burghley between

2 and 5 September 1971. However, her lack of experience meant that she wasn't shortlisted to join the British team, which would be defending the European title. Riding as an individual, she would be one of twelve in addition to the team of four.

With the prospect of riding in such a prestigious competition beckoning, Anne went back to her public duties and in June was able to attend events at Hampton Court and Ascot. Then, with just weeks to go before Burghley, she became ill and was diagnosed as having an ovarian cyst. After undergoing an operation, she was sent to Balmoral to recuperate. She was determined to get back to full fitness as quickly as possible, however, and in July she was well enough to take part in the Eridge Horse Trials, at around the same time as her father was playing polo for England and her mother's horse Westward Ho! won the Stonehill Handicap at Goodwood. The Queen also enjoyed success in France once more with Example, who won the Prix de Royallieu at Longchamps, and Albany, who won the Prix de Psyche at Deauville. Anne arrived at Burghley, tense but excited. Nor were her nerves helped by the fact that she was arriving to a background of opinion that she wasn't good enough. She was becoming used to having to justify her right to compete before the competition itself.

On the first day of the European Championships, Anne had an early lead with Doublet and sustained it, leading the field with 41.5 penalty points after dressage. Day two was cross-country, and again Doublet finished the day in the lead.

Then, on day three, Anne rode in the show-jumping event. She was more nervous than she had been on day one. There was silence as she rode the course, and when she finished clear, the crowd erupted in applause. She was now European champion for 1971, securing the Raleigh Trophy and was presented with a gold medal and a cheque for £250 by her mother. Mark Phillips, meanwhile, had come sixth.

Anne had earned a place with the British Olympic team for Munich in 1972, but again she was judged by many not to be good enough to participate. Undeterred, she resolved to ride two younger horses in novice horse trials in the autumn while Doublet, who was suffering leg trouble, was rested. In the event, Britain did well in the summer Olympics of 1972, the equestrian team securing two gold medals on 1 September, while Anne and her father watched Mark Phillips ride a clear round.

Meanwhile, her reputation for being a proficient rider was spreading far and wide. Back in 1971 she travelled with her father to Iran to attend the Shah's coronation, and while she was there she was shown the Royal Stables at

Farahabad, just outside Tehran, where she was invited to ride the Shah's three-year-old stallion which was part thoroughbred, part Persian and part Jadran Arab. Anne's hosts were impressed by her horsemanship, and when she left she was presented with a colt named Awtash (Arabic for 'fire'), of the same Pahlavan breed. After quarantine, Awtash was sent to Robert Hall's Fulmer School of Equitation in Buckinghamshire.

At the beginning of November 1971, Anne was nominated for the title of Sportswoman of the Year by the Sports Writers' Association for her successes in horse trials and received 360 votes – 123 more than her nearest competitor, Ann Moore – to secure the title on 6 December. The *Times* reporter who covered the event described her as a 'runaway winner' and observed sagely that she'd had to work hard for her result. The votes were cast on the basis of each nominee's impact on her chosen sport internationally, he said, and predicted that, with Anne's success, the world of horse trials would become less exclusive.[34]

Also in 1971, the Duke of Edinburgh decided to give up polo after spending 22 years in the saddle and enduring many injuries as a result of bumps, crashes and collisions, not to mention being catapulted over the head of his horse. He'd taken these falls with good humour, however, but in recent years the injuries had taken longer to heal. One such injury to his right wrist had caused the joint to become arthritic. For a time he took Butazolidan (a drug normally used for ponies) to relieve the discomfort, but after a while he began to suffer side-effects from taking the drug and decided that enough was enough. His career ended on a high note, however, with a handicap of five – which was excellent, considering that he hadn't been able to devote as much time to polo as those who had made a living out of it. He now intended to turn his attention to carriage driving, a new interest that he'd adopted the previous year and that provided the perfect substitute for polo, involving speed and competition. That autumn, he went to Budapest to watch the first European Driving Championships.

On 28 May 1972, while the royal family prepared for the Trooping of the Colour, the Queen's uncle, the erstwhile King Edward VIII, Duke of Windsor, died at his home in France. His wife, Wallis, brought his body back to England for interment at Windsor. The next day, it was announced that, while the Duke's death and the preparations for his funeral were dominating the week, the Trooping of the Colour would nevertheless go ahead that Saturday, before the Duke's funeral on the Monday. The ceremony would also include an act of remembrance. The Duchess of Windsor would not be there, although she approved the arrangements.

That Saturday, the Queen took her position on the parade ground. Everyone there that day wore black armbands, and colours and drums were draped in black. There was a roll of drums, followed by a minute's silence, and then another drum roll, followed by a lament played by the pipers. A royal salute followed, and then the trooping continued. Finally, the Household Troops, with whom the Duke had served, were given the opportunity to pay a final tribute.

The public would remember Edward, Duke of Windsor, primarily for giving up the throne in 1936 so he could be with the woman he loved. Few would remember his passion for sports and his determination to prove himself on the field, whether he was competing against his brothers or pushing his own limits.

Meanwhile, the Prince of Wales continued to play polo, competing in another match that June. While studying at Cambridge, his polo handicap had gone up to two, and by the time he entered the navy it had risen to three. Within twelve months he was playing high-goal polo, an extremely dangerous sport. He was getting nervous at the idea of riding steeplechases, but he found he couldn't discuss his concerns and the technicalities of horsemanship with his mother in the same way that his sister, Anne, could. Even so, he was quite happy to improve his skills at his own pace, and he also enjoyed hunting, a sport that had played a large role in his family's history and that was to be the source of much debate in the future.

Prince Philip, meanwhile, was devoting himself to his new sporting interest of carriage driving. Just as he'd been with polo when he had taken up the sport back in 1949, the Duke was a total novice at carriage driving; indeed, until the late sixties, he'd hardly been aware that it existed. He was first introduced to the sport by a Polish delegate of the FEI (International Equestrian Federation) named Eric Brabec while both were on a visit to the Aachen International Horse Show. Impressed by what he saw, on his return to England the Duke set up a carriage-driving committee with show-jumping expert Sir Michael Ansell and the two men drafted a rule book together. Then, in 1970, the Duke suggested that the Crown Equerry, Lieutenant-Colonel Sir John Miller, compete with a team of Windsor greys under the new rules. Thus a competition was established at the Royal Windsor Horse Show, providing a further extension of the use of the Royal Mews, where much of the required equipment was stored, so keeping expenses down to a minimum.

In 1972, the Duke entered numerous carriage-driving competitions, but he soon discovered that he had a great deal to learn. In one contest, the pair of horses he was driving refused to complete the course and eventually had to be coaxed along with the aid of sugar lumps. The Duke wasn't put off, though, and in fact had ideas of competing in four-in-hand carriage driving, although here he had to start from scratch as he knew no one who knew anything about the sport. He therefore sent for David Muir, who looked after the stalking ponies at Balmoral, and both set about learning how to harness four horses together while the Duke read up extensively on the subject.

In January 1973, the Duke took six bays from the Royal Stable at Sandringham and, with Major Tommy Thompson – a retired riding master of the Household Cavalry and a man who'd been at the Royal Mews since 1971 – trained both the team of horses and himself. The two men began to prepare for the following season, beginning in April, and on the 19th of that month it was announced that the Duke would be competing in carriage driving two weeks later at Lowther, near Penrith, Cumbria. In that event he would be driving one of the Queen's entries, the other driven by the Crown Equerry, Lieutenant-Colonel Sir John Miller.

On this occasion, not much went the Duke's way and his drive was full of errors, largely because the ground was boggy after a night of rain. Even so, he managed to improve his position and eventually finished fourth. It was an encouraging start and he felt confident enough to carry on with the sport.

On 27 April 1973, Anne rode Doublet at a series of horse trials at Powderham Castle, near Exeter. Just a couple of days before the trials, she'd been shortlisted for the British team in the European Championships that September in Kiev, where she hoped to ride Doublet and her other horse, Goodwill, to defend her title. For the first time in the event's history, the shortlist for the British team comprised solely women, while Anne was the only woman on the list of ten to have entered two horses in the competition.[35]

That May, the Duke participated in the second European International Driving Championships at Windsor, where he came sixth in the preparation and dressage rounds. He was also one of three to go clear in the obstacle driving event, where he came second, but his carriage hit an obstacle and was damaged, and his position slipped to seventeenth out of nineteen. He left the tournament aware that he still had much to learn.

1974 also brought ill fortune for the Royal Stud. In the previous October, the Queen's mare Example had been sent to America to be covered by Nijinsky, standing at the Claiborne Stud in Kentucky. As Sir Michael Oswald recalled, 'By the 1970s, many of the best stallions were in America. We started keeping three or four mares in Kentucky to visit stallions there, bringing the foals back after they had been weaned.'[36] Months later Example gave birth to a foal, later called Pas de Deux, but in a terrible twist of fate Example died from a ruptured colon after the foal put its foot through her uterus. As Ian Balding recalls in his autobiography, *Making the Running: A Racing Life*, the Queen took the news calmly, aware that such a terrible occurrence was proof of how unpredictable the business of horse-breeding could be. After approaching the English National Foaling Bank, Sir Michael was able to secure a foster mother for the foal and both were transported to Wolferton.

At least with the rough came the smooth, however, and that year the Queen had success with Highclere, a two-year-old bred by her (by Queen's Hussar, out of Highlight) and trained by Dick Hern. Highclere turned out to be one of Her Majesty's best horses as a two-year-old, coming second in a maiden race at Newmarket and again in the Princess Margaret Stakes at Ascot but winning the Donnington Stakes at Newbury. Trainer Dick Hern and jockey Joe Mercer, however, believed that she wasn't of sufficient standard to run in the Classics, although this opinion wasn't shared by Her Majesty's racing manager, Lord Porchester. He did recommend, however, that she be returned to Highclere Stud for a couple of months for a change of scenery. This break proved to be beneficial, as Hern soon noticed when Highclere returned to his training establishment West Ilsley, and he decided to enter her in the 1,000 Guineas, scheduled for May of that year.

On 20 March 1974, with the Amberley horse show and trials just days away, Princess Anne was the victim of a kidnap attempt. Her bodyguard was shot and injured in the attack, but Anne managed to fight off the assailants. She refused to let the attack put her off attending the Amberley event, however, and both she and Mark Phillips – her husband since the previous year – arrived at Cirencester Park on the 23rd.

In that year's event, Anne and Mark had nine entries between them, one of whom was Doublet, despite breaking down in 1972 and being eliminated from the final trial at Osberton for the 1973 European Championships in Kiev, where Goodwill had defended Anne's title in his stead. Anne also rode Flame Gun, who had won dressage at the same show the previous year, along with two novice horses: Blackjack and Arthur of Troy. Mark, meanwhile, had entered his dual Badminton winner, Great Ovation, and the Queen's horse Columbus, in addition to Laureate II, Persian Holiday and High Flyer.

Soon after Anne's attempted kidnap, her father suffered an accident while carriage driving when his carriage hit a tree stump and turned. He was thrown and the horses ran off. Badly shaken and bruised, he was driven back to the castle but soon recovered and before long was driving once again.

Then, on 2 May 1974, Joe Mercer rode Highclere in the 1,000 Guineas and won in a determined finish. Despite her success, however, the Queen knew that where the Newmarket course suited Highclere, the one at Epsom would not and decided that instead she should run for the Prix de Diane at Chantilly, the French equivalent of the Oaks. In the meantime, she went on to win the King George VI and Queen Elizabeth Stakes.

Another success in May could easily have turned out differently. One of the Queen's hopefuls for the Oaks that year was a horse named Escorial, by Royal Palace out of Asturia, who was a favourite for the Musidora Stakes at York on 15 May, after winning a fillies' mile race at Ascot in the previous autumn. The plan was for Lester Piggott to ride her at York, but Escorial, a temperamental beast, had other ideas. On the day of the race she managed to get loose from the lads walking her and galloped off down the racecourse, much to the Queen's amusement. She was eventually cornered, taken back to the start and won the race, but later failed to win the Oaks.

Princess Anne is noted for displaying calmness during competition, but an event on 13 May 1974 devastated her. While riding Doublet at Smith's Lawn, she heard a loud crack and, on examining her horse, discovered that he'd broken his leg. Sadly, Doublet had to be put down, and Anne never really got over his death. Nevertheless, she carried on eventing throughout the year and was shortlisted for the European Championships again that September at Burghley, where she rode Goodwill. Some believed that Doublet wasn't a very robust horse and might have been past his prime when he died, even though he was still capable of performing well. All the same, Anne had lost a valued teammate and would grieve his loss for some time to come.[37]

At Chantilly on 16 June, there was a very impressive turnout to watch the Prix de Diane and see the Queen in attendance. That day, Joe Mercer rode Highclere, who was at her best and, indeed, was the British favourite, alongside French favourites Comtesse de Loi and Hippodamia. The Queen led her into the enclosure, but there was such a crush of admirers that Lord Porchester and Sir Michael Oswald had to link arms to keep the crowds back. Highclere went on to win the race, and the strength of the crowd's applause signalled just how far British success on French soil had risen in estimation since the nineteenth century. Later, back at Windsor, a dinner party was held and the winner's trophy – presented by Marcel Boussac – took pride of place in the centre of the table.

With confidence in Highclere's potential now running high, she was entered for the Prix de l'Arc de Triomphe at Longchamps on 6 October, but this time she failed to make the grade. Buffeted during the race, she lost ground and was several lengths back by the time the winner crossed the line. This defeat signalled the end of her racing career and she was soon retired to stud, although she is still remembered today as having been one of the Queen's best racehorses.

While the Queen was being praised for the success of her stables, her daughter was coming in for some criticism. Every event Anne took part in at this time was seen as preparation for the Montreal Olympics of 1976, but she was now accused of putting sport before royal duty. She protested that she had three brothers before her in the line of succession, so why should she go out of her way to curry favour with the press and public? And when she was told that, at her age, she should have been thinking about starting a family, she retorted that first she wanted to get used to married life and realise her ambitions.

Towards the end of 1975, the Queen Mother and Princess Margaret attended Ascot to watch two of the Queen Mother's horses participate. On that occasion Game Spirit, one of her best, won the Sardan Handicap Steeplechase and Sunnyboy won the Sardan Novices Hurdle, bringing the Queen Mother's list of wins up to eighteen, seventeen of which had come from horses resident at Fulke Walwyn's Saxon House in Upper Lambourn.[38]

By this time, the Duke of Edinburgh had become a member of the British carriage-driving team and participated in that year's European and World Championships in Poland. In fact, he was proving to be quite popular in Eastern Europe and was also becoming more adept at carriage driving, learning how better to cope with the inevitable falls from hitting obstacles, as well as how to deal with harness failures and being hurled aloft while being kicked by stumbling horses.

1976 got off to an auspicious start when, in January, it was reported that, if Anne was chosen for the Olympics, she would remain with the team. This was excellent news for the Princess, and one in the eye for her critics. Then, on 18 February, Sunyboy became the Queen Mother's 300th winning racehorse in the Fernbank Hurdle at Ascot, a success followed by her horse Game Spirit winning the Hermitage Chase, bringing his total of race wins for the Queen Mother up to 21.

The good start didn't last, however, and on 22 April, during a series of horse trials at Durweston, Dorset, Anne fell at a fence and her horse rolled onto her. Fortunately, Mark was on the course at the time, but by the time he reached her she was unconscious, so he covered her with a rug and helped to carry her to a waiting ambulance. It was later discovered that one of Anne's vertebrae had suffered a hairline fracture, an injury from which it would take her a long time to recover. When suggestions appeared in the press that her injury signalled the end of her hopes to compete at the Montreal Olympic Games, however, she set her mind to proving them wrong and underwent several gruelling weeks of physiotherapy. Eventually, she recovered well enough to be chosen for the British team, along with her husband (as reserve) and three others: Hugh Thomas, Richard Meade and Lucinda Prior-Palmer. Anne would ride Goodwill while Hugh Thomas would ride Playmar, Richard Meade would ride Jacob Jones and Lucinda Prior-Palmer would ride Be Fair.

That year the Queen travelled to Montreal to see her daughter participate in the summer Olympics. Unfortunately not everything went well and, during the cross-country event, Anne suffered another bad fall, yet, although dazed, she remounted and managed to finish. To make matters worse the press was hounding her every move, causing her to decide after the Games to end her eventing career. This was unfortunate because she had the determination to reach the very top of her profession. She continued to enter events, but ever since that time she has concentrated more on her royal duties than her equestrian pursuits, although she sometimes manages to combine the two, for example sponsoring the charity Riding for the Disabled.

The following year, on 15 November 1977, Princess Anne gave birth to a son, Peter, and four years later, on 15 May 1981, her daughter Zara came along. Both children have an interest in sport, but Zara has followed in her mother's footsteps most closely, participating in events and following horse-racing closely.

For the Queen Mother, March 1977 was a month of ups and downs. On the 5th Bill Smith rode her horse Game Spirit in the Geoffrey Gilbey Chase at Newbury, but the horse fell and later had to be destroyed, which was a blow for Elizabeth as he'd been a popular horse and had loved to run at Newbury.

Also that month, Newmarket trainer Jenny Pitman – today a well-known racing commentator – attended Sandown Park for the Grand Military Gold Cup and, to her surprise (not realising it was the Queen's custom), was invited with the other trainers and jockeys to a cocktail party at Royal Lodge in Windsor Great Park. She and her husband Richard had a great time and found the Queen Mother charming, and at one point Jenny spotted a woman in a red dress and spent some minutes racking her brains, trying to remember who she looked like. Then, to her shock, she realised that the woman in red was the Queen! The two were introduced, and during their following conversation Jenny, like others before her, had the impression that the Queen would have quite liked to have been a trainer herself.[39]

At around this time, the Queen's new jockey, Willie Carson, was preparing to ride the Queen's horse Dunfermline in the Oaks at Epsom two months later, on 4 June. Carson had never been very impressed with this horse and noted later in his autobiography, *Willie Carson Up Front: A Racing Autobiography*, that she wasn't a very feminine-looking animal; in fact, she wasn't good-looking at all, and had little character.

On the day of the race, Willie was unavoidably detained and almost missed it while trainer Dick Hern cast about in a panic for a substitute jockey. Finally, though, he appeared and within minutes was riding in the race, which to his shock Dunfermline won. As he wrote in his autobiography, he very often wanted to let rip after winning a race, but as he was among conservative people that day felt that he had to behave, and his discretion paid off. It hadn't been the best of races, but nevertheless it was a notable triumph. After the race, he met the Queen Mother, who was delighted, and received a set of cuff links for his efforts. He later rode Dunfermline to victory again on 10 September in the St Leger, making 1977 the best racing year to date for the Queen.[40]

Nor was 1977 a bad year for Prince Charles, who in July of that year captained the Young England polo team against France. By now, his horsemanship was being taken to a new level and he was receiving tuition from Australian Sinclair 'Ten Goal' Hill, one of the world's best polo players. Over recent years, Charles's confidence had grown immeasurably and he'd played polo in Brazil, India, America, Australia, New Zealand, Malta and Ghana, yet he was still nervous about going over jumps and in an attempt to overcome this enlisted the help of his sister, who taught him from scratch on a horse named Pinker. He decided that hunting might help him to overcome his fear, also seeing it as a way of getting to know the ins and outs of country life. Anne's efforts to help him overcome his fears paid off, however, and later he took part in the Vale of the White Horse event, riding as an ordinary member and quite content to carry out instructions.[41]

Unfortunately, the same couldn't be said for the Queen's horse Milford – trained by Dick Hern and ridden by Lester Piggott – who, on 6 June 1980, failed to secure the 200th Epsom Derby, finishing tenth while the race was won by several lengths by Troy, ridden by Willie Carson. Had Piggott won, it would have been his ninth Derby win and his first for the Queen. Sadly, on that occasion there was an act of hooliganism when, after the runners passed Tattenham Corner, a roll of toilet paper thrown by a spectator became tangled in the legs of a horse named Accomplice, ridden by Yves Saint-Martin. Fortunately, both horse and rider escaped unscathed.[42]

The following month, in July, Milford redeemed himself by winning the Prince of Wales Stakes in record time, but sadly failed to win anything further after this. Rather than being retired to stud at Sandringham, he was sold to Baeton Stud before being sent to Japan.

At the end of the 1970s, the Royal Stud had survived tragedy, vast changes to management and structure, and competition, thanks largely to the visionary outlook of the Queen and her managers, none of whom had been introspective in their dealings with the stud and had taken the long view in order to ensure its survival. Even so, the stud still had a considerable competitive gap to bridge over the coming decades.

Meanwhile, the level of sportsmanship enjoyed by Anne, Charles and their father reflected a new openness not seen during the era of the Duke of Windsor, back when he'd still been Prince of Wales. Sadly, the Duke of Windsor died just as his great-nephew and -niece were coming into their own as competitors, achieving through sport what he had been prevented from achieving.

But it wasn't just the younger generation who were enjoying success in sport. In 1980, the Two-Mile Champion Chase at Cheltenham – a race that promoted the highest standard of speed and jumping – became thereafter known as 'the Queen Mother'. Then, in February, the Duke of Edinburgh was re-elected President of the International Equestrian Federation. The year would prove to be his best in sport yet, seeing him win a gold medal with his team at Windsor and three bronzes in other world-championship events.

On Tuesday 4 March, the Prince of Wales rode in a flat race for the first time at Plumpton and enjoyed himself immensely. Four days later he was due to ride Sea Swell in the Gloucester Memorial Trophy Steeplechase but finished last, the race being won by Ten Up.[43] Despite this failure, Charles's confidence in the sport was growing daily and he found that another of his horses, ten-year-old Allibar, suited him perfectly.

That year was the Queen Mother's eightieth, but her interest in her horses and horse-racing in general hadn't waned. She still made visits to Saxon House to see her horses at work and to the racecourses to see them run, and whether they won or lost she took great pleasure in seeing them race. As has been previously noted, she'd already enjoyed many successes, with five of her horses sired by Colonist winning a staggering 33 steeplechases and hurdles events between them by the end of the season, fourteen of which were by popular royal favourite Inch Arran alone. That year, the Jockey Club presented her with a horse named Master Andrew as a birthday present.

The Queen Mother had always felt that horse-racing should be fun, but with that fun came responsibility. With this in mind, on 2 September 1980 Anne opened the British Equine Veterinary Association in London. There had been criticisms at the time that too many horses were being injured over high fences, but in her opening speech the Princess gave her opinion that this was the fault of humans rather than horses, some of whom weren't up to competing in top-class competitions. There were many horse owners out there who hadn't grown up on farms or in similar environments, she observed, and these people needed to be educated.[44]

On 20 February 1981, the day before Prince Charles took part in the Cavalry Hunters' Chase at Chepstow, a certain Lady Diana Spencer was present to watch the workout at Lambourn. Unfortunately, that day was one of Charles's worst; his horse, Allibar, after completing the workout, buckled on the way back and died of a ruptured aorta. Charles was devastated but had to concentrate on finding a replacement. Nevertheless, a few days later, his and Lady Diana's engagement was announced at Buckingham Palace.

On 13 March the Prince of Wales took part in the Grand Military Gold Cup at Sandown Park on Good Prospect, who had been chosen by trainer Nick Gaselee. He was a good stayer but had to be ridden into the fences, and Charles didn't find him as smooth a ride as Allibar. At the eighteenth fence, with Charles and Good Prospect lying in sixth place, the horse stumbled and threw the Prince. The next day's edition of *The Times* included a rather undignified picture of Charles landing on the ground with his legs in the air, but fortunately he suffered nothing more than a bloodied nose. It was a very disappointing result, though, especially for Nick Gaselee, but as always Charles refused to blame the horse for his own mistake. Even when he was thrown again the following week at Cheltenham, he put it down to his own lack of experience. He was coming to the conclusion that, although he enjoyed steeplechases and the camaraderie of the weighing-in room, racing was much harder than polo, and he found show jumping to be even more of a challenge.

That June, his mother was presented with a challenge of an altogether more serious nature at the Trooping of the Colour where someone fired six blank shots at her as she rode her Canadian mare, Burmese. The Household Cavalry sprang into action as Burmese reared up – not, said the Queen later, because of the shots but because of the sudden appearance of other horses. She was later praised for her ability to calm her horse, an ability that came from years of experience.

It soon became clear that Anne wasn't about to take things easy after the birth of her daughter, and indeed in August 1981 she announced that between 10 and 13 September she would be attending the Burghley Horse Trials at Stamford, Lincolnshire, a large event where she would be riding Stevie B in the Raleigh Trophy. Owned by the Queen, Stevie B had recently injured his leg while participating in an event in Derbyshire, but Anne hoped that he'd be fully fit for the trials. Meanwhile, her husband, Mark, had two horses entered: Town and Country and Classic Lines.[45]

That year's Ascot was held on 24 September, which wasn't the best of days for weather, with wind and rain aplenty, but it was a good day for the Queen, whose horse Height of Fashion won the Hoover Fillies' Mile, having led from the start and maintaining her lead to the finishing line. It was a great accomplishment, given that she was up against some tough competition, and caused many to hope that she would be able to run for the Oaks in 1982. That year, noted *The Times*, was the first in which the Queen had stepped forward to receive her statuette as winning owner since 1974, when Highclere, Height of Fashion's dam, had won the Prix de Diane.

Throughout the 1980s, both the Queen and her mother continued to keep in close touch with their managers and trainers, including Sir John Miller, former Keeper of the Royal Mews, who was also impressed, like many others before him, by her knowledge and ability to read a race. Talking about her horses relaxed her, too, and Miller would often call on her on a Tuesday evening, which he found was always the best time to do so.

By February 1982 the Queen Mother had seven horses in training at Lambourn, one of whom, Sindebele, had been bred in New Zealand and brought to Saxon House at the beginning of the previous year. Sindebele was sweet-natured yet slow to mature and wouldn't be hurried. On 20 February, he damaged his shoulder while running at Chepstow and finished unplaced. Fortunately he recovered, but his luck proved somewhat thin on the ground when he later ran at Cheltenham and broke his off right fetlock joint just as he was well placed to win.

Meanwhile, the Duke of Edinburgh's enthusiasm for competitive driving was still high. As well as taking part in individual trials, he also took part in team trials between 1979 and 1981, a year in which he enjoyed wins at Norwich and Tatton Park. Then, in 1982 he won both the International Driving Grand Prix and the World Driving Championships, held at Apeldoorn in Holland, in the same year that he wrote a book titled *Competition Carriage Driving*. In the past, he'd often been criticised for getting involved in a sport considered by many to be dangerous, but he argued that the danger was minimal as long as the driving was undertaken sensibly. In fact, the number of crashes he'd suffered was relatively small, considering how much he'd been driving, as far afield as Hungary, Switzerland, Holland and Poland.

By this time, too, the Duke had become very interested not only in the technicalities of carriage driving but also in the different breeds of horses. He was particularly interested in the Caspian horse, descended from the ancient and small Persian horse, which for 2,000 years had been thought to be extinct. While visiting the Shah of Iran at the time of his coronation in 1971, the Duke had offered to take charge of some of his stock in order to help preserve the breed – a prudent move, as it turned out, as shortly afterwards Iran returned to fundamentalist Islam, a doctrine whose adherence would have seen the species killed off for good.

Then, in December 1982, it was announced that Princess Anne was to give a Persian Arab foal to a stud in Canada in the hope of starting a new bloodline there.

It wasn't just the future of bloodlines that was on the minds of the royals; they were also concerned about the care and welfare of those involved in equestrian sports. As a demonstration of this, the Queen Mother became a patron of the Injured Jockeys' Fund and in 1983 the Prince of Wales opened a Paralympics event during the charity fundraiser Royal Ascot Spectacular. On that occasion he and his father, the Duke of Edinburgh, wandered about the course, meeting and talking with the 1,100 competitors from forty countries.

The heritage of horse-racing was always on the royals' minds, of course, and in April 1983 the Queen visited Newmarket to open the new National Horseracing Museum in the town's High Street. On display there was the skeleton of Eclipse, one of the fastest racehorses ever to grace a racecourse and originally bred by the Duke of Cumberland, the Queen's ancestor.

Two months later, in August, Willie Carson was informed that he would be made an OBE and was invited to a reception in Downing Street. While he was there, he tried to pick an argument with Prime Minister Margaret Thatcher about the world of racing needing government funding, but she was more than a match for him. Earlier, at his visit to Buckingham Palace, he'd spoken about horses for a precious fifteen seconds with the Queen, who that day had to stand for four hours, handing out medals.

Another proud royalist is Jenny Pitman, who in 1984 had the chance to meet the Queen Mother again when her horse Burrough Hill Lad won the Cheltenham Gold Cup by three lengths. Still in a state of shock, Jenny managed to pull herself together as she approached the winners' enclosure and tried not to faint when the Queen Mother presented her with the trophy. Then, when the Queen Mother invited her into the royal box,[46] she was delighted but confessed that she needed to see to her horse first, much to the shock and disbelief of those present. The Queen Mother, however, understood and asked Edward Gillespie, the racecourse's manager, to escort Jenny back to her horse and to return her to the royal box when she was done. As they walked back to Burrough Hill Lad, Jenny couldn't understand why Gillespie was so reticent – until they returned to the royal box, she removed her coat and realised what he must have noticed: she was still wearing her favourite jumper, which had a large hole in it.

Towards the end of 1984, Jenny ran Burrough Hill Lad again in the King George VI Chase – a nerve-racking race, according to Jenny – and won. Suddenly, Jenny found herself surrounded by journalists and well-wishers, and on turning around noticed a small, elderly lady peering at her. It was, of course, the Queen Mother. Jenny stepped forward, received her trophy and once again went to the royal box for a drink, this time with her parents – although, of course, after she'd attended to Burrough Hill Lad.[47]

In the same year, the Queen Mother's horse Special Cargo won the Whitbread Gold Cup in one of the best races at Sandown that year. He also won the Grand Military Cup that year and would go on to win it again in 1985 and 1986. By this time, his trainer, Fulke Walwyn, had trained 150 winners for the Queen Mother, of which Special Cargo was possibly the most popular.

Meanwhile, since reducing her eventing commitments, Princess Anne had participated in her first race on the flat at Epsom on 24 April 1985 in a charity event to raise money for Riding for the Disabled, of which she was patron. On that occasion, she finished fourth on Against the Grain while the race was won by No U Turn under Elaine Mellor. The Princess's weak position hadn't been the horse's fault, she declared, noting that he would probably have made greater progress if he'd been ridden by someone else. Despite her modesty, Anne ran a good race, completing the course in two minutes and fifty seconds – an abrupt change of pace after her eventing career and altogether too quick for her to feel afraid. The event raised £20,000 for Riding for the Disabled.

Then, on 19 February 1986, *The Times* published a small announcement stating that the Princess would be riding one of her mother's horses in the upcoming flat-racing season, effectively scotching rumours that she'd been expecting another baby. At around this time, she also became president of the International Equestrian Federation following her father's retirement from the position.

On 25 July of the same year, Anne won the Dresden Diamond Stakes on Ten No Trumps (trained by Michael Stoute) at Ascot, beating the favourite, Tahilla, by four lengths, whereupon she was presented with a gold necklace chain bearing a 0.77ct diamond. She later admitted that she'd just let Ten No Trumps stride on at his own pace, since he'd seemed capable of carrying on without her instruction. She'd known that she was ahead, she said, but hadn't wanted to look around in case she got told off later.[48]

Also in 1986, the Duke of Edinburgh finally decided to retire from carriage driving. He was 66 years old, after all, and was finding it increasingly difficult to control a team of horses, so he changed to riding ponies instead. Over the years, he'd amassed a great deal of knowledge concerning the technicalities of the sport, including the engineering side of it, and in later years promoted metal carriages and came up with ideas for developing them further. He would communicate some of these ideas – including one for special light alloy wheels – to Sir George Edwards, managing director of the British Aircraft Corporation, who would then construct what the Duke had designed. Prince Philip also designed a cross-country vehicle that has since been adopted worldwide.

At Ascot the following year, on 21 November 1987, Kevin Mooney rode the Queen Mother's horse Sun Rising in The Rip Handicap Chase while another of her horses, Insular, came third in the Snow Hill Handicap Hurdle under Richard Dunwoody. Many jockeys rode Insular, including Princess Anne, who steered him to victory on 11 June 1988 in the Queen Mother Cup at York in the Lady Amateur Riders class. This triumph seemed to break the deadlock that had impeded his progress thus far and he went on to win again at Sandown on 2 July in the Commonwealth Handicap. But then, on 22 July at Ascot, he came third in the Brown Jack Handicap, and five days later at Redcar he came fourth in the Sea Pigeon Handicap.

Also in 1988, the Queen's three-year-old Unknown Quantity raced for the first time at Kempton, coming fourth in the Laburnum Stakes, and then at Ascot on 15 June he came ninth in the Jersey Stakes. He then managed to improve on this position by coming third in *The Mail on Sunday* Three-Year-Old Series Handicap at Newmarket on 30 July, but he proved unable to maintain this new-found form and on 20 August at Sandown he came fourth in the Air Europe Stakes Handicap. Following this poor performance, he came fifth in the Golden Jubilee Challenge Trophy Handicap at Great Yarmouth, and in his final race of the year, on 29 October, he came seventh in the final of *The Mail on Sunday* Three-Year-Old Series Handicap at Newmarket.

Sometime after this, tragedy struck and Unknown Quantity was hit by a car. Fortunately, the crash wasn't fatal and he recovered at William Hastings-Bass's stable, but it remained to be seen how he would fare in 1989 as a four-year-old.

As it turned out, Unknown Quantity did well in the next season. His first race of 1989 was at Lingfield on 3 June, where he achieved a win in the *Daily Mail* Casino Handicap. Then, four days later, Bruce Raymond rode him to victory in the Gulf Palace, Royal Hong Kong, Jockey Club Stakes at Sandown. These two successes marked a brilliant start to his season.

At the beginning of 1990, a bronze statue of George III's horse Eclipse, sculpted by James Osborne, was nearing completion and would eventually stand in the garden of the National Horseracing Museum at Newmarket. If ever there was a horse to justify the existence of the thoroughbred industry, Eclipse was it. Osborne's two-thirds life-sized model was constructed from details taken from the horse's preserved skeleton (reconstructed by Dr Juliet Jewell of the Natural History Museum, where Eclipse's remains had been stored since the 1920s), as well as extant prints and a thesis on the horse by the King's Equerry, Charles Vial St Bel. The unveiling of the model in October, on the 200th anniversary of Eclipse's death, was a proud moment for all concerned, not least for the Queen, whose ancestor William Augustus, Duke of Cumberland, had bred him in the first place.[49] And, as Sir Michael Oswald pointed out, 'Over ninety per cent of all thoroughbreds in the world are descended from Eclipse.'[50]

Sadly, at around this time the abuse of horses was becoming a serious issue in horse training and, indeed, in equestrian sports in general. Consequently, there was a general consensus in the industry not only that the problem had to be tackled but also that those involved in the racing, training and breeding of horses needed to present a reassuring image to the public. For this reason, in her capacity as President of the International Equestrian Federation, the Princess Royal announced that a commission was being set up charged with the aim of forming codes of practice, hopefully by March of 1991.[51]

On 18 January of that year, as British and American troops fought in the first Gulf War, one writer for *The Times* argued that sport wasn't important, given what the armed forces were going through. In response to such accusations, protesting its benefits toward morale, Princess Anne found herself in the same position as those who had spoken on behalf of sport in the First and Second World Wars. Also in that year, she launched the 1991 Year of Sport after receiving backing from the Minister for Sport, Robert Atkins.

In the early years of the 1990s, the Queen Mother's best horse was Nearco Bay, trained by Nicky Henderson. On 30 May 1994, he became the Queen Mother's 400th winner when he triumphed under John Kavanagh in the Neville Lumb Silver Jubilee Handicap Chase at Uttoxeter, the final race of the season. At the start of that year, however, he hadn't looked too promising, being pulled up in the Party Politics Handicap Chase on 3 January and then again on the 25th in the Ollerton Handicap Chase. Nothing more was heard of him until 4 April, when he came first in the Newton Williams Handicap Chase, having chased the leaders before pulling out to take the lead. He then repeated his success on 30 April to secure the Knight, Frank and Rutley Handicap Chase, and then won once again, this time on 11 May at Hereford, where he won the Canon Pym Handicap Chase. When the season recommenced later in the year, he came third at Chepstow on 1 October in the Mercedes Benz Handicap Chase, and then eleven days later he came first in the Trent Bathrooms Handicap Chase, where he pushed along unchallenged.

In fact, 1994 began well overall for the Queen Mother, whose six-year-old Bass Rock, trained by Ian Balding, came third in the Foxhills Open National Hunt Flat under J Frost. Less than a month later, on 2 February, he came third again, this time in the Brocas National Hunt Novices' Hurdle at Windsor, again with J Frost riding. Then, on 23 March, his prospects improved further at Exeter when he came first in the EBF National Hunt Novices' Hurdle Qualifier.

Inevitably, though, when things were going so well for Bass Rock, he fell at Exeter on 19 May in the Lapford Novices' Hurdle, but by 12 October, however, he'd recovered sufficiently to pull off a creditable first in the Dean and Dyball Handicap Hurdle, ridden this time by J Osborne, but after that race he wouldn't run again for the rest of the year and, in fact, wouldn't be seen on the course at all for over twelve months.

The following year, on 24 February 1995, Anne prepared to compete in a desert race – proof of her willingness to ride all terrains – in Dubai, where a local hotelier named Khalef al-Habtoor had spent £50,000 on buying five horses and shipping them to the Persian Gulf for her to ride. This was a horse race with a difference. It was run on a course 21 miles long and lasted for two hours, rather than the two minutes or more of those in which Anne was used to riding, and was named – appropriately enough – the Desert Challenge Endurance Race. She would also be competing against many Arab riders who were experienced desert riders. The Princess was expected to do well, however, and would be riding a five-year-old chestnut gelding named Keor, owned by one of racehorse owner and breeder Sheikh Mohammed al-Maktoum's daughters, while the Sheikh himself would be riding a nine-year-old gelding. In the event, the Princess – one of forty starters – completed the course in 68 minutes, finishing in sixteenth place.[52]

Later, on 3 May 1995, the Queen's horse Phantom Gold had her first appearance at Ascot, where she came third in the Insulpak Conditions Stakes with J Weaver up. Sixteen days later, she came sixth in the Vodafone Group Fillies' Trial Stakes at Newbury. Then, on 22 June, on her return to Ascot, Frankie Dettori had the honour of riding her and managed to turn her fortunes around when the pair came first in the Ribblesdale Stakes. Dettori was so pleased that he asked the Queen's permission to kiss the horse's muzzle.

Phantom Gold's next appearance was in 1996 as a four-year-old at Sandown, where she came ninth in the Spillers Brigadier Gerard Stakes. Her form had improved only moderately by 21 June, when she came fifth in the Hardwicke Stakes at Ascot. Then, at Haydock on 6 July, she came second in the Letheby and Christopher Lancashire Oaks, but she couldn't sustain this improved performance and on 28 July, in the Deutschlandpreis 50 Jahre Nordheim-Westfalen (Group 1) race at Düsseldorf, she came fifth. On her return to England, however, she teamed up again with Frankie Dettori at Newbury on 17 August to win the Triplepoint Geoffrey Freer Stakes.

In 1997, at the age of 97, the Queen Mother took as much delight in attending races as she had done when she'd been a young woman, but from that year onwards she moved about in a chauffeur-driven, motorised buggy – which, of course, was adorned with her racing colours. Even so, at Ascot on 17 June she chose to walk about rather than be driven and chatted to owners and trainers before walking unaided the 300 yards from the paddock to the royal box. By this time, she'd been attending Royal Ascot for some seventy years and might have thought she'd seen pretty much all there was to see at race meetings, but that year a man wanted by the police was spotted in Ascot High Street. They moved in, but the target managed to evade them.[53]

In the following year, it was announced on 9 October that Sir Michael Stoute and Richard Hannon would be employed as the Queen's new trainers after Lord Huntingdon decided to retire. Both men have maintained special traditional lines – with Sir Michael at Cecil Boyd Rochfort's place and Hannon having trained for Carnarvon, a friend of the Queen.[54]

Then, in 1999, Sir Michael Oswald retired from the royal studs, although he still had a great deal to contribute, continuing to manage the Queen Mother's horses until her death. In the same year, the Queen enjoyed one of her final wins of the century with Blueprint, who won the Duke of Edinburgh's Stakes at Ascot to give Her Majesty her seventeenth win there since 1953.

The year 2000 heralded a new century and a new millennium, and in that year the Queen was presented with the Carter Millennium Award – not only in recognition of her contribution to horse-racing as an owner and breeder but also for the achievements of the royal stables in the twentieth century. That year, the Queen had eleven winners, although at the beginning there was little sign of the year being particularly promising in this regard, with Brandy Snap coming fourth in the European Breeders Fund National Hunt Novices Hurdle at Plumpton on 17 January and then coming third on 24 February in the Yorkshire Dales Trekking Centre (Malham) Mares-Only Maiden Hurdle in Huntingdon.

In the same year, only four days before the Queen Mother's 100th birthday, she was at Kingsclere. On that visit, as indefatigable as ever, she insisted upon getting out of her Land Rover so that she could view the horses on the hill. Towards the end of her life she increasingly appreciated the views that Kingsclere boasted, and on that occasion, remembers trainer Ian Balding, she just wanted to enjoy them and the company of the horses in peace.

In 2001, the Queen and Queen Mother reduced the numbers of horses that they owned. This left the Queen with eighteen horses in training for the flat (fourteen fewer than the previous year) while the Queen Mother reduced her complement to thirteen (half the number that she'd had the previous year), although the Queen still had 26 mares in breeding at Sandringham.

Much has changed in the few years since. In September 2001, for instance, Henry George Reginald Molyneux Herbert, Lord Porchester, 7th Earl of Carnarvon, died of a heart attack. He'd been the Queen's racing manager since 1970 and a first class breeder of horses, while he'd also been involved in local government, planning and conservation and, in 1985, had become the chairman of the Newbury Race Committee. The following year, he'd become chairman of the Equine Virology Research Foundation and had twice been president of the Thoroughbred Breeders' Association – first between 1964 and 1974 and then between 1986 and 1991. With Porchie's death, the Queen had lost a good friend, someone she had known for much of her life. Worse, though, was to follow.

Some months later, during the first week of February 2002, Princess Margaret suffered a stroke and during the early hours of Saturday 9 February, three days after the fiftieth anniversary of her father's death, she died at the age of 62. Then, less than two months later, on 30 March at 3.15 p.m., her mother died with the Queen by her side. The Queen Mother's death truly signalled the end of an era and hundreds of thousands of people filed past her coffin as it lay in state. Her funeral was held a few days later, and in fact before her death the Queen Mother had been involved in its planning, even deciding which horses should take part.

Soon the tributes were pouring in from all over the globe, praising not only her devotion to public service, particularly during World War Two, but also her devotion to horse-racing. Christopher Spence, senior steward of the Jockey Club, noted her contribution as an owner and breeder as well as a racegoer,[55] while Sir Michael Oswald recalled that she was as good a loser as she was a winner and that her approach to horse-racing was based on the assumption that it should be fun. On 3 April 2002, there was a minute's silence at Ascot in her honour as people remembered a dignified lady who had contributed so much to the image and appeal of horse-racing – especially steeplechasing – for over fifty years.

On the Queen Mother's death, her daughter inherited her horses. As Sir Michael recalls, 'She kept four broodmares and four horses in training. There are now six horses in training for racing over jumps, all home bred.'

That year, 2002, was Golden Jubilee year for the Queen, and in celebration of her fifty years on the throne the annual race meeting at Ascot – starting on 18 June – was extended to five days. That year's event showed just how much the monarchy had changed over the last fifty years. The first day went well enough, and on the second the Queen went down to the paddock to see her horse Approval just prior to his run in the first race. On the third day, however, a whirlwind – what the Met Office referred to as a 'dust devil' – hit the course, tossing up chairs, hats, a gazebo – anything, in fact, that wasn't nailed down – into the air and sending people scurrying in all directions. Two people were taken to hospital, one with a suspected heart attack and the other with minor injuries. The Queen and the Duke had only just arrived when the dust devil struck and saw all kinds of debris flying past from their position in the royal box. It wasn't exactly the kind of fly-past they were used to![56]

Matters didn't improve much when the Queen's horse Green Line – the favourite for the Britannia Handicap – finished well behind the winner, Ian Balding's Pentecost. He hadn't improved much by 1 August, either, when he came fourth in the Stanley Racing Stakes on the third day of Goodwood. But then, on 7 September at Kempton, he came third in the Milears Ruislip Handicap and he ended his season by coming thirteenth at Ascot in a Showcase Handicap.

A week later, Captain Ginger came fifth in the Battle of Britain Nursery at Doncaster, but he improved on this performance on 21 September at Warwick, where he won the Stan James Nursery, and had his final run of 2002 on 10 October at York, where he came seventh in the Green Howards Cup Nursery Handicap.

Meanwhile, another of the Queen's horses, Snow Bunting, competed in the Teletext Racing 'Hands and Heels' Apprentice Series Handicap on 11 September at Leicester and won.

In the following year, the Queen unveiled a bronze statue of the Queen Mother at the Cheltenham Meeting, while the Champion Chase was renamed in the Queen Mother's honour.[57]

The 2003 flat season began well for the Queen when Green Line won the Stratstone Aston Martin Rated Stakes at Chester on 8 May with Kieran Fallon up. Then, on the 12th, in his first run of the season Right Approach came first in the Agfa Royal Windsor Stakes for colts and geldings, also with Kieran Fallon up. Another of the Queen's horses, Promotion, won his owner the treble by finishing in first place in the Join the Revolution Maiden Stakes at Sandown on the 27th, again with Kieran Fallon.

For the Queen and the Duke of Edinburgh, attending Ascot is a family affair, and they and their children are usually there for the event's entire four- or five-day duration. Their visits are semi-private, as they like to relax and enjoy the races while they're there, but they also spend some time entertaining guests. On these occasions, the party begins with lunch at Windsor Castle and is a precisely timed affair. At the appointed hour, they all drive down to Windsor Great Park, and just before they reach the course at Ascot they disembark and get into landaus (four-wheeled carriages with folding hoods) ready for the royal procession.

Ascot is one of the Queen's favourite events, whether or not she has success there – but she's had a few. In fact, until 2003, she'd had nineteen winners there, although none since 1995, when Phantom Gold won the group-two heat of the Ribblesdale Stakes. In 2003, Green Line began as favourite for the Buckingham Palace Stakes on 20 June – day four – but finished twelfth, the race being won by Attaché. And Captain Ginger didn't fare much better five days later at Kempton, where he finished ninth in the British–Saudi Friendship Classified Stakes.

July, too, proved to be a mixed month for the Queen's horses. At Windsor on the 7th, under Kieran Fallon, Promotion came third in the extravagantly named Tote Supports The Great Ormond Street Hospital and Trinity Hospice EBF Classified Stakes. Four days later, at York, Green Line (under Pat Eddery) was pulled up in the Danepak Classic Rated Stakes, whereupon it was discovered that he'd gone lame. Then, on the 12th, there was some consolation at Ascot when Right Approach came third in the Michael Page International Silver Trophy Stakes. Captain Ginger, too, managed to improve on his performance when he came third in the Pinnacle Insurance Classified Stakes at Epsom on the 17th. And on the 25th, Royal Warrant came fourth in the *Salisbury Journal* Maiden Stakes.

On 24 June, Captain Ginger came eighth in the Seafrance Dover-Calais Ferries Classified Stakes at Goodwood, and four days later he came fourth in the Skybet Vegas Rated Stakes Showcase Handicap at Bath, with Martin Dwyer up. The following day, Green Line – running for the first time since his injury at York in July – came in at a creditable second place in the Moss Bros Shergar Cup Mile, while on the same day Right Approach came fifth in the Petras Race of the Lancaster Stakes at Haydock.

Royal Warrant, too, was experiencing a season of mixed results. At Windsor, on 11 June, he came third in the Harpon Louise-Windsor Maiden Stakes, under Martin Dwyer, and then on the 22nd he came first in the European Breeders' Fund Maiden Stakes at Thirsk.

Green Line's next run wasn't until 10 September, at Del Mar, where he came second out of three runners in the Live The Dream Handicap, with Julie Krone riding. Ten days later, Royal Warrant came ninth in his last race of the season, the Stan James Nursery at Warwick, and on 14 October another royal newcomer – two-year-old Magnetic Pole, trained by Sir Michael Stoute – came third in the EBF Soar Maiden Stakes under Pat Eddery.

In 2004, a month before he retired, it was announced on 8 January that Michael Norris, who'd been stud groom at the Queen's private stud at Polhampton Lodge Stud Farm in Hampshire, was being recognised in the New Year's Honours List, with a silver bar being added to his Royal Victorian Medal. Originally from Ireland, Norris came over to England in 1954 as a student at Sandringham, then progressed to stallion man and later stud groom at Hampton Court, where he stayed for eleven months before moving on to Polhampton Stud. Indeed, his career almost spans that of the Queen as monarch.

On 21 February, Right Approach came first in the al-Rashidiya Unfuwain Stakes at Nal al-Sheba, Dubai, while on the same day at Lingfield Royal Warrant came first in the Littlewoods Bet Direct Handicap and a week later came third at the Bet Direct On 0800 32 9393 Conditions Stakes (how's that for a mouthful?), again at Lingfield.

In 2004, the Queen's horse Magnetic Pole enjoyed only moderate success, making his first appearance that year on 27 April at Bath, where he came second in the MJ Church Maiden Stakes. Then, on 16 May, he came third in the True Temper Maiden Stakes under Kieron Fallon but didn't do quite so well the following day at Ripon, where he came eighth in the Ripon Bell-ringer Stakes. He did, however, come second in the Special Package Deal Maiden Stakes at Catterick on 7 September, and then second again on the 16th in the Lady Ball Maiden Stakes at Pontefract. His final appearance of that season was on 15 October at Brighton, where he came first in the 3R Red Online Casino Maiden Stakes under Dane O'Neill.[58]

Over the years, the Royal Stud has faced tough competition from other owner/breeders, particularly those from Saudi Arabia, who continue to dominate the thoroughbred industry. As Sir Michael Oswald observes, 'The large Arab owner/breeders may each own over 200 broodmares, and they have many of the best stallions in the country. Their operations are, in each case, ten times larger than the Queen's. They have excellent stud farms.'

Meanwhile, over the last 200–300 years, the nature of thoroughbreds has changed significantly, especially with regards to stamina. 'The modern thoroughbred may not be as tough as his predecessors and tends to be more specialised,' Sir Michael notes. 'They are either sprinters, milers, mile-and-a-half horses or stayers. The quality is as high as ever but is possibly levelling out. Record times are broken less frequently, possibly explained by improvements in grass management by racecourses. A thick grass surface can slow times down. Veterinary techniques have also improved, resulting in basically unsound horses being kept in action longer.'

Throughout the ages, however, the thoroughbred's place within the Royal Stud has been sustained, and today, with the Queen as custodian, the Stud has not only survived but has moved into the 21st century and looks set to endure for a while yet. And with the 1,000th anniversary of the Battle of Hastings just sixty years away at the time of publication, things have come full circle.

Notes:

1. Fitzgerald, p221
2. *The Times*, 20.08.1952
3. *News Chronicle*, 02.02.1953
4. *Daily Telegraph & Morning Post*, 03.06.1953
5. Mortimer, Onslow and Willet, pp33–4; *The Times*, 19.07.1954
6. *The Times*, 09.10.1954
7. *The Times*, 27.11.1954
8. *The Times*, 17.03.1955
9. Francis, pp190–1
10. Francis, p192
11. Francis, p193
12. Francis, pp195–6
13. Francis, p196
14. Francis, pp196–7
15. Ibid.
16. Francis, p198
17. Francis, p199
18. *The Times*, 28.03.1956
19. *The Times*, 08.05.1957
20. *Daily Herald*, 05.10.1957; 30.10.1957
21. *The Times*, 13.06.1960
22. *The Times*, 29.05.1961; 17.06.1961
23. *The Times*, 05.10.1961: 30.09.1961
24. *The Times*, 12.05.1962; 14.05.1962
25. *The Times*, 23.06.1962
26. Fitzgerald, p240

27. Fitzgerald, p244
28. *The Times*, 20.03.1965; 29.03.1965
29. *The Times*, 12.06.1967; 25.07.1967
30. *The Times*, 27.05.1968
31. Sir Michael Oswald
32. Ibid.
33. *The Times*, 25.05.1970; 29.05.1970
34. *The Times*, 06.11.1971
35. *The Times*, 26.04.1973
36. Sir Michael Oswald
37. *The Times*, 14.05.1974
38. *The Times*, 11.04.1975
39. Pitman, pp128–9
40. Carson, p96
41. *The Times*, 24.07.1978
42. *The Times*, 07.06.1979
43. *The Times*, 08.03.1980
44. *The Times*, 03.09.1980
45. *The Times*, 18.08.1981; 25.09.1981
46. Pitman, pp209–10
47. Pitman, pp229–30
48. *The Times*, 27.07.1987
49. *The Times*, 04.04.1989; 06.10.1989
50. Sir Michael Oswald
51. *The Times*, 18.01.1991
52. *The Times*, 24.02.1995; 25.02.1995
53. *The Times*, 18.06.1997
54. *The Times*, 10.10.1998
55. Christopher Spence www.bbc.sport.co.uk
56. www.bbc.co.uk
57. Ibid.
58. Ibid.

Epilogue

The royal family's deep-rooted interest in everything to do with horses is stronger now than it was almost 1,000 years ago, when William of Normandy and his followers landed in England and set in motion an equine evolution that saw the relationship between monarch and steed transformed from one of soldier and warhorse to one of thoroughbred-owner and racer. Over the years, as well as being used for war, hunting and racing, horses have been used politically as vehicles of diplomacy, social responsibility and morale-boosting during times of war. They serve as an expression of confidence, wealth and prestige, and have become an integral part of the nation's identity and a representative of its own self-confidence, while also helping to bring the monarchy and its subjects closer together, in the process enjoying a connection with the nation's ruling family that has never been lost but has, in fact, gained in strength. As each century has passed, so each monarch has kept the nation aware of its responsibility towards horses, no more so than during the last 100 years, an era in which a dazzling array of new ideas and technology has been embraced. The Royal Mews, for instance, is constantly evolving; in this new century it provides email and internet access and gives its visitors an opportunity to get a glimpse of the place's history by allowing them to see its prized coaches and uniforms.

Hampton Court, too, has been turned into a museum and, after a long and rich history of housing many of England's monarchs' horses, now houses carriage horses and cream-coloured ponies descended from those brought over from Hanover by King George I.

Today, King George's descendant Queen Elizabeth II is the custodian of the Royal Stud, and her involvement is as personal as ever. She regularly visits her horses (all of whom she names herself), and in between such visits views video footage sent to her covering their progress and welfare. Indeed, she has set a new standard in the care and management of horses, and it is a standard that looks set to continue well beyond 2066, the thousand-year anniversary of the Norman Conquest.

Bibliography

Adams, Simon: *Leicester and the Court: Essays on Elizabethan Politics*, Manchester University Press, 2000

Appleby, John: *Henry II*, G Bell & Sons Ltd, London, 1962

Appleby, John: *The Troubled Reign of King Stephen*, G Bell & Sons Ltd, London, 1969

Ashley, Maurice: *The Life and Times of King John*, Weidenfeld & Nicolson, London, 1972

Astley, Sir John: *Fifty Years Reminiscences*, Hurst & Blackett Ltd, London, *c.*1893

Bagley, J J: *The Earls of Derby 1485–1985*, Sidgwick & Jackson Ltd, London, 1985

Balding, Ian: *Making the Running: A Racing Life*, Headline Book Publishing, London, 2004

Barber, Richard: *Edward, Prince of Wales and Aquitaine: A Biography of the Black Prince*, Allen Lane, Penguin Books Ltd, London, 1978

Bartlett, Robert: *England Under the Norman and Angevin Kings, 1075–1225*, Oxford University Press, 2002

Bates, David: *William the Conqueror*, George Philip Ltd, London, 1989

Baxter, Stephen B: *William III*, Longmans, Green & Co Ltd, London, 1966

Beatty, Laura: *Lillie Langtry: Manners, Masks and Morals*, Chatto & Windus, London, 1999

Bedford, Julian: *The World Atlas of Horseracing*, Hamlyn Publishing Group Ltd, London, 1989

Bevan, Bryan: *James, Duke of Monmouth*, Robert Hale & Co, London, 1973

Bevan, Bryan: *Henry IV*, Rubicon Press, London, 1994

Bland, Ernest (editor): *Flat Racing Since 1900*, foreword by Earl of Rosebery, Andrew Dakers Ltd, 1950

Browning, Andrew (editor): *English Historical Documents, Volume III 1660–1714*, Eyre & Spottiswoode, 1953

Burnet, Alistair (with Tim Neligan): *The Derby: The Official Book of the World's Greatest Race*, Michael O'Mara Books Ltd, London, 1983

Byrne, M St Clare (editor): *The Letters of King Henry VIII*, Cassell & Co Ltd, London, 1968

Campbell, Judith: *Royal Horses*, New English Library, London, 1983

Carson, Willie and Scott, Brough: *Willie Carson Up Front: A Racing Autobiography*, Stanley Paul & Co Ltd, Random House, London, 1993

Chifney, Samuel: *Genius Genuine*, 1804

Chrimes, S B: *Henry VII*, Methuen London Ltd, London, reprinted 1984

Clark, John (editor): *The Medieval Horse and its Equipment*, HMSO Copyright Unit, Norwich, 1995

Clive, Mary: *This Sun of York: A Biography of Edward IV*, Macmillan, London, 1973

Clower, Michael: *Mick Kinane: Big Race King – The Authorised Biography*, Mainstream Publishing Company (Edinburgh) Ltd, Edinburgh, 1997

Crouch, David: *The Reign of King Stephen, 1135–1154*, Pearson Education Ltd, Essex, 2000

Crouch, David: *The Normans: The History of a Dynasty*, Hambledon & London, London, 2002

Curling, Bill: *All the Queen's Horses*, Chatto & Windus, London, 1978

D'Arcy, Fergus A: *Horses, Lords and Racing Men*, Turf Club, Curragh, County Kildare, 1991

Davis, R H C: *The Medieval Warhorse*, Thames & Hudson Ltd, London, 1989

Dettori, Frankie: *The Autobiography of Frankie Dettori*, Collins Willow (an imprint of

BIBLIOGRAPHY

HarperCollins Publishers), London, 2004

Dimbleby, Jonathon: *The Prince of Wales: A Biography*, Warner Books (a division of Little, Brown & Co, UK), London, 1995

Dizikes, John: *Yankee Doodle Dandy: The Life and Times of Tod Sloan*, Yale University Press, New Haven and London, 2000

Donaldson, Frances: *Edward VIII*, Weidenfeld & Nicolson Ltd, London, 1974

Douglas, David C: *William the Conqueror*, Eyre Methuen Ltd, London, 1999

Douglas, David C: *English Historical Documents: Volume X, 1714–1783*, Eyre & Spottiswoode (General Edition)

Douglas, David C and Greenaway, George W: *English Historical Documents: Volume II, 1042–1189*, Eyre & Spottiswoode, 1968

Earle, Peter: *Henry V*, Sphere Books Ltd, London, 1975

Edwards, Elwyn Hartley: *Horses: Their Role in the History of Man*, William Collins Sons & Co Ltd, 1987

Ennor, George and Mooney, Bill: *The World Encyclopaedia of Horse Racing: An Illustrated Guide to Flat Racing and Steeplechasing*, Carlton Books, 2001

Evelyn, John: *John Evelyn's Diary and Correspondence*, Edited by William Bray, 1906

Fitzgerald, Arthur: *Royal Thoroughbreds: A History of the Royal Studs*, Sidgwick & Jackson Ltd, London, 1990

Francis, Dick: *The Sport of Queens: A Champion Jockey's Personal Story*, Michael Joseph Ltd, Pan Books Ltd, London (second printing, 1976)

Fraser, Antonia: *Cromwell Our Chief of Men*, Mandarin Books, 1993

Fraser, Antonia: *King Charles II*, Mandarin Paperbacks, 1993

Fraser, Antonia: *Mary Queen of Scots*, Arrow Books, Random House UK Ltd, London, 1995

Fulford, Roger (editor): *Darling Child: Private Correspondence of Queen Victoria and the German Crown Princess 1871–1878*, Evans Brothers Ltd, London, reprinted 1981

Gilbey, Sir Walter: *Racing Cups 1559 to 1850*, Vinton & Co, London, 1910

Gillingham, John: *Yale English Monarchs: Richard I*, Yale University Press, New Haven and London, paperback edition, 2002

Girouard, Mark: *Windsor: The Most Romantic Castle*, Hodder & Stoughton, Kent, 1993

Given-Wilson, Chris: *The Royal Household and the King's Affinity: Service, Politics and Finance in England 1360–1413*, Yale University Press, 1986

Goldman, Paul: *Sporting Life: An Anthology of British Sporting Prints*, British Museum Publications Ltd, London, 1983

Gravett, Christopher: *Hastings 1066: The Fall of Saxon England*, Osprey Publishing Ltd, Campaign Series, London, 1992

Gregg, Edward: *Queen Anne*, Routledge & Kegan Paul Ltd, London, 1980

Green, Reg: *A Race Apart: The History of the Grand National*, Hodder & Stoughton, 1987

Green, Reg: *National Heroes. The Aintree Legend*, Mainstream Publishing Company, 1997

Green, Reg: *The Grand National: Aintree's Official Illustrated History*, Virgin, London, 2000

Green, Reg: *Kings for a Day: Aintree's Bravest Sons*, Mainstream, 2002

Greville, Charles C F: *The Greville Memoirs: A Journal of the Reigns of King George IV and King William IV: Volume I*, edited by Henry Reeve, Longmans, Green & Co, 1875

Greville, Charles C F: *The Greville Memoirs: A Journal of the Reigns of King George IV and King William IV: Volume II*, edited by Henry Reeve, Longmans, Green & Co, 1875

BIBLIOGRAPHY

Greville, Charles C F: *The Greville Memoirs*, edited by Christopher Lloyd, 1958

Hallam, Elizabeth: *The Plantagenet Chronicles*, Weidenfeld & Nicolson Ltd, London, 1986

Hallam, H E: *Rural England 1066–1348*, Harvester Press Ltd, Sussex, 1981

Hamilton, Elizabeth: *Henrietta Maria*, Hamish Hamilton Ltd, London, 1976

Hamilton, J S: *Piers Gaveston: Earl of Cornwall, 1307–1312 – Politics & Patronage in the Reign of Edward II*, Harvester Wheatsheaf (a division of Simon & Schuster), Hertfordshire, 1988–1992

Harrison, G B (editor): *The Letters of Queen Elizabeth I*, Cassell & Co Ltd, 1968

Hatton, Ragnhild: *George I: Elector and King*, Thames & Hudson Ltd, 1978

Heald, Tim: *The Duke: A Portrait of Prince Philip*, Hodder & Stoughton, 1991

Hibbert, Christopher: *George III: A Personal History*, Penguin Books Ltd, London, 1998

Hibbert, Christopher: *Queen Victoria in her Letters and Journals: A Selection*, John Murray, 1984

Hicks, Michael: *Richard III: The Man Behind the Myth*, Collins & Brown Ltd, London, 1991

Holland, Anne: *Steeplechasing: A Celebration of 250 Years*, Little, Brown & Co (UK), London

Howard, Philip: *The Royal Palaces*, Hamish Hamilton Ltd, London, 1970

Hutchinson, Harold F: *Edward II: The Pliant King*, Eyre & Spottiswoode Ltd, London, 1971

Johnson, Paul: *The Life and Times of Edward III*, Weidenfeld & Nicolson, London, 1973

Judd, Denis: *King George VI*, Michael Joseph Ltd, London, 1982

Keen, Maurice: *Chivalry*, Yale University Press, London, 1984

Kitson, Frank: *Prince Rupert: Portrait of a Soldier*, Constable & Co Ltd, London, 1994

Laird, Dorothy: *Royal Ascot: A History of Royal Ascot From its Founding by Queen Anne to the Present Time*, Hodder & Stoughton, 1976

Lambton, The Hon George: *Men and Horses I Have Known*, Thornton Butterworth Ltd, London, 1924

Leapman, Michael: *Inigo: The Troubled Life of Inigo Jones, Architect of the English Renaissance*, Headline Book Publishing (a division of Hodder Headline), London, 2003

Lee, Christopher: *This Sceptred Isle: 55 BC–1901*, Penguin Books Ltd, London, 1997

Lee, Christopher: *This Sceptred Isle: Twentieth Century*, Penguin Books Ltd, London, 1999

Lees-Milne, James: *The Age of Inigo Jones*, B T Batsford Ltd, London, 1953

Lockyer, Roger: *Buckingham: The Life and Political Career of George Villiers, First Duke of Buckingham 1592–1628*, Longman Group Ltd, Essex, 1981

Longrigg, Roger: *The History of Horse Racing*, Macmillan London Ltd, London, 1972

Lord, Graham: *Dick Francis: A Racing Life*, Warner Books (a division of Little, Brown & Co), London, 2000

McCarthy, Justin: *A History of the Four Georges, Volume 1*, Chatto & Windus, London, 1903

McFarlane, K B: *Lancastrian Kings and Lollard Knights*, Oxford University Press, London, 1972

Magee, Sean (with Sally Aird): *Ascot: The History*, Methuen Publishing Ltd, London, 2000

Marsh, Richard: *A Trainer to Two Kings: Being the Reminiscences of Richard Marsh, MVO with a foreword by the Right Hon The Earl of Durham, KG*, Cassell & Co Ltd, 1925

May, Peter: *The Changing Face of Newmarket 1600–1760*, Peter May Publications, 1984

Montgomery-Hassingberd, Hugh: *Atlas of Royal Britain*, Windward Publishers, 1984

Mortimer, Roger: *The Jockey Club*, Cassell & Co Ltd, London, 1958

Mortimer, Roger: *The History of the Derby Stakes*, Cassell & Co Ltd, London, 1962

Mortimer, Roger, Richard Onslow and Peter Willett: *The Biographical Encyclopaedia of British Flat Racing*

BIBLIOGRAPHY

Mortimer, Roger and Peter Willett: *More Great Racehorses of the World*, Michael Joseph Ltd, London, 1972

Musgrave, Clifford: *The Fascinating Story of Prinnie's Pleasure House: Royal Pavilion*, Leonard Hill Books Ltd, London, 1959

Muir, J B: *Ye Olde Newmarkitt, Calendar of Matches, Results and Programs from 1619 to 1719*, published by the author at his Sporting Fine Art Gallery, London, 1892

Museum of London: *The Medieval Horse and Its Equipment: Medieval Finds from Excavations in London*, HMSO Copyright Unit, Norwich, 1995

Myers, A R: *English Historical Documents 1327–1485*, Eyre & Spottiswoode, London

Nash, Roy: *Hampton Court: The Palace and the People*, MacDonald & Co, 1983

Oaksey, John: *A Racing Life: Mince Pie for Starters*, with foreword by Dick Francis, Headline Book Publishing (a division of Hodder Headline), London, 2003

Oaksey, Lord and Bob Rooney (editors): *A Racing Companion*, W H Smith Ltd, 1992

Onslow, Richard: *The Squire: George Alexander Baird: Gentleman Rider 1861–1893*, Harrap, 1980

Onslow, Richard: *A History of Newmarket and its Racing Headquarters*, Great Ouse Press, Cambridge

Onslow, Richard: *Royal Ascot*, Crowood Press, Wiltshire, 1990

Painter, Sidney: *William Marshal*, Johns Hopkins Press, Maryland, US (third reprinting), 1966

Painter, Sidney: *The Reign of King John*, Johns Hopkins Press, Geoffrey Cumberledge; Oxford University Press, London (second printing), 1959

Parissien, Steven: *George IV: The Grand Entertainment*, John Murray Ltd, London, 2001

Parker, Geoffrey: *Philip II*, Hutchinson & Co, London, 1979

Parker, John: *The Princess Royal*, Hamish Hamilton Ltd, 1989

Phillips, G M: *Horses in Our Blood*, Turf Newspapers Ltd, London, 1974

Pierson, Peter: *Philip II of Spain*, Thames and Hudson, London, 1975

Piggott, Lester: *The Autobiography of Lester Piggott*, Transworld Publishers Ltd, London, 1995

Pimlott, Ben: *The Queen: Elizabeth II and the Monarchy* (Golden Jubilee edition), HarperCollins, London, 2001

Pitman, Jenny: *Jenny Pitman: The Autobiography*, Bantam, 1999

Pocock, Tom: *Sailor King: The Life and Times of William IV*, Sinclair-Stevenson Ltd, London, 1991

Ponsonby, Sir Frederick: *Recollections of Three Reigns*, Quartet Books Ltd, London, 1988

Portland, 6th Duke of: *Memories of Racing and Hunting*, Faber & Faber, London, 1935

Powicke, Sir Maurice: *The Thirteenth Century: 1216–1307*, Oxford University Press, Oxford

Prestwich, Michael: *Edward I*, Methuen London Ltd, London, 1988

Ramm, Agatha (editor): *Beloved and Darling Child: Last Letters between Queen Victoria and her Eldest Daughter 1886–1901*, Alan Sutton Publishing Ltd, Gloucestershire, 1990

Richards, Sir Gordon: *My Story*, Hodder & Stoughton, 1955

Roberts, Philip (editor): *The Diary of Sir David Hamilton 1709–1714*, Oxford University Press, 1975

Robinson, John Martin: *Royal Residences*, Macdonald & Co, London, 1982

Rose, Kenneth: *King George V*, Weidenfeld & Nicolson Ltd, London, 1983

Ross, Charles: *Edward IV*, Eyre Methuen Ltd, London, 1974

Rothwell, Harry (editor): *English Historical Documents, Volume III: 1189–1327*, Eyre & Spottiswoode, 1975

St Aubyn, Giles: *The Year of Three Kings: 1483*, Collins, London, 1983

St Leger, Moya Frenz: *St Leger: The Family and the Race*, Phillimore & Co, Sussex, 1986

BIBLIOGRAPHY

Sainty, J C and Bucholz, R O: *Officials of the Royal Household 1660–1837, Part II: Departments of the Lord Steward and the Master of the Horse – Office Holders in Modern Britain XII*, University of London, Institute of Historical Research, London, 1998

Saul, Nigel: *Richard II*, Yale University Press, New Haven and London, 1999

Saul, Nigel: *The Reign of Edward III*, Tempus Publishing Ltd, Gloucestershire, 2000

Sinclair-Stevenson, Christopher: *Blood Royal: The Illustrious House of Hanover*, Jonathan Cape Ltd, London, 1979

Smith, Doug (in collaboration with Peter Willett): *Five Times Champion*, Pelham Books Ltd, London, 1968

Smith, E A: *George IV*, Yale University Press, London, 1999

Smith, Sean: *Royal Racing: The Queen and Queen Mother's Sporting Life*, BBC Worldwide Ltd, London, 2001

Smyley, Patricia: *Encyclopaedia of Steeplechasing*, Robert Hale & Co, London, 1979

Stacey, Robert: *Politics, Policy and Finance Under Henry III 1216–1245*, Oxford University Press, Oxford, 1987

Stewart, Alan: *The Cradle King: A Life of James VI and I*, Chatto & Windus, London, 2003

Storey, R L: *Chronology of the Medieval World 800–1491*, Helicon Publishing Ltd, Oxford, reprinted 1995

Tanner, Michael: *The Champion Hurdle 1927–2002*, Mainstream, 1989

Tanner, Michael and Gerry Cranham: *Great Jockeys of the Flat: A Celebration of Two Centuries of Jockeyship*, Guinness Publishing Ltd, Middlesex, 1992

Thompson, Laura: *Newmarket: From James I to the Present Day*, Virgin Publishing Ltd, London, 2000

Thurley, Smith: *Hampton Court: A Social and Architectural History*, Yale University Press, London, 2000

Trease, C: *Portrait of a Cavalier: William Cavendish, First Duke of Newcastle*, Macmillan London Ltd, 1979

Trevor, Meriol: *The Shadow of a Crown. The Life Story of James II of England and VII of Scotland*, Constable & Co Ltd, London, 1988

Tyrrel, John: *Running Racing: The Jockey Club Years Since 1750*, Quiller Press Ltd, London, 1997

Van Der Kiste, John and Bee Jordaan: *Dearest Affie: Alfred, Duke of Edinburgh, Queen Victoria's Second Son*, Alan Sutton Publishing Ltd, Gloucestershire, 1984

Van Der Kiste, John: *Edward VII's Children*, Alan Sutton Publishing, Gloucestershire, 1989

Van Der Kiste, John: *Queen Victoria's Children*, Sutton Publishing Ltd, Gloucestershire, 2003 (revised edition)

Van Der Kiste, John: *William and Mary*, Sutton Publishing Ltd, Gloucestershire, 2003

Van Der Kiste, John: *George III's Children*, Sutton Publishing Ltd, Gloucestershire, 2004 (revised edition)

Waldstein, Baron: *The Diary of Baron Waldstein: A Traveller in Elizabethan England*, translated and annotated by G W Groos, Thames & Hudson, London, 1981

Walker, Stella A: *Sporting Art: England 1700–1900*, Studio Vista, London

Walpole, Horace: *Memoirs of the Reign of George the Third, Volumes 1, 2, 3 and 4*, Lawrence and Bullen, 1894

Walwyn, Peter: *Handy All the Way: A Trainer's Life*, Metro Books (an imprint of Metro Publishing Ltd), London, 2000

BIBLIOGRAPHY

Warren, W L: *King John*, Eyre Methuen Ltd, London, 1978

Warren, W L: *Yale English Monarchs: Henry II*, Eyre Methuen Ltd, first published 1973; new edition 2000

Weatherby, C J and J P: 'The Racing Calendar for the Year 1873', *Races Past Vol 101*, Publishers' Office, London, 1873

Weatherby, C J and J P: 'The Racing Calendar for the Year 1875', *Races Past Vol 103*, Publishers' Office, London

Weatherby and Sons: 'The Racing Calendar': *Steeplechases Past for the Season 1935–1936*, Volume 69, Publishers' Office, London

Weintraub, Stanley: *The Importance of Being Edward: King in Waiting 1841–1901*, John Murray Ltd, London, 2000

Weir, Alison: *Lancaster and York: The Wars of the Roses*, Jonathan Cape (Random House), London, 1995

Weir, Alison: *Children of England: The Heirs of King Henry VIII*, Jonathan Cape (Random House), London, 1996

Weir, Alison: *Britain's Royal Families: The Complete Genealogy*, Pimlico (Random House), London, 1996

Weir, Alison: *The Six Wives of Henry VIII*, Pimlico (Random House), London, 1997

Weir, Alison: *The Princes in the Tower*, Pimlico (Random House), London, 1997

Weir, Alison: *Elizabeth the Queen*, Jonathan Cape (Random House), London, 1998

Weir, Alison: *Henry VIII: King and Court*, Pimlico (Random House), London, 2002

Weir, Alison: *Eleanor of Aquitaine*, Pimlico (Random House), London, 2000

White, John: *The Racegoers' Encyclopaedia*, HarperCollins, London, 1996 (revised edition)

Wilder, F L: *English Sporting Prints with 95 Colour Prints*, Thames & Hudson Ltd, London, 1974

Wilkinson, David: *Early Horse Racing in Yorkshire and the Origins of the Thoroughbred*, Old Bald Peg Publications, York, 2003

Williams, Dr Ann and Professor G H Martin (editors): *Domesday Book: A Complete Translation*, Penguin Books Ltd, London, 1992

Wilson, Derek: *Sweet Robin: A Biography of Robert Dudley, Earl of Leicester 1533–1588*, Hamish Hamilton Ltd, London, 1981

Wilson, Julian: *Little Brown Book: The Great Racehorses*, Little, Brown & Co, London, 1998 (revised edition)

Wilson-Fairfax, John: *General of Parliament's Forces in the English Civil War*, John Murray Ltd, London, 1985

Windsor, Edward, Duke of: *A King's Story: The Memoirs of HRH The Duke Of Windsor, KG*, Cassell & Co Ltd, 1953

Woodham-Smith, Cecil: *Queen Victoria: Her Life and Times, Vol 1, 1819–1861*, Hamish Hamilton Ltd, London, 1972

Wright, Howard: *The Encyclopaedia of Flat Racing*, Hale, London, 1986

Wyndham, Violet: *The Protestant Duke: A Life of the Duke of Monmouth*, Weidenfeld & Nicolson, London, 1976

Wynn Jones, Michael: *The Derby: A Celebration of the World's Most Famous Horse Race*, Croom-Helm Ltd, 1979

Ziegler, Philip: *William IV*, William Collins Sons & Co Ltd, London, 1971

Websites

www.abcgallery.com
www.aro.co.za
www.attheraces.com
www.badminton.horse.co.uk
www.balmoralcastle.com
www.berksfho.org.uk
www.bloodlines.net
www.british-history.ac.uk
www.bwpics.co.uk
www.camelotintl.com
www.classics-betting.com
www.countrylife.co.uk
www.england-in-particular.com
www.equine.behaviour.com
www.equi.net
www.equiworld.net
www.expage.com
www.framlingham.com
www.genie.co.uk
www.geraldsegasby.co.uk
www.goracing.co.uk
www.hiddenlondon.com
www.highflyersupanet.com
www.horseandhound.co.uk
www.horseguild.com
www.hra.net

www.ihrinfo.ac.uk
www.ihr.sas.uk/office
www.irishhistorysociety.com
www.knaresborough.co.uk
www.lincolnshirelife.co.uk
www.lynnews.co.uk
www.magnacharta.org
www.neroche.net
www.newmarket.org.uk
www.nhrm.co.uk
www.nicomorgan.com
www.npg.org.uk
www.number10.gov.uk
www.pepysdiary.com
www.questria.com
www.racingpost.co.uk
www.regency.town-house.org
www.royal.gov.uk
www.somerleyton.co.uk
www.spartacus.schoolnet.co.uk
www.tauntonracecourse.co.uk
www.tbheritage.com
www.thamesweb.co.uk
www.thenewforest.co.uk
www.touruk.co.uk
www.tudorplace.com

Index

INDEX

INDEX

INDEX

INDEX

INDEX